INFORMATION SOURCES
FOR RESEARCH AND DEVELOPMENT

Use of
Management and Business Literature

INFORMATION SOURCES
FOR RESEARCH AND DEVELOPMENT

A series under the General Editorship of

R. T. Bottle, B.Sc., Ph.D., F.R.I.C., M.I.Inf.Sc.,
and
D. J. Foskett, M.A., F.L.A.

Use of
Management and
Business Literature

Editor
K. D. C. Vernon
Librarian, London Business School

BUTTERWORTHS
LONDON AND BOSTON

THE BUTTERWORTH GROUP

ENGLAND
Butterworth & Co (Publishers) Ltd
London: 88 Kingsway, WC2B 6AB

AUSTRALIA
Butterworths Pty Ltd
Sydney: 586 Pacific Highway, NSW 2067
Melbourne: 343 Little Collins Street, 3000
Brisbane: 240 Queen Street, 4000

CANADA
Butterworth & Co (Canada) Ltd
Toronto: 2265 Midland Avenue,
    Scarborough, Ontario, M1P 4S1

NEW ZEALAND
Butterworths of New Zealand Ltd
Wellington: 26–28 Waring Taylor Street, 1

SOUTH AFRICA
Butterworth & Co (South Africa) (Pty) Ltd
Durban: 152–154 Gale Street

USA
Butterworth, 161 Ash Stréet,
Reading, Boston, Mass. 01867

First published 1975

© The several contributors named in the list of contents, 1975

ISBN 0 408 70690 2

Photoset, printed and bound in Great Britain by R. J. Acford Ltd, Chichester,
Sussex

Preface

This book seeks to open some doors for users of the literature. It is intended primarily as a guide for managers who need to find information and understand the theories and ideas which can be applied to business problems; for teachers and students of business who must use the literature and learn from it; for research workers who require signposts through the jungle of published information; for market researchers, economists, social scientists and others for whom management literature is relevant; and lastly for the information 'handlers'—librarians and information officers —who need to be expert in providing services for their clients.

The Harvard Business School Library, the largest of its kind in the world, contains nearly half a million books and has been built up over the past 65 years as a great information resource for people studying management. It is a daunting thought that so much should have been written about a subject which is largely concerned with practical things—the organisation of people and resources in enterprises many of which exist in order to produce things for sale. But it is because so much has been written that a guide-book like this is necessary.

The book is in three parts. The first is concerned with the subject content of the literature, with the libraries which store it and arrange it for use, and with the bibliographical tools which are the keys to the store. The second part deals with business information in three different forms—research materials, statistical publications and company information—written by experts who have specialised in these types of information. The third part consists of six subject surveys of the literature which are presented by people, mainly business school teachers, with wide experience of their various subject areas. These surveys together cover the main aspects of management literature.

But there are other important subject areas which are not discussed here. Economics has been omitted because its vast literature has already been surveyed in *The use of economics literature*, by John Fletcher (Butterworths, 1971); but managerial economics has been touched on in Chapter 17 by Howard Thomas. The literature of the social sciences is being surveyed in another book shortly to be published in this series under the editorship of Norman Roberts. Business and industrial law comes into Chapter 14, by Loveridge and Timperley, but no attempt has been made to survey the full range of business law literature. The literature of production and of research and development management have also not been discussed in detail but are briefly surveyed in Chapter 18, while office management has been omitted altogether. This book in fact makes no attempt to cover all aspects of an ever-broadening subject area. It concentrates instead on trying to help executives, teachers and management students to understand what the literature has to offer, the various forms in which it is published and how to find information by using libraries and other sources. It also emphasises British publications and British library practices in Part 1 because they are not so well known as their American counterparts. American management literature is far more voluminous, better publicised and better documented.

Furthermore the book has, hopefully, got a message for its readers. This message is not spelled out anywhere in capital letters because it is intended to be caught and not taught—Chapter 4 provides the clue. The message says this: of course there is far too much management and business information being published, and indeed shouted at us, for anybody to absorb even its main aspects; but there is no reason to give up hope and merely deplore its quantity. Published information can be effectively used to help solve business problems; it is stored in libraries and can be obtained when it is wanted; but those who want information must make an effort to understand *how* it can be found. They must acquire the skills needed to use libraries and other information resources effectively—once learned, these skills can be of immense value to busy managers and hard-pressed students.

Part 1 concentrates on this theme. It is not written by a librarian for librarians: it is written specifically for users of libraries. The writer, in his capacity as Librarian of the London Business School, has frequently seen users of his library go away frustrated because they have not found what they wanted—a better understanding of sources of information how to use reference works, catalogues and indexes, and how to communicate with the library staff can avoid many, although obviously not all, of the frustrations. A skilled library user knows how to start the hunt for information and has a good chance of finding it. Business graduates are beginning to master the art, but they must continue to practise it in their jobs because the answer to many business problems can be found in the literature.

Librarians who use this book may perhaps be able to improve their knowledge and understanding of management literature and business information, the wide ramifications of its subject content, and the many and varied forms in which it is published. The documentation and control of the literature in this subject area has been badly neglected by the library profession. This situation must change and much more attention must be given to studying what kinds of information are needed, how the information can be better indexed and retrieved, and how computers can be used not so much for library housekeeping jobs as for solving the problems of information retrieval. There is much scope for research into some of these problems, and users of the literature—businessmen, teachers, research workers and others—must take more interest in problems of documentation so that a better dialogue with librarians can be promoted. A good start has been made in this direction by the courses which are run jointly by librarians and statisticians under the auspices of the Library Association.

Part 2 of this book, which examines three different forms of business and commercial information, aims to reveal some of the innumerable sources which can be used to find statistical data and company information. In an increasingly complex world more and more people want facts and figures, so it is essential to know how to find them. Joan Harvey, writing with many years of experience as Librarian of the Statistics and Market Intelligence Library of the Department of Trade and Industry, has surveyed the main sources of statistics which are available to us. George Henderson, an acknowledged expert on company information, has not only discussed the sources, but also described the relevance and importance of company information to business and financial transactions. Computers are now increasingly being used to handle this kind of information, and data banks of financial information are being set up to serve the needs of investment analysts. The rapidly developing business information services which are being provided by the *Financial Times* and others, which are far removed from books and conventional library services, are particularly valuable for those who need information about companies. Much valuable information, ranging over the whole field of management and business, also lies hidden away in the growing number of working papers and discussion papers prepared by research workers. This semi-published material, which contains the first results of research, is sometimes only relevant for a limited period until the results are fully published, but it has been badly neglected by many people who could use the information. John Fletcher, who has done much to make this kind of material more readily accessible in microform, has discussed the sources which are available for discovering what research work is being undertaken.

In Part 3 the literature of six important subject areas has been surveyed by experienced teachers from business schools and by David Dews, Librarian of Manchester Business School, who is doubly qualified to write on the literature of computers and management. With the ever-mounting volume of publications which threaten to engulf us, it is essential to have reviews of the literature to select for us the most significant publications in important subject areas. It is in these reviews that the interdisciplinary nature of the literature is particularly stressed. Anthony Hopwood shows how the literature of corporate finance is concerned with all aspects of a company's operations—accounting, investment, long-range planning, marketing, personnel management, and decision-making. John Child, Ray Loveridge and Stuart Timperley concern themselves with guiding us through the vast literature of organisational behaviour, manpower management and industrial relations, and they show how the literature is related to other aspects of the social sciences, to psychology and to law. Marketing literature is reviewed by Philip Law, and he shows how marketing relies heavily on using quantitative methods and draws on the principles of economics, policy-making and consumer behaviour. David Dews relates the literature of computers to the need for managers to appreciate how the power of the computer can be harnessed to a wide range of business activities, how it can affect people and handle a firm's information and control systems. And finally, Howard Thomas, in his chapter on the theory and applications of quantitative methods, illustrates how these methods are used in marketing, production, finance, business policy, managerial economics, organisational behaviour, research and development, and management information systems.

The book therefore attempts to guide managers and others through a complex subject area of published information and to provide a work of reference to many sources related to business and management. It concentrates on English-language publications because English has been the basic language for management writings. But we need a similar guide-book to management literature which will concentrate instead on writings in other languages. Perhaps a suitably qualified compiler will take on this task.

K.D.C.V.

Contributors

John Child, MA, PhD(Cambridge), Professor of Organisational Behaviour, Management Centre, University of Aston in Birmingham

J. D. Dews, MA(Cantab.), FLA, Librarian, Manchester Business School

John Fletcher, BA(Econ.), ALA, Assistant Librarian, Economics and Business Studies, University of Warwick

Joan M. Harvey, MA, FLA, Senior Lecturer, School of Librarianship, Loughborough Technical College

G. P. Henderson, Managing Director, C.B.D. Research Limited

Anthony G. Hopwood, BSc(Econ.), MBA(Chicago), PhD(Chicago), Member of the Senior Staff of the Administrative Staff College, Henley

P. J. S. Law, BA(Cambridge), Dip.Bus.Admin.(Manchester), Lecturer in Marketing, London Business School

Ray Loveridge, MA(Cambridge), MSc(London), Professor of Manpower Management, Management Centre, University of Aston in Birmingham

Howard Thomas, BSc, MSc(London), MBA(Chicago), PhD(Edinburgh), Senior Lecturer in Statistics and Operational Research, London Business School

Stuart R. Timperley, BA(Strathclyde), BScSoc(London), MBA(Strathclyde), PhD(Liverpool), Lecturer in Organisational Behaviour and Manpower Studies, London Business School

K. D. C Vernon, FLA, Librarian, London Business School

Contents

Contents

PART 1

The literature, the library and
the bibliographical tools

1

Management Literature and Business Information: its Subject Content, Characteristics and Terminology

K. D. C. Vernon

Management literature is largely the product of management education, and much of the writing has been done by teachers and research workers in the business schools. This chapter must therefore cover a wide canvas by surveying not only the subject content and terminology of the literature, but also the general influence of management and education upon it.

The boundaries of this subject area are imprecise and difficult to define; in fact they are so imprecise and the amount of published literature is growing so rapidly that any definition can be disputed. Oscar Wilde, as one would expect, disliked definitions. He said, 'to define is to limit'; and it is true that any rigid delineation of the boundaries of management literature and business information would limit it in an unrealistic way. Nevertheless some broad definition must be attempted in order to explain the content of the subject area as it is understood at present. So perhaps one can define it best by saying that it is concerned with three things— business activities, techniques, the environment within which business must operate. Or, to be more explicit, management literature and business information is concerned with (a) the activities of enterprises and organisa- tions, especially those concerned with manufacture, trade and commerce, and the control and organisation of these activities and the people engaged in carrying them out: (b) the techniques and methods available for use in managing and carrying out these activities: (c) the environment as it directly affects these enterprises and organisations.

It would be unrewarding to pursue this definition further, because it

1

deals with such a wide and heterogeneous field of study. It is obviously, and of necessity, an arbitrary definition. So it is better to let the various chapters in this book be taken as parts of the whole and together provide the over-all coverage of the subject. However, it should be remembered, as Alice reminded her friends, that when I speak, albeit dogmatically, of *management literature,* I mean published or readily available information relevant to the process of managing organisations and people. When I speak of *business information,* I mean published and readily available information, often statistical data, about trade, commerce, manufacture and aspects of the environment related to these activities. But the term *management information,* on the other hand, usually has a specific meaning of its own and is not used here in relation to books, periodicals and libraries—in fact it is accepted to mean financial and other operating data supplied to a manager so that decisions can be taken.

Even though this subject area is so difficult to define, it can at least be broken down into meaningful terms to show the subject content. It is helpful to consider business information and management literature as containing three broad streams, each of which can be further subdivided using terms taken from the *London Classification of Business Studies*:

1. Management responsibility in the enterprise	*2. Environmental studies*	*3. Analytical techniques*
Management	Economics	Operational research
The enterprise	Transport	Statistics
Marketing	Industries	Mathematics
Production	Behavioural sciences	Automation and
R & D	Communication	computers
Finance and accounting	Education	O & M and work study
Manpower planning and personnel	Law	
Office services	Political science	
	Science and technology	
	Philosophical logic and scientific method	

If it is accepted that the manager's job is, in conjunction with others, to plan and decide policy, to organise his resources to achieve agreed objectives, to motivate and communicate with people and to control operations, then the literature in stream 1 above is concerned with the functioning of the enterprise and the manager's part in it. The general term 'management', in this context, refers to the writings about the theory, principles and practices of management, and includes corporate planning and policy formulation. 'The enterprise' is a term used here to cover writings about the company—private and public, small and large. Stream 2 relates to the influence of the environment on the functioning of the enterprise. It obviously covers a vast field of literature and human knowledge, but only those aspects of these subjects which influence and impinge on business and the managing process are relevant. And so while much of the literature of economics, transport, industries and the behavioural sciences has a close bearing on business and management, only small sections of the total literature of communication, education, political science, science and technology and philosophical logic is directly relevant. Stream 3, on the other hand, is directly related to the decision-making process, providing by the use of quantitative methods the techniques for analysing problems and the means for solving them. Again it is obvious that much of the vast literature of mathematics, as an academic discipline, is not directly related to management and decision-making, but nevertheless mathematical methods and statistical mathematics are the very basis on which operational research and optimal decision-making rests. Statistical methods are essential for market research, forecasting and quality control, for example, but other aspects of the literature of statistics, such as the theoretical aspects, are less directly concerned with business and management.

And so it can be seen that the literature of this subject area has a central core, but it is difficult to define it in words. In Chapter 2 the core of the literature will be discussed in terms of books and periodicals. Spreading out from the core there is an enormous amount of published information on economics, social science, technology and other subjects which becomes relevant to research and the study of aspects of business and management problems. In fact the study of management is inter-disciplinary, with its foundations broadly based in economics, the behavioural sciences, statistics and accounting. This can clearly be seen in the stock of books in a business school library which illustrate well the ramifications of the subject area. To browse around the shelves of such a library can help to provide a 'feel' for the nature of the literature—more students should be encouraged to do this in order to learn, for themselves, how much published material is available and how management is concerned with and influenced by so many 'non-business' topics.

MANAGEMENT EDUCATION AND THE LITERATURE

Management education has led directly to the growth of the literature as teachers and research workers have published the results of their thinking, experience and research. Business schools as we know them today have a short history, dating back only to 1881. Before that time there was no systematic study of management methods in industry. Good managers in the eighteenth and early nineteenth centuries—men such as Richard

Arkwright, Boulton and Watt—were practical men who spent their time managing their factories. They were far too busy coping with the new problems of the Industrial Revolution ever to think of writing about their concepts and understanding of the management process. There were a few others, however, who realised early in the nineteenth century the need for a scientific approach to the study of management—men such as Charles Babbage and Andrew Ure, for example—and who did publish books on the subject. But it was not until the end of the century that management education began to get a foothold in American universities.

In 1881 the Wharton School of Finance was founded at the University of Pennsylvania in Philadelphia, and it was there that the idea of teaching business skills at a university level of education first took root. But American universities were reluctant, at first, to accept into their academic circles businessmen and students of management. They did not fit easily into the usual organisation of faculties and departments. The same attitude persisted much later in British universities in the 1960s, when business schools were beginning to establish themselves in this country.

Seventeen years later, in 1898, the Universities of Chicago and California set up their business schools. Others soon followed and in 1908 the most famous of all, the Harvard Business School, was founded. The first period, when business schools were struggling for a foothold in American universities, lasted from 1881 to 1914, but it was not until the 1920s and 1930s that the need for management education was widely recognised in America and the business schools began to flourish at many centres. Frequently they developed out of the economics departments in the universities. Research into business problems started, ideas began to germinate and books began to be written. The business world and the academic world could in fact talk together. American managers realised that they had much to learn 'away from the job'.

There are now hundreds of graduate business schools in America, and the number of academic staff in these schools, many of whom are voluminous writers of books and articles, is very large. It is therefore not surprising, but nevertheless worth noting, that most of the seminal books and articles upon which the main ideas for management education are based, have been written by outstanding teachers and thinkers in American business schools. Between the years 1930 and 1950 the writings of such men as Elton Mayo, Chester Barnard, F. J. Roethlisberger, Peter Drucker and Herbert Simon, to mention but a few, were compelling the attention of a new breed of educated managers who could see the relevance of their ideas to business and management methods in a changing society. But these leaders in thought owed much to the earlier ideas and practices of people such as Frank and Lillian Gilbreth and F. W. Taylor, the pioneer of scientific management, who advocated fair pay by measuring work accurately and implemented his system in many American factories between 1880 and 1909. His ideas are expounded in his books *Shop management* (1903) and *Principles of scientific management* (1911). They were taken up and developed by his contemporary Henry L. Gantt in several papers and books which were published about the same time, and the concept of scientific management was given academic recognition through the efforts of an early business school teacher, H. S. Person of the Amos Tuck School at Dartmouth. But it was a Frenchman, Henri Fayol, who was the first to conceive a general theory of management in his book *Administration industrielle et générale* in 1916.

In addition to books, the American business schools have been responsible for starting and editing some of the most influential periodicals concerned with management—periodicals such as the *Harvard Business Review* and the *Journal of Business*, for example. These will be discussed in greater detail in Chapter 6, but their influence over a period of many years is evident from the fact that so many of the articles in them are cited as references in books and other articles. They contain the first results of many important research findings, writings which have subsequently been taken up and developed further and frequently used in improving management and business practices.

On the other side of the coin, however, it must be stated that there is a great disparity in standard and value between the best and the worst American management books and articles. An unfortunately large number of them must inevitably be rejected by British and European managers but the best are essential for study and teaching. In addition, many American writings, even the best, are wordy and unattractive in style to British readers, so a natural resistance is sometimes built up against them, perhaps unfairly, for this reason alone.

The dominance of American literature, good and bad, is especially evident to British and European librarians and library users, who can see so clearly on the shelves of their business and management libraries the high proportion of books written and published in America. The best textbooks, written by American teachers, have been used extensively not only in the American business schools, but also in the more recently established British and European business schools, universities and other institutions where business studies are pursued. Once a book has been taken up as a textbook in business schools, the publishers have the happy prospect of a big demand for several years and the consequential financial gains. It is small wonder, then, that the larger American publishers in particular have earnestly wooed the best teachers in the business schools to write more and more. The acceptance of management education as a 'good thing' has led directly to a very rapid growth in the numbers of books and periodicals, and of libraries to house them.

The American business schools have also greatly influenced the form of the literature. They have given it two particular characteristics—case studies and collections of readings—which publishers have promoted.

The first of these was fathered by the Harvard Business School, where the teaching has always been based on case studies of real situations and problems which management has had to meet. The case studies have been compiled and written up by teachers, who have used them as material for study and discussion by students. This method of teaching, which has always been used so effectively at Harvard, is now widely accepted as a means of teaching management. It led to the establishment of the great Intercollegiate Case Clearing House at Harvard, which started operating in 1956 and which now runs a big business by issuing over 3 000 000 copies of cases annually. Teachers from all over the world in business schools and colleges get much of their teaching material from the Clearing House and use it in their classes. The cases are all listed annually in the *Intercollegiate Bibliography: cases in business administration* (ICCH, Boston)—an invaluable tool in every business school library and essential to management teachers everywhere.

Many of the cases have been collected together and published as books. These books of cases are one of the hallmarks of management literature. They are often based on some aspect of management—business policy, marketing or personnel problems, for example—and they usually contain a text on the subject followed by the cases. Sometimes the publishers also provide a teacher's manual to go with the book. Many case books of this nature are also listed in the *Intercollegiate Bibliography*.

The second characteristic of the literature is the large number of books of readings which have been published. So much of the best writing on any management topic is scattered in a large number of articles, pamphlets, reports and books that it can sometimes be a convenience to republish a selection of these in one volume. The compilers of such books are usually well-known experts in their subject. They select the articles or other writings which they consider important to the subject; each article is called a chapter; an introductory essay on the subject which links all the writings together is written by the compiler; and, hey presto! there is another book ready for publication. This idea became very popular with American publishers. It can rightly be said, from a librarian's point of view, that this large-scale reprinting of previously published writings, which are still available in periodicals and elsewhere, is increasing the number of books unnecessarily by duplication. But on the other hand, just because there is so much published material on business and management, a well-selected distillation of writings is a great convenience to busy people and provides useful texts for study purposes.

This dominance of American writings is now becoming less pronounced in British and European business schools and libraries. The development of management thinking in the UK is well described in *British management thought: a critical analysis,* by John Child (Allen and Unwin, 1969). He traces the way in which British managerial thinking has slowly been built up into a body of knowledge during the past 50 years, and boldly concludes by giving an assessment of that body of knowledge, recorded as it is in books and periodicals. He points out that as educational programmes in general are supported by the published literature, the recorded British management thought was, at the time of writing, deficient for management educational purposes. Hence, with the establishment of the London and Manchester Business Schools in 1965 and the impetus to management education which their founding imparted, it was necessary to rely at first largely on American ideas and publications, while meeting the challenge of establishing a British body of systematic knowledge. Now, 10 years later, there is a considerable amount of British- and European-based teaching materials, case studies, etc., which is increasingly being used in business schools. A British Case Clearing House has recently been established at Cranfield to distribute cases to teachers. Mildred Wheatcroft in her book *The revolution in British management education* (Pitman, 1970) has surveyed the remarkable change in attitudes towards management education which took place in this country during the decade of the 1960s.

New ideas flow from research and the business schools have provided the environment within which research can be conducted. The results usually appear first as articles in periodicals or as theses or dissertations, and then subsequently the results and ideas are often developed and enlarged into books and become absorbed into the literature. The publication of research results is discussed in Chapter 8. It is sufficient here merely to recognise the fact that the increasing volume of research has been one of the main influences on the growth of the literature. There has been far too little research yet into business problems in the UK and in Europe to provide a new body of knowledge which can take the place of American ideas and publications. But the situation is slowly changing.

The relevance of management literature to all aspects of managing far beyond the confines of 'business' is now widely recognised. Management principles, evolving as they always are, together with decision-making techniques and quantitative methods of problem analysis, are being widely used in government, public services and organisations of all kinds. If management is concerned with 'getting things done through people', then its literature is certainly relevant to a very wide spectrum of human activity. And similarly important opinion-forming books of wide general interest, such as Galbraith's *New industrial state*, Rachel Carson's *Silent Spring*, Schumacher's *Small is beautiful*, de Bono's *Use of lateral thinking* and McLuhan's *Understanding media*, for example, are highly relevant to management. So the boundaries of management literature are constantly shifting and being influenced by writings concerned with many aspects of the environment within which business operates. At the present time there is a growing amount of writing about the social responsibility of business, pollution and the need to conserve natural resources.

The business schools in the UK and in Europe are producing a growing number of professionally educated managers, while companies and other organisations are increasingly training their own executives and supervisors to understand and adopt modern, evolving management methods. More and more people therefore are studing the literature of management, using the books—still frequently American books—and periodicals, distilling from them the ideas which can be practically applied and learning to realise that 'practical' men and women, as all good managers must be, can in fact turn to the literature for assistance in solving management problems. This is having a profound effect on libraries which are concerned with this subject area and on publishers, who realise that there is a new and growing market for books and periodicals. In the prefaces and introductions to many new books concerned with varying aspects of management and business the authors state that the book is intended for executives and business students. Thus it is becoming accepted that today's managers need to make use of the literature, and the growing number of business graduates coming from the business schools have been accustomed to using their libraries. They know that they must continue to rely on the literature if they are to keep up to date with new ideas.

Professionally educated managers know that information relevant to their problems exists. They may not all be expert library users, but as their numbers continue to expand they will increasingly require access to libraries and information services. They will expect the libraries they use to provide the most important books, to subscribe to the leading management and business periodicals, to have statistical publications readily available and to maintain a relevant collection of information about companies. They need librarians who can help them to find the information they require at the time they want it. In fact there is an increasing need for users of management literature and business information to take a more active interest, in co-operation with librarians, in the documentation and bibliographical control of their information resources.

K. G. B. Bakewell in his recent thesis *The Development of management documentation services in the United Kingdom* (Queen's University of Belfast, 1973) has made a careful study of our documentation and information services, libraries, organisations and both the form and content of the literature. He has rightly concluded that the over-all picture is one of slow development; and although the problems of indexing and classification are being tackled, progress is not yet rapid enough. Significantly he goes on to say: 'the greatest difficulty is perhaps that of making managers, management teachers and management research workers aware of the information sources which are available and it is here that the librarian has a vital role to play'.

TERMINOLOGY

The orderly use of meaningful words and terms is very necessary in management writing: without it bibliographical control is difficult. New ideas must be expressed simply and terms must be used consistently. The terminology used in management books and articles is described by librarians and information scientists as 'soft'. Scientific terms, on the other hand, are 'hard'—they describe known facts, people accept them as precise words and there is no argument about their meaning. This statement about terms being 'soft' or 'hard' may not seem, to the average library user, to be of much significance—why should it be? Its significance lies in the fact that when one uses indexes for finding information precise terms are more likely to produce relevant references to books or articles than imprecise ones. It is easier to find relevant references in an index to, say, a chemical formula than it is to a term like 'organisation'. In mechanical information retrieval systems this fact becomes significant because one does not want to be presented with a string of references from a computer store which are not relevant to one's requirement. The problem is a semantic one and will not be solved satisfactorily so long as we use arbitrary and imprecise terms in management writings.

There is a great need for those who write, teach and study the literature of management to take an interest in the meanings of some of the words and terms they use. The word 'organisation' is a case in point, because it is so important. In an article called 'Semantic hay—the word *organization*', by L. F. Urwick (*Omega*, 1(1), 97–105, 1973), the author discusses the importance of semantics and shows that the term 'organisation' has been given two different interpretations by people with different claims to the subject. He argues that the use of the term 'organisation' of an institution as a whole has diverted attention from the study of organisation structure, and that this diversion leads to faulty communication in the literature—a librarian would also argue that it causes confusion in indexing and classification and, hence, makes information retrieval difficult. We need better bibliographical control of the literature, and writers must begin to assist librarians in this respect.

Other examples will readily spring to mind. 'International business' is a term widely used in the literature, but writers frequently call it by other names, such as 'multinational business', 'international marketing', 'international trade', 'foreign commerce', 'world business' or 'overseas business'. It would be much better for all concerned if confusion could be avoided and the term 'international business' were accepted to mean all business activities abroad. Donald F. Mulvihill in his short article 'Terminology in international business studies—order out of chaos' *(Journal of International Business Studies*, Spring, 87–91, 1973) has recognised the problem and suggested a group of terms which could lead to a more orderly approach in the use of words concerned with business abroad. With the growing volume of international trade and business some standardisation of terms among the various languages is also required if misunderstanding in communication is to be avoided.

This is not the place for a full discussion of the problem of terminology in the literature, but it is patently clear that writers, teachers and librarians should begin to grasp this nettle and try to reach some agreement on terms which cause confusion. Some useful work has been done by compilers of thesauri such as J. F. Blagden's *Management information retrieval: a new indexing language* (Management Publications, 1971) and glossaries such as *Management glossary*, by H. Johannsen and A. Robertson (Longman, 1968), which attempt to provide acceptable definitions of management terms. But much remains to be done to standardise, to a greater extent, the imprecise language which is used so needlessly in American and British books and articles. We are liable to sink into a sea of confusion as the quantity of management literature increases, the jargon jungle grows ever faster and writers on management subjects invent more and more repellent words to express their ideas. We must totally reject abominable and pompous phraseology such as 'a dynamic conceptual framework capable of accommodating the complex interactions inherent in the management process' and stick to simple meaningful English.

Management literature is spreading out more and more to comprehend the broad environment within which business must work and also towards the literature of 'people'—psychology, social science and behavioural sciences in general. The growing awareness of the need for industrial companies to be socially accountable for their operations is opening up the need to study urban and community problems, pollution and waste disposal. As the boundaries spread, the central core remains, but the core of the literature, which we will now consider in Chapter 2, has to be used and interpreted.

2

The Core of the Literature

K. D. C. Vernon

In the previous chapter the subject content and very wide ramifications of management and business literature were considered. This chapter will discuss the core of the literature—the nucleus or central part which contains the generally accepted concepts, principles and methods upon which practices have been based—but it will only discuss it in terms of books and other publications.

There are several very good reasons why it is necessary to identify the books and periodicals which contain the writings essential to an understanding of management, its purposes, practices and principles. In science one accepts that certain publications contain explanations of principles and natural laws which are essential to man's understanding of nature. They are explained in definitive books and papers such as Newton's *Principia,* for example, which was published in 1687 and contained the laws of motion and gravity on which much of the science of physics was based for nearly 300 years; Faraday's writings on electromagnetic induction, which enunciated the main principles on which modern electrical engineering is based; or Rutherford's books and articles on the atom, which have so influenced our twentieth-century hopes and fears. Management obviously cannot claim publications of such great significance for mankind, but nevertheless many valuable seminal books have been written and they have contributed, to a greater or lesser extent, to an understanding of the management of organisations, people and resources.

Unlike science, it is hard to identify with confidence the concepts which have been generally accepted as fundamental to the development of management thought, not only because the subject is so difficult to define, but also because it changes and develops rapidly and people have different concepts of it at different times. Nevertheless, if management is becoming a profession, as many people believe, there must be a central body of published knowledge which is basic to those who study it. This is one reason why an acceptable core list of publications is needed, even though it must always be an arbitrary list and one which must constantly be revised as new concepts and ideas are developed, tested and accepted.

Another reason is that the subject is widely studied in business schools, particularly in America and Europe, in universities and colleges and on a multitude of courses. In addition to this large educational input, there is all the internal management training organised by companies and training boards and much of this also has to be based on the same central body of published knowledge. Teachers and course organisers must have information about the basic publications which can be used for business studies and courses.

A third reason for a core list is to enable libraries, especially small collections, to be set up. Libraries are obviously essential for educational establishments and, with the increasing demand for the literature of management, librarians are being pressed to provide that literature by adding the 'most important' books and periodicals in this subject field to their libraries. More and more companies and training establishments are seeing the need to set up small collections of books and periodicals on management. Special libraries concerned with technological, industrial, commercial, scientific and professional subject fields are all required to add management literature to their specialised collections because of its pervasive relevance. Public libraries, too, are now required by the demand to add an increasing number of books and periodicals on management to their stocks, and many of the larger cities provide excellent commercial reference libraries run for the general benefit of the local business community.

The need for core lists, then, is essential, but how is it possible to compile lists and bibliographies of selected publications which contain only titles of books and periodicals which are 'essential' to all who wish to study management or aspects of it? The answer to this question is that a lot more work and effort must be undertaken by librarians, teachers in business schools, research workers and practising managers in examining, assessing, listing and documenting the literature before agreement can be reached on the real core publications. We need more guides to sources of information; more surveys and reviews of the literature in selected subject areas by specialists in these fields; more carefully selected bibliographies which boldly reject the bad and the superficial writings, many of which have emanated from America, the cradle of management thinking; more analytical surveys of how the literature is being used; so that our libraries can be built upon known facts about the publications they should contain. This book provides some guidance to those who are concerned with assessing and using the literature. Hopefully it will also provoke them to examine some of the problems raised.

Many useful bibliographical tools designed to help those who want to know what publications are available already exist, and some of these are discussed in Chapters 5 and 7. A core list, however, is basic to all—other bibliographies are important for the various specific purposes they are designed to serve. But for the sake of a definition let us say, quite arbitrarily, that 'a core list of basic books about management contains only those titles which are essential to a person wishing to understand the concepts, principles and generally accepted practices of the subject. It must include some of the "classics" and also the best expressions of the latest developments.' The size of the list can be quite small to start with—100 titles, for example—if it is required for establishing a small library in a company or other organisation. Or it can be more comprehensive—1000 titles should be sufficient—if it is required either as a book-selection tool for a medium-sized library or as a guide to the literature of the main fields of study relevant not only to management and its functions, but also to its environment—economic, technical, socio-logical, behavioural, educational and legal.

It is common practice in the libraries of educational establishments, including business schools, to segregate a 'reserved collection' of books which contain all the essential and recommended reading which students have to undertake in their courses. Lists of the titles in these reserved collections are in fact 'core lists' to the college or school concerned. Few such lists, however, have been published and widely used. They are regarded mainly as domestic lists which represent primarily the opinions of individual teachers in a particular establishment on what management students should read for their course. If a selection of these lists from, say, 10 different business schools were compared, it is probable that some of the titles would appear on all the lists. An acceptable core list might be prepared on this basis, but it would of course be a 'teaching list' and so far there has been little concerted effort to reach agreement in this respect. But a start should be made.

The famous Baker Library at Harvard Business School has published a list of its core collection which is now being revised and updated annually, *Core Collection: an author and subject guide* (Baker Library, Harvard Business School). This list of 4000 titles was compiled by reference librarians who examined reading lists used on courses at Harvard and various other bibliographies, and then selected from these a representative collection of recent books in all subject fields studied at the School. It is thus an important bibliography and guide for librarians, teachers, students, managers and others concerned with the literature of management. It provides one answer to the question previously posed—how can an acceptable core list be compiled? But valuable though this list is, and it undoubtedly contains most of the currently available seminal books and textbooks, it is composed mainly of American publications.

Various British and European lists and bibliographies also provide good guidance to the literature, and the British Institute of Management's list *A basic library of management* (BIM, 1974) is particularly useful. It represents a conscious attempt to compile a list of the best books for managers in industry, for training officers and for organisations wishing to form a small collection of management books to add to their own internal library service. The need remains, however, for an impartial list which includes important British and European books, as well as the best American books, on the main aspects of management and business studies. Ideally the list should be broadly acceptable as a sound basis for study and reading in this subject area. It must be regularly updated and revised, and inevitably individual managers, teachers and librarians will regard it, as indeed they should, as a series of recommendations.

Lists of 'best-sellers' in management and business studies have often been compiled by consulting or publishing firms. These lists are usually based on reported sales of books and therefore cannot provide more than a guide to the current popularity of individual books. Nevertheless they act as a means of calling attention to a few important books and thereby probably help to add a few titles to the core of the literature each year.

Another possible way of identifying important core publications is by means of use-surveys which are sometimes carried out in libraries. Unfortunately there have not been many assessments of this kind which have been made for management literature. They are difficult to make and must of necessity extend over a considerable period of time. Even when they are completed, their results are often influenced by external events which may lead people to use particular books in a library heavily for a short period. In an academic library, for instance, the way the books are used is greatly influenced by the courses which are being taught at the institution concerned and by the teachers' recommendations. Surveys of this kind are therefore difficult to analyse accurately.

Despite these and other limitations to their usefulness as a means of assessment, several surveys do give valuable guidance to the way the literature is being used. *What managers read* (BIM Occasional Paper, new series OPN3, 1969) is a report by J. F. Blagden which assesses the reading habits of managers on the basis of a particular sample— namely, all the books out on loan from the BIM Library on a particular date in November 1967. The primary assumption was that if a busy manager decides to read up a subject, it is pretty certain that he has a problem in that area. The survey therefore gives a broad picture of what problems or subjects were attracting most attention at that time. It includes a list of the 'top 20' titles and some interesting tables which indicate how the literature was then being used. The survey indicates that most managerial reading lies in the field of human problems, followed by general management, marketing and production management in that order. It also shows very clearly that the demand is for recent publications —the demand for books published within the past 5 years was 70% of the total.

The list of 100 books which follows is grouped for convenience under a few main subject headings and has been compiled by the author, using his experience of the literature and drawing on other lists and bibliographies in the same subject field. The list is therefore very short, arbitrarily chosen and inevitably open to criticism, but nevertheless it is put forward as a basis for an agreed core list. It may be an acceptable list in the first instance for executives who wish to set up a collection of management books in a company, for example, or for librarians faced with the task of forming small libraries or special collections in this subject field. They can then refer from this list to Chapters 12–17 for other titles in the various subject areas reviewed in this book. Books on economics, sociology, psychology, mathematics and other disciplines are excluded unless they are specifically related to business.

Some quite new books have been included, not because they are widely accepted yet as seminal publications, but because they appear to have added important new thinking to the subject. Some textbooks have been included because of their undoubted practical value. A few books of readings have also been incorporated in the list because they include seminal and conceptual writings culled from periodicals and other publications. Each main section of the list therefore contains basic books relevant to modern management thinking, important new books, textbooks or introductions. It does not contain many of the older books which influenced pre-war thinking on management.

It is hoped that this list will provide others, better qualified than the author, to spot omissions and enjoy the game of improving its usefulness! The limit of 100 books is entirely arbitrary and has no merit apart from the fact that it provides a convenient starting point, a budget limit of £350 (or $840) at 1973 prices and a rule for the game!

A CORE LIST OF 100 BOOKS

Paperback editions are now so frequently published that users of this list should check for themselves the details of publishers and dates which are given here. No prices are stated because of the frequent changes which occur, but for £350 (in 1973) most of these books could be purchased. The 10 subject divisions under which the books are grouped should not be taken as a rigid classification of the subject field; they are used here merely as a convenient method of arranging the list. The section on organisational behaviour is larger than any of the others because so many books on the subject of organisations have had a big influence on the development of management thinking.

1. General management

Many general books on business, economic conditions and society have greatly influenced management thinking, but they have been excluded because this section is limited to books on the principles and practice of management. Books by Galbraith, Jay, Spiegelberg and Tugendhat, for instance, would undoubtedly find a place in a larger core list which included books on the economic and sociological environment of business.

Child, J.: *British management thought: a critical analysis* (Allen and Unwin, 1969)
The best available assessment of British managerial thinking during the past 50 years.

Drucker, P. F.: *Managing for results* (Pan Books, 1967)
First published by Harper and Row in 1964. A practical book which achieved great popularity.

Drucker, P. F.: *Practice of management* (Heinemann, 1963)
First published by Harper and Row in 1955, this book established Drucker as one of the most influential writers on management.

Jay, A.: *Management and Machiavelli* (Penguin Books, 1970)
First published in 1967.

Koontz, H. and O'Donnell, C.: *Principles of management: an analysis of managerial functions* (4th ed., McGraw-Hill, 1968)
First published in 1964. Provides a conceptual framework for management.

Revans, R. W.: *Theory of practice in management* (Macdonald, 1966)
Introduces new European ideas on management.

Sloan, A. P.: *My years with General Motors* (Sidgwick and Jackson, 1965)
A management classic of American entrepreneurship.

Stewart, R.: *Reality of management* (Pan Books, 1970)
First published in 1963. An important examination of management in practice based on the results of 1500 interviews.

Urwiek, L. and Brech, E. F. L.: *The making of scientific management* (3 vols., Pitman, 1945)
A management classic.

2. Business Policy and International Business

Ansoff, H. I.: *Corporate strategy: an analytic approach to business policy for growth and expansion* (Penguin, 1970)
First published in 1965 by McGraw-Hill.

Chandler, A. D.: *Strategy and structure: chapters in the history of industrial enterprise* (MIT Press, 1963)
Analyses the development of the 70 largest American companies.

Dean, J.: *Managerial economics* (Prentice-Hall, 1964)
First published in 1951. Has been influential in promoting the use of economic analysis in formulating business policies.

Kindleberger, C. P.: *The international corporation: a symposium* (MIT Press, 1970)

Learned, E. P., Aguilar, F. J. and Valtz, R. C. K.: *European problems in general management* (Irwin, 1963)
Based on cases used at IMEDE, the Swiss business school, by teachers from Harvard. The companion volume *Business policy: text and cases*, by Learned, Christensen and Andrews (Irwin, 1969), has been widely used for teaching.

Robock. S. H. and Simmonds, K.: *International business and multinational enterprises* (Irwin, 1973)

Steiner, G. A. ed.: *Managerial long-range planning* (McGraw Hill, 1963)
Describes how long-range planning programmes have been used in American companies.

Stopford, J. M. and Wells, L.T.: *Managing the multinational enterprise: organisation of the firm and ownership of the subsidiaries.* (Basic Books, 1972 and Longman, 1972)

3. Marketing

Bartels, R.: *Development of marketing thought* (Irwin, 1962)
Covers the period 1900–1960.

Britt, S. H.: *Consumer behavior and the behavioral sciences* (Wiley, 1966)

Ehrenberg, A. S. C.: *Repeat Buying: theory and applications* (North-Holland, 1973)

Green, P. E. and Tull, D. S.: *Research for marketing decisions* (3rd ed., Prentice-Hall, 1970)
First published in 1966.

Howard, J. A.: *Marketing theory* (Allyn and Bacon, 1965)

Kotler, P.: *Marketing management: analysis, planning and control* (2nd ed., Prentice-Hall, 1972)
Generally accepted as the standard text on this subject. First published in 1967.

Kotler, P. and Cox, K. K.: *Readings in marketing management* (Prentice-Hall, 1972)
Includes many important writings by leaders in marketing thought.

Levitt, T.: *Innovation in marketing: new perspectives for profit and growth* (McGraw-Hill, 1962)
An American book which has influenced the development of marketing.

Levitt, T.: *The marketing mode: pathways to corporate growth* (McGraw-Hill, 1969)

4. Production

Ammer, D. S.: *Materials management* (Revised ed., Irwin, 1968)
First published in 1962.

Buffa, E. S.: *Modern production management* (4th ed., Wiley, 1973)
First published in 1963. His other book, *Readings in production and operations management* (Wiley, 1966), is a collection of papers which have influenced production concepts.

Moore, F. G.: *Manufacturing management* (5th ed., Irwin, 1969)
First published in 1953.

Nicholson, T. A. J.: *Optimization in industry* (2 vols., Longman, 1971)
Vol. 1. reviews procedures for solving optimisation problems.
Vol. 2. reviews their application in industrial practice.

Timms, H. L. and Pohler, M. F.: *The production function in business: decision systems for production and operations management* (3rd ed., Irwin, 1970)
First published in 1962.

5. Corporate finance and management accounting

Anthony, R. N.: *Management accounting: principles* (Revised ed., Irwin, 1970)
His other book, *Management accounting: text and cases* (4th ed., Irwin, 1970), is widely used for teaching.

Argyris, C.: *The impact of budgets on people* (Cornell University Press, 1952)
The first study to recognise the significance of the human element in the budgetary process.

Brealey, R. A.: *An introduction to risk and return on common stocks* (MIT Press, 1969)

Clarkson, G. P. E. and Elliott, B. J.: *Managing money and finance* (2nd ed., Gower Press, 1972)
The best introduction to the creative nature of the financial manager's task.

Fama, E. F. and Miller, M. H.: *Theory of finance* (Holt, Rinehart and Winston, 1972)

Horngren, C. T.: *Accounting for management control* (2nd ed., Prentice-Hall, 1970)
First published in 1965.

Merrett, A. J. and Sykes, A.: *Capital budgeting and company finance* (2nd ed., Longman, 1973)
This and their other book, *Finance and analysis of capital projects* (2nd ed., Longman, 1973), have been widely used in practice and teaching.

Parker, R. H.: *Management accounting: an historical perspective* (Macmillan, 1969)
An authoritative discussion of the development of accounting concepts.

Reid, W. and Myddleton, D. R.: *The meaning of company accounts* (2nd ed., Gower Press, 1974)
A practical presentation of analytical accounting techniques.

Shillinglaw, G.: *Cost accounting: analysis and control* (3rd ed., Irwin, 1972)
An essential textbook first published in 1961.

Sizer, J.: *Insight into management accounting* (Penguin, 1969)
Probably the best British introduction to the financial aspects of management.

Solomon, E., ed.: *Management of corporate capital* (Free Press, 1959)
Includes many of the pioneering articles on this subject.

Solomon, E.: *Theory of financial management* (Columbia University Press, 1963)

Van Horne, J. C.: *Financial management and policy* (Prentice-Hall, 1971)

6. Personnel and industrial relations

The books in this and the following section on Organisational Behaviour are divided arbitrarily rather than significantly into two sections.

Bain, G. S.: *Growth of white collar unionism* (Clarendon Press, 1970)

Clegg, H. A.: *System of industrial relations in Great Britain* (2nd ed., Blackwell, 1972)
The most authoritative book on this subject.

Flanders, A.: *The Fawley productivity agreements: a case study of management and collective bargaining* (Faber, 1964)
A pioneering book on participative methods of bargaining.

Flanders, A.: *Management and unions: the theory and reform of industrial relations* (Faber, 1970)

Jaques, E.: *Equitable payment* (Penguin, 1967)
Based on his research on the Glacier project.

Lowndes, R.: *Industrial relations: a contemporary survey* (Holt, Rinehart and Winston, 1972)

Lupton, T. and Gowler, D.: *Selecting a wage payment system* (Kogan Page, 1969)

Paul, W. J. and Robertson, K. B.: *Job enrichment and employee motivation* (Gower Press, 1970)

Pigors, P. and Myers, C. A.: *Personnel administration* (7th ed., McGraw-Hill, 1973)
A classic in this subject field. First published in 1947.

Report of the Royal Commission on Trade Unions and Employer Associations (Donovan Report) (Cmnd. 3623, HMSO, 1968)
The most lucid analysis of industrial relations in the UK.

Strauss, G. and Sayles, L. R.: *Personnel: human problems of management* (2nd revised ed., Prentice-Hall, 1972)
First published in 1960.

7.   Organisational behaviour

Argyle, M.: *Social psychology of work* (Allen Lane, 1972)

Argyris, C.: *Personality and organization: the conflict between the system and the individual* (Harper and Row, 1970)
One of several influential books by Argyris.

Barnard, C. I.: *The functions of the executive* (Harvard University Press, 1964)
A management classic, first published in 1938.

Bennis, W. G.: *Organisation development: its nature, origins and prospects* (Addison-Wesley, 1969)
Other writings by the same author have also influenced thinking in this subject.

Blake, R. and Mouton, J. S.: *The managerial grid: key orientations for achieving production through people* (Gulf Publishing Co., Houston, 1964)

Blau, P. M. and Scott, W. R.: *Formal organisations: a comparative approach* (Routledge and Kegan Paul, 1964)

Brown, W.: *Exploration in management* (Penguin, 1972)
First published in 1960. Describes the Glacier Metal Company's project led by Elliott Jaques.

Burns, T. and Stalker, G. M.: *Management of innovation* (Tavistock Press, 1966)
A pioneering study of Scottish electronics companies moving into more dynamic environments.

Cyert, R. M. and March, J. G.: *A behavioural theory of the firm* (Prentice-Hall, 1963)

Follett, M. P.: *Dynamic administration: the papers of Mary Parker Follett*, ed. by H. C. Metcalf and L. Urwick (Pitman, 1963)

Herzberg, F., Mausner, B. and Synderman, B. B.: *The motivation to work* (Wiley, 1959)
A pioneering work in the theory of job satisfaction.

Katz, D. and Kahn, R. L.: *Social psychology of organisations* (Wiley, 1966)

Lawrence, P. R. and Lorsch, J. W.: *Organisations and environment: managing differentiation and integration* (Harvard Graduate School of Business Administration, 1967)

Leavitt, H. J.: *Managerial psychology* (3rd ed., University of Chicago Press, 1972)
First published in 1958.

Likert, R.: *New patterns of management* (McGraw-Hill, 1961)
Contains the results of his influencial research work.

Lupton, T.: *Management and the social sciences* (2nd ed., Penguin, 1971)
First published in 1966.

McGregor, D.: *Human side of enterprise* (McGraw-Hill, 1960)
A book of classic importance.

March, J. G. and Simon, H. A.: *Organisations* (Wiley, 1965)

Miller, E. J. and Rice, A. K.: *Systems of organisation: the control of task and sentient boundaries* (Tavistock Press, 1967)
First published in 1958.

Pugh, D. S., Hickson, D. J. and Hinings, C. R.: *Writers on organisations* (2nd ed., Penguin, 1971)
A compact collection of summaries of the work of the main writers on organisations.

Roethlisberger, F. J. and Dickson, W. J.: *Management and the worker* (Harvard University Press, 1939)
The classic report on the famous Hawthorne Experiments.

Schein, E. H.: *Organisational psychology* (2nd ed., Prentice-Hall, 1972)
First published in 1965.

Vroom, V. H.: *Work and motivation* (Wiley, 1964)

Woodward, J.: *Industrial organisation: theory and practice* (Oxford University Press, 1965).

8. Business law

This short section lists only a few British and European law books. Different titles would obviously have to be selected for American business law and the law of other countries.

Charlesworth and Cain: *Company law* (10th ed., Stevens, 1972)
First published in 1932.

Cheshire, G. C. and Fifoot, C. H.: *Law of contract* (8th ed., Butterworths, 1972)
First published in 1945.

Gower, L. C. B.: *Principles of modern company law* (3rd ed., Stevens, 1969)
First published in 1954.

Mitchell, E.: *Businessman's guide to commercial conduct and the law* (Business Books, 1972)

Zaphiriou, G. A.: *European business law* (Sweet and Maxwell, 1970)
Provides basic information and general concepts.

9. Operational research and quantitative methods

Ackoff, R. L. and Sasieni, M. W.: *Fundamentals of operations research* (4th ed., Wiley, 1970)
First published in 1968.

Bierman, H., Bonini, C. P. and Hansman, W. H.: *Quantitative analysis for business decisions* (3rd ed., Irwin, 1969)
First published in 1968.

Duckworth, E.: *A guide to operational research* (Methuen, 1967)
First published in 1962. A very readable introduction.

Moore, P. G.: *Statistics and the manager: the use of statistics and probability in managerial decisions* (Macdonald, 1966)

Raiffa, H. and Schlaifer, R.: *Applied statistical decision theory* (Harvard University Press, 1961)

Rivett, P. and Ackoff, R. L.: *Manager's guide to operations research* (Wiley, 1963)
An introduction intended for executives.

Schlaifer, R.: *Analysis of decisions under uncertainty* (McGraw-Hill, 1969)

Wagner, H. M.: *Principles of management science: with applications to executive decisions* (Prentice-Hall, 1970)
An essential textbook.

10. Information control and computers

Beer, Stafford: *Cybernetics and management* (2nd ed., English Universities Press, 1967)

Dearden, J.: *Computers in business management* (Irwin, 1966)

Hertz, D. B.: *New power for management: computer systems and management science* (McGraw-Hill, 1967)

Mumford, E. and Banks, O.: *The computer and the clerk* (Routledge, 1967)
This and other books by Enid Mumford have influenced management attitudes towards computers.

Simon, H. A.: *Shape of automation for men and management* (Harper and Row, 1965)
Brings together much of the author's original thinking on systems and automation in the 1950s.

Stewart, R.: *How computers affect management* (Macmillan, 1971)
Based on case studies.

Wiener, N.: *Human use of human beings: cybernetics and society* (Houghton Mifflin, 1949)
Contains the author's basic concepts on cybernetics and control.

PERIODICALS

So far we have only considered books which contain the core of the literature. But periodicals are no less important; in fact they are more so for the growing number of managers, teachers, research workers and students who need to keep up to date with the latest developments in management thought and practice, or with the results of research into business problems. Chapter 6 is devoted to periodicals within our subject field, but in order to complete the picture we have been trying to form of those publications—books and periodicals—which contain information essential to an understanding of management, a core list of periodicals is included here. Perhaps librarians who are handling large numbers of periodicals daily realise more clearly than their academic colleagues that some periodicals are far more important and are in much heavier demand by library users than others. It is these periodicals that we are concerned with now.

The following core list of periodicals has been compiled as a joint project by an informal group of librarians from British and European business schools and edited by J. D. Dews. It was first published in *Management Education and Development*, Dec., **4**(3), 170–177 (1973). The intention was threefold: (1) to provide new business schools, university departments and colleges with a guide to the periodicals to which they should consider subscribing, and existing schools and colleges with a list against which they may review their subscriptions; (2) to provide a similar guide for company and other libraries which find themselves responsible for giving services to a management department; (3) to provide teachers, students, businessmen and other users of management literature with an indication of the important journals in the subject area.

The aim has been to present a balanced collection, covering the important branches of the field, while keeping the total number of journals as small as possible.

The list is arranged in sections, in order to show the structure of the selection process. The 'Main' list consists of journals which any library providing for the study of business and management might be expected to have and which represent the core. There are then subsidiary lists of the main journals in five subject areas which are relevant to management: economics, sociology, psychology, computers and systems analysis, and the 'environment'. These lists have been deliberately restricted to a few important journals, since the number of journals acquired in these topics would depend very much on the bias of interests among the users of a particular library. The third section lists the journals which are considered relevant and important to libraries in particular countries, or with an interest in those countries. The complete list is then given in one alphabetical sequence. The main list consisting of 56 titles and the subsidiary list of the most important journals in five subject areas relevant to management are given below.

Core list of periodicals

Academy of Management Journal (School of Business Administration, University of Oregon)

Accounting and Business Research (Institute of Chartered Accountants in England and Wales)

Accounting Review (American Accounting Association)

Administrative Science Quarterly (Graduate School of Business Administration, Cornell University)

British Journal of Industrial Relations (London School of Economics and Political Science)

Business Horizons (Graduate School of Business, Indiana University)

Business Topics (Bureau of Business and Economic Research, Michigan State University)

California Management Review (Graduate School of Business Administration, University of California)

Columbia Journal of World Business (Graduate School of Business Administration, Columbia University)

European Business (INSEAD)

European Journal of Marketing (University of Bradford)

European Marketing Research Review (European Society for Opinion and Marketing Research)

European Trends (Economist Intelligence Unit)

Financial Analysts Journal (Financial Analysts Federation)

Financial Executive (Financial Executives Institute)

Fortune (Time Inc., Chicago)

Futures: the journal of forecasting and planning (IPC Science and Technology Press)

Harvard Business Review (Graduate School of Business Administration, Harvard University)

Human Relations (Plenum Press)

Industrial and Labor Relations Review (New York State School of Industrial and Labor Relations)

Industrial Relations (Institute of Industrial Relations, University of California)

International Journal of Production Research (Institute of Production Engineers)

International Labour Review (International Labour Office)

Investment Analyst: journal of the Society of Investment Analysts

Journal of Accounting Research (Institute of Professional Accountants, Chicago)

Journal of Advertising Research (Advertising Research Foundation)

Journal of Business (Graduate School of Business, University of Chicago)

Journal of Business Finance and Accounting (Blackwell, Oxford)

Journal of Business Policy (University of Bradford)

Journal of European Training (University of Bradford)

Journal of Finance (American Finance Association)

Journal of Financial and Quantitative Analysis (University of Washington Graduate School of Business Administration)
Journal of Industrial Economics (Blackwell, Oxford)
Journal of Management Studies (Blackwell, Oxford)
Journal of Marketing (American Marketing Association)
Journal of Marketing Research (American Marketing Association)
Long Range Planning (Society for Long Range Planning)
Management Accounting (Institute of Cost and Management Accountants)
Management Accounting (National Association of Accountants)
Management Decision (University of Bradford)
Management Education and Development (Association of Teachers of Management)
Management International Review (European Foundation for Management Development)
Management Science (Institute of Management Science)
Management Today (British Institute of Management)
Operational Research Quarterly (Operational Research Society)
Operations Research (Operations Research Society of America)
Organizational Behavior and Human Performance (Academic Press)
Personnel Journal (Swarthmore, Pennsylvania)
Personnel Management (Institute of Personnel Management)
Personnel Review (Institute of Personnel Management)
Quarterly Review of Economics and Business (Bureau of Economic and Business Research, University of Illinois)
R & D Management (Manchester Business School)
Research Management (Industrial Research Institute)
Sloan Management Review (Sloan School of Management, Massachusetts Institute of Technology)
Technological Forecasting (American Elsevier, New York)
Vision: the European business magazine (Geneva)

Related subject lists

Economics

American Economic Review (American Economic Association)
Econometrica: Journal of the Econometric Society
Economica (London School of Economics and Political Science)
Economic Journal (Royal Economic Society)
Journal of Economic Literature (American Economic Association)
Quarterly Journal of Economics (Harvard University Press)

Environment

Journal of Political Economy (University of Chicago Press)

New Scientist (New Science Publications, London)
Public Opinion Quarterly (American Association for Public Opinion Research)
Science Policy (Science Policy Foundation)
Scientific American (Scientific American Inc., New York)

Psychology

Journal of Applied Psychology (American Psychological Association)
Journal of Personality and Social Change (American Psychological Association)
Occupational Psychology (National Institute of Industrial Psychology)
Personnel Psychology (Ohio State University)

Sociology

American Journal of Sociology (University of Chicago Press)
American Sociological Review (American Sociological Association)
Behavioural Science (Mental Health Research Institute)
British Journal of Sociology (London School of Economics and Political Science)
Journal of Applied Behavioral Science (Institute for Applied Science)
Sociology (British Sociological Association)
Sociological Review (University of Keele)

Computers and Systems Analysis

Computer Journal (British Computer Society)
Data Processing (IPC Press, London)
Data Systems (Business Publications, London)
Journal of Systems Management (Association for Systems Management)
Journal of Systems Engineering (Department of Systems Engineering, University of Lancaster)

The total subscription cost for the main list of 56 titles was about £365 (or $870) p.a. at 1973 prices. But every librarian knows that the real cost of keeping periodicals in libraries lies hidden in the continuing work of registering, filing and binding them. Nevertheless, for their incalculable information value to a company or educational institution, the cost is small, while the potential benefits of having these periodicals available for constant use are very great.

This core list of periodicals is therefore a definite suggestion for providing an essential starting point around which libraries and other information resources can be established. But as with the suggested core list of books, the list must be constantly scrutinised and up dated as new periodicals appear and become established in their particular subject area.

CONCLUSION

The acceptance of a core list of books and periodicals is basic to an understanding of the parameters of the subject and the concepts on which management thought is based. There is a real need for the list to be broadly accepted by all concerned—managers, teachers, librarians and others.

It should be widely recognised that the literature is not 'controlled' from a bibliographical point of view, partly because its boundaries are so difficult to define, but more particularly because not enough people who use the literature have realised the necessity of good documentation. Users of management literature and librarians must co-operate in literature assessment and documentation problems.

A small basic management library, composed of the books and periodicals included in these core lists, can be purchased initially for about £700 (or $1680) at 1973 prices.

3

Management and Business Libraries and Management Associations

K. D. C. Vernon

The previous chapters have been concerned with describing the literature and its central portion, the core. In this chapter we shall be discussing the various kinds of libraries which contain the literature and make it available for people to use. The libraries vary greatly in size and in the services they give, but they all exist for the purposes of providing information about management and business. Of course libraries are not the only means of collecting information and making it available for use— there are many other types of organisations, societies and people with specialist skills (consultants, for example), who do this—but it is the libraries which contain the main resources of published information. There are many guide-books and directories which provide the basic lists and facts about 'who knows what'—some of them are mentioned in Chapter 7.

This chapter is in fact a brief guide to business libraries concentrating mainly on the UK and Europe. It emphasises the libraries of business schools, because these are still very young in Europe compared with America, and indicates other types of libraries—government, public and special—by describing a few selected libraries of each type. It should be supplemented if necessary by reference to some of the well-known comprehensive directories and guides to libraries, which include business libraries. The *Aslib Directory* (2 vols., Aslib, London, 1968–1970) is the standard UK library guide and the *Directory of Special Libraries and Information Centers*, edited by Anthony T. Kruzas (2nd ed., Gale Research Co., Detroit), is the best of several guides to American libraries. Others are available for most major countries. The intention of this brief guide therefore is not to provide a mass of detailed information about hundreds of libraries, but to emphasise, through a few examples, the need for businessmen to realise that information available in libraries can be used to good effect. Despite the fact that management education has developed so rapidly in the UK and Europe during the past decade, the potential value of the libraries which contain the fruits of thinking, research and writing has clearly not been widely understood or even adequately considered yet. Library users and businessmen, as well as librarians, must give some thought to the problem of how to organise published information for effective use. The libraries of British and some European business schools, for example, have established information resources which are only gradually, even now, being fully exploited by today's new breed of graduate managers. This list provides a brief over-all picture of these libraries in the belief that a list of the resources available will help those who need to use business information and management literature.

The commercial and business departments of the great public libraries are quite invaluable to the business community, but comparatively few executives in the UK and even fewer management teachers and research workers, in universities and colleges, realise their potential value as sources of information—business information which is sometimes painfully and expensively gathered by companies because nobody had thought of using the public library. The provision of more generous financial resources for the development of commercial public libraries in the UK would benefit many small businesses and local centres of commerce.

In striking contrast to the slow realisation of the need for business libraries in the UK and Europe, the library resources of the many large American business schools, public libraries, government departments, companies and specialist organisations have been richly developed and well used for 50 years or more. They have contributed greatly to the information needs of American businessmen and to the study of management.

The libraries selected for mention in this chapter are listed in four main groups according to their purpose. The first group comprises academic libraries belonging to educational institutions, notably the business schools in the UK, Europe and America. They aim to provide the literature and information required mainly for academic purposes by teachers, research workers and students of management; but there is no really defined division between theory and practice, and the libraries are much used also by businessmen, particularly by those who have participated in courses at business schools. Hence, these libraries are equally concerned with all aspects of management literature and business information. The second group is composed of government libraries and four UK examples are briefly described. The third group is the public libraries, which are freely available to everybody for all kinds of literature and information; but especially because of the nature of management and business literature, they are invaluable to businessmen and other specialists—they do in fact provide, through their commercial reference services, excellent information resources which are not always fully appreciated. The fourth group is the larger number of special libraries both big and small whose purpose it is primarily to serve the people within their own organisation, although they are usually available to other bona fide information seekers. Outstanding in this group is the library of the British Institute of Management, which is probably the best library of its kind in Europe. It is described in more detail later in this chapter.

LIBRARIES OF BUSINESS SCHOOLS

The libraries which have been established to serve business schools, or management centres at universities, polytechnics and technical colleges, all cover much the same subject areas, although obviously they vary greatly in their size and in the depth of coverage provided by their stock. Some of these libraries are departments of a larger university or college library, financed directly by the parent body, while others are more independent units.

The rapid development of British management education which followed the establishment of the London and Manchester Business Schools in 1965 has led to an equally rapid development in libraries dedicated to the service of management education and research into business problems. In 1966 both these business schools realised that they could not provide the high quality teaching and research which was their objective without equally high-quality library services. Hence, these two libraries are now, some 8 years later, probably the best of their kind east of the Atlantic. A very good survey of British management education, its development in the 1960s and its future potentialities is given in *The revolution in British management education*, by Mildred Wheatcroft (Pitman, 1970). Although the author does not concern herself with libraries, it is easy to see that such a quick change in attitudes to and thinking about management education led to an immense surge of publications and a desire by many people to use the literature. Hence, they demanded library services.

In Chapter 1 we discussed the subject content of management literature and business information. It is that literature and information which is contained in the libraries of business schools. It is published in varying forms: in books and pamphlets; in periodicals and serials of all kinds; in newspapers, research reports, discussion papers; in theses and dissertations; in information bulletins and works of reference; in government and statistical publications; in company reports and financial card services; in films, microfilms, microfiches and cassettes. It is all presented at different levels of speciality and for different purposes—academic, research, informative, general interest and practice. And so the libraries of business schools are challenged to collect, arrange, disseminate and exploit all these kinds of information for the benefit of teachers and research workers, for doctoral, postgraduate or undergraduate students; for managers and businessmen who are either attending courses or using the library because it is relevant to their business problems. They therefore must provide services at varying levels according to the needs of their users and they must be flexible enough to change their method of service as needs and interests alter or fluctuate.

The following short annotated list of nine libraries, selected because they are all supported by active business schools, indicates the growing wealth of library services and information resources which are available. But it should be remembered that no library can aspire to provide a complete service to its users from its own resources. All are dependent on one another and so it is that library co-operation, particularly in the UK, has been developed to a high degree of efficiency. Chapter 4 discusses the need to appreciate that libraries are interdependent. These brief notes illustrate the information resources which are available in a few places where management is studied. Details about the availability of these libraries can be obtained from the libraries.

British business schools

London Business School, Sussex Place, Regent's Park, London NW1 4SA

The library was started early in 1966 and moved to its present beautiful situation overlooking Regent's Park in 1970. It has seating accommodation for 110 readers and now contains some 23 000 books and pamphlets, and 550 current periodicals covering all aspects of management and business studies and related subject fields; a special corporate library containing a large collection of British and foreign company reports and other company and financial information, including the Extel card service; a good collection of statistical publications—economic, financial and social; government publications, newspapers, information files on most industries and countries; an extensive collection of research reports and working papers from other business schools; reprints of articles; and a wide range of reference works of all kinds, including bibliographies, and indexing and abstracting publications.

Classified by the *London Classification of Business Studies*, a new classification for this subject area compiled at the LBS and published in 1970. Services include a monthly list of new accessions to the library, current-awareness services covering the contents of periodicals, a series of sources of information, and occasional bibliographies and reading lists on special topics. An index of articles in periodicals is maintained jointly with the Manchester Business School Library.

Manchester Business School, Booth Street West, Manchester, M15 6PB

The library was started in 1966 and moved to its present excellent situation in the modern University Precinct in 1971. It contains some 25 000 books and pamphlets, and 650 current periodicals, covering all aspects of management and business studies, with good collections in related subject fields, such as economics and sociology. There is a collection of the annual reports of some 1300 major companies, supplementing the Extel card service and files of newspaper clippings on topics related to management, and a growing collection of 'working papers'. The main English newspapers are held on microfilm since 1960, and a good collection of statistical publications is maintained, as well as numerous abstracting and indexing services.

Publications of the library include an accessions list (monthly), periodical holdings (annual), library bulletin (6 per annum), information notes (irregular), and reading lists and bibliographies (occasional). The library also publishes *Current Contents in Management* (weekly, subscription £10.00 ($5.00) per annum, including quarterly and annual author indexes).

University of Bradford Management Centre, Emm Lane, Bradford, Yorkshire, BD9 4JL

The library was started in 1963 and moved into a new and more spacious building in 1974. The stock consists of about 17 000 books and pamphlets, 1800 bound volumes of periodicals and 420 current periodicals dealing with all subjects of interest to students, teachers and researchers in management studies, including company and financial information, statistical publications, reference works and bibliographies. The collection is particularly strong in the areas of marketing and research methods, and there is a good selection of abstracting and indexing publications.

The library is classified partly by the Dewey Decimal Classification and partly by the Universal Decimal Classification, with some local modifications. Services include a weekly recent additions bulletin, current-awareness services and occasional bibliographies on special topics. There is a strong emphasis on helping the reader to exploit the resources of the library, and to this end a programme of instruction in library use and literature-searching is being developed.

Cranfield Institute of Technology, Management sub-library, Cranfield, Bedfordshire

This library, a subsidiary of the main college library, was started in 1970. It now contains some 5000 books and pamphlets, 180 periodicals and a substantial reference collection of directories, bibliographies and abstracting publications. A collection of European and American company reports and company information files is currently being developed, as is a source index to published case material.

The collection is classified by the *London Classification of Business Studies*. A subject index to the books and pamphlet collection is maintained, and this is based on John Blagden's *Management information retrieval* (BIM, 1969). An index to periodical articles is also maintained.

Services include a monthly accessions list, a fortnightly current contents service based on periodicals received in the library and a series of reading lists on special topics.

Graduate Business Centre, The City University, Lionel Denny House, 23 Goswell Road, London EC1M 7BB

The library has undergone a period of rapid expansion since 1970 and now contains a stock of 11 000 books and subscribes to about 200 journals. Special collections include reports of the quoted companies listed in *The Times 1000*, industry and country studies extracted from the national press, a Short Loan Collection of books in heavy demand and a collection of recommended journal articles.

The book-stock is classified by the Dewey Decimal Classification. Services include *Contents of Recent Journals* (weekly), personalised SDI service to a small number of academic staff undertaking research projects, the preparation of specialised bibliographies on request, and a series of short seminars on information-searching techniques to postgraduate students about to embark upon business appreciation projects.

A library guide, which includes lists of books and articles in heavy demand, is available from the Librarian.

Oxford Centre for Management Studies, Kennington Road, Kennington, Oxford OX1 5NY

The Oxford Centre for Management Studies, founded in 1965 and now part of the University, moved into its striking modern building just south of Oxford in 1969. The library, a large galleried area with all teaching, seminar and lecture rooms leading off it, was designed as the core of the working life of the Centre, and this focal position ensures a valuable integration of library, teaching and research activities. However, for students who require a quieter ambiance, it has been found necessary to include a separate reading room in the new wing to be completed in 1974.

Currently (1973) the library has some 7000 books and pamphlets, 180 journals, a collection of important journal articles for loan, a sequence of ephemera files (classified but uncatalogued material that is judged likely to have a short useful life), and a Statistical Data Section. The Company Records Section provides reference material, files of reports and accounts of some 350 companies, and the Moodie British Card Service (updated daily). The library subscribes to the valuable *Business International European Research Service* and receives a substantial number of indexing and abstracting publications.

Books, pamphlets and ephemera in the OCMS library are classified by the *London Classification of Business Studies*. Information services provided by the library include an accessions list and a management education information service circulated to academic staff.

Administrative Staff College, Greenlands, Henley-on-Thames, Oxon, RG9 3AU

Since the library does not set out to be a comprehensive library of business and management, but aims to be an active working unit geared closely to the work of the College, the material is carefully selected and reviewed with this aim in mind. Thus the library, now reclassified and recatalogued by the *London Classification of Business Studies*, has grown slowly from its origin in 1948 to its present size: 10 000 books, pamphlets and government publications; 280 periodical titles; annual reports of some 300 companies; press cuttings relevant to the topics in the Course of Studies; a reference collection of a wide selection of directories, statistical works, bibliographical tools and company histories; plus the College archives.

The College library is responsible for the provision of multiple sets of prescribed publications for syndicate and group study. The Library staff work closely with the Directing staff in the selection of new material for inclusion in the reading lists and their subsequent preparation.

A monthly accessions list and an annual list of periodical holdings are produced. Bibliographies and reading lists on selected topics are compiled at the request of staff and course members, and these can be made available to other enquirers.

Polytechnic of Central London (PCL), School of Management Studies, 35 Marylebone Road, London NW1 5LS

Since the move to this site in 1970, the Management Library has expanded to such an extent that the new premises are hardly adequate to contain its stock of some 9000 books, 2000 pamphlets and 190 periodicals. In addition to standard texts on all aspects of management, a small but up-to-date reference collection which includes several important bibliographical aids and a rapidly growing collection of bound periodicals, the Library contains a special collection of books and magazines relevant to the PCL course in the administration of the arts. Following the introduction of the CNAA Master's degree in management, the Library has acquired a considerable amount of important material in the behavioural science area.

The Library was classified by the *London Classification of Business Studies* but has recently changed to Dewey, in line with other libraries of the Polytechnic. To members of the academic and research staff it provides both current-awareness and SDI (selective dissemination of information) services, and members of the Library staff are happy to provide bibliographies when these are needed. A new venture is the compilation of a fortnightly digest of articles on management education which is issued to anyone who is particularly interested in this subject.

University of Warwick, Coventry CV4 7AL

The first graduate students for the School of Industrial and Business Studies came in 1967, and undergraduate courses began in 1969. Senior library staff are organised on a subject specialisation basis, one group being responsible for economics, business studies and industrial relations. There is no separate business studies library, the 20 000 books and pamphlets and 250 periodicals being integrated with the other social science material. Home-made classification schemes are used for the social sciences and classified card catalogues provided for each subject area.

Some special collections worth noting are a very large Statistics Collection (about 2000 current serials and almost 10 000 titles in all) and a small collection of company reports; the Extel Card Services are taken. The collection of unpublished working papers in economics and management contains over 7000 papers from more than 150 institutions throughout the world, and new additions are listed weekly in *Contents of Recent Economics Journals* (HMSO) and in *Current Contents in Management* (Manchester Business School). From 1973 a quarterly *Bibliography of Economics Working Papers* and a microfiche service has been published by Trans-Media Publishing Co., based on the Warwick Collection.

There is a growing number of other similar libraries, such as those at the universities of Bath, Lancaster, Durham and Strathclyde, for example, and at numerous polytechnic and technical colleges and at independent centres such as Ashridge Management College. Information about these libraries can readily be found either in the university and college brochures or handbooks or in reference works and directories of libraries. The pattern is much the same and varies only according to the kind of education offered by each school—postgraduate, undergraduate or shorter courses for executives.

European business schools

The libraries of European business schools tend to exist rather more in isolation than their British counterparts because, on the whole, the national, university and public library services of these countries are less organised for inter-library lending and giving other co-operative information services. Some of the business schools are not university-based and are geared more to the provision of courses for managers and businessmen rather than the longer undergraduate or postgraduate degree courses. These schools therefore have not needed to develop their libraries to the extent which would have been required by academic institutions which grant degrees and carry out research, but recent educational developments are leading towards greater emphasis being placed on the need to provide adequate library and information resources.

Some European countries, such as France, Switzerland, Spain, Italy and Scandinavia, for example, have been developing centres for management education very rapidly during the past few years. Frequently and inevitably they tended to be based on the American patterns at first, but are now rapidly developing their own 'styles'. Others, however, notably Germany, have not felt the need to establish educational centres dedicated to the study of management at undergraduate or postgraduate level on the American business school style. They have preferred to follow different methods of developing management personnel. A good general description of the European business schools is given in 'European management education: history, typologies and national structures', by Ian McNay (*Management Education and Development*, **4**(1), 3–13, 1973). With the establishment of the European Foundation for Management Development in 1971 there is now an opportunity for representatives of European business schools to co-operate and discuss problems of mutual concern.

The librarians of several European business schools, realising the need for more co-operation, now meet together with librarians of British business schools for discussions on mutual problems and for developing closer ties which are now beginning to lead towards better co-operative library services. Informal co-operation of this kind is a valuable means of sharing information which should be available, but yet has hitherto been difficult to get because librarianship in this subject area has not been sufficiently internationally minded.

The following examples of 10 European business school libraries are given, not because they are necessarily the most important, but because they are good examples of library services which are well developed and ready to provide new services for new needs in the study of management. Other business schools in Scandinavia, Spain and elsewhere provide similar library facilities for their staff and students, but they cannot be included in this brief list.

Centre d'Enseignement Supérieur des Affaires, Jouy-en-Josas, France

The CESA Library serves the three constituent bodies—l'Ecole des Hautes Etudes Commerciales, l'Institut Supérieur des Affaires and the Centre de Formation Continue. After several transformations, it was restructured and reorganised in 1970 and is now one of the most important libraries of its kind in Europe.

It has accommodation for 250 readers and it is open to present and former students in the three programmes within CESA and can also be used by outsiders. It is remarkably well stocked in up-to-date works on business management. In 1973 the Library contained some 30 000 books and nearly 500 current periodicals, a third of which are in English. About 2000 volumes are added every year.

Abstracting and indexing of reviews and bibliographical materials together with a system of inter-library information services with French and foreign institutions support the School's teaching and research work.

Centre d'Etudes Industrielles (Centre for Education in International Management), 4, chemin de Conches, 1211 Conches-Geneva, Switzerland

The CEI library was started in 1946, the year the School was founded. In 1958 it moved to its present site, called 'Le Mesnil', in Conches, on the edge of Lake Geneva.

The collection includes some 10 000 books and monographs and 260 periodicals, both with a representation of French and some German publications; a broad selection of company reports and related sources of information; and a file of business schools calendars. A vertical file covering major business topics, countries and industries is organised in straight alphabetic order, using the same subject headings as the index of articles.

The classification used for the books is the UDC, with adjustments in the 65 sections. A monthly selective accessions list is being circulated, and faculty members receive photocopies of the contents pages of selected journals. Special reading lists are prepared for the Industry Study Trips and for individual readers.

European Institute for Advanced Studies in Management, Place Stephanie 20, B-1050 Brussels

The Institute's library was started in April 1972. It is designed as a small highly specialised library to serve the research and teaching missions of the Institute and to complement and enhance doctoral education in management. Books, periodicals and other materials are mainly devoted to management research. This specialisation causes a considerable dependence on inter-library co-operation.

The library contains about 1500 books and 120 current periodicals which include the most important titles in management research. Other collections are a series of working papers from a number of European and US business schools, reports from many European companies, American doctoral dissertations on microfilm, reprints of articles, bibliographies, and indexing and abstracting publications.

A collection of European doctoral dissertations on management subjects is being built up and is designed to become an information service system for doctoral works in Europe.

The books are classified by the *London Classification of Business Studies*. This classification scheme is used for indexing books, for arranging books on the shelves and for filing catalogue cards systematically.

Services include a photocopy service and a current contents service.

Helsinki School of Economics Library, Runeberginkatu 22–24, 00100 Helsinki 10, Finland

The Library was started in 1911. It now contains some 110 000 books and 950 current periodicals on economics and business, a collection of company reports from all Scandinavian countries, statistical publications, dissertations, research reports and a large collection of bibliographies, indexing and abstracting publications. There is also a collection of 12 different card services of company information from various countries available in the library.

The classification used is Universal Decimal Classification. The wide range of services include publications of the Helsinki School of Economics Library Series, an index of articles from Finnish periodicals, SDI service for researchers and teachers of the School, a monthly list of accessions, a union list of periodicals in the fields of economics and business sciences, and occasional reading lists on special topics.

Besides the main library there is also a textbook library in a separate building containing 10 000 volumes, including multiple copies of books required for the various courses in the curriculum.

IFAP Centro IRI per lo Studio delle Funzioni Direttive Aziendali (IRI Centre for the Study of Management Functions), Piazza della Repubblica 59—00186 Roma, Italy

IFAP is an Institute established by IRI (Institute for Industrial Reconstruction) financial companies and by some of the major business concerns of the Group, with the purpose of integrating individual company programmes in the field of personnel training. IFAP carries on its work through the activities of the IRI Centre for the Study of Management Functions, which organises and runs courses, seminars and meetings intended for the Group's company management.

In 1967 the Documentation Section and the Library were reorganised and a new classification was compiled.

The Library now consists of approximately 8400 volumes and 350 current periodicals covering all aspects of management and social sciences. Furthermore it contains a collection of Italian company reports; national, foreign and EEC statistical publications; research reports; documentation open files and up-dated bibliographical open files; indexing and abstracting publications, reference works, and conference proceedings.

All the material is classified according to the internal classification plan; the catalogue, arranged by author, title and subject, contains cards with abstracts and cross-classification for all the material available.

Library services include: a monthly bulletin, *Segnalazioni Bibliografiche*, containing index cards with abstracts for all volumes acquired during the month; and occasional bibliographies, reading lists, summaries of articles, etc.

Other services offered by the Documentation Section are: a monthly publication titled *Segnalazioni e Informazioni* containing organic presentation of topics of current interest in management; transcripts of reports on conferences and round tables held at IFAP; publications of books translated at IFAP, etc.

IMEDE, Management Development Institute, 23 chemin de Bellerive, 1007 Lausanne, Switzerland

The IMEDE library is situated among the trees and lawns of the park of Bellerive, in full view of the ,Alps, on the shores of Lake Leman. It was started in 1957.

The library houses approximately 8000 books and subscribes to over 200 periodicals covering the several aspects of business administration and international economics. The majority of books and periodicals are in English, the Institute's official teaching language. However, in keeping with the international character of IMEDE, there are considerable holdings of material published in a number of other languages.

Books are classified according to a decimal system based on the main subjects taught at IMEDE. The library receives some 200 company reports and also stores the complete collection of IMEDE case studies (now numbering about 900).

The library publishes a *Monthly Bulletin of Abstracts* summarising articles selected from over 200 periodicals and includes lists of new acquisitions. This publication is available also to persons and organisations not connected with the Institute. In addition, the library prepares a separate yearly cumulative list of new acquisitions.

Institut Europeen d'Administration des Affaires (INSEAD), Boulevard de Constance, 77305 Fontainebleau, France

The library of this famous international business school was started in 1959. It contains 22 000 books and pamphlets and 550 periodicals covering all areas of management and relevant domains, such as psychology, sociology, operational research, information technology and political sciences. This collection is completed by publications of the European Communities, OECD and other international organisations and by publications of a statistical character.

The books are a selection of the best works published in English, French and German; 60% are in English, approximately 25% in French and the rest in German. The periodicals are also in English, French and German. Their use is made easier by numerous indexes which are at the disposal of readers.

Some important developments in documentation and indexing have been tested and promoted in this important library.

International Institute of Management, 1 Berlin 33, Griegstr. 5–7, Germany

The library, together with the Institute, was started in 1970 and is located on the ground floor of a beautiful old Grunewald residence.

It contains over 6500 books and 250 journals in the field of management science, with supporting literature on economic theory, public administration, mathematics and statistics. Although quite small, the library has a well-documented section of reference material. Books and pamphlets are classified according to the *London Classification of Business Studies*.

Services include a monthly current-awareness service covering the contents of all the periodicals held by the library, and an inter-library loan service reaching over the whole of Germany.

Interuniversitair Instituut Bedrijfskunde, Poortweg 6–8, Delft, Holland

The library was started in 1966 as a department of the 'Stichting Bedrijfs-kunde', being an institute for organising post-graduate courses in business administration and carrying out management research. The 'Stichting' is sponsored by some large international firms, the Rotterdam School of Economics and the Technological University, Delft. In 1970 the Interfaculty for Graduate Studies in Management was established in the same building in Rotterdam. Both the 'Stichting' and the Interfaculty are now joined in the 'Interuniversitair Instituut Bedrijfskunde' (IIB), from 1974 onwards operating in Delft.

The library, for budgetary reasons a formal department of the Inter-faculty, contains 10 000 books and 400 current periodicals. It also inherited, from the International University Contact for Management Education (IUC), a collection of research projects, cases, games and curricula.

A *Documentation Bulletin* is published under the aegis of the European Foundation for Management Development (EFMD) in Brussels, giving desk information on recent books in the field of managerial sciences. Three times a year a file of abstracts of 30 recommended articles from periodicals is distributed, offering the opportunity for ordering photocopies of the indicated articles for personal use.

Stress is laid on rendering qualified service to the clients, helping them to find relevant literature for teaching, learning and researching purposes.

Irish Management Institute, 186 Orwell Road, Rathgar, Dublin 14

The Institute's library, which was established in 1955, holds a comprehensive book-stock of some 11 000 titles, providing exclusively for its staff and members a borrowing, reference and bibliographical service, and a reference service to non-members. In addition to the book-stock, which is classified by Universal Decimal Classification, the library holds a large collection of abstracts and reports, and some 300 current periodicals emanating from many parts of the world.

The scope of the library covers a wide field of management techniques in the main functional areas of finance, marketing, production, personnel management, training and development, and data processing.

Services include a monthly list of accessions, which is circulated to staff, local special libraries and members (company libraries), bibliographies, reading lists and occasional publications.

Much of the more recently acquired material relates directly to conditions in Europe and the EEC countries. Directories, guides, year-books, glossaries and other reference works have been added to cope with an anticipated increase in inquiries about conditions in Europe, particularly in the Common Market countries. This expansion of the reference section to approximately 1000 items and some 30 new journal titles has been one of the major developments during 1972/73.

In addition to its own resources, the library has a wide range of outside contacts, including the full range of library and information services of the British Institute of Management.

In its relatively short life the IMI library has made four moves to more spacious accommodation. In 1974 the library made what is expected to be its final move to the Institute's new training centre at Clonard, Sandford, County Dublin.

American business schools

American librarians have always been very professionally conscious and have therefore realised the value of meeting together and forming associations and groups which are subject-centred. The American Association of Collegiate Schools of Business has a libraries section which provides the librarians with the opportunity to meet, to share problems and to act together when problems need to be solved co-operatively.

The great libraries of the leading American business schools have been built up over a period of 50 years or more. Many of them are more than 10 times the size of the London and Manchester Business Schools, which are large libraries by British and European standards, and they are all under the direction of the university library of which they form a part, even though they exist to serve primarily a particular business school. In sharp contrast to their British and European counterparts, they have mostly been generously financed and their great collections of books and periodicals therefore approach a comprehensiveness which would be inconceivable, or even desirable, in the UK and Europe. At the top of the league there is the famous Baker Library at Harvard Business School, which is by far the largest business school library in the world, being nearly twice the size of most of the other libraries belonging to the main business schools. Its importance as a vast information resource for scholarly research has been widely recognised and its influence on business studies can never be adequately measured. Other business school libraries, which form important parts of the numerous great American university libraries, at Chicago, California, New York and Indiana, for example, may vary in size between 100 000 and 200 000 volumes.

These American business school libraries serve the teaching and research needs of large academic staffs, and many hundreds of doctoral, post-graduate and undergraduate students. Their services are well organised and closely controlled by efficient, professionally educated library staffs, and their facilities often include discussion rooms, typing facilities and ample equipment for reading microfilms and microfiches. The largest libraries sometimes have their own computer facilities for producing their catalogues or handling their circulation records.

The American business school libraries illustrate vividly, by their size and intense activity, how immense the information resources are and how much accumulated knowledge has been collected during the past 90 years or so since undergraduate business education first started at the Wharton School in 1881. The intense use which is made of these libraries illustrates, better than any verbal description can, the active relationship between publications, on the one hand, and business education and practice, on the other.

The following brief notes indicate the resources of a few of the leading business school libraries. They are examples which illustrate the pattern of American library development in this subject area. Details of others can be found in various reference books and in the brochures of the business schools.

Baker Library, Harvard Business School, Cambridge, Mass.

Baker Library serves primarily the Graduate School of Business Administration at Harvard University. The faculty and administration of that school determined some 50 years ago to build a historical and research library in the field of business and economics. As a consequence Baker Library now has, in addition to its central collection, extensive collections in its Reference, Manuscripts and Corporation Records Divisions, and a purely historical collection—the Kress Library of Business and Economics.

Baker Library is a part of the Harvard University Library, but is administered within the Business School. It occupies approximately 60 000 ft^2 of space and houses 480 000 volumes and 33 000 microfilms.

After organising its collections, this library has extended their use to the scholarly world through publication of catalogues and specialised indexes, and has now initiated the publication, by a commercial firm, of the entire Kress Library, in microfilm. Two annual cumulative catalogues are issued: the catalogue of the *Core Collection* and *Current Periodical Publications*, an index to all serials held in the library. A commercial firm has issued the *Author-Title and Subject Catalogs of Baker Library* in 32 volumes. Other publications include 27 in the *Reference List* series, 21 *Kress Publications* and a *List of Manuscripts in Baker Library*.

A new classification was designed for the library some years ago and has been published as *A Classification of Business Literature.*

Reference services have been developed to serve students, faculty and alumni, and these are extensively used by the business community. Reference librarians now issue *Mini-Lists* covering bibliographical sources, a monthly *Current Contents* (copies of tables of contents) and a monthly *New Books in Business and Economics.*

An historical account of the formation and growth of this great library is given in Chapter 12 of *And mark an era: the story of the Harvard Business School*, by Melvin T. Copeland (Little, Brown, 1958).

Graduate School of Management Library, University of California, Los Angeles

The Management Library was authorised in 1958 and first opened for service on 16 September, 1961. Its collection at present numbers some 100 000 monographs and 5000 subscriptions to current journals and newspapers in English and over 20 foreign languages.

Among its areas of subject concentration are accounting and information systems, business economics, finance and investments, international management theory and policy, management in the arts, marketing and advertising, production and operations research management, sociotechnical systems and behavioural science, and urban land economics.

The Management Library accommodates 300 students, and has open stacks, a microfilm—microcard reading room, photocopying machines, a business records area, and assigned carrel study space for graduate management students.

Among the special collections of the library are the Robert E. Gross Collection of rare books in business and economics, made possible by the generous gifts of the Lockheed Leadership Foundation and of Mrs. Robert E. Gross in 1963; the Arthur Young & Company Accounting Collection established in 1961; an extensive collection of annual reports of major American and foreign corporations; and a corporate history collection.

Thomas J. Watson Library of Business and Economics, Columbia University, New York

The library was established in 1920 and moved to its present location in Uris Hall in 1964. It houses a collection of about 300 000 volumes on business and economics, 2300 American and foreign periodical titles, and files of current US government documents and pamphlet materials. The current collection is being classified in the Library of Congress system.

Extensive collections of annual reports and other financial records of public companies in the US and Canada are maintained. The Marvyn Scudder Financial Collection consists of financial records of more than half a million companies from 1821 to the present. Among the materials contained in the collection are annual reports, by-laws, charters, communications to security owners, histories, prospectuses, proxy statements, indentures, leases and contracts, recapitalisation plans, reorganisation material, underwriting documents, voting trust agreements and other corporate instruments.

Services include individual consultations for PhD candidates, tours for new faculty members and students, and compilation of subject and faculty publication bibliographies.

The library is open to Columbia University faculty, students, alumni and staff.

Graduate School of Business and Public Administration, Cornell University, Ithaca, New York 14850

The BPA Library began in 1946, but until 1953 was primarily an undergraduate, course-orientated collection. It was located in McGraw Hall, one of the oldest of the Cornell University buildings. A new emphasis and a new direction were taken in 1953, and significant growth began. Both the School and its library have made their major contributions to academic and research programmes since that date. In 1964 the School moved into new quarters in Malott Hall, where books and readers are comfortably accommodated. The library supports a curriculum and research programmes in the internal workings of organisations and, as well, in the economic, social and political environments in which management must function.

There is a special strength in the area of finance and investments. In addition to books and journals, there are collections of corporate reports in both microfiche and hard copy. Also, there is a small collection of computer tapes supporting various research projects.

The library has a collection of 108 000 volumes and journal subscriptions number 1100. All are classified in the Library of Congress system, Corporation files are uncatalogued, as are a current 3-year file of business and economic research working papers.

During academic sessions an *Acquisitions List* is published monthly. A list of periodicals received and specialised bibliographies are published on an occasional basis.

Dewey Library, Sloan School of Management, MIT, Cambridge, Mass.

Dewey Library, the largest of the five main libraries in the MIT Library

System, is located within the complex housing the Sloan School of Management and the Departments of Economics and Political Science and the Center for International Studies. It serves students and faculty in these departments and other MIT students who elect to take courses in these areas. Because of its extensive business reference sources, Dewey Library is also used by many students from other universities in the Boston area, and by personnel from many of the larger private corporations located in the area. The library provides reference and information services for classes and research; ample, quiet study and reading facilities; as well as inter-library loans, microfilms, microfiche and microreproduction facilities.

Since 1965, Dewey Library has classified its collection according to the US Library of Congress classification system. The library's catalogued collections now total approximately 400 000 volumes, more than half of which are in the subject areas of economics and management.

Among the several specialised collections in Dewey Library, the most important is the Industrial Relations Collection. This is one of the largest and oldest collections in the United States dealing with employer–employee relations, labour law and related subjects. The Industrial Relations Section publishes a bi-monthly Accessions List.

J. Hugh Jackson Library of Business, Stanford University, Stanford, California

The J. Hugh Jackson Library of the Graduate School of Business, Stanford University, was established in 1933 to serve the needs of students and faculty of the Graduate School of Business. It is still primarily a working laboratory for the School, although it has long been open to members of the University community.

The reference collection of financial and business services, directories, statistical sources, etc., is maintained and professionally staffed to provide assistance and guidance to students in the preparation of reports and in independent research.

Special areas are devoted to current periodicals, reserve books, reference and special collections. Numerous areas throughout the library are provided for study. Located within the library are case discussion, calculating machine, computer terminal, typing and visual aids rooms, as well as photocopying facilities.

The collection contains over 182 500 volumes as well as federal and state documents, reports and pamphlets; over 400 000 corporate annual reports of companies listed on the several stock exchanges; 152 000 micro-text and microfilm; and 4895 current periodical titles and continuations, including 32 newspapers.

The J. Hugh Jackson Library issues a bi-monthly publication, *Selected Additions to the J. Hugh Jackson Library*.

Lippincott Library, Wharton School, University of Pennsylvania, Philadelphia

Founded in 1927, the Lippincott Library moved in 1966 to its present location in the Dietrich Graduate Library Center adjoining the Van Pelt Library (main University Library). Accommodations are provided for about 450 users, including individual study carrels, group study areas, small conference rooms, typing cubicles and informal seating. It provides a collection of over 160 000 volumes—books, pamphlets, periodicals, and a variety of highly specialised materials—in the fields of business and applied economics. Classified by the Library of Congress system since 1966 and prior to that time by a modified Dewey Decimal system.

Emphasis in the Lippincott Library has been placed on the subjects included in the Wharton School curriculum. Indexes, directories and general guides to sources are provided in recognition of the user's need to acquire source materials and statistical data. Many federal and state government documents, publications of international organisations, selected business and financial services, and a collection of over 1600 business periodicals are assembled for special reference.

The Peck Corporation Room houses the Library's collection of over 57 000 annual reports published by 2700 US and foreign corporations during the past 130 years. Also included in this special collection are stock prospectuses, proxy statements, mortgages, articles of incorporation, corporate histories, and a variety of other corporate and financial publications.

Publications include a library handbook, *The Pilot*; a monthly list of selected acquisitions; lists of information sources for various business disciplines; and occasional brief bibliographies on business topics.

GOVERNMENT LIBRARIES

The difference between information for management, which is largely business and commercial information, and information about management, i.e. management literature, is clearly apparent if one considers the reason for governments setting up libraries and documentation centres. Government libraries concerned with business, trade and employment exist in order to provide the vast amounts of information needed for modern complex government activities devoted to organising and supervising the economic life of the industrialised countries of the world—at least 25 000 US government publications are issued each year. These libraries therefore are not concerned so much with management literature, which is the prime concern of business school libraries, for example, as they are with official and business information. Businessmen should be well aware of the help which they can receive from these libraries.

In all countries the libraries of government departments and agencies contain not only official economic and business information but also other, statistical, commercial and marketing information relevant to the work of their departments. These libraries serve primarily their own departments but the information they contain is widely available to others, particularly through the provision of information about official regulations and government documents of all kinds. In the USA the enormous libraries of the Department of Commerce and the Department of Labor, for example, are the information storehouses for the large-scale government operations in the areas of trade and employment. In Canada, Australia, Europe and elsewhere the libraries of government departments are similarly important sources of business information required primarily by civil servants in their work of organising and controlling the economic activities of their countries.

Details about government libraries are easily available in directories such as the *Directory of Special Libraries and Information Centers*, edited by Anthony T. Kruzas (2nd ed., Gale Research Co., Detroit, 1968) for the USA and Canada; the *Repertoire des Bibliothèques d'Etude et Organismes de Documentation* (Bibliothèque National, Paris) for France; the *Directory of Special Libraries in Australia* (Library Association of Australia, Sydney); and similar publications for other countries.

British government libraries

Numerous government departments such as the Department of Employment, the Department of the Environment and the Treasury, for example, are concerned with various aspects of business and commerce, but it is primarily the Departments of Trade and Industry which watch over the private sector of industry. This great joint Department has for many years provided excellent library and information services for businessmen. The main Central Library, with its very large collection of books, periodicals, pamphlets and government publications, is particularly strong in all aspects of applied economics, including industry, trade and commerce throughout the world. The *Department of Trade and Industry, Statistics and Market Intelligence Library* aims to provide complete coverage for all countries of statistical publications on foreign trade and production and includes a vast range of economic, financial and social statistics, market surveys and development plans. As a statistical collection it is unrivalled in western Europe, and, being open to the public, it provides a store of information which is invaluable to business, trade and industry. Together these two great libraries contain the main information resources upon which most government economists rely and which serve the whole business community of the UK.

In 1970 the *Central Management Library* of the Civil Service Department (Whitehall, London SW1A 2AZ) was started. It provides services to the Civil Service Department and to a number of agencies and sub-departments in the central public sector. It contains about 32 000 books and pamphlets, and subscribes to some 1600 serials. Its subject coverage includes the behavioural sciences, personnel management, computers, public administration, management science and management services. It contains a substantial collection of specialised bibliographies, abstracts and indexes relating to its subject area, as well as a large classified collection of reading lists on specific topics. Its journal holdings embrace the major English-language periodicals on management and related topics. The library also contains a good collection of government publications. Its current-awareness service, *Policy Science Documentation*, comprises five sub-series: New books; Contents of current journals; Semi-published research; Reading lists; and Bibliographies. The library is classified by the *London Classification of Business Studies*. Information retrieval is achieved by means of a thesaurus allied to an articulated subject index, linked to an authority file. Research into computer linkage is currently in progress.

The *Civil Service College*, which is under the direction of the Civil Service Department, was opened in 1970 with its headquarters at Sunningdale, Berkshire, and centres in both London and Edinburgh. At each centre there is a library with a growing collection of multi-media material reflecting the interests of the centre it serves; the library at Sunningdale is being developed as the headquarters library for the rest of the College. Sunningdale is specialising in public administration, personnel mangement and some other fields of management, excluding management for profit and related fields. London specialises in economics, sociology, statistics and European Institutions. Edinburgh has a more general collection to meet the requirements for middle management courses. The combined number of periodicals taken by the College is about 324. The total book stock for all three centres, excluding multiple copies, is about 30 000. The total stock of films is about 60, with about 12 audio tapes. The Libraries use the *London Classification of Business Studies*.

Although now discontinued the *Guide to Government Department and Other Libraries and Information Bureaux* (Ministry of Defence, 1971) is still an invaluable handbook to the many government libraries in London and elsewhere. Considerable detail is provided for each library, and the helpful subject arrangement used for grouping the libraries listed means that the user can quickly see which libraries are likely to be able to answer a subject enquiry. Another useful small guide is *Librarians in*

Government Service (Civil Service Commission, 1971), which describes the library services in 20 government departments.

PUBLIC LIBRARIES

In most countries with a public library service it is recognised that business and commercial information should be freely available, particularly in the larger cities and industrial regions. The usual pattern is to set up a special department in the public library which specialises in this type of information, by providing directories, statistics, commercial reference works of all kinds, books and periodicals. But it is true to say that in many countries the standard of service in public commercial libraries falls far below the needs of the business communities and much more could be done to improve their services.

In the USA, however, the need for public business libraries has long been recognised and impressive collections have been built up in many cities. The Cleveland Public Library in Ohio and the Business Library of Newark Public Library in New Jersey provide outstanding services. Both are particularly active in compiling and issuing bibliographies on many aspects of business, guides to the literature and other useful services announcing new publications and promoting the use of business sources of information. Other American public libraries provide the same kind of services and information about them is readily available through library directories such as *The American Library Directory* (Bowker, New York). Other countries have similar library directories.

British public libraries

A wealth of information resources for business and management is available through British public libraries, particularly those in the larger cities. Although they are not specifically geared to serve academic communities and the needs of today's modern business graduate, they complement and extend the resources provided by the libraries of universities, business schools and colleges. They provide all the economic, trade, commercial and background information without which many local business activities could not be effectively carried on. Their undoubted value to small firms and to the community is proved by the way in which these libraries are so well used; but unfortunately there are many regions in the UK which are still very poorly served.

The following notes on four selected libraries illustrate the kind of service provided and the immense range of information which is available through these great collections. Details of all the other fine services, particularly in the larger cities, are readily available in the *Aslib Directory* and other guides to libraries.

Birmingham Commercial Library was opened in 1919 with a stock of about 2000 volumes, its chief object being to provide businessmen with a ready means of finding markets for their goods or information about the makes of articles they may require. During the following years the stock was increased to include all Patent Office official publications as well as textbooks on commerce, economics, accountancy, banking and allied subjects.

In 1968 it was decided that the public would be better served if the Patents and book stock at the Commercial Library were separated from the commercial stock of directories, year-books and statistical material and the quick reference stock at the Reference Library added to the Commercial material to form a Quick Reference and Commercial Information Department. Further premises were leased at this time which made it possible for the newly formed Department to be opened on the ground floor of the Reference Library in March 1969.

During recent years the stock has been added to considerably, and on 6 June 1973 the Quick Reference and Commercial Information Department was opened on the ground floor of the magnificent new Central Library building, which must surely be rated as one of the largest and best examples of modern library architecture in the country. There is seating accommodation for 100 readers.

The service provides many general reference works such as year-books, atlases, gazetteers, encyclopaedias, dictionaries, etc.; town directories and plans; hotel lists and timetables; trade and industry directories of all kinds; telephone directories for the UK, Europe and most of the major cities of the world; company information; newspapers; and a large collection of information for market intelligence research.

City Business Library (Gillett House, 55 Basinghall Street, London EC2V 5BX) was opened in 1970, having evolved from the Commercial Reference Room in Guildhall Library. It is a public service department of the City Corporation, freely available to all without formality, but does not lend material. Some 5500 directories of all kinds and from all parts of the world constitute an important part of the collection, and there are some 8000 books and pamphlets on business law, finance, taxation and market intelligence sources. Management as a subject is to receive less emphasis than formerly, regard being paid to alternative collections in the London area as well as to the fact that the City of London Lending Libraries now specialise in this field within the Metropolitan Special Collections Scheme. Over 900 periodicals and nearly 100 newspapers are taken regularly, as well as many statistical services. Financial and market research reporting and abstracting services issued by Moodies, Extel, Extract, McCarthy, MIRO and Predicasts are held. In addition, there are collections of maps, atlases, timetables, town guides and street plans.

Basically the classification used is Dewey, in a simplified form in the case of area and product market research data. The Library uses its own classification for directories and current periodicals.

Issued twice a year in February and August, *City Business Courier* is largely a listing of new items received. There is also a list of periodicals and newspapers taken, a guide to the classification used in the library, a general descriptive brochure, and others on company information and market research sources. All these are free on application.

Manchester Commercial Library was formed as a separate department of the Manchester Public Libraries in 1919, with the stated aim of providing 'any and every kind of Commercial information which may be obtained from printed matter, and such additional information as it may be possible to procure from public or private sources'. The emphasis is on current material; superseded items and the more academic studies of management, economics and finance are housed in the Social Sciences Library in the same building.

Displayed in the Library are 1300 periodicals and some 40 overseas newspapers. All periodicals are kept for a minimum period of 3 years and 500 are bound for permanent preservation. Complementary to this collection is a vertical file containing many thousands of newspaper clippings and pamphlets maintained under some 800 subject headings. The stock of current directories, numbering 4500, is probably the largest in the Provinces and includes a complete set of alphabetical and classified telephone directories for Western Europe as well as for many other parts of the world. A notable collection of financial services covers both British and overseas companies. Statistics, both official and non-official, for many countries are displayed separately, and all sale publications of the Stationery Office, European Communities, OECD, GATT and United Nations are taken. Over 13 000 sheet maps, foreign and British timetables, town plans, gazetteers, atlases and guides provide topographical information.

The number of visitors using the library exceeds 200 000 annually, and the information service is also available by telephone, telex and post. Publications include *Business Bibliographies: brief guides to business sources*, a monthly *Management Digest* for local government and miscellaneous lists.

A detailed report on the use and users of the library has been made by Averil Osborne for Aslib—*Report on a pilot study at the Commercial Library, concerning the use and users of publicly available business and commercial information* (Aslib Research Department, 1973).

Sheffield City Libraries of Commerce, Science and Technology. The City Libraries' service to industry began in 1916. By 1932, with the establishment of Sheffield Interchange Organisation (SINTO), the provision of business and commercial information to the public was further extended. In 1972 the Sheffield quick reference Business Library was opened as a separate department within the Central Library.

The Business Library, like those of the other large city libraries described above, provides a comprehensive service of information. It contains a large collection of directories of all kinds; indexes of trade names; information about companies, with particular emphasis on the development of local companies; travel information; newspapers; commercial journals; and extensive current-information files on industries and countries.

The Sheffield Interchange Organisation is an association of over 50 industrial, research, university, commercial and government libraries in the Sheffield area. Membership is open to any library or information unit in the region with a minimum of 50 books and 10 current periodicals. The Organisation is a practical example of the value of inter-library co-operation.

SPECIAL LIBRARIES

The term 'special libraries' is usually taken to mean that very large group of libraries which are not supported by public funds and which are concerned with a particular branch of knowledge or belong to a privately supported organisation. Thus the libraries of all companies, professional institutions, learned societies, research organisations and all kinds of associations can, for the sake of convenience, be called special libraries. They are naturally intended primarily for the members of the organisations to which they belong, but most of them participate to a greater or lesser extent in formal or informal inter-library co-operative arrangements.

There are several useful guides to these libraries and some are listed in Chapter 7. The *Aslib Directory*, although it is now nearly 6 years old and needs updating, is still probably the most comprehensive guide to special libraries in the UK, and gives details of the availability of these libraries, their hours of opening and their subject coverage. The *Directory of Special Libraries and Information Centers*, edited by Anthony T. Kruzas (Gale Research Co.), which has previously been mentioned, is one of several American library directories. It gives information on more than 11 000 special libraries and information centres in the USA and Canada belonging to business organisations and companies, government agencies, educational institutions and non-profit organisations of all kinds. The *Special Libraries Association*, which was founded at Bretton Woods in New Hampshire in 1909, is an association of more than 6000 professional librarians and information experts who provide specialised services to business and industrial organisations, government agencies and organisations in the field of science and technology. Through its various divisions it has done much to promote the use of business information by compiling guides and bibliographies on a wide range of specialised subjects. In the UK *Aslib*, which was founded in 1924, has performed the same kind of service, although it has been far more concerned with science and technology than it has with business.

Invidious though it is to select so few, the following three libraries are of interest to British businessmen, and they are briefly described here as representative of the whole group of special libraries within the scope of this subject field.

British Institute of Management, Management House, Parker Street, London WC2B 5PT

The Institute was founded in 1947 following the recommendations of the Baillieu Committee that a central institution be set up to deal with all questions concerned with managment. In 1952 the Institute of Industrial Administration merged with the BIM.

The Library now contains some 55 000 books and pamphlets, subscribes to about 300 periodicals covering all aspects of management and business studies, and provides services which are intensively used by BIM members and others. It also collects information on management films, and has a salary unit which maintains up-to-date information on executive salaries in the UK and Common Market.

The Library is classified by UDC and uses a co-ordinate indexing system to retrieve periodical articles. The thesaurus used has been published under the title *Management information retrieval: a new indexing language*, by John Blagden (Management Publications, 1971). A short selection of new titles added to the library's stock appears in *Management Review & Digest*, which is distributed to all members. The Library maintains 170 bibliographies on various management topics and will compile special bibliographies on request.

Confederation of British Industry, 21 Tothill Street, London SW1

The function of the expert special committees of CBI is to monitor the work of policy-making bodies, inform Members, advise government and international institutions such as EEC and ILO, and act as spokesman for the views of industry as a whole. Matters of outstanding interest include national economic policy, taxation, international trade and monetary policy, industrial relations and conditions, safety and welfare, education and training, company law, industrial effluent water resources and the impact of the European Communities on industry. The library is concerned with all these subject areas. It provides a current-information service, including a fortnightly bulletin to the secretariat of these committees, and concentrates on acquiring material from government bodies both national and international, learned societies and related institutions, and pressure groups which seek to influence policy.

In addition to a small central collection of pamphlets, books, journals and newspapers, the library has special sections of statistics, company reports, trade and employers' association reports and trade directories.

Trades Union Congress, Congress House, Great Russell Street, London WC1B 3LS

The Library was started in 1915 and from 1922 till 1956 was shared jointly by the TUC and the Labour Party. In 1956 the greater part of the stock was moved from Transport House when the TUC took over its new premises at Congress House.

Primarily the library exists to serve the staff of Congress House, who are concerned with education, international relations, organisation of labour, the press, research and economic problems, social insurance and industrial welfare, and production. In addition, the library serves the research departments of affiliated trade unions and the TUC Centenary Institute of Occupational Health. Since the TUC holds an almost unique collection of labour history materials, including the John Burns Collection of eighteenth and nineteenth century books and pamphlets, together with publications dealing with contemporary trade union organisations and industrial relations, access to the Library is given to academic researchers. Normal inter-library co-operation is also part of the library service.

These three important libraries have been singled out because no detailed survey can be given here of the many special libraries which together make up this group. Many of them have valuable collections of publications and information in their own chosen subject fields. *The Institute of Personnel Management*, for example, has an active and important library service concerned with many aspects of personnel administration, organisation and manpower planning, payment and employment conditions, training and industrial relations. *The Institute of Chartered Accountants* has a very comprehensive library on accounting. The *Institute of Banking* has an unrivalled collection on all aspects of banking. The *Institute of Marketing* has an important library in this field. The *Consumers Association*, the *National Institute of Economic and Social Research*, the *Industrial Society* and the *Tavistock Institute of Human Relations* are other active organisations which provide library services. The larger advertising and management consulting firms all run their own libraries and information services, and outstanding in this group is the large and efficient library of the *Urwick Management Centre* at Slough, which is in many respects similar to the libraries of the business schools.

Enough has been said to indicate the resources available in special libraries and to underline the fact that these resources, together with those of the libraries of business schools, government departments and the public libraries, exist in order to serve those who need to use business information and management literature of all kinds.

MANAGEMENT AND BUSINESS ASSOCIATIONS

The many important management and business associations, societies and institutes which provide services for their members, in addition to their library services, also supply information in many ways and of various kinds. The *British Institute of Management*, for example, runs a whole range of services designed to give specialised advice and information on many practical aspects of management, executive remuneration, consulting services and training. It issues several series of publications based on surveys and investigations carried out with the co-operation of member firms. It is also well known for its meetings, conferences and courses, which have had a very beneficial effect on the development of British management during the past decade. The *Institute of Marketing*, the *Institute of Personnel Management*, the *Industrial Society*, the *Institute of Directors* and many other organisations operate in much the same way within their own chosen area of activity.

In the USA, Canada, Europe and other countries there are many similar organisations serving management and business interests. The *Conference Board,* which organises conferences, carries out an active research programme into business problems, issues a valuable series of reports and numerous other publications and provides a comprehensive business information service for its members, is one of the best-known American organisations in this field. Another is the *Small Business Association,* an American government agency devoted to helping small firms with their management and business problems.

Through these and similar organisations people engaged in business and management can meet to exchange ideas, discuss problems and develop acceptable policies. The organisations therefore become focal points for people with common interests, and so it is natural for them to become information centres also. This custom of forming societies and institutions is at least 400 years old and began to flourish especially in Italy in the late sixteenth and early seventeenth century with the formation of scientific societies such as the Accademia dei Lincei, the society which encouraged Galileo and published some of his writings. From Italy scientific leadership passed to France, Germany and England in the seventeenth Century. The Académie Royale des Sciences and the esteemed Royal Society of London were formed in 1666 and 1662, respectively, and before long scientific societies were springing up everywhere—they have done and still do much to promote and develop ideas. And societies are particularly associated with professions—science, medicine, law, art, engineering and librarianship, for example.

The discussion on whether management is or is not a viable profession is still continuing, but there are the management associations which provide focal points for people to meet and exchange ideas, share problems and discuss developments either at meetings or through publications. The *American Management Association,* formed in 1923 by the merger of several earlier management societies, aims to be, as its official statement says, 'a non-profit educational organisation dedicated to finding, developing and sharing better methods of management'. It promotes, in pursuit of this aim, conferences, courses, seminars, information and publication services, and its 61 000 members come from large and small firms in all industries, from government and education, and from every kind of administration. It operates in many centres in the USA, in South America and, more recently, in Europe. With the rapid development of European management education during the past decade, the *Management Centre Europe,* founded in 1961, is currently very active in promoting short courses at its headquarters in Brussels. The MCE is linked with the American Management Association through the *International Management Association,* which is a subsidiary of the parent AMA and operates as the membership division in Europe.

The *British Institute of Management* (see p. 57) performs the same kind of function for its 45 000 individual members and 14 000 collective subscribers as the American Management Association and its offshoots. So together these societies provide cohesiveness to the management profession; they influence and encourage the development of management skills and promote management training, which in turn is linked with the education provided by the business schools. And the extensive information services of both the AMA and the BIM have proved invaluable to a multitude of managers for many years.

Other countries, notably in Europe, have formed management associations within recent years somewhat on the lines of the AMA and BIM but with a tendency to be rather more closely tied initially to the development of management education rather than concentrating on helping the practising manager with his daily problems, although the former aim divorced from the latter would obviously be pointless. Thus the *Irish Management Institute,* the *North European Management Institute* in Oslo, the *Finnish Institute of Management* and the *Indian Institute of Manage-*

ment, to mention but a few, are growing sturdily and expanding their activities.

Management teachers have also realised that they need to meet together, share ideas and discuss problems. They do this of course mostly through their own informal and professional contacts with one another, and as colleagues within their own academic institutions; but they have, additionally, formed associations which enable contacts to be extended. And so the *Association of Teachers of Management* was formed in the UK in 1960. It was a weak and ailing infant in its early days but has now struggled up on to its feet with the firm aims of encouraging the development of management education and research and providing teachers with the means for communicating ideas and exchanging experiences. Its journal, *Management Education and Development* (see p. 114), is one means of communication, and its meetings and conferences have done much to raise the professional standards of management teaching. The Business Graduates Association, founded in 1967, is active in promoting graduate business education as an important method of developing and improving management.

On the continent of Europe management teachers have only started to come together even more recently, and after early struggles to form an association the *European Foundation for Management Development* was established in Brussels in 1971, through a merger between the former *European Association of Management Training Centres* and the *International University Contact for Management Education.* The Foundation was formed with the blessing of the EEC and the OECD, and has quickly won the support of the main European and British business schools, management and business organisations and some of the leading companies. It has started to publish a journal, and aims to encourage a dialogue on management development, to help national bodies and to study needs and problems in European management education of all kinds.

In contrast to these two young associations, the adult and professional *American Association of Collegiate Schools of Business* was established as long ago as 1916, and exists to promote and improve higher education for business and administration. It is widely recognised as the accrediting agency for business schools and colleges in America, and thus ensures that all its accredited member institutions run business administration programmes which are of a high educational standard. It operates through an Assembly which organises national and regional meetings, and publishes reports, proceedings of meetings and the *AACSB Bulletin.* The AACSB typifies the 'profession' of management education, and it is true to say that the younger institutions in the UK and Europe are now developing a new and fresher image than the older and vastly more experienced image of their adult American sister institution.

CONCLUSION

So there is no lack of information! The problem is to find it and get it at the time when it is wanted and to ensure that it is relevant information. The libraries, information services and management associations can do much to help. By using a directory or a reference work such as *Social Science Research and Industry,* by A. T. M. Wilson and others (Harrap, 1971), one can easily find which library, which information service or which organisation to use.

The libraries of British, European and American business schools provide for the needs of management education and research and for the study of management and business problems. The government libraries serve the increasing requirements of the departments concerned with industry and commerce. The public library resources provide the essential quick-reference information and data essential to business activities. The special libraries and specialist organisations supply the information needed by particular groups of people engaged in a variety of activities.

Together these information resources are very comprehensive in their subject coverage, but it is fundamentally important to learn how to use libraries effectively. And that is the subject discussed in the next chapter.

4

Using Libraries as Information Resources

K. D. C. Vernon

Every library, from mammoth collections such as the US Library of Congress, the Bibliothèque Nationale or the British Museum Library, to the small shelf of books in an executive's office, is an information store. It provides a resource which can be used for a wide variety of purposes— for education, pleasure or general interest, or out of sheer necessity when facts and knowledge are essential for solving problems. And the people who use libraries together represent a microcosm of human activities— learning, living, working and pursuing the real meaning of individual lives— seen through the information or the books they want or collect around them. Libraries therefore exist to fulfil needs, and it is the purpose of this chapter to discuss the ways in which libraries concerned with business and management can be used.

In the previous chapter we discussed some of the library resources which are available in our subject field, but before considering how to use these resources it is as well to remember that basically there are four kinds of libraries, apart from the private collections of books belonging to individuals which are kept in so many homes.

1. *National libraries*, which are the largest collections and represent each nation's attempt to provide its citizens with a storehouse of knowledge —in the UK, for example, our copyright laws require all publishers to deliver one copy of every published book, pamphlet, periodical, etc., to the British Museum Library within one month of publication and, on demand, to the National Library of Scotland, the Bodleian Library at Oxford, Cambridge University Library, the National Library of Wales and the Library of Trinity College Dublin. These great libraries, which

are primarily reference and not lending collections, therefore approach comprehensiveness in their holdings of British publications. Until recently we have in the UK also had two national lending services, known as the National Central Library and the National Lending Library, and in addition there have been other great nationally owned reference collections, such as the libraries of the Patent Office and Science Museum. Our national bibliographical recording service is known as the British National Bibliography. All these excellent services have in the past been operating independently, but in 1972 the new British Library Act was passed by Parliament and under its provision we now have one co-ordinated national library service controlled and managed by a board appointed by the government. The British Museum Library will be the focal point of the service and becomes the main reference collection with various other services and subsidiary collections related to it (*Figure 4.1*). The National Lending Library at Boston Spa, which is described on p. 77, has now merged with the former National Central Library and becomes the lending division of the British Library. When the whole system is fully operational and the plans for computerised catalogues and bibliographical records have been put into effect, we shall have an integrated national library service unrivalled in the world.

The national libraries of many countries provide services suited to national needs. The enormous and immensely active Library of Congress in Washington, which was founded in 1800, provides a whole range of services, including the preparation of MARC tapes, which are computer tapes containing bibliographical details of all English-language monography publications currently being received in the Library. The tapes are available to other libraries and thus provide the data for their catalogues. The great Lenin State Library of the USSR in Moscow, the Bibliothèque Nationale in Paris, the National Library of Australia, the National Library of India, to mention but a few, each provide bibliographical services and foster inter-library co-operation in their own countries.

2. *Academic libraries*, which range in size from the enormous collections at Harvard and Yale in America or at Oxford and Cambridge in this country, down through the more modest collections of most universities to the small and sometimes specialised libraries of colleges and schools, form a large part of the total library resources. This great group of libraries aims to provide for the educational and research needs of the members of the academic institutions concerned. Most American Universities possess immense libraries and devote a realistic proportion of their funds to the upkeep and development of their libraries. In the UK the universities, which together have a total stock of over 30 000 000 volumes, have never been very generously funded, but they do provide excellent services and place considerable importance on inter-library co-operation,

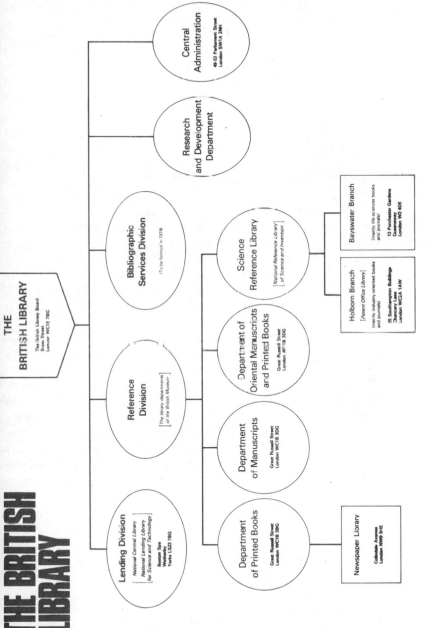

Figure 4.1

(Reproduced with permission from the British Library)

which means that each can call on the much wider resources of other collections. *The World of Learning* (Europa Publications) is one of the best annuals for providing brief information on the world's universities and their libraries.

3.   *Public libraries*, which stand for the principle that all men should have free access to books, also vary greatly in size, from the vast New York Public Library with its stock of over 5 000 000 volumes down to tiny local community libraries. In the UK the public library system provides a very high standard of service and contains book-stocks which together amount to over 114 000 000 volumes. In the larger cities the public libraries provide very good information resources for business and management— a fact which is often not fully appreciated in the business world. Some indication of these services has been given in Chapter 3.

4.   *Special libraries*, which, broadly speaking, are all other types of libraries not publicly owned. They include company libraries and the libraries of individual institutions such as the British Institute of Management. In the UK and even more so in the USA there is a vast number of special libraries owned by a wide variety of organisations and providing information resources for many groups of people with similar interests. Accountants, architects, doctors, engineers, lawyers, musicians, scientists and statisticians, for example, all have their own professional special libraries. And so too do many other groups of people linked by mutual interests—anthropologists, chemists, directors, geologists, mountaineers, photographers, surveyors, town planners, trade unionists and women's lib supporters. Together these libraries have immense information resources. The *Aslib Directory*, edited by B. J. Wilson (Aslib, 1968–70), is the best guide to British special libraries. It is published in two volumes, the first covering information sources in science, technology and commerce, and the second covering information sources in medicine, the social sciences and the humanities. Each volume gives details of the stock, subject coverage and availability of about 2500 libraries; and although many of the details are now rather out of date, the *Directory* is still of considerable value to librarians and others who need to find out about sources of information. The *Directory of Special Libraries and Information Centers*, edited by A. T. Kruzas (Gale Research Co.), which has previously been mentioned in Chapter 3, is one of several guides to immense resources of information available in American special libraries.

Most of the major countries of the world have developed extensive and efficient library systems, but on the whole their potential value, as sources of information for trade, business and management, has not yet been realised, largely because most people have never learnt how to use a library properly or purposefully. It is a skill which should be taught in our schools so that young people can approach the task of finding information with confidence.

USING LIBRARIES

Businessmen in general and executives in particular are at considerable disadvantage if they do not know how to use libraries as sources of information. In *Scanning the business environment*, by Francis J. Aguilar (Collier-Macmillan, 1967), there is a valuable survey of the methods by which managers obtain the information they need. It shows clearly that library resources are not regarded, at least by Aguilar's sample, as important in the manager's information gathering process. Could this fact, if it is true, be the result of not knowing how to use libraries and not realising their potential value as information resources?

Several guide-books include sections on how to use libraries and give helpful advice on classification systems and on using catalogues and indexes. John Fletcher in his book *The use of economics literature* (Butterworths, 1971) devotes two chapters to this subject, including a description of various types of libraries and their characteristics, and advice on making a literature search and on using the economics library in particular. *How to find out: management and productivity*, by K. G. B. Bakewell (2nd ed., Pergamon, 1970), also has a chapter on using libraries which offers similar helpful advice. There are several parallel American publications such as *How to use the business library, with sources of business information*, by H. W. Johnson (4th ed., South-Western Publishing Co., 1972). The author is Professor of Marketing at Wayne State University, and in the preface to this useful guide-book he makes the point that: 'The business library can be most useful to those who know how to take advantage of its many sources of business information. It is an institution of great value . . . but the sources and tools it provides are no more effective than the skill of the user.' That is written, not by a librarian trying to get more people to use his library, but by a person who has discovered the benefit of using a library as an information resource.

For busy people it may be helpful to forget that their library is mostly full of books and periodicals and to consider it instead as a place where thousands and thousands of units of useful information are stored. The probability is that some of those units of information are relevant to the current business or management problem and might help to solve it, or at least provide ideas which can be applied to the problem.

These units of information are contained in many forms of publication—in books and periodicals, in statistical publications and market surveys, in newspapers and their supplements, in encyclopaedias, directories, and reference works of all kinds, in the multitude of government reports, laws and papers, in company reports or research reports, in conference proceedings or in semi-published documents such as stockbrokers' reports, discussion papers or theses. Written communication in the modern world demands that all these different forms of publication be used, and some of them may be in microform or even on cassette tapes. But whether the problem is concerned with finance, marketing, industrial relations, research and development, organisational structure, production control or a wide range of other business activities, one can be confident that information about it probably exists in some form or other. Armed with the knowledge of that probability the information-seeker only has one problem left—to find it!

In the light of these considerations it is evident that the person who knows how to tap libraries as sources of information has a big advantage. It is necessary to have the right attitudes to the task of finding information and to approach it with confidence. The person who gives up after one brief look at the card catalogue and then goes away frustrated and muttering to himself about the uselessness of libraries will never reap much benefit from their resources. Of course many businessmen have little time to use libraries themselves to find information, but there is a rapidly growing number who do, and they are beginning to accept the necessity of having to understand the system before its full potential can be utilised. It is really no good assuming that 'of course I know how to use this or any other library and I don't need a librarian to tell me either', because such an assumption may well be incorrect. It is much better to start with an open-minded questioning attitude towards the library and to approach it in the spirit of finding out about its resources and how best to use them. Learning how to use a library is not time wasted for most businessmen: it is a process of acquiring a new skill which may be required for use at any time.

KEYS TO THE INFORMATION STORE

Catalogues and indexes are the keys to the store of information in any library: they should not be regarded as the private possessions of librarians, even though librarians do, on occasions, tend to surround these things with a kind of mystique which can only be penetrated if one possesses certain secret bibliographical powers! The confident library user, who has spent a little time in learning how to look up information in a catalogue or index, knows how valuable they can be.

All libraries, whether they be large or small, operate as a system composed of four main parts which can be simply illustrated in diagrammatic form:

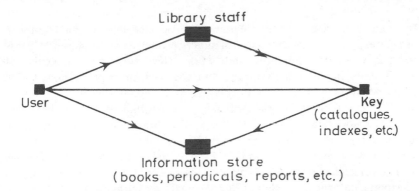

The user therefore has three options open to him when he goes to a library for information—he can go straight to the shelves if he knows exactly what he wants and where to find it; he can look up the information he requires in the catalogue and then go to the shelves to find it; or he can ask the library staff to help him and they will probably use the catalogue on his behalf and, if they are kind or not too busy, will get the information (book, article, etc.) for him from the library shelves, or will at least point the user in the right direction! Obviously this over-simplifies the problem of getting information from a library, because, as everybody knows, there may be frustrations and difficulties which can be caused by books and periodicals being out on loan to somebody else, or they may have been sent to the bookbinder, or they may even be missing—regrettably the number of books and periodicals stolen from universities has increased rapidly in recent years. The catalogue or index may be difficult to use quickly or it may not contain the information required, or the item wanted may not be in the library. The libray staff may all be very busy or they may fail properly to understand the question asked (but did the questioner really state clearly what he wanted?). Never-theless, accepting the fact that all libraries are inevitably imperfect instru-ments for supplying the information needs of every user all the time, the onus clearly rests on the user to understand the library system. He must (a) appreciate that because there are so many different forms of publication the total information on one subject cannot possibly be shelved neatly all in one place; (b) spend a short time learning how to use the catalogues and indexes, because by doing this he will save himself much time in the future; (c) ensure that he phrases his enquiries to the library staff clearly and adequately, so that they can correctly interpret each question into subject terms and headings used in catalogues and indexes. The person who uses his library in this way stands a good chance of getting the best out of it.

CATALOGUES

It would be tedious indeed to attempt a detailed description of how to use library catalogues, but lack of practice often causes people to forget what they are for and how they work. They are bibliographical tools which must be used in libraries, and the user must learn how to use them, not from a book such as this but by going to a library and finding out for himself. Library staff will normally be glad to explain how their catalogue works and there are textbooks for library students which explain in detail both the theory and practice of cataloguing and classification. The following brief description is given merely as a reminder of a few general principles which are relevant to the seeker after business information —expert catalogue users should skip the next four paragraphs!

The catalogue of any library is the record of its holdings and the guide which indicates where to find individual publications. It is an inventory of the stock and it normally records all books, pamphlets, government publications and serial publications in the library. It may, but does not always, record other things such as selected articles in periodicals, research reports, microfilm and microfiche publications, tape cassettes, films, etc. But the catalogue can never include details of all the 'units of information' which the library contains. It is a record of published items but *not* a record of all the contents of each item.

Most library catalogues are still on cards, which are usually arranged under the names of authors, subjects or titles. Obviously there must be one or more author cards for every item in the library and each card must give details of the author, title, publisher and date of publication and its location in the library. These details are the bibliographical records, which can now be easily handled by a computer. Some libraries have all their catalogue cards arranged in one alphabetical sequence which includes authors, subjects and titles—catalogues of this kind are called dictionary-catalogues. Others have separate sequences for authors and subjects and, less frequently, for titles also. Subject catalogues may be arranged under subject headings or they may be arranged in classified order according to the classification scheme used, in which case it is necessary to have an index of the subject headings in the classification scheme.

An author catalogue does not often confront the library user with too many difficulties, but problems do arise with finding publications which have no single person as the author—government publications or conference proceedings, for instance. Librarians have to catalogue these kinds of publications under the name of the corporate author, i.e. the body responsible for producing the publication, and it is here that the fun begins! Frequently the library user does not know the exact name of the corporate author—was it a special committee, a select committee or just a committee? Was it appointed by the Department of Trade and Industry, in which case would the catalogue card be under D or T, or would that wretched librarian be trying to confuse me on purpose by putting it under Great Britain, Trade and Industry, Department of, Select Committee on . . .? These are problems which must be faced, and they do present difficulties not only to library users, but to librarians also. After all we live in a complicated and confused world, so it is only to be expected that perfect clarity and simplicity cannot be achieved even in apparently unimportant things like author cards in a library catalogue. The best advice to follow is try to understand the system and get the library staff to help when problems arise. The purpose of library catalogues really is, truthfully, to help people to find things in libraries, not to confuse them. The author catalogue helps one find items in the library when the author's name is known, and it displays together all the publications of each author.

The subject catalogue aims to display, for the benefit of the library user, the contents of the library in order of subjects. Each card in the subject catalogue gives the same bibliographical details for each item as the author catalogue. The subject headings, or terms, which are chosen to group all publications on the same subject together in the catalogue serve as a means of finding what books or other publications a library has on a chosen subject. Thus in a dictionary-catalogue all the books on market research, for example, will be identifiable from the cards which have been given that subject heading. In a classified subject catalogue, on the other hand, each subject has been given a classification number or letters according to the classification system which is being used in the library, and the cards are arranged in the catalogue in the order of that classification. The classification number therefore is the 'address' on the library shelves where the publication will be found. The starting point, however, for the user of the classified subject catalogue is the index to the classification scheme. First he must look up the subject in the index, then he must note the numbers (or letters) allotted to that subject, then he must look under those numbers in the card catalogue to find the items he wants on his chosen subject. Market research is classified by the letters BD in the *London Classification of Business Studies*, so all books on that subject, in a library using that classification, would have subject cards filed in the catalogue under the letters BD.

That brief description of author and subject catalogues has grossly oversimplified their real use for the skilled library user and has ignored the fact that catalogues are complicated instruments, and information retrieval is a rapidly developing specialised science based on theoretical concepts which are evolving from empirical research. The developments which have occurred during the past 20 years have revolutionised many traditional library practices, and it may well be that within the next 20 years the card catalogue as we know it today will be a thing of the past. Many of our larger libraries already use computers to print out, edit and maintain their catalogues, so library users must become accustomed to using a print-out form instead of 5 × 3 in cards in a catalogue cabinet. But remember, a computer-printed catalogue has no special merit for overcoming catalogue-using problems. The computer in this case is helping the library housekeeping business and not necessarily the person trying to find a particular publication or piece of information.

CLASSIFICATION

Much has been written on this evolving subject, so it is only necessary now to relate it firstly to using library catalogues and secondly to management literature. In computer-produced catalogues the classification system is used as a convenient means of locating individual items on library shelves and not as an ideal tool for retrieving all kinds of specialised business information contained in management literature. We have not yet reached the stage when this kind of specialised information in libraries can be mechanically retrieved in a satisfactory manner suited to the modern needs of business.

Most traditional library card catalogues use one of the general classification systems — the Dewey Decimal Classification, the Library of Congress Classification or the rather more specialised Universal Decimal Classification. These well-established systems will continue to be used in libraries for many years to come merely because it is too expensive for large libraries to change their systems even if they wanted to. But all these classification schemes are very unsuitable for the rapidly developing needs of libraries which specialise in the subjects of business and management, but they are nevertheless being used in large computerised catalogues because it is necessary to standardise the classification for a mechanical system.

Only two specialised classification schemes for the ill-defined subject area of business and management have been produced and published for use in libraries. The first is the Harvard Business School's *Classification of Business Literature* (2nd ed., Shoe String Press, 1960); the second is the *London Classification of Business Studies*, by K. D. C. Vernon and Valerie Lang (London Business School, 1970). The Harvard Classification, which was first published in 1937, has, for various reasons, never been adopted to any extent by other libraries despite its merits, and has not been developed as a practical tool even in the great Baker Library at Harvard. The London Classification, on the other hand, was born of necessity when libraries for business studies started to develop rapidly in the UK in the late 1960s at the time when management education burst on the scene in this country. This classification is now used in some 45 libraries in Britain and overseas, although not to any extent in America.

The outline of the *London Classification* has been given in Chapter 1, but it is repeated here in more detail in order to show its broad coverage and to illustrate how business studies impinge and draw upon a wide spectrum of subjects and disciplines (*Table 4.1*). The classification

Table 4.1.

SYNOPSIS OF THE SCHEDULES

Facets and classes are combined in alphabetical order, with the exception of A which always comes second. The schedules of Personnel (F) and Labour economics (JW) have recently been modified and extended by the Institute of Manpower Studies, but they appear here in the original form.

MANAGEMENT RESPONSIBILITY IN THE ENTERPRISE		B	MARKETING
		BA	Marketing
		BB	Classes of Goods Marketed
		BC	International Marketing
A	MANAGEMENT	BD	Marketing Research
		BF	Sales Forecasting
AA	Management	BG	Marketing Campaigns
AB	Management Personnel	BH	Product Planning
AC	Management Education	BK	Advertising
AD	Corporate Strategy	BM	Pricing
AE	Managerial Activities	BN	Channels and Systems of Distribution
AF	Managerial Functions		
AH	Project Management	BNZ	Physical Distribution
		BP	Sales Force Control
		BQ	Personal Selling
AZ	THE ENTERPRISE	BR	Sales Promotion
		BT	Shopping
AZA	Business Enterprise		
AZB	International Enterprise		
AZC	Private Enterprise		
AZD	Mixed Enterprise	C	PRODUCTION
AZE	Public Enterprise		
AZG	Interfirm Studies	CA	Production
AZH	Small Businesses	CB	Types of Production
AZK	Large Businesses	CD	Production Development
AZL	Industrial and Commercial Associations	CE	Production Planning and Control
AZM	Environment of the Enterprise	CF	Value Analysis

CG	Production Methods		GC	Secretarial Work
CH	Production Equipment		GD	Correspondence Activities
CM	Factory Management		GF	Copying
CP	Production Services		GG	Calculating
			GJ	Document Maintenance
			GK	Translating
D	RESEARCH AND		GM	Registry Activities
	DEVELOPMENT		GP	Invoicing

DA	Research and Development
DB	Research
DC	Development
DD	Results of Research
DE	Patenting
DF	Research Facilities (physical)

ENVIRONMENTAL STUDIES

J	ECONOMICS

JA	Economics and Economic History
E	FINANCE
JB	Comparative Economic Systems

EA	Finance			
EB	Financial Markets		JC	Principles of Economics
EC	Financial Institutions		JD	Microeconomics
EE	Business Asset Management		JE	Costs
EF	Portfolio Investment		JF	Demand
EG	Business Formation and		JG	Price Mechanism
	Liquidation		JH	Market Structure
EH	Land and Property Finance		JJ	Distribution Theory
EJ	Personal Financial		JK	Economic Conditions
	Management		JL	Macroeconomics
EL	Accounts and Accounting		JM	Econometrics
			JN	Investment and Growth
			JP	Monetary Economics
F	PERSONNEL		JQ	International Economic Relations
FA	Personnel Administration		JR	Public Finance
FB	Selection of Personnel		JS	Economic Planning
FC	Personnel Training		JU	Local Government Finance
FD	Status of Personnel		JW	Labour Economics
FE	Conditions of Employment (non-financial)			
FF	Remuneration			
FG	Financial Benefits		JZ	TRANSPORT
FH	Social Benefits			
FJ	Employee Communication		JZA	Transport
FK	Industrial Relations		JZB	Land Transport
FL	Working Conditions		JZC	Water Transport
			JZD	Air Transport
			JZE	Space Transport
G	OFFICE SERVICES		JZG	Transport Termini
			JZH	Vehicles
GA	Office Services			

JZJ	Traffic	LC	Sociology
JZL	Traffic Studies	LE	Population Studies
JZN	Public Transport	LG	Social Stratification
	(passenger)	LJ	People
JZP	Freight Transport	LN	Informal Groups
JZR	Accidents and Accident	LQ	Formal Organisations
	Prevention	LU	Social Control
JZS	Navigation	LW	Social Administration
		LX	Psychology

K INDUSTRIES

M COMMUNICATION

KA	Agriculture, Forestry and	MA	Communication
	Fishing Industries	MC	Information
KB	Extractive Industries	ME	Communication Skills
KBZ	Manufacturing Industries	MG	Group Communication
KC	Food, Drink and Tobacco	MJ	Mass Communication
	Industries	MP	Communication Media
KD	Chemical Industries	MS	Signs
KE	Metal Industries	MU	Codes of Communication
KF	Engineering Industries		
KG	Shipbuilding and Marine		
	Engineering	**N**	**EDUCATION**
KH	Vehicles Industries		
KJ	Other Metal Goods Industries	NA	Education
KK	Textile Industries	NB	Education at School
KL	Leather and Fur Industries	NC	Further Education
KM	Clothing and Footwear	ND	Curriculum
	Industries	NE	Teaching Methods
KN	Building Materials Industries	NF	Teaching Aids
KP	Timber and Furniture	NH	Students' Work
	Industries	NK	Educational Assessment
KQ	Paper, Printing and Publishing	NL	Staff
	Industries	NN	Educational Administration
KR	Other Manufacturing	NR	Careers
	Industries		
KS	Construction and Civil		
	Engineering Industries	**P**	**LAW**
KT	Power Industries		
KU	Water Engineering Industry	PA	Jurisprudence
KV	Postal and Telecom-	PB	General and Comparative Law
	munications Services	PC	International Law
KW	Service Industries	PF	Public Law
		PG	Private Law
		PL	Law and Legal Systems of
L	**BEHAVIOURAL SCIENCES**		Europe
		PN	Law and Legal Systems of
LA	Behavioural Sciences		Africa

PQ	Law and Legal Systems of Asia and the Pacific
PT	Religious Legal Systems
PV	Ancient and Mediaeval Law

Q	POLITICAL SCIENCE
QA	Political Science
QB	The State
QC	Government
QD	Constitutions
QE	Legislation and Legislative Bodies
QG	Administration of Government
QL	International Relations
QM	Dependent Territories
QQ	War
QS	Practical Politics
QU	Local Government

R	SCIENCE AND TECHNOLOGY
RA	Science and Technology
RB	Science
RC	Astronomy
RD	Physics
RE	Chemistry
RF	Geography
RG	Geology
RH	Paleontology
RJ	Biology
RK	Botany
RL	Zoology
RM	Medical Sciences
RN	Technology

S	PHILOSOPHY, LOGIC AND SCIENTIFIC METHOD
SA	Philosophy
SB	Fundamentals of Logic
SC	Conclusions
SD	Logical Calculation
SE	Theory of Knowledge
SF	Logical Standpoints and Trends
SH	Scientific Enquiry
SJ	Scientific Systemisation

ANALYTICAL TECHNIQUES

TA	Operational Research
TB	Systems Analysis
TC	Scheduling
TD	Sequencing
TE	Search Theory
TF	Statistical Decision Making
TG	Simulation
TH	Queuing Theory
TJ	Resource Allocation
TK	Mathematical Models
TL	Game Theory
TM	Network Analysis
TN	Heuristics

U	STATISTICS
UA	Statistics
UB	Statistical Evaluation
UC	Statistical Distribution
UD	Sampling
UE	Statistical Analysis
UG	Probability Theory
UH	Estimation
UJ	Statistical Testing
UK	Statistical Dispersion
UL	Statistical Relationships

V	MATHEMATICS
VA	Mathematics
VB	Arithmetic
VC	Algebra
VD	Mathematical Analysis
VF	Homology
VG	Calculus
VH	Potential Theory
VJ	Special Functions
VK	Trigonometry
VL	Geometry
VM	Differential Equations
VN	Integral Equations
VP	Series
VR	Preferred Numbers
VS	Numerical Analysis
VT	Graphical Methods
VU	Slide Rule Methods

VV	Mathematical Programming	XC	Organisation and Methods
VW	Metrology	XE	Work Study
		XG	Method Study
W	AUTOMATION	XK	Work Measurement
WA	Automation	XP	Ergonomics
WB	Computers		
WC	Data		
WD	Input-output Media		AUXILIARY SCHEDULES
WE	Computer Operating Systems		
WF	Programming	1	People and Occupational
WG	Programming Language		Roles
WH	Computer Installation and Operation	2	Industrial Products and Services (To be used with K.)
		3	Common Properties
X	ORGANISATION AND METHODS AND WORK STUDY	4	Common Activities
		5	Geographical Divisions
		6	Time
XA	Organisation and Methods and Work Study	7	Form Divisions
		8	Languages

is based on the following arbitrary definition of business information which is concerned with:

1.   The activities of enterprises and organisations, especially those concerned with trade, commerce and manufacture; the control and organisation of these activities and of the people engaged in carrying them out.

2.   The techniques and methods available for use in managing and carrying out these activities.

3.   The environment as it directly affects these enterprises and organisations.

The list of the main classes and their sub-divisions is given in *Table 4.1*. It will be seen that they are grouped into three large categories which correspond to the three parts of the above definition: (1) management responsibility in the enterprise, (2) environmental studies, (3) analytical and quantitative techniques. The classification was developed in the Library of the London Business School and has been designed for use in libraries concerned with the whole or with part of the broad field of business studies. It is a flexible system which was constructed by using the method of analysing subjects by their 'facets' or characteristics. It is explained in more detail in an article 'The London Classification of Business Studies and management literature', by K. D. C. Vernon and Valerie Lang (*Aslib Proceedings*, March, **24** (3), 187–198, 1972).

Like all classifications of developing subjects, this classification is kept up to date by amendments which are issued periodically, and a more extensive revision of parts of it has been compiled by Miss Lang and published as a pamphlet entitled *A Classification for Manpower Studies: introduction to the I.M.S. development of the London Classification of Business Studies* (Institute of Manpower Studies and London Business School, 1972).

The *London Classification* is not, and can never be, the perfect answer to the problems of retrieving information in this interdisciplinary subject area, but it is a useful and practical library tool. Like the Philosopher's Stone, the search for perfection must go on, and research into methods of information retrieval in business studies urgently needs to be undertaken. Not enough serious attention has been paid to this problem.

Catalogues and classification schemes can never completely satisfy the specialised needs of library users who thirst for specific information. These needs are not yet properly understood, but it is evident that new methods of indexing and retrieving information must be devised, and the library user must be prepared to look beyond the conventional library catalogue even when it is computer-produced.

There are, for example, the published indexes and abstracting publications, which are discussed in Chapter 5. These can often be regarded as the next step in the search for information if the library catalogue fails to reveal any relevant publications. Or there are the special indexes which most libraries compile to assist their users—these may be subject indexes of articles in periodicals which are known to be relevant to particular groups of users. It is often accepted as part of a good library's services that the staff should compile and maintain indexes· which are known to be needed, bibliographies or lists on topics which are important and which are outside the scope of the general card catalogue. An example of this kind of service is the series of bibliographies and reading lists compiled and issued by the Library of the British Institute of Management.

The compilation of special subject indexes, or indexing as librarians call it, is becoming an increasingly complex and skilled task and has led to some important advances in documentation and information control. One method is known as co-ordinate indexing, and the best example in the field of management literature is described in *Management Information Retrieval: a new indexing language,* by John Blagden (2nd ed., Management Publications, 1971). This system is used for indexing articles in the BIM Library and is based on a thesaurus of terms which can be used singly, or in combination, to retrieve references to articles which are recorded on optical coincidence cards.

INTER-LIBRARY CO-OPERATION

No modern library can exist successfully in isolation from other libraries, nor can it possibly aspire to provide comprehensive subject coverage—there is too much published information in the world for this to be possible. And so libraries must co-operate. They do in fact do this in most countries, but library co-operation in the UK has been developed to such an extent that it is probably the most effective system in the world. It is based on the principle that access to published information should be possible wherever it is located. In the UK library co-operative activities are on three levels: national systems; regional and local arrangements between libraries; the 'old boy network' which operates widely between individual libraries.

Under the auspices of the British Library, the British Lending Library, which is situated at Boston Spa in Yorkshire, currently receives over 40 000 periodicals and, since its recent amalgamation with the National Central Library, now contains about $1\frac{1}{4}$ million books. It provides a very comprehensive, efficient and quick postal loan service to other libraries. Applications may be made by any approved library which purchases BLL forms either for the loan of books and periodicals or for photocopies of articles, and so effective has the service become that over 1 400 000 applications were made in 1972. Most of these were dealt with on the day of receipt; and because the library is so comprehensive, particularly for periodicals, it manages to satisfy nearly 90% of the requests it receives. This fine service is much appreciated by all who use it. Loans are made only on a library-to-library basis and not to individuals. A good readable description of the BLL and its services is *Out of the dinosaurs. the evolution of the National Lending Library for Science and Technology*, by Bernard Houghton (Clive Bingley, 1972).

The formation of this remarkable service was undoubtedly one of the most signficant events in British librarianship. The Library was scientifically planned and developed. It comprises a massive central collection of documents of all kinds and is organised on the lines of a mail-order store with a conveyor-belt system which is used to carry books and periodicals from the shelves to the packing and dispatching points. Its collection of Russian and Chinese scientific periodicals is the most comprehensive in the western hemisphere and has done much to reveal for the first time the extent of scientific research in these great countries. The Library costs about $£1\frac{1}{2}$ million a year—its value to the community is inestimable.

Regional and local library co-operative arrangements have reached a high level of efficiency in many areas, particularly around our large towns. They depend for their success primarily on the determination of librarians within a particular area to work together, so far as their organisational structures permit, to provide easy access on a local level to information which is available in the libraries of that area. The libraries usually vary greatly in size, availability and subject specialisation, and co-operative arrangements may include the public library, the university library, the libraries of technical and further education colleges, local institutions and societies, companies and industrial organisations. The librarians who operate these local arrangements have considered their library resources, the needs of their users, the advantages, snags and costs of co-operation, and have accordingly set up systems which suit local requirements.

Many very effective local library co-operative systems now exist—for example, at places such as Liverpool, Sheffield, Nottingham and Newcastle, to mention but a few of the largest. They are usually based on the central public library, and the libraries in the system jointly provide valuable information services for local industries, companies, banks, insurance offices, businesses of all kinds and teaching establishments, besides serving the 'man in the street', that well-known but distinctly vague public figure. Library users in these areas are fortunate in having access to such well-organised information resources. Much credit for these systems should be given to the librarians who have been far-sighted enough to set them up. A good description of the Hertfordshire system is contained in a booklet *The development of HERTIS,* by G. H. Wright (Hatfield Polytechnic, 1969).

The third type of library co-operation is entirely informal and exists merely because librarians realise that they can help to meet the needs of their library users by sharing their library resources wherever possible. This does not mean that small libraries latch on to big ones like fleas on an elephant, but that librarians get to know one another as people and accept the fact that it is reasonable to look to other libraries for information which is outside the scope of one's own library. It would be both selfish and ineffective if librarians conceived co-operation as being a means of saving money by using somebody else's resources. A good librarian, who knows about the resources of other libraries and their availability, can greatly extend the service he provides in his own library. But the personality of the librarian and his ability to communicate with his colleagues in other libraries is the all-important keystone to the successful operation of the 'old boy network'. Well operated, it can be an effective service and one which is beneficial to the users of a library.

This is not the place for a discussion of inter-library co-operation in other countries, but many countries have developed systems of inter-library lending and co-operation based on their existing library systems, and on their union and regional catalogues. Library co-operation, in most countries, is centred on the national library, and the richer industrialised countries of the world have provided the necessary resources in money and personnel for promoting co-operation. The poorer, developing countries are restricted by their limited resources, but countries such as Nigeria, for example, are taking active steps to develop their library systems.

LIBRARY STAFF–LIBRARY USER RELATIONSHIPS

One of the four points in the model of a library system given on p. 67 is the library staff. By communication between the library user and the library staff the information store and the keys to the store are used to their best effect. Like any other organisation, a library depends on the people who operate it — without them the organisation would have no life.

The person who has learnt to use a library in the way I have described above realises that the staff are there to help the user. And so they are, because librarianship is a service. Probably few library users, however, realise that the library staff cannot help much if an enquiry is put to them in vague and indefinite terms or in an impatient and perhaps aggressive manner. For example, the person who asks 'where are your books on the chemical industry?' when what he really wants is the name of the managing director of ICI (Dyestuffs Division) is wasting his own time and that of the library staff; but yet that kind of request is made all too frequently. Or there is the other kind of user who puts a highly specific enquiry couched in professional jargon to a junior member of the library staff and then stands impatiently peering over the young librarian's shoulder while he or she nervously, and probably unsuccessfully, consults the catalogue.

The regular library user who gets to know the staff of his library will be able to communicate with them when he wants assistance and he will get it readily. The regular library user who walks into another library which he has never used before and puts his query to the staff member clearly and concisely should get the same assistance. The library staff should use their knowledge of the information store and their ability to handle catalogues, indexes and other bibliographical tools to answer the enquiries of their clientele. But they should do far more than this. They should devise ways of telling people what is available in the library — they should disseminate information actively to their users through book displays, reading lists on selected topics, lists of new books and other forms of publication recently added to the library. In smaller libraries they can get to know their clients as people and hence provide a more personal service tailored closely to the users' needs. This is positive librarianship and we need more of it.

In business and management libraries the library staff should have the ability to use the information resources described in this book to meet the needs of their library users. They should be imbued with the desire to ensure that their library resources are used to serve business and management. Equally businessmen who know how to use libraries should provide adequate financial resources in their companies to establish and run library services — their money will be well invested.

CONCLUSION

There are many different types of libraries in all countries relevant to the needs of business and management. They can probably provide considerable help in solving problems and supplying both facts and information, but the library user must make an effort to understand how to use the library effectively. The library network in the UK is very extensive, being based on the British Library. It is available to all libraries and because it is so comprehensive most requests can be satisfied.

Using libraries can be summed up as the process of understanding the nature of published information and its storage and establishing good channels of communication between the information user and the librarian who provides the keys to the store and assistance in using them.

5

Abstracts, Indexes and Other Similar Bibliographical Tools

K. D. C. Vernon

Suppose that a small library has been regularly receiving 100 periodicals for the past 5 years, that each periodical publishes an average of 10 parts a year and that each part contains, say, five articles. The total number of articles which are available to users of that small library will be $100 \times 5 \times 10 \times 5$, i.e. 25 000 articles. That number, large though it is, would probably be quite inadequate to satisfy the information needs of even a medium-sized company. It would certainly not be sufficient for most companies with good R & D departments, for a business school or college, for a government department or a good public library. The Baker Library at Harvard Business School regularly receives at least 4000 periodicals: over a 5-year period it accumulates 1 000 000 articles, and in the past 25 years has therefore acquired the staggering number of five million articles!

In the face of such numbers how is the library user to find the one article he wishes to read? It may seem daunting at first but this is the question with which we are now concerned—we will not discuss, tempting though it is to do so, other wider issues, such as the total quantity of published information which pours forth each year from the world's printing presses, or the problem which faces libraries as they attempt to store all that information and make it available for use. We will consider here only the problem of finding articles in periodicals.

The answer to our question is that we have abstracting and indexing publications which are the keys to the mass of published information. Of course they are very imperfect bibliographical tools, because they can never supply all the answers, but nevertheless they do very frequently provide the answer we need, and so they are important. No regular library user in fact can afford to ignore them.

There is a clear difference between an abstracting and an indexing publication. An abstracting publication is one which contains short summaries (abstracts) of articles contained in a selected number of periodicals. The abstracts are usually grouped under carefully chosen subject headings, and each item states the author's name, the title of the article and the reference to the periodical concerned—title, volume number, page number and date. There is also usually an index of the abstracts arranged by author's names and by subjects. The abstracts are either *indicative*, i.e. they give brief summaries of the original articles and thus indicate the possible value of the articles to the user, or they are *informative* and give a fairly full précis of each article.

An indexing publication, on the other hand, is one which merely lists articles from a selected number of periodicals, usually under carefully chosen subject headings, and gives the full bibliographical reference for each article. It does not indicate the contents of each article in the way that an abstracting publication does.

An abstracting publication therefore gives more information but includes fewer references to articles than an indexing publication, while an indexing publication provides references to a larger number of articles but gives less information about each. Both types of publication are invaluable for the person trying to find information on a particular subject, because they enable him to 'search' a large number of periodicals (i.e. all those indexed or abstracted) in a short time by looking at one publication only. They are therefore keys to the literature and can save the busy person an enormous amount of time—they often enable the library user to find the proverbial needle in the haystack.

The other similar kind of key is the bibliography. The first distinction between an abstracting or indexing publication, on the one hand, and a bibliography, on the other, is that the latter is not normally a continuing serial publication—it is an individual compilation. The second distinction, which is now rapidly disappearing, and rightly so, is that an abstracting or indexing publication is primarily concerned with articles in periodicals, whereas a bibliography is not. The library user wants information and should not normally be concerned with its form—whether it is in a book, periodical, newspaper, report or pamphlet. It is therefore increasingly becoming the practice to publish bibliographies which are in fact annotated lists of books and articles which perform the same function as abstracting publications.

Inevitably the next stage of 'publishing' potted information is now emerging, and tape cassettes summarising information contained in periodicals and books are already on the market. These have many obvious and attractive uses, particularly for the busy manager, but they will not take over the role of abstracting and indexing publications, at least for many years to come.

The following list of abstracting and indexing publications covering management and business was originally compiled in the library of the London Business School in 1970. It has recently been extended to include some European publications of the same kind and therefore provides guidance on a wide range of basic bibliographical tools. The list is now sponsored and updated by the European Business Schools Librarians' Group, and is available from the London Business School. It is by no means a comprehensive list but it provides ample information for most purposes. All the publications in it are designed to help people to find information in other publications—they are guides to finding one's way through the literature. The list does not include publications which are solely or mainly concerned with books such as the excellent *Documentation on books*, which is published by the European Foundation for Management Education in Brussels, nor does it include lists of dissertations and theses, apart from the *Dissertation Abstracts*, because these are discussed by John Fletcher in Chapter 8.

ABSTRACTING AND INDEXING PUBLICATIONS ON MANAGEMENT AND BUSINESS: A LIST COMPILED ON BEHALF OF THE EUROPEAN BUSINESS SCHOOLS LIBRARIANS' GROUP

1. *Accountants Index: a bibliography of accounting literature* (American Institute of Certified Public Accountants, New York)

A standard reference work in book form published as a service to the accounting profession. Arranged under subjects, authors and titles in one alphabetical sequence. Mainly articles from periodicals—but includes books, sections from books, reports, pamphlets, papers from conferences. Now published quarterly. Started in 1921. Each annual supplement includes over 11 000 references from more than 300 periodicals and other publications. Up to 1973 there was always a long time-lag between date of original article and publication of the Index, but from 1974, when the quarterly Service started, this has been largely eliminated.

Very useful for retrospective searching of the literature, but not intended for latest current information prior to 1974.

2. *Accounting and Data Processing Abstracts* (Anbar Publications Ltd, London)

Published eight times a year in association with the Institute of Chartered Accountants. Started publication in 1971, when the Anbar Management Services Abstracts was split into four sections. Like the other Anbar services, this publication is very prompt and the abstracts, which are selected and evaluated from over 200 of the most important periodicals published in the UK, USA and Europe, usually appear within 1–2 months of the original publication.

Articles are selected for abstracting because, in the opinion of the editors, they add something new on the subject. The service includes a half-yearly and annual index.

Essential for accountants and for most business libraries.

3. *Accounting Articles* (Commerce Clearing House, Inc., Chicago)

A comprehensive loose-leaf monthly service covering all aspects of accounting and related subjects. Arranged under major accounting topics — principles and practices, statements and reports, cost accounting, budgeting, auditing, management services, public accounting, education. In addition to articles in periodicals, the service covers books, government publications and conference proceedings. Includes author and subject indexes.

Gives much the same coverage as *Accountants Index*.

4. *Analyses des Revues Françaises et Etrangères sur l'Economie et la Gestion* (Centre de Documentation Productivité, 38 Grenoble)

A monthly abstracting bulletin with a keyword subject index and author index. Each entry is clearly laid out to occupy the same space and in the same style with the reference details, keywords and abstract. Classified under 22 main headings. Abstracts cover articles from French periodicals and books. Monthly issues are circulated annually with an annual index. Started publication in 1971.

A useful journal covering French publications.

5. *Anbar Management Services Abstracts* (Anbar Publications Ltd, London)

Probably the best British abstracting service in the field of management. Started publication in 1961. In 1971 the service was divided into four parts — top management, personnel and training, marketing and distribution; accounting and data processing. In 1973 *Work Study and O & M Abstracts* began publication. Each part is issued eight times a year with a cumulative index. An annual volume, *The Compleat Anbar*, No. 1 covering the year 1971–72, has now become part of the service and is now appearing regularly.

The abstracts not only summarise the articles, but also add critical comments. Over 200 periodicals are regularly scanned and the abstracts are arranged in a well-organised decimal classification system which is easy to use. Abstracts are well up to date, usually appearing within 1–2 months of the original articles. An annual bibliography listing books, pamphlets and films which have been reviewed is also published.

This valuable service is essential in libraries for current information on most aspects of management.
See also Nos. 2, 36, 44, 55, 58.

6. *British Humanities Index* (Library Association, London)
Quarterly indexing service cumulated annually with author index. 380 British periodicals, many of which are of wide general interest, and important national newspapers are regularly scanned. Covers all aspects of the humanities, including business studies. Articles indexed are listed under well-chosen subject headings. Average time lag, 3–4 months.
Frequently useful for finding general articles.

7. *British Technology Index* (Library Association, London)
Monthly indexing service cumulated annually. Scans nearly 400 British scientific and technical periodicals and indexes about 28 000 articles p.a.
An effective up-to-date service for technical and industrial information with an average time lag of 2 months. Includes OR, systems engineering, work study and ergonomics. Started publication in 1962.

8. *Bulletin Signalétique, No. 528 Science administrative* (CNRS Centre de Documentation Sciences Humaines, Paris)
Quarterly abstracting publication covering all aspects of administrative science. The abstracts, all of which are in French, are arranged according to a classified system with six main sections. Includes articles, books and government publications. About 100 periodicals, mainly French, are regularly scanned. Subject and author index.
Provides good coverage of European periodicals and includes a photocopying service.

9. *Business Periodicals Index* (H. W. Wilson Co., New York)
This well-known publication indexes articles from about 170 periodicals concerned with most aspects of business management, including industries, transport, trade and economic conditions in countries. It is published monthly with quarterly and annual cumulations. About 55 000 articles are indexed each year. They are arranged under clear well-chosen subject headings with numerous cross-references to other subject headings. Average time lag, 2–3 months.
This American indexing service, which began in 1958, provides the best available means of finding recent information across the whole field of business and industry. It does not, unfortunately, index many British or European periodicals, and some of the American trade journals included are not readily available in the UK. Nevertheless BPI is an essential source of information for all business libraries.

10.   *CIRF Abstracts* (CIRF Publications, ILO, Geneva)

A quarterly selective abstracting service on vocational training for personnel in industry and all sectors of economic activity, manpower planning, general and technical education and management development. About 300 abstracts are published each year from articles in periodicals, books, pamphlets and reports. Good international coverage. Abstracts are in English but are taken from publications in several European languages. Average time lag, 5 months.

This is a well-arranged specialised loose-leaf service concerned with all aspects of vocational training. It is easy to use.

11.   *Computer Abstracts* (Technical Information Co., Jersey, C.I.)

First published in 1960, this monthly publication provides some 2500 abstracts p.a. of articles in about 140 periodicals, conference proceedings, etc. Also includes abstracts of US government research reports, British and US patents and books. Time lag, about 5 months. Arranged under 18 main subject headings, with a separate section for books. Monthly and annual subject and author indexes.

An important abstracting service in this subject field.

12.   *Computer and Control Abstracts* (Inspec., Institution of Electrical
       Engineers, London)

Aims to cover all aspects of computers and control, including systems and control theory and applications, programming, information science and documentation, computer systems. Abstracts information from a wide range of sources covering about 2000 journals, books, reports, dissertations, patents and conference papers published in all countries and languages. About 30 000 abstracts are published each year by use of a computer system.

Monthly, with subject and author indexes and 6 monthly cumulations. Abstracts are arranged in classified order. Started publication in 1966 under the title *Control Abstracts* and changed to present title in 1969.

Gives good coverage for the technical literature but is not closely concerned with management and business aspects of computer usage.

13.   *Dissertation Abstracts International—A. The humanities and social
       sciences* (University Microfilms, Ann Arbor)

These are abstracts of doctoral dissertations which are available on microfilm or as xerographic reproductions. Dissertations come from about 270 American and Canadian universities and colleges. A few dissertations from Australian and European universities are also included.

Monthly with keyword title index and author index, and annual cumulative index. Abstracts are arranged under principal subject categories, which include accounting, business administration, economics, public administration and sociology.

This is an important source for identifying recent research work. All dissertations listed in this publication since 1970 are available on loan from the British Lending Library.

Supplemented by *American Doctoral Dissertations,* which is a complete listing of all doctoral dissertations accepted by American and Canadian universities.

14. *Documentation Economique: revue bibliographique de synthèse* (29 Quai Branly, Paris viie)

A bi-monthly publication issued under the auspices of the Centre National de la Recherche Scientifique. Started publication in 1934. Provides classified abstracts of articles from leading economics journals and from books.

15. *Economic Abstracts* (Martinus Nijhoff, The Hague)

A fortnightly review of abstracts on economics, finance, trade, industry, foreign aid, management, marketing and labour. Compiled by the Library of the Dutch Ministry of Economic Affairs. Includes abstracts in the original language of articles from about 400 periodicals as well as from reports and books. Time lag, about 6 months. Arranged in classified order by UDC with a subject index to each fortnightly issue. Also annual author and subject indexes. Started publication in 1953.

A useful service which concentrates more on British and European than on American literature. Retrospective searching with the subject index is sometimes difficult.

16. *Economic Titles* (Martinus Nijhoff, The Hague)

A fortnightly review compiled by the Library and Documentation Center of the Economic Information Service (Ministry of Economic Affairs) at The Hague. It extends the service already given by *Economic Abstracts.*

This new computer-processed information service, which started publication in 1974, scans about 2500 leading periodicals in the field of economics and business. Each issue contains about 600 short abstracts of articles, reports, monographs and reference works. Abstracts are in the language of the original publication, with English keywords and a thesaurus-controlled index in English.

An essential service for most business and economics libraries.

17. *Fichier Bibliographique de l'Entreprise* (Dunod, Paris)

Quarterly publication edited under the auspices of Centre d'Etudes et de Recherches Economiques, Statistiques et Comptables.

Contains long and informative abstracts of articles and other publications related to management of the firm, use of statistical methods in management, economic and social environment of the business. Abstracts are classified under nine broad subject headings, each of which is further subdivided.

Ceased publication in 1973.

18.　*FT Abstracts in Science and Technology* (Microinfo Ltd, Alton, Hants.)

A monthly review of developments and significant events in science and technology reported in the daily columns of the *Financial Times* since 1972. Short abstracts arranged under 40 subject headings. Photocopies of original articles may be purchased from FT Business Information Service.

Provides very up to date information and acts as an index, within this subject area, to the FT.

19.　*F & S Index of Corporations and Industries* (Predicasts Inc., Cleveland, Ohio)

This well-known American index is issued monthly with quarterly and annual cumulations. It covers US company, product and industry information, which is indexed from over 750 financial and business newspapers, journals and other publications. Similar information for the rest of the world is indexed in *F & S Index International.*

Section 1, which covers industry and product information is arranged in major industry groups subdivided by the *Standard Industrial Classification.* Section 2 deals with companies and is arranged alphabetically. Section 3 lists companies by the *SIC* and thus enables the user to relate information from the company section to the industry and product section.

A very useful and comprehensive service, which is particularly valuable for US company information. Unfortunately many of the American trade journals which are indexed are not readily available in British and European libraries. The annual hard-back cumulated volume is sufficient for most libraries.

20.　*F & S Index International* (Predicasts Inc., Cleveland, Ohio)

Started in 1968, this international index is more generally useful than the *F & S Index of Corporations.* Section 1 covers industry and product information arranged by the *SIC.* Section 2 contains the same information as in Section 1, but arranges it alphabetically by countries within regional groups—Latin America, EEC, other Western Europe countries, Eastern Europe, Africa, etc. Section 3 deals with company information and is arranged alphabetically by names of companies.

Issued monthly with quarterly and annual cumulations in the same style as the *Index of Corporations.* The hard-back annual volume is a valuable reference work which is essential in most business libraries, but many of the trade journals indexed are not always readily available.

21. *Gestion des Entreprises: directions et structures. Guide Documentaire Nos. 18–21* (Chambre de Commerce et d'Industrie de Paris)

These are four of the series of 50 documentary guides published by the Centre de Documentation de la Chambre de Commerce on a wide range of business activities. They are loose-leaf indexing publications which index articles from periodicals, books or extracts from various publications. Uses a classified system for the entries combined with keywords.

Each guide covers a different aspect of management.

22. *Index of Economic Articles* (Richard D. Irwin, Inc., Homewood, Illinois)

Prepared by the American Economic Association, this annual publication, which is in book form, indexes English-language articles which have appeared in the major economic journals and in collective volumes such as conference proceedings. Each volume is in three parts: (1) list of books indexed; (2) a classified index in which material is arranged by subject according to the AEA Classification; (3) an author index.

The *Index of Economic Articles* is very useful for retrospective searching of the literature covering the long period since 1886. Volume VII A is an index of articles in collective books published in 1964 and 1965, i.e. conference proceedings, collected essays, readings, etc. Unfortunately volumes always appear several years after the original articles were published; for example, the 1968 volume was published in 1971. It includes only articles in English.

23. *Industrial Marketing Research Abstracts* (Industrial Marketing Research Association, London)

Covers only the years 1969 to 1971, when it ceased publication. Published twice a year. Complements *Market Research Abstracts* (No. 34). Covers market and industry information, industrial marketing research techniques and methodology, industrial marketing research, case studies and histories. About 100 abstracts were published in each issue, with a subject index.

A useful specialist bibliographical tool covering publications issued between 1969 and 1971.

24. *International Abstracts in Operations Research* (North Holland for International Federation of Operational Research Societies)

Quarterly publication arranged under a system of subject headings with cross-references to other related subjects. Author and subject index in each issue and also annual cumulative indices. About 50 periodicals are regularly scanned and 1400 abstracts published each year. Includes reports and books as well as articles. A useful feature is the Digest at the beginning of each issue which lists abstracts under their various subject headings for quick reference purposes.

An important publication for all concerned with OR.

25. *International Bibliography of the Social Sciences: Economics*
    (Tavistock Publications, London)

Prepared by the International Committee for Social Science Information and Documentation, which is financed by UNESCO. This is one of the four sections which make up this large and important annual bibliography, the others being Sociology, Political Science, Social and Cultural Anthropology. Started publication in 1952. Arranged in classified order with author and subject indexes.

The Economics section of this extensive bibliography indexes articles selected from over 1500 periodicals, and the latest volume included references to nearly 8000 articles. It is thus a comprehensive survey of the literature, but its chief drawback is that articles are 2–3 years old by the time each volume is published.

An important publication for larger libraries.

26. *International Executive* (Foundation for Advancement of Inter-
    national Business Administration, Hastings-on-Hudson, N.Y. 10706)

A quarterly reading service for those concerned with international business. Each issue contains fairly lengthy notes on a few selected books and articles, followed by an extensive list of books and articles arranged under broad subject headings. Regularly scans about 230 periodicals.

A very useful publication for keeping up to date with the literature of international business. Unfortunately there are no author or subject indexes.

27. *International Labour Documentation* (ILO, Geneva)

This is a fortnightly computer-produced list of publications—books, papers, reports, articles, etc.—added to the ILO Library. It forms part of the large mechanical information retrieval system, covering all aspects of labour, which has been developed at the ILO.

An important publication for all concerned with this broad subject field.

28. *Journal of Economic Literature* (American Economic Association,
    Cambridge, Mass.)

Up till 1968 this publication was known as *Journal of Economic Abstracts*. Each quarterly issue contains articles (frequently review articles), communications, book reviews and annotated list of new books, followed by an extensive section on current periodicals. The latter has sections on (a) contents of about 180 current periodicals; (b) subject index of articles; (c) selected abstracts of articles. Arrangement is by AEA Classification.

A valuable publication for academic libraries.

29. *Library and Information Science Abstracts* (Library Association, London)

Bi-monthly, with author and subject indexes cumulated annually. Covers all aspects of library science, including information retrieval and use of computers in libraries. Scans about 230 periodicals. 1–2 months time lag.

Title changed from *Library Science Abstracts* in 1969.

30. *Literatuurservice Bedrijfskunde* (Interuniversitair Instituut Bedrijfskunde, Delft)

Published three times a year, this service aims to help busy managers to decide what to read. Each issue contains abstracts of one book and 30 articles from periodicals, together with a list of additions to the Interuniversitair Instituut Library. About 100 of the most important management periodicals are scanned regularly.

Although this useful service is intended primarily for Alumni of the IIB, it is available to others on a subscription basis.

31. *Management Abstracts, Digests and Reviews* (British Institute of Management)

This well-known quarterly publication has the virtue of being small and highly selective rather than large and comprehensive. Publishes about 250 abstracts annually. Arranged under broad subject headings, with annual author and subject indexes. Time lag, about 5–6 months. Includes book reviews, and notes on management research (usually research which has been completed and published) and new management films.

Particularly useful for small libraries and for companies. Photocopies of articles abstracted may be obtained from the BIM.

Now incorporated in *Management Review and Digest* (BIM).

32. *Management Documentation* (INSEAD, Fontainebleau)

A monthly service which ceased publication in 1973. It indexed and abstracted articles and books in English, French and German. The service is still useful for scanning European management literature up to 1973, as it covers a wide range of important periodicals.

It is not easy to use for retrospective searching, because it has undergone too many changes.

33. *Management Review* (American Management Association, New York)

Although this monthly periodical is not strictly an abstracting or indexing publication, it performs a useful, but rather superficial, function by providing digests of a few articles of management interest each month. Feature articles and shorter summaries of other articles are also included. Started publication in 1923.

34. *Market Research Abstracts* (Market Research Society, London)

Published half-yearly as a complementary service to *Industrial Marketing Research Abstracts* (No. 23). Emphasis is on research. Covers survey techniques; statistics; models and forecasting; attitude and behaviour research; personality and social psychology; communications; applications of research; industrial market research; market research; and new product development. It is highly selective. About 250 abstracts are published annually, with author and subject indexes.

Owing to infrequency of publication, there is a lengthy time-lag between the original publications and the appearance of the abstracts.

35. *Marketing Abstracts* (Published quarterly in the *Journal of Marketing*: (American Marketing Association, Chicago)

About 100 abstracts of articles are published each quarter, arranged under 23 subject headings. Significant selected articles are abstracted from a wide range of periodicals and not only those specifically concerned with marketing.

No index is published, so retrospective searching is not easy.

36. *Marketing and Distribution Abstracts* (Anbar Publications, Ltd)

Published eight times a year in association with the Institute of Marketing. Started publication in 1971 as one of the four sections of Anbar Management Services Abstracts. Follows the same arrangement and policy as the other Anbar abstracting services and covers the whole wide field of marketing and distribution.

Essential for most business libraries.

37. *Marketing Information Guide* (Trade Marketing Information Guide Inc., Washington)

Monthly annotated bibliography formerly published by US Chamber of Commerce. Includes abstracts of articles, reports, government publications and books covering marketing functions and operations, areas and markets, industries and commodities. About 2000 items are abstracted annually. Monthly and annual subject indexes.

A very useful publication for keeping up to date with the literature of marketing.

38.   *Monthly Bulletin* (IMEDE, Lausanne)
Comprises abstracts from the main European and American management
and business periodicals, including economics. Also lists recent acquisitions
to the IMEDE Library in a separate section.
  Although no index is issued, this is a useful publication for scanning
the current literature of management and business.

39.   *New Literature on Automation* (Het Nederlands Studiencentrum voor
       Informatica, Amsterdam)
Monthly international classified abstracts journal which started publication
in 1961. Abstracts in English, French, German or Spanish arranged in
subject classified order, with monthly author and subject indexes. Cumulative indexes covering several years are published at intervals.
  This is an important abstracting service in this subject area and provides
a good survey of recent literature, including books, reports, articles and
proceedings concerned particularly with automation and the application
of computers to business and industry. Good coverage of the main
European periodicals.

40.   *Operations Research/Management Science* (Executive Sciences Inst.,
       Whippaney, N.J.)
A loose-leaf service providing highly informative abstracts of articles
selected from the main periodicals concerned with OR and management
science. Arranged in classified order, with annual author and subject
indexes.
  It is intended primarily for specialists in this subject field.

41.   *Personnel and Training Abstracts* (Anbar Publications Ltd, London)
Published eight times a year in association with the Institute of Personnel
Management. Started publication in 1971 as a section of the Anbar
Management Services and follows the same arrangement as the other
sections. Covers all aspects of this broad subject area.
  Like the other Anbar publications this is an important publication
for all business libraries.

42.   *Personnel Literature* (US GPO, Washington)
A monthly service containing abstracts of selected books, pamphlets,
dissertations and microforms received in the Library of the Civil Service
Commission in Washington. Items are selected for their interest and
significance to the Commission and its research projects. Arranged under
subject headings. Annual author and subject indexes.

43.   *Personnel Management Abstracts* (Bureau of Industrial Relations,
       University of Michigan)
A quarterly publication primarily concerned with personnel administration

and industrial relations. Includes abstracts of books and articles. Scans about 100 periodicals. Time lag, about 4 months. Quarterly index arranged under authors, titles and subjects. Started publication in 1955.

An important source of information on personnel management.

44. *Psychological Abstracts* (American Psychological Association)
This well-known publication provides non-evaluative summaries of the world's literature in psychology and related disciplines. Monthly, with semi-annual author and subject indexes. About 750 periodicals are regularly scanned and 25 000 items abstracted each year. Includes abstracts of books, reports and dissertations. Average time lag, 6 months.

Because of its comprehensiveness, this is an important publication for searching the literature, particularly for personnel and industrial psychology, but it is probably too large and academic for smaller business libraries.'

45. *Public Affairs Information Service Bulletin* (PAIS Inc., New York)
A selective subject list of the latest books, pamphlets, US Government publications, reports and articles from periodicals, relating to economic and social conditions, public administration and management, and international relations. About 1000 English-language periodicals are regularly scanned and some 30 000 items p.a. are indexed and listed.

This service, which was originally started in 1913 by a group of librarians, is still run by an association of librarians. It is a weekly publication cumulated quarterly and annually. The subject headings are well chosen and easy to use.

In 1971 the PAIS *Foreign Language Index* was started covering a similar subject field for publications in French, German, Italian, Portuguese and Spanish.   •

A very important bibliographical tool which can be used to complement and extend the more limited coverage of *Business Periodicals Index* (see No. 9).

46. *Research Index* (Business Surveys Ltd, Wallington, Surrey)
A fortnightly index of articles and news items, mainly of financial interest, which have appeared in about 100 newspapers, business, economic and trade periodicals during the previous fortnight. Arranged in two sections covering (a) industrial and commercial news and reports arranged under about 100 subject headings; (b) companies arranged alphabetically by names.

Research Index is the best available means of tracing recent information in the *FT*, *The Times*, *Economist*, *Investors Chronicle* and many other important business publications. No cumulative index was published until 1973, so retrospective searching is tedious. From 1973 *Research Index Amalgamation* is an annual cumulation of the news section. There is no cumulation yet for the company information.

A very important publication for finding recent information published in the press. Essential in all business libraries.

47. *Research into Higher Education Abstracts* (Society for Research into Higher Education, London)
A quarterly publication, based on a regular survey of 160 journals and books. Intended for use by administrators, librarians, research workers, students, teachers, etc. Classified under 10 main headings and arranged alphabetically by author. It abstracts articles, research reports and books.
  Only of marginal interest to business libraries.

48. *Selected Rand Abstracts* (Rand Corporation, Santa Monica, Cal.)
Issued quarterly as a guide to the important Rand Corporation unclassified publications — books, reports, memoranda and papers. Mainly scientific and technical, but includes management, the social sciences, economics and quantitative methods. Cumulated throughout the year with annual author and subject indexes.
  All Rand publications are available from the British Lending Library.

49. *Social Science Citation Index* (Institute for Scientific Information, Philadelphia)
This is the latest development in citation indexing and covers some 1000 of the world's most important social science journals, including business and management. Three related indexes are provided — citation index, permuterm-subject index and source index. Two tri-annual issues and an annual cumulation for each index are published.
  A very important publication for research workers and large libraries but not for small business libraries. It is necessary to understand the principles of citation indexing in order to use *SSCI* effectively.

50. *Sociological Abstracts* (Sociological Abstracts, Inc., New York)
This well-known publication is issued six times a year with an annual cumulative index. About 800 periodicals are regularly scanned and some 7000 abstracts are published each year, categorised under 28 main headings. Covers a very wide subject area and includes many foreign-language periodicals.
  Provides a very comprehensive coverage. An important publication for larger business libraries.

51. *Source Directory of Predicasts Inc.* (Cleveland, Ohio)
This is the latest information service from Predicasts, having started publication in 1973. It is not an abstracting or indexing publication as such but is, as its title indicates, a directory to sources of business information.

Published quarterly with an annual cumulated volume. Composed of four basic parts: (1) alphabetical list of over 4000 publications, including US Government documents, business newspapers and periodicals, bank letters, trade journals, directories, special reports and books; (2) list of titles by region and country; (3) list of titles by subject, product or industry; (4) index to subjects and countries.

It is designed to answer the question 'Where can I get information on . . .?' rather than to give references to individual articles or publications, and so is, in effect, a bibliographical guide. Heavily biased towards American publications.

This will become an important publication for most business libraries.

52. *Statistical Theory and Method Abstracts* (Longman Group for International Statistical Institute)

Aims to give complete coverage of papers with contributions to the theory and method of mathematical statistics, theory of probability and immediately related subjects. Also includes abstracts of relevant research reports and reports of conferences, symposia and seminars, together with a list of statistical algorithms.

Quarterly, with annual index supplement. Divided into 12 main sections arranged by own classification scheme. Although the time lag between original publication and publication of the abstract is often very lengthy (over 1 year), this is a most valuable bibliographical tool for searching the literature of statistics.

53. *Stock Market Research Reviews* (39 Hall Croft, Beeston, Notts.)

Privately published by Professor C. W. J. Granger of the University of Nottingham, this valuable specialist abstracting journal confines itself to the subject of the behaviour of capital markets and investment analysis. It is issued three times a year and includes about 30–40 reviews and abstracts of articles, theses and books in each issue. Started publication in 1967.

An important specialist publication for financial institutions and business libraries.

54. *Technical Education Abstracts* (Information for Education Limited, Liverpool)

A quarterly abstracting service which publishes about 600 abstracts p.a. of articles selected from some 50 periodicals. Includes management education and training for industry, methods of instruction and teaching aids. Classified by an adapted UDC system. Time lag, 2–3 months.

A very useful and up-to-date service for educational articles.

55. *Top Management Abstracts* (Anbar Publications Ltd, London)

Like the other Anbar abstracting services, *TMA* has been published eight times a year since 1971 in the same style and with the same promptness. It is published in association with the British Institute of Management and covers articles likely to be of interest to senior managers, including brief abstracts of articles about companies.

Essential for all business libraries.

56. *Training Abstracts Service* (Information for Education Limited, Liverpool)
A monthly card service, formerly prepared and published by the Training Department of the Department of Employment. The service covers training at all levels from operatives to managers. Abstracts are published on 6 × 4 in cards and are prepared from new books, articles, research reports and other publications relevant to training. Some of the abstracts are taken from other abstracting journals rather than from the original publications—a practice which inevitably leads to delays.

Cards are arranged by a special classification scheme which provides sufficient detail to ensure that information can be readily retrieved. A separate guide explains the classification. The abstracts themselves are frequently long and informative. The time-lag for abstracts from British periodicals is quite short but much longer for other publications.

This useful service provides a large and valuable store of information on all aspects of training. Ceased publication in 1975.

57. *What's New in Advertising and Marketing* (Special Libraries Association, New York)
A monthly list of new American publications. Includes books, pamphlets, reports and reprints.

Essentially a current-awareness service, but useful for identifying advertising and marketing publications which are often scattered in numerous other indexes and bibliographies.

58. *Work Study and O & M Abstracts* (Anbar Publications Ltd, London)
This is the latest Anbar sectional abstracting journal, having started publication in 1973. It is published eight times a year in association with the Institute of Work Study Practitioners and in the same style as other Anbar publications.

A very useful and prompt service.

USING ABSTRACTING AND INDEXING PUBLICATIONS

A small library or information service obviously needs only a few abstracting and indexing publications—perhaps four from our list would suffice. By subscribing to one or more of the Anbar services, *Business*

Periodicals Index, International Executive and *Research Index*, for example, and by making full use of them, it would be possible for a large number of people in a firm or other organisation to find information, and to keep abreast of new ideas, developments and current news across the whole field of management and business. The benefit of having this facility available in a firm could be immense, yet the annual subscription cost of these four publications is probably only about £150 (or about $350)—a small investment for such potentially valuable tools.

The following examples are typical questions which can be answered by using abstracting and indexing publications. They indicate how these publications can be used.

To answer a subject enquiry

Q.   What is human resource accounting? I want one or two articles which will help me to understand it.

A.   Try the index to *Personnel and Training Abstracts* (Anbar). Turn to a few of the abstracts which seem to be most relevant and select the ones which appear to provide the best introductory articles on human resource accounting. Then look up the articles chosen in your library, or order photocopies of the articles direct from the Anbar Service.

To make a retrospective search

Q.   What has been published during the past 3 years on job enrichment?

A.   Use *Personnel Management Abstracts*. Start with the most recent index to this publication and work backwards, listing all the apparently relevant books and articles. In this way a short bibliography can quickly be prepared and each item can be consulted in the library if required.

To keep abreast of new developments

Q.   How can I keep myself informed on what is being written about multinational companies?

A.   Look regularly at *International Executive*, which publishes notes on important new books and articles concerned with international business. Thus the whole field can be quickly scanned and items chosen for further reading can be obtained through the library.

To keep up to date with news

Q.   How can I follow developments in a current business merger?

A.   Look at *Research Index* every fortnight. It is a most useful index to recent business news in the main newspapers and general business journals. It is very up to date and lists news items under the subjects, such as 'mergers', and also under the names of individual companies.

Using abstracting and indexing publications, however, is often a frustrating and time-consuming exercise, particularly if one is trying to do a retrospective subject search for information. Of course these publications can be used systematically and often effectively for scanning quickly a large number of periodicals covering a specified period of years; but problems arise frequently because the subject headings used in one index may be different from those used in another. For example 'management by objectives' is used as an indexing term in *Anbar Management Services Abstracts* but not in *Business Periodicals Index.* The latter indexes articles on management by objectives under the broader term 'management', and consequently one has to pick out references to articles on management by objectives from a large number of more general articles. And again, it is often frustrating to find that the articles chosen from these publications are contained in periodicals which are not easily available in one's own library, and so delays occur while the articles are obtained from another library. Or, worse still, a person may select articles from an abstracting or indexing publication, then ask for them from his library; and when they arrive, they may turn out to be less relevant to the problem in hand than he had expected.

To get the best out of these publications it is necessary to learn how to use them, to accept the fact that they are not infallible guides, and to rely mainly on a few abstracting and indexing publications which seem most likely to suit the purpose in hand—a subject enquiry, a retrospective search or a means of keeping up to date with new publications. Advice from an experienced librarian on where to look can often save a great deal of time and fruitless searching in irrelevant publications.

CURRENT CONTENTS LISTS

Because of the vast number of new publications it is now virtually impossible for anybody to keep up to date with regular reading even in a fairly narrow subject area, and so, in order to help people in this respect, many libraries and information services provide some kind of current-awareness service. The service can take various forms and is usually tailored to the needs of a particular group of users. Some libraries produce a regular bulletin listing new books, articles and other publications received, and circulate it within the organisation. Others prefer to concentrate on periodicals and provide photocopies of the contents pages, which are batched together into groups as the periodicals arrive in the library, and to circulate these to the library users. In this way it is easy to scan the contents pages of a lot of periodicals and select articles for reading.

Most of these services are informally produced in photocopy form primarily for 'domestic' use in a particular organisation. The following are a few examples.

Contents of Current Journals (London Business School) is issued monthly in six subject sections, each covering a selection of the most important journals received in the LBS Library. The subject sections are for (a) general management and business; (b) economics; (c) finance and accounting; (d) marketing; (e) organisational behaviour and industrial relations; (f) quantitative methods.

Current Awareness Bulletin: Human Sciences and Management (University of Surrey Library) is a monthly typescript list of articles taken from about 160 periodicals received in the Library. The list is divided into 10 main subject headings, each being further subdivided as required, and includes economics, management, planning, psychology and sociology. It is a good example of how a library can disseminate information to its users about current articles which may be relevant to their work. It is issued to members of the academic staff of the departments concerned.

Policy Science Documentation (Central Management Library, Civil Service Department) is produced monthly and covers a wide selection of journals concerned with political science, law, public administration, business management, sociology and contemporary political history.

Some libraries publish their current contents lists for a wider clientele than their own readers, because they believe that the lists are relevant to the work of people in many other places. The following are two examples of this type of service.

Contents Pages in Management (Manchester Business School) is a weekly service with a quarterly and annual author index which is available on a subscription basis. It covers about 20 journals each week as they arrive in the MBS Library and provides a very good current-awareness service for management. It also includes a useful list of working papers received in the library of the University of Warwick (see p. 151).

Contents of Recent Economic Journals (HMSO) is available on a subscription basis and is prepared by the Department of Trade and Industry Library Services. It is published weekly and covers about 10 journals each week from a selection of some 200 journals received in the DTI Library, and also includes the Warwick University list of working papers. This service is intended for economists and others in government and business.

The same idea, but in printed form, is provided by some publishers. For example, *Current Contents: Behavioral, Social and Educational Sciences* (Institute for Scientific Information, Philadelphia) is a very comprehensive, but rather expensive weekly service, covering a total of some 1100 journals dealing with these subject areas. Each issue has an author index and an address list of the journals. But commercially produced contents lists are not often as useful, for the average library user, as the more informal domestic lists, which can be closely related to the actual periodicals available in the library.

CONCLUSION

Abstracting and indexing publications are valuable bibliographical tools designed as guides which scan a large number of publications. They are time-savers which enable the user to search the literature and navigate his way through the jungle of information on management and business which is churned out by the world's printing presses. They must be used with perception and understanding and their shortcomings must be accepted. By their nature, they can never be completely comprehensive nor can they be entirely up to date.

Current-awareness services and current contents lists disseminate information rapidly but superficially. They are useful for browsing and for keeping up to date with the latest articles in periodicals, because they enable people to skim quickly through the contents of a lot of periodicals. They can be circulated to the staff of an organisation.

6

Periodicals

K. D. C. Vernon

Wonder breeds curiosity, curiosity investigation, investigation discovery.
Hugo de S. Victore

This chapter is concerned primarily with the periodicals on general management and business and with those covering a wide subject scope. In particular it stresses the important publications emanating from the business schools. In the chapters comprising Parts 2 and 3 other contributors have discussed periodicals in their subject areas, and in Chapter 5 of his book *The use of economics literature* John Fletcher has discussed economics journals; so they are excluded from this discussion, relevant though many of them are to management and business. This chapter is concerned also with problems of using periodicals in libraries and is in fact a continuation of Chapter 5, which discussed how to find articles through abstracting and indexing publications. Periodicals purposefully scanned can awaken curiosity, and lead to investigation and perhaps even to discovery of better ways to manage.

Journals, magazines, newspapers, periodicals, proceedings, reviews, transactions and sometimes bulletins and papers also, are all 'periodicals', and we will regard them all as synonymous in this chapter. No longer is a journal merely a record of daily events, or a review necessarily concerned only with the criticism of other publications. They are all means of communicating information in a continuing form. They are in fact 'serials', and we can best define the term 'periodical' as a serial publication issued in parts at stated or regular intervals under the same title and usually containing articles by several authors in each issue. A periodical can even be an annual publication, but we will confine ourselves to publications which appear more frequently than once a year.

The first scientific periodical was the *Journal des Sçavans,* which was published in Paris in January 1665, and the second was the *Philosophical Transactions of the Royal Society,* which closely followed it in March 1665. Before that time men of science used to give accounts of their work and experiments and discuss their ideas by writing letters to one another. Now there are more than 50 000 scientific periodicals and probably about the same number of social science periodicals. Dolby and Resnikoff have estimated in *Interfaces,* 1 (4), 23–30 (1971), that by 1985 25 000 000 scholarly papers will be published each year. Some scientists and social scientists, when faced with the mass of literature which they are expected to read nowadays, might understandably long for a return to personal letter-writing as a means of communication! Librarians, on the other hand, might lose their jobs in such a situation. However, although the *Journal des Sçavans* finally ceased publication in 1828, the *Philosophical Transactions of the Royal Society* is still being published and is therefore the oldest periodical in existence today, with a life of over 300 years. Such longevity must surely indicate a continuing need for periodicals as a means of communication.

Management periodicals have no such historical record. They can claim no outstanding writers of articles who were able, like Faraday or Rutherford, to describe the results of their researches with elegant clarity, simplicity and lucidity of phrase. They have had no great editors such as Henry Oldenburg, the first editor of the *Philosophical Transactions,* or Justus Liebig, the founder of *Annalen der Chemie,* for example—men who felt a burning need to provide a means of communication between scientists. The management periodical, as such, is a very new phenomenon originating in America with a life-span to date of little more than 50 years and a literary style which is on the whole so lamentable that it is almost non-existent. There is a vital need for those who write about management to appreciate how important it is to express themselves by using simple forms of words free from clumsiness, obscurity and padding, so that their articles are not, at least, repugnant to the reader. If all writers of articles in our management periodicals could be concise and simple in style, the problem we have today in finding information would diminish dramatically because there would be less of it! The periodical would no longer be the terror of the research worker, who has to search the literature, with its mass of obscure and verbose articles, for the grains of information he needs.

Management periodicals perform various functions. Some are published with the intention of providing, in a popular and readable form, news and articles for busy executives who need to keep up to date with events, and new ideas and developments in management thought and practice. Others are more academic in their approach and contain the results of recent research and discussions of new theories and techniques. But whether they are popular or scholarly, they all provide a means of fairly rapid and continuous communication.

A third group, commercially published, are those journals which act as a means of communication within a trade or industry or between groups of businessmen engaged in a particular aspect of business. They cater for an enormous range of interests and there are hundreds of them all aiming to provide information within a defined field—banking, insurance, advertising, distributive trades, chemical and engineering industries, for example. Some of them are obviously important and well known to business-men within these industries, but they are outside the scope of this chapter. Many of them are included in the lists of periodicals mentioned on pp. 121–123. Financial newspapers too are excluded from this chapter. They are of prime importance and few businessmen do not read the *Financial Times*, *Wall Street Journal* or the financial section of some other news-paper, but they perform a different function from that of the periodicals with which we are concerned here. There is a comprehensive review of the financial press and other sources of investment information in Chapter 3 of *Investment analysis and portfolio management,* by J. B. Cohen and E. D. Zinbarg (Irwin, 1967). The services of the *Financial Times* are described in detail in a booklet called *Guide to FT statistics* (Financial Times, 1973).

There are few, if any, descriptive lists of periodicals in this subject area and so the following annotated list is presented in order to help the selection process. It reviews only the main business and management periodicals, which are quite general in their scope and which aim to cover all aspects of this broad subject. Other lists of the more specialised periodicals are readily available in reference works and some are mentioned in Part 3 of this book. The core list of periodicals given in Chapter 2 can be used in conjunction with the following notes.

The preponderance of American publications in the section devoted to academic periodicals is less now than it would have been if the list had been compiled 10 years ago. But it takes a long time for a new periodical to gain academic standing and to attract authors to publish articles in it—most writers prefer to get their articles published in those journals which are best-known and therefore quoted most widely in other publications. There are also considerable economic hazards for publishers who launch new periodicals in an already over-crowded market.

GENERAL BUSINESS AND MANAGEMENT PERIODICALS

Business Week (McGraw-Hill, New York)
This is the leading news magazine for businessmen. It is widely read, particularly in the USA, and contains short articles on aspects of American

and international business events, in-depth articles and reports on current business matters, and comment on economic conditions and related political developments. It is well known for its pithy and perceptive reports and comments.

An essential periodical for business libraries of all kinds. Started publication in 1929.

CBI Review (21 Tothill Street, London SW1)
A general management and business journal which aims to discuss matters of concern to industry, to management and to CBI policy in particular. Contains general articles on a wide range of topics relevant to the business private sector, the UK economy and to international trade.

Director—Journal of the Institute of Directors (London). Monthly
A general management 'glossy' which provides a good over-all look at business affairs from the executive's point of view. Includes short articles on topical subjects, comments on current economic, political and commercial events, book reviews and matters of interest to members of the Institute of Directors, including information on leisure activities.

A useful periodical in any library concerned with management. It started publication in 1947.

Dun's Review (666 Fifth Avenue, New York, N.Y. 10019). Monthly
Like *Business Week,* Dun's is one of the oldest and best-known general management journals. It is a Dun and Bradstreet publication, which was first started in 1893 and is intended, as the publishers say, for 'business executives in top and middle management'. It has a circulation of 200 000.

The contents, which have maintained a remarkably consistent pattern over the years, are mainly concerned with American business, and include short but pertinent articles on management matters and methods as practised in American companies and topics of current general interest. Includes also notes and comments on the contemporary economic, political and business scene.

Articles are indexed in the main indexing and abstracting publications.

Economist (25 St. James's Street, London SW1A HG). Weekly
Founded in 1843 and therefore probably the oldest general business journal still in existence, its well-known, authoritative reports and comments on all aspects of economic, business and political affairs are very widely read. Each issue contains sections reporting on Britain, the World, business and economic events. Regular book reviews and notes are an important feature.

With a circulation of over 100 000, this journal is essential reading for businessmen.

Entreprise: revue d'information de l'économie et des affairs (13 Rue Saint-Georges, Paris). Weekly

The French equivalent of *Business Week*. Contains lively news and comment sections on all aspects of French business and economic affairs, articles and book reviews. This is an important news publication for all business libraries and for businessmen who wish to keep in touch with developments in French and European business. Special issues, known as *Les Dossiers d'Entreprise*, are published from time to time on selected topics. They include occasionally an extensive directory of French and European companies.

Expansion: premier journal économique Française (78 Rue Olivier de Serves, Paris 15). Monthly

Includes news and comment and articles on a wide range of subjects related to the French economy and business and to international trade and commerce. Special studies on selected topics are published at intervals.

Forbes (60 Fifth Ave., New York). Twice Monthly

A chatty general-interest business journal with a financial bias, which started publication in 1917. It is widely read in the USA, with a circulation of over 600 000, and concentrates mainly on news and short articles about American companies and the executives who run them.

On the whole this journal tends to be too exclusively American and its articles too 'newsy' for most British businessmen, but it gives a lively insight into American business methods.

Fortune (Time Inc., 541 North Fairbanks Court, Chicago). Monthly

The largest and best-known American business glossy, with a circulation of over 500 000. Being a Time-Life publication, it is lavishly illustrated. In addition to current reviews on the business scene, news and comment, it publishes significant, topical and readable articles on a variety of American and international economic business subjects. It often includes biographical articles and studies of companies. The well-known *Fortune Directory*, which is published at regular intervals, contains ranking lists of companies arranged by size, industry and profitability, etc.

An essential publication for all business libraries. It started publication in 1930.

Industrial Management (Embankment Press Ltd, Hutton House, Hutton Street, London EC4Y 8AQ). Monthly

Formerly called *Business Management*, this readable general management journal publishes short articles on a wide range of business and management topics, including articles on selected companies.

International Management (McGraw-Hill House, Shoppenhangers Road, Maidenhead). Monthly
Aimed at directors and senior executives of major industrial companies outside the USA, to whom it is available on a complimentary basis. Available to others by subscription. Started publication in 1947. As this is mainly a market-directed publication, it has a very high controlled circulation stated to be 100 000.

A very readable general management journal covering a wide range of topics, including frequent articles on individual companies. Provides interesting general articles for executives who want to be well informed.

Investors Chronicle (30 Finsbury Square, London EC2A 1PJ). Weekly
The best-known British financial weekly. Started publication in 1860 and now amalgamated with the *Stock Exchange Gazette*. Each issue contains well-informed economic and financial comment, investment prospects, company news and results, and stock-market information. Also publishes frequent comprehensive surveys covering a wide range of industrial, financial, economic and international topics.

Essential reading for most businessmen, particularly those concerned with finance and investment.

Le Management: direction (5 rue d'Alger, 75001 Paris). Monthly
The articles in this lively French journal cover all aspects of management, and are intended for general reading by executives. Includes comment on economic affairs, book reviews and reports on special studies into business problems. Occasional special issues are mainly devoted to one general topic, e.g. marketing.

Management Review and Digest (British Institute of Management). Quarterly
This is the BIM's new quarterly journal, which started publication in 1974 and replaces the former members' *Bulletin*, *Quarterly Review* and *Management Abstracts*. It includes short articles on management problems, features and news items, in addition to book and film notes, abstracts of articles from periodicals and notes about BIM activities.

An informative, readable journal for all concerned with management.

Management Today (Haymarket Publishing Ltd. On behalf of Management Publications Ltd, a company owned by the British Institute of Management, the *Financial Times*, the *Economist* and Haymarket Publishing Ltd). Monthly
The best-known UK glossy periodical for managers, with a circulation of over 50 000. It is the British equivalent of *Fortune* and is widely read in this country. Formerly known as *The Manager*, which was the journal of the

BIM, it changed its title in 1966 to *Management Today* in order to present, in a more attractive and authoritative manner, the new ideas and concepts of management which were then gaining general acceptance. Since then *Management Today* has continued to publish lively feature articles on current and new management practices used in companies. In addition to these company studies, this journal includes other articles of general management and business interest, economic news and comment, biographical articles and BIM news and reports.

Management Today is an essential periodical in all business libraries, and its articles are included in most indexing and abstracting publications.

Rydge's (74 Clarence Street, Sydney 2000). Monthly
The best-known Australian general business journal, with a circulation of about 43 000. Started publication in 1928. Each issue contains special feature articles on financial and investment matters, and a section devoted to articles on a wide range of business management topics.

Includes news, comment and book reviews.

Successo (Piazza Cavour 1, 2012 Milan). Monthly
Now in its fifteenth year, *Successo* is the main Italian glossy journal for managers and is widely read in most European countries, being published in two editions—Italian and English. Contains Italian and international economic and business news and comment, well-illustrated feature articles on a wide range of management and business topics, and special reports in depth of recent studies into specific management problems.

An important periodical for most business libraries.

Vision: the European business magazine (13 Rue Saint-Georges, 75 Paris 9e). Monthly
Published in French, German, Italian and English editions. A lively journal which includes feature articles of interest to European businessmen, news and comment, and book reviews. Each issue also includes a study of one topic in more depth.

Provides good general reading on European management matters.

ACADEMIC PERIODICALS

Academic periodicals can be roughly divided into two groups: (1) those which emanate directly from the business schools; (2) others which do not, but yet are scholarly in their approach. The distinction is not important, but it is interesting to reflect that the American business schools have been publishing, over a period of about 50 years, journals which have greatly influenced business thinking first in America and then internationally and, hence, presumably have affected the management and economies of many countries. These journals, led by the well-known *Harvard Business Review*, still hold pride of place wherever people are studing management and business problems. They are widely available in libraries and their articles have been cited in thousands of books and other publications. It is only since about 1965, or even later, that British and European journals have begun to dent the American monopoly in this field, and publications such as *European Business* and the *Journal of Management Studies* are now exerting a growing influence on business thinking.

Periodicals emanating from business schools

The following annotated list of 22 titles includes only the main general management journals.

Academy of Management Journal (Department of Management, Bowling Green State University, Ohio). 3 times each year

Started publication in 1958, and now edited under the supervision of a board drawn from a number of American business schools. Publishes scholarly articles in the fields of business policy and planning, most aspects of general and international management, organisational behaviour and functional management problems. It also includes research notes. It is a well-produced and well-documented journal.

Administrative Science Quarterly (Graduate School of Business and Public Administration, Cornell University, Ithaca, New York)

Started publication in 1956 and has consistently concentrated on developing administrative science and organisational behaviour. Its high-quality articles have undoubtedly contributed to a better understanding of administrative processes.

Widely available in academic libraries. A cumulative index to the first 12 volumes was published in 1969.

Business Horizons (Graduate School of Business, Indiana University, Bloomington, Indiana). Bi-monthly

This is another of the group of high-quality periodicals published by the leading American business schools. It started publication in 1958 and covers the whole field of management. Includes a useful series of notes, entitled 'Research Clearinghouse', of current research projects of interest to business executives. Articles are indexed in the main abstracting and indexing publications.

Business Quarterly: Canada's management journal (University of Western Ontario, School of Business Administration)

This Canadian periodical is very similar in the high standard of its articles to the periodicals of the leading American business schools. It is both scholarly and practical in its approach to the wide range of subjects which impinge on modern business and management. Started publication in 1933 and so is now one of the oldest general management academic journals. Cumulated indexes covering several years are published from time to time, and a reprint service for obtaining multiple copies of individual articles is also available.

California Management Review (Graduate School of Business Administration, University of California, Berkeley). Quarterly

One of the outstanding publications in this field, the *Review* publishes articles concerned with all aspects of management and is intended for businessmen and scholars. It aims to interpret the results of research, to stimulate thinking and to contribute to the advancement of management. It is widely available in libraries and is indexed in the main abstracting and indexing publications. Started publication in 1958 and has a circulation of over 15 000 copies.

Columbia Journal of World Business (Graduate School of Business, Columbia University, New York). Quarterly

A comparative newcomer among the academic periodicals edited by the leading American business schools, the *Columbia Journal* started publication in 1965, its original publishers being Pergamon Press. It has concentrated, from the beginning, on international business, and its objectives are stated in somewhat ponderous terms to be 'to serve as a means of communication for members of the global business community and university scholars; to deepen understanding of significant developments of concern to business wherever they occur; to keep executives and students of business abreast of important advances in business thinking throughout the world; to provide a platform from which authorities can speak freely on business and related issues of our time'.

Publishes high-quality articles by leading businessmen, teachers and research workers from universities and business schools. The *Columbia Journal* is certainly one of the best publications on all aspects of international business. It is widely available in libraries and its articles are indexed in the main abstracting and indexing publications.

European Business: the international management review (Société Européenne d'Edition et Diffusion, Paris). Monthly

This is the leading European management periodical and is essential to all business libraries. It started publication in 1964 and originated from INSEAD, the international business school at Fontainebleau. It has received wide support from European and British business schools. Its aim is to study the enterprise and its development in a European context and to foster a dialogue among European businessmen, researchers and educators.

European Business has led the way in helping to establish the European, in contrast to the American, style of management education and development. It is widely available in libraries and its articles are indexed in the main abstracting and indexing publications.

Harvard Business Review (Graduate School of Business Administration, Harvard University). Bi-monthly

Undoubtedly the leading scholarly management periodical in the world, with a circulation of over 100 000 copies. It is widely read by businessmen, teachers, research workers and students, and is available in all libraries concerned with business, management and economics. Its articles are indexed in many abstracting and indexing publications and are frequently quoted in other books and periodicals. Annual, 5 yearly and 10 yearly cumulative author and subject indexes are published, and these make it easy to find articles quickly. In addition, an excellent reprint service for individual articles is available and also a service which provides reprints grouped into series by subjects. This service has enabled teachers in business schools to make frequent use of articles for classroom use on courses. The famous '*HBR*' has always followed a very active editorial and publishing policy which has developed over the years and is perhaps reflected in the change of sub-title from 'the magazine for thoughtful businessmen' to 'the magazine of decision makers'.

First published by the young and growing Harvard Business School in October 1922, it was in fact the first 'professional' management journal. Its policy from the start has been to maintain an analytical, exploring, thought-provoking approach towards problems of business administration —a policy which was similar to the School's approach to teaching management. It rapidly gained support, and articles, not only by leading business school teachers at Harvard, but also by teachers from other universities and business schools, by professional and business men, were soon being published. It has set a high standard for other periodicals to follow.

It publishes the results of recent research and innovative thinking, and it is noticeable that articles on aspects of business responsibility are now becoming an increasingly topical subject.

Journal of Business (University of Chicago Press). Quarterly

After the *Harvard Business Review* the *Journal of Business* is probably the next most significant scholarly management journal. It was founded as early as 1920 and is edited by the Faculty of the Graduate School of Business at the University of Chicago. It is devoted to professional and academic thinking and research over the broad range of business and related subjects. It has a circulation of about 5000 and is widely available in libraries. Its articles are indexed in the main indexing and abstracting publications.

The Chicago Business School has for many years been the leading school for research into problems of finance and investment analysis, and so the *Journal of Business* has, over the years, reflected this research interest and its articles have tended to be rather mathematical and statistical in their content; but the aim of the editors has been to publish articles which contribute to both the theory and the practice of business and management, and the *Journal of Business* is renowned for the number of important research reports it has published which have led to significant advances in subsequent practice. Book reviews and lists of recently completed university dissertations are a useful feature.

Journal of Business Administration (Faculty of Commerce and Business Administration, University of British Columbia, Vancouver, Canada). Half-yearly

This newly established academic journal in an unpretentious format, which started publication in 1969, aims to communicate to its readers the results of research and theoretical enquiries. It is intended for teachers and research workers rather than practising businessmen. Articles are concerned with the functional areas of business, management science and aspects of the behavioural sciences related to business.

Journal of Contemporary Business (Graduate School of Business Administration, University of Washington, Seattle). Quarterly

This new journal, which started publication in 1972, makes a practice of devoting each issue to a chosen theme—financial reporting, social responsibility, computers, organisation development, etc. Articles are usually concise and are mainly written by teachers or research workers from American business schools and universities.

Journal of International Business Studies (School of Business Administration, Georgia State University and the Academy of International Business). Half-yearly

This new journal, which started publication in 1970, concentrates on international business in its widest sense, and articles are concerned with problems of management and education, finance, overseas investment, marketing, trade, economics and the role of international firms.

An important periodical for most business libraries.

Journal of Management Studies (Basil Blackwell, Oxford). 3 times a year

This was the first British journal of a scholarly nature concerned with the study of management. It started publication in 1964, shortly before the rapid development in management education in the UK began, and during recent years has been edited from the Manchester Business School. Its stated aim is to contribute to the advance of knowledge directly related to the practice of management. Articles cover all aspects of management.

It is an essential journal for business libraries and is probably the leading British publication of its kind.

Management Decision: the European review of management technology (Bradford). Quarterly

Originated from the University of Bradford Management Centre in 1967, when it succeeded the former journal *Scientific Business*. It aims to provide through its articles practical advice to managers faced with unfamiliar problems and to give them a basic understanding of management techniques. Like the *Journal of Management Studies,* it largely reflects British thinking and is an important publication for management libraries.

Management Education and Development: journal of the Association of Teachers of Management. 3 times a year

The ATM is a group of teachers in universities, technical colleges and industry which was founded in 1960 with a view to raising the standards of British management teaching. '*M.E.A.D.*', as the Journal is now called, aims to provide a means of communicating developments in teaching, research findings and the exchange of experiences.

M.E.A.D. started publication in 1961 as the *ATM Bulletin* and changed to its present title in 1970. There is usually a main theme for each issue and articles reflect the developments taking place in many schools and universities. Book reviews are also included.

This is an essential journal for any library concerned with management education. A new section devoted to sources of information was started in 1973.

Management International Review (Betriebswirtschaftlicher Verlag, 62 Wiesbaden, Fed. Rep. of Germany). 6 times a year

This authoritative international review for management and managerial sciences is in three languages—English, French and German. Most of the articles are in English, with French and German summaries. It is published under the auspices of the European Foundation for Management Development with an international editorial board and aims to promote the comparative study of management practice, management sciences and education.

It started publication in 1961 and is an essential periodical for all libraries concerned with management and business.

Management Science: journal of The International Institute of Management Science (146 Westminster Street, Providence, Rhode Island 02903). Monthly

The best-known and most widely used academic journal concerned with quantitative methods. It started publication in 1954 and has a circulation of nearly 10 000. Published in two parts—Theory and Application. The editor and most of the associate editors come from American business schools, and the articles in both parts report on original work and are subject to approval by referees.

Management Science is an essential periodical for academic business libraries.

MSU Business Topics (Graduate School of Business Administration, Michigan State University, East Lansing, Michigan). Quarterly

Similar in scope and coverage to other periodicals from American business schools. Started publication in 1953. Articles are indexed in the main abstracting and indexing publications.

Omega: the international journal of management science (Pergamon Press). Bi-monthly

This new journal, which started publication in 1973, is edited from the Department of Management Science at Imperial College, London, and has an editorial board drawn mainly from British, European and American business schools. The aim is to publish high-quality review papers, to report developments in management science and managerial economics, and to provide a rapid means of publication for short research papers. It also includes useful abstracts of selected research reports and theses.
An important new periodical for business libraries.

Sloan Management Review (Alfred P. Sloan School of Management, MIT, Boston). Monthly

Started publication in 1959 and changed its name from *Industrial Management Review* in 1970. It is the professional journal of the Sloan School of Management and aims to promote an exchange of information between the academic and business worlds. Articles cover all aspects of management and describe current research and its application to business problems. The *Review* is widely available in academic libraries and is indexed in the main indexing and abstracting publications.

University of Washington Business Review (Graduate School of Business Administration, Univ. of Washington, Seattle). Quarterly

Not so well known as some of the other business school periodicals, although it started publication in 1941. Publishes academic articles on a wide range of business, economics and management topics.

Wharton Quarterly (517 Franklin Building, 3451 Walnut Street, Philadelphia, Pa. 19174)
Although coming from such a famous business school, this journal is not so well known as some of the other periodicals from American

business schools. Started publication in 1966. Publishes articles, some based on current research, on a wide range of topics concerned with business and the social sciences. Includes the important *Wharton Economic Newsletter* prepared by the Econometric Forecasting Unit, which gives quarterly forecasts of the US economy.

These periodicals covering the whole field of business studies, many of which are almost household names in the management world, indicate how the business schools, primarily the American ones, have stimulated management thinking and provided the platforms needed for the development of new concepts and practices based on research. But this list is by no means exhaustive and does not, for example, include the lesser-known publications, such as the *Arizona Review,* the *Michigan Business Review* or the *Pittsburgh Business Review.* Nor does it include the various 'alumni bulletins' which many of the business schools publish primarily to keep former students in touch with the school and its work and with one another. Examples are:

Alumni Gazette (University of Western Ontario)
Harvard Business School Bulletin
Issues /Ideas (University of Chicago)
London Business School Journal
Stanford Business School Alumni Bulletin

Some of these, such as the *London Business School Journal,* contain important articles of interest to all executives and are also very useful as a means of communication. On the other hand, some alumni bulletins are little more than jolly house journals intended for the old boys of business schools.

Finally, to complete the picture of the now extensive publishing activities of the business schools, there are the numerous high-quality periodicals which are devoted to a more specialised field than any of the titles so far mentioned. Some of these publications are discussed in the subject chapters in Part 3 of this book, but it is worth noting here that these periodicals, based as they are primarily on research groups in the business schools and universities, are publications of outstanding importance in their subject fields. The following short list of examples, which exclude journals on economics and social sciences, indicates the range of subjects of these periodicals—some of the titles will be well known to executives, professional people, teachers and librarians. The titles are followed by the name of the business school or university to which they are affiliated.

British Journal of Industrial Relations (London School of Economics)
Business History (Liverpool)

Business History Review (Harvard)
European Journal of Marketing (Bradford)
European Training (Bradford)
Industrial and Labor Relations Review (Cornell)
Industrial Relations Journal (Nottingham)
Journal of Accounting Research (Chicago)
Journal of Financial and Quantitative Analysis (Washington)
Journal of Retailing (New York)
Personnel Management Abstracts (Michigan)
Personnel Review (Manchester)
Quarterly Review of Economics and Business (Illinois)
R & D Management (Manchester)

Other academic periodicals concerned with general management

Again, in this context the word 'academic' should not be misconstrued, as it sometimes is by businessmen, to mean theoretical and divorced from practice or reality. It merely means that these periodicals are not popular light reading but are scholarly in their general style, and the articles either report on new work and ideas or new approaches to business problems, or they review current issues in some depth. Most of the articles contain lists of references to other publications relevant to the topic under discussion, which indicates that they are based on the study of other ideas and that the readers are people who might wish to pursue further reading noted in the references given.

The few periodicals in this group are either commercially published, with editors and editorial advisory boards who frequently come from academic institutions as well as from industrial organisations, or are published by an institute or society. They are similar therefore to the group of periodicals emanating from business schools, and the publishers rely heavily on support from teachers and research workers at business schools.

These six titles, covering general management and matters of business policy, may therefore be considered as an extension of the preceding list. The two lists together provide details of most of the main academic periodicals in the general field of management.

Advanced Management Journal (Society for Advancement of Management, 135 West 50th Street, New York, N.Y. 10020). Quarterly

This is the official journal of the Society for Advancement of Management, which became a division of the American Management Association in

1972. Started publication in 1936. Publishes short articles on a wide selection of management topics, including papers given at the SAM annual conference.

Business and Society Review /Innovation (89 Beach Street, Boston, Mass. 02111). Quarterly

The subtitle states that this is a 'quarterly forum on the role of business in a free society'. Started publication in 1972. It is particularly concerned with the social responsibility of companies and publishes lively articles on this and related topics. A wide range of matters of social and business concern are discussed. Includes a good collection of book reviews in each issue.

Conference Board Record (845 Third Avenue, New York, N.Y. 1022). Monthly

The Conference Board, now over 50 years old, is an independent, non-profit, business research organisation concerned with business economics and management. It publishes a series of research studies and reports. The *Record*, which started publication in 1939 and now has a circulation of 34 000, publishes short articles on a wide range of management subjects and economic affairs.

Futures (IPC House, 32 High Street, Guildford, Surrey). Bi-monthly

An international journal, edited by the IPC Science and Technology Press and the Institute for the Future, USA, which started publication in 1968. It aims to present forecasts, case studies and the results of investigations so that probable trends and developments can be evaluated by management and government. Articles have been concerned with natural resources, economic assessments, research trends and all aspects of industrial, social and economic forecasting. Includes book reviews and news.

An important periodical for business libraries.

Journal of General Management (Mercury House Business Publications Ltd, Mercury House, Waterloo Road, London SE1 8UL, in association with the Administrative Staff College, Henley). Quarterly

This new periodical, which started publication in 1973, is concerned with the job of the senior management team who have the problem of integrating the functions of management—finance, marketing, production, industrial relations, etc.—and of relating the organisation to its environment. Its aim is to foster new thinking and research relating to problems of general management in the private and public sectors. It focuses attention on the over-all management of the enterprise, whether it be small or large, and aims to encourage a dialogue between academics and senior management on an international basis; hence, the editorial advisory board has representatives from British, European and American business schools, industry and the nationalised industries.

This periodical has replaced the *Journal of Business Policy*, which was issued by the same publishers for 3 years from 1970 to 1973.

Long Range Planning: journal of the Society for Long Range Planning (Pergamon Press). Quarterly

Aims to focus attention on the concepts and techniques in the development of strategy and the generation of long-range plans. Intended for senior managers, administrators and academics. Articles are concerned with the techniques of forward planning in business and government and especially with new thinking, recent practical developments and the results of research into the problems of long-range planning. Started publication in 1968.

An important periodical for business libraries.

USING PERIODICALS

We do not in fact know much about how management and business periodicals are used in libraries. We know, from subjective observation, which ones are most used, which ones are covered by the indexing and abstracting publications, and which ones are kept because they are 'important' or academically respectable. We also know which ones are of current topical interest and which ones are so specialist that they are of interest only to a small group of people. In addition, the publishers' circulation figures give factual information on the numbers of copies sold, and some publishers know, with considerable accuracy, who their subscribers are and what they do. But very few comparative studies have been made in any depth on who uses which business and management periodicals and why. *The use of information sources by teachers and research workers in the field of business studies: a report to the Office for Scientific and Technical Information*, by J. D. Dews (Manchester Business School, 1970), is a valuable piece of research based on a detailed survey of how nearly 400 business teachers and research workers used information sources. Although not concerned, in any depth, with periodicals, the Report did list 32 periodicals which are apparently used most by this group of people. Top of the list was *Management Today*, followed by *Harvard Business Review* and *Journal of Management Studies*.

The only other British published studies in the social sciences which are relevant to the use of business and management periodicals are 'A view of the literature of economics', by John Fletcher (*Journal of Documentation*, **28**(4), 283–295, 1972), the *Investigation into information of the social sciences*, by M. B. Line and others (Bath University, 1971), and 'The use of social science periodical literature', by D. N. Wood and C. A. Bower (*Journal of Documentation*, **25**(2), 108–122, 1969). Fletcher has shown that there is a high degree of concentration in the use of economics titles and that 70% of the use, reckoned by citations to periodicals made by authors in nine selected economics journals, was concentrated on 20 important periodicals. Wood and Bower in their study, which was based on the use made of periodicals at the National Lending Library in 1968, showed, among other interesting results, that the three most frequently used periodicals in the whole of the social sciences were the *Harvard Business Review*, *Management Science* and *Operations Research*.

Research into these problems is not of immediate relevance to most library users, but they should at least know that efforts are being made to base methods of organising and managing libraries on facts elucidated by research. Survey methods are frequently used to provide facts and other information about libraries and how they are used—on such facts library management and policy decisions can be based. Surveys also sometimes enable librarians to understand what their clientele thinks of the services provided and they are, for example, one method of discovering which periodicals are considered to be most useful. But surveys of this kind are a fairly superficial means of investigation—many library problems require more scientific or social science research methods to be employed.

Most people using periodicals in a business or management library want either a particular article or else information about a subject, i.e. they want 'information units'. If the author and the journal reference is known, there is obviously no problem in finding it provided the library takes the journal that is wanted. If it does not, the enquirer must ask the librarian to get the article he wants from elsewhere and that usually means sending an application to the British Lending Library at Boston Spa (see p. 77). The article will then, in all probability, come from Boston Spa within three or four days—either it will be a photocopy or it will be the issue of the periodical which contains the required article.

If an enquirer wants to discover what articles a particular author has written, he must search the author indexes of abstracting and indexing publications and compile his list from these. If, on the other hand, he wants one specific article and he knows the name of the author and also the title of the periodical in which it was published, but not the exact title of the article or the reference, he must use the index to that periodical. Bibliographies can also sometimes help with author enquiries of this kind, but, broadly speaking, it is not easy to find long lists of articles in different journals arranged by authors.

If information on a subject is required, the enquirer (or probably the librarian who may act for him) has three choices open to him in making a search. First, he can look in the indexes of likely journals for the past few years—a task which does not take long if the indexes are easily available, but which becomes increasingly time-wasting if one has to search a lot of journals, some of which may not have indexes, in the vague hope that each may be the right one. Any search of this kind must be systematic and should start with the most recent years and work backwards. Some journals provide cumulative indexes covering a number of years, and when these are available one can save a great deal of time by using them. *Harvard Business Review* and *Administrative Science Quarterly,* for example, are journals which do publish good cumulative indexes. But it is very noticeable to librarians that publishers of periodicals do not, on the whole, spend nearly enough money and effort on producing good indexes for their periodicals. The next choice for the enquirer looking for subject information is to use indexing and abstracting publications (see Chapter 5). By doing this he can quickly scan a large number of periodicals by searching for articles listed in an indexing or abstracting publication under the most likely subject headings and by noting those which appear to be relevant. Again the search should be conducted systematically, starting with the most recent years. The third choice is to find out whether any recent relevant subject bibliographies exist (see Chapter 7). Many libraries make a point of collecting bibliographies and some are even kind enough to compile them on request, provided the request is a serious one. Most bibliographies include articles as well as books.

There are of course many other ways of finding subject information apart from using printed publications—research workers, for instance, usually know people working in the field and can ask their advice, but we are not concerned here with these personal sources of information, invaluable though they may be.

LISTS OF PERIODICALS

With the vast number of periodicals which exist in the world today it becomes increasingly meaningless to the average library user to be confronted with an enormous list of titles the vast majority of which are completely irrelevant to him. But there are a few published lists, which, although obviously not fully comprehensive, are nevertheless very extensive, and these large lists do have their uses, particularly for identifying titles and for finding who publishes a particular periodical. They are mainly useful to research workers and to librarians.

The best known list is *Ulrich's International Periodicals Directory* (15th ed., Bowker, New York, 1974). This is a classified guide listing about 55 000 periodicals on all subjects and from all countries. It provides details of frequency, and publisher and price for each periodical, and usually includes some indication of the contents and format and the circulation figures if available. It also provides lists of new periodicals and periodicals which have ceased publication. *Ulrich* is an essential tool for all libraries. Most business journals of any significance are included.

Other useful lists are *Willing's Press Guide,* an annual list of British newspapers and periodicals which is especially valuable for trade and technical publications; *Willing's European Press Guide* is a companion volume listing similar publications in western European countries. More useful, however, is the Library Association's second edition of *Guide to Current British Journals,* by David Woodworth (Library Association, 1973). This is published in 2 volumes and surveys over 4700 current titles, giving publication details and notes on the contents. The *World List of Social Science Periodicals* (3rd ed., UNESCO, 1966) includes details of about 2000 academic periodicals arranged under countries, with title and subject indexes.

Slightly different in purpose are the union lists of periodicals, which not only give all necessary publication details but also indicate the main libraries which hold each periodical. In the early days of library co-operation —35 years ago or more—lists of this kind were invaluable reference works for scholars, research workers and librarians, and publications such as the *World List of Scientific Periodicals,* published in the years 1900– 1960, edited by P. Brown and G. B. Stratton (4th ed., Butterworths, 1963–65), which included the periodicals holdings of 300 major British libraries, have been immensely valuable reference works. The *World List* has now ceased as a separate publication and is incorporated in *BUCOP.* But the situation is changing, particularly in the UK, and union lists, although useful for many purposes, are becoming less important because periodicals, or photocopies of articles, are readily obtainable from large comprehensive national resources. In the UK we are splendidly served in this respect by the British Lending Library with its comprehensive collection of periodicals at Boston Spa in Yorkshire, and so the need to try to find which library holds a particular periodical has diminished. We can now rely instead on the British Lending Library with its enormous stock of 45 000 current periodicals—the BLL, being so comprehensive, operates on the principle 'you ask for it, we've got it'. The last list of current periodicals received in this great library was published in 1974.

There is, however, one union list which, because of its comprehensiveness, is a valuable all-purpose bibliographical tool. It is *The British Union-Catalogue of Periodicals* (Butterworths) which was originally published in 4 volumes in 1955–58, with a supplement in 1962. Generally known as *BUCOP*, it lists over 140 000 periodicals which are held in about 440 British libraries and since 1964 it has been kept up to date with new titles, which are listed in a quarterly supplement with a cumulated annual volume. *BUCOP* is now part of our national bibliographical service operated by the British Library.

In America there is a similar publication in 5 volumes—*Union List of Serials in Libraries of the United States and Canada* (H. W. Wilson Co., New York, 1965). This is continued by *New Serials Titles*, which is published monthly by the Library of Congress in Washington, with an annual cumulated volume.

Despite their comprehensiveness, these great lists are hardly likely to be of much use to the average user of management and business libraries. He is better served by the list of periodicals held in his own library or by the lists of other business and management libraries. The lists of periodicals in the libraries of the British Institute of Management, the London and Manchester Business Schools and the City Business Library are sufficient for most purposes, and each contains details of some 500 journals relating to business and management. More extensive still is *Current Periodical Publications* in the Baker Library (Graduate School of Business Administration, Harvard University), which is issued annually and lists about 7000 serials received in this, the largest business school library in the world.

In 1973 the informal group of librarians from European business schools, which has already been referred to in Chapter 3, produced a combined list of their holdings of periodicals under the title *Union List of Periodicals in European Business Schools* (Manchester Business School Library, 1973). This computer-produced list, which was compiled only for members of the group initially, was edited and prepared by J. D. Dews and others at the Manchester Business School Library. It contains over 2600 titles held in 20 libraries in the UK and other European countries.

CONCLUSION

The vast number of periodicals published today has greatly complicated the task of those who want frequently to find information in them, and so it is necessary to learn how to make the best use of the various aids which are available. For new ideas, techniques and analytical discussions of problems ranging over the whole field of management there are about 25 periodicals emanating mainly from business schools in

America and Europe which are important. In addition, there is a growing number of good academic journals published in the UK concerned with a wide spectrum of management problems, and these compare well with their more numerous and older-established American counterparts. For general reading business executives have a choice of about 18 weeklies or monthlies—one or more of these are essential for keeping up to date with management news and events.

The core list of periodicals in Chapter 2 is a good starting point either for a library user to assess quickly what is available or for a librarian about to start a management library; in contrast, this chapter has concentrated on periodicals concerned with the whole general field of management and business and has provided a selected and annotated list of these so that the various titles can be assessed for their usefulness. In Part 3 the chapters on the various subject fields which follow indicate which are the most significant periodicals in the main subjects with which management is concerned.

The quotation with which this chapter began is a gentle reminder to those who, in our paper-filled world, no longer trouble to read periodicals because too many are published, to retain a sense of curiosity. A few periodicals and a knowledge of how to 'gut' them can reward the library user and the 'curious' manager.

7

Reference Works and Bibliographies

K. D. C. Vernon

Some books are to be tasted, others to be swallowed, and some few to be chewed and digested.

Francis Bacon

We all need reference works in order to find facts and answer questions quickly—they are, as Bacon suggested, to be tasted. Without them we would indeed flounder hopelessly whenever our memories failed us. One has only to consult a great work such as the *Encyclopaedia Britannica*, for example, to realise how little even the most widely educated person can ever hope to know of man's accumulated store of knowledge. To stand alone in a great library and to ponder on its contents can be both a humiliating and an inspiring experience for the thoughtful man—how much effort goes into the writing of even one book. To be surrounded by thousands is to realise the industriousness of many men and their desire to communicate their thoughts to others. With so much information in the form of books and other publications available to us it becomes increasingly important to know where to look for relevant facts whenever they are required. And so in this chapter we must address ourselves to the use of reference works and concentrate on those which are particularly significant to the needs of management and business.

There are several useful general guides which discuss, evaluate and list reference works, organisations and publications of all kinds. *How to find out: a guide to sources of information for all,* by G. Chandler (4th ed., Pergamon Press, 1974), is an introduction to general and subject-based reference works of all kinds and gives much useful advice to library users. *How to use the business library, with sources of business information,* by H. W. Johnson (4th ed., South Western Publishing Co., Cincinnati,

125

Ohio, 1972), is much more specific and is an important guide for all users of business information. It covers handbooks, directories, business and financial services, dictionaries, encyclopaedias, government publications, research reports and audio-visual aids of all kinds. It also includes sections on sources of information for small business, data-processing and business and market forecasting. The author is Professor of Marketing at Wayne State University and so he writes with the experience of a knowledgeable user of information. His guide, although mainly concerned with American sources, is an essential reference tool for all business libraries.

Another similar and valuable guide-book is *How to find out: management and productivity*, by K. G. B. Bakewell (2nd ed., Pergamon, 1970). It provides a wealth of information on all aspects of business and management literature, and supplements Johnson's book by concentrating more on British and European sources. It has chapters on management education and training, advice on using libraries, bibliographies and reference books, periodicals and abstracts, and sections on information sources for financial management, personnel, production, marketing and statistical publications.

Social science research and industry, edited by A. T. M. Wilson, J. Mitchell and A. Cherns (Harrap, 1971), emphasises the growing importance for business of economic and social research. It aims to provide a British reference work which helps to close the gap in contact between producers of relevant research and executives who may become its sponsors, developers and users. It begins with four introductory chapters on industry and the social sciences; the utilisation of social science research in industry; economic research and the executive; social science research as the study of industrial relations. These are followed by the main part of the book, which is an extensive directory of social science research activities in over 600 government departments and public bodies, universities and colleges, independent research institutes, firms and consultants, trade unions, societies and professional organisations.

There are numerous American directories of research and one of the best is *Research Centers Directory* (Gale Research Co., Detroit). It is regularly updated and is a guide to university sponsored and other non-profit research organisations carrying on research in most subject areas including business, economics, transport and social science. It covers a wider field than Wilson's British book, but the latter has more specialised objectives.

The guide-books by Johnson and Bakewell are of vital importance to every company and business library and Wilson's book, or its American equivalent, is equally important for all concerned with research. If properly understood and effectively used, they can save an enormous amount of valuable time which can otherwise be easily wasted in frantic and aimless searching for information which is in fact readily available. Two other source-books, although older, are still available in most business libraries — *Sources of business information*, by Edwin T. Coman (University of California Press, Berkeley, Los Angeles, 1964), is a mine of information particularly on American business statistics and financial services, and the more recent *Literature of executive management*, edited by Charlotte Georgi (Special Libraries Association, New York, 1969), is a well-chosen annotated list of books, periodicals and reference sources for the international businessman, prepared by an experienced group of American business school librarians. A successor to Coman's *Sources of business information* is being compiled by Lorna M. Daniells of the Baker Library at Harvard Business School and will be published by the University of California Press in 1976.

There are many other useful but more specific guides to sources of information related to industries and to particular aspects of management. The Gale Research Company in Detroit publishes a series of helpful management information guides which are continually being updated and extended in their coverage. Although primarily concerned with American publications and information-providing organisations, they are nevertheless valuable tools in most business libraries. The following are a few of the titles in this series:

Accounting Information Sources, by R. R. Demarest, 1970
Electronic Industries, by G. R. Randle, 1968
International Business and Foreign Trade, by I. I Wheeler
Investment Information, by J. B. Woy, 1970
Packaging, by G. Jones, 1967
Public and Business Planning, by M. B. Lightwood, 1972

Other organisations and publishers, notably Pergamon Press, have sponsored the compilation and publication of guidebooks to sources of information on certain industries and on various aspects of business, and many of these have been compiled by librarians who are well acquainted with the literature. The textile industry, for example, is served by *A guide to sources of information in the textile industry* (Aslib and the Textile Institute, 1970). For rubber and plastics there is *Sources of information on the rubber, plastics and allied industries*, by E. R. Yescombe (Pergamon, 1968). There are several guides to the chemical industry, but R. T. Bottle's *The use of chemical literature* (2nd ed., Butterworths, 1969) is probably the best. Another is *How to find out about the chemical industry*, by R. Brown and G. A. Campbell (Pergamon Press, 1969). For the wool industry there is *How to find out about the wool textile industry*, by H. Lemon (Pergamon, 1968).

Other aspects of business have been treated in the same way, and a helpful range of guide-books to information sources is available — they are important reference works which should be readily available in business libraries and offices. Marketing, in particular, relies heavily on published data and information, and most market researchers are skilled in finding the facts they want, but *Sources of UK marketing information*, by Gordon Wills (Nelson, 1969), is of wider scope and can be used effectively not only by marketeers, but also in most business offices and libraries. It has directory-type sections on prime sources, market data, media data, marketing research services, marketing journals and information for marketing outside the UK. Unfortunately the arbitrary division into these various sections has made this otherwise useful book rather confusing as a work of reference, but the indexes are helpful.

BIOGRAPHICAL REFERENCE WORKS

Information about people is constantly required in almost every business organisation. Executives and their secretaries need to know, frequently at short notice, a few facts about the people they have to meet or write to, or with whom they have to conduct their business. It is particularly important for secretaries to know where to look for this kind of information, and there is no shortage of reference works available to help them. The company library should of course be well stocked with books of this kind, and they should be kept up to date by ensuring that the latest edition is regularly purchased—the cost is minimal compared with the time and efficiency which can be easily lost without them. But in addition to the library copies of bibliographical reference works, it is necessary for any well-run office to be equipped with its own copies of the most important ones relevant to the work of the office.

The universally known British annual *Who's Who* (A. and C. Black) is essential in every office and library. Corresponding volumes are available for most other countries, and of these *Who's Who in America* (Marquis Who's Who, Chicago), now published in 2 volumes, is the most important for business libraries. With a wider coverage there are several international directories, and *International Who's Who* (Europa Publications) is one of the best. It is revised annually.

More specifically there is a whole range of similar works relevant to management and business organisations. Best-known is the annual *Directory of Directors* (Thomas Skinner Directories), which lists the directors of the principal public and private companies in the UK, giving the names of the concerns with which they are associated. This essential reference work now contains the names and appointments of some 40 000 men and women and provides a wealth of useful information about the direction of British companies. Another similar British biographical reference work is *Leviathan: the business who's who* (Leviathan House, 1972), which is a biographical dictionary of chairmen, chief executives and managing directors of British-registered companies, cross-referenced by an alphabetical index of the companies. It can be used to supplement the more limited information in the *Directory of Directors*. A similar directory with an international coverage is *International Businessmen's Who's Who* (Burke's Peerage Ltd), latest edition 1970.

A whole range of British 'who's who-type' publications is now available covering various aspects of business, such as finance, personnel management, marketing, production, etc. Gower Press in the UK is a publisher who has recently been active in publishing reference works of this kind. *Who's Who in Finance* (Gower Press) first appeared in 1972 and now includes biographical information about some 3500 British executives. *Who's Who in Finance and Industry* (Marquis Who's Who, Chicago) is the much larger American counterpart, which appears annually and very sensibly excludes many 'biographees' whose names appear in the widely used *Who's Who in America. Who's Who in Personnel Management and Industrial Relations, Who's Who in Marketing* and *Who's Who in Production Management* are three more Gower Press publications which provide very useful biographical information about British businessmen engaged in these activities. Similar reference works are published in a number of other countries, particularly in America.

All good public reference libraries are well stocked with biographical dictionaries of various kinds, but no efficient company or business organisation should fail to equip itself with sufficient copies both for its own library and for the people in the organisation who most need this kind of information—and who doesn't want biographical information sometimes? The editors and compilers of such information source-books perform a real service in facilitating communication, besides assuaging the thirst which many people have to find out facts about their fellows—'so-and-so really is 5 years older than I am, after all!'.

ENCYCLOPAEDIAS

It is not surprising that there are so few encyclopaedias of management. An encyclopaedia, by its very name, attempts to present a comprehensive coverage of knowledge and provide summaries of current knowledge in each subject, but management is not an amenable subject for such treatment, because its boundaries cannot be adequately defined. For large-scale multi-volume encyclopaedias one therefore has to turn to economics and the social sciences. The best and most recent is the *International encyclopaedia of the social sciences*, edited by David L. Sills in 17 volumes (Macmillan and Free Press, 1968), which includes many authoritative articles relevant to management and business which are of lasting importance. In contrast to this great work there are only two one-volume management encyclopaedias which give anything more than a superficial coverage of the subject area. The *Encyclopaedia of management*, edited by Carl Heyel (2nd ed., Van Nostrand Reinhold, 1973), is an authoritative and useful American publication which provides a concise picture of the state of the art as it was at the time of publication. It has been completely revised since the first edition appeared in 1963. Major articles are by acknowledged American experts in the subject and each article is followed by a list of references. There are ample cross-references to provide complete coverage of a subject area, and a systematic reading course is presented covering the articles in the encyclopaedia in a planned sequence. *Heyel's Encyclopaedia* is an essential reference work for most business libraries. The other encyclopaedia, which trails far behind Heyel in quality and scholarship, is *Newnes encyclopaedia of business management*, edited by Oliver Standingford (Newnes, 1967). It is naturally better than Heyel for information on British business practice and is still a useful reference work for larger libraries, but it is now getting rather out of date in some sections.

Apart from these two management encyclopaedias the cupboard is bare and one has to rely on dictionaries, glossaries and handbooks.

DICTIONARIES AND GLOSSARIES

It is convenient to consider dictionaries and glossaries in two groups— language dictionaries and subject dictionaries and glossaries. The distinction between a dictionary and a glossary is unimportant, but the word 'glossary' does cause doubt in some people's minds. It means in fact a small or partial dictionary—a list of explanations and definitions often added at the end of a technical or specialised textbooks. A 'gloss' was a word inserted between the lines or in the margin as an explanatory rendering of a word in the text, and so a glossary was a collection of such explanations.

Language dictionaries

Of the few language dictionaries compiled specifically for the business and management subject area the well-produced *Delmas business dictionary*, by G. and G. S. Anderla (J. Delmas et Cie. in association with George Harrap, 1972), is a new and reasonably comprehensive English–French and French–English dictionary consisting of some 70 000 entries for the most widely used English or French business words and phrases. It also includes a bilingual list of basic weights, measures and conversion coefficients and abbreviations in common use. A useful but smaller German equivalent is *Management dictionary*, by W. Sommer and H. M. Schonfeld (Walter de Gruyter, 1968), which is in 2 volumes. To be really with-it, however, the businessman, struggling with his French, should carry the most useful pocket *Glossary of French and English management terms*, by J. Coveney and S. J. Moore (Longman, 1972), actually in his pocket, not only because it conveniently measures $7\frac{1}{2} \times 3\frac{1}{4}$ in, but also because the two lexicographers have provided a thoroughly up-to-date and well-selected list of management terms in French and English. Many new terms describing techniques and concepts not found in general language dictionaries, but drawn from all main areas of management interest, have been included. S. F. Horn's *Glossary of financial terms* (Elsevier, 1965) is a valuable multilingual dictionary for English/American, French, Spanish and German, and covers the wide field of finance, banking and accounting.

Apart from these dictionaries which cover the main business languages, there are others of course for economics and social science and business dictionaries for Italian, Spanish and other languages. Any good public library with a commercial department will be well stocked with dictionaries for all languages. With all the facilities for language courses which are now widely available and the many translation services which can be used, the language barriers for businessmen are slowly diminishing in western European countries.

Subject dictionaries

Turning now to subject dictionaries, it is worth remembering that because many management terms are imprecise and ambiguous they cannot be adequately explained in short precise definitions. Some of the larger management handbooks, which we will discuss later, are more valuable for most purposes than subject dictionaries, which have little scope for the necessary longer explanations which are often needed. But there are a few dictionaries and glossaries which are useful for reference purposes. Probably the best is *A management glossary*, by H. Johannsen and A. Robertson (Longmans, 1968). It contains brief definitions of more than a thousand significant and commonly used terms taken from all areas of management. By the clarity of its short definitions this glossary helps to dispel the fog of doubt which surrounds many management terms. *Pitman's Businessman's guide: a comprehensive dictionary of commercial information*, edited by L. F. Nelson (14th ed., Pitman, 1968), is a cross between a small encyclopaedia and a dictionary, but it attempts to cover too wide a field. However, this Guide, together with a few other economics dictionaries such as the *McGraw-Hill Dictionary of modern economics* (McGraw-Hill, 1965), *Penguin Dictionary of commerce*, by M. Greener

(Penguin, 1970), and *Dictionary of economic terms,* by A. Gilpin (2nd ed., Butterworths, 1970), supplement the lack of dictionaries on general management.

Management techniques were much in vogue a few years ago and have been widely discussed on management courses and in the literature. They are specialised tools which managers can use to solve certain problems, but it is in fact difficult to isolate them from other aspects of management practice. However, they have been listed and briefly explained in *A new glossary of management techniques,* by John Argenti and Crispin Rope (Management Publications Ltd, 1971)—a useful pamphlet of 32 pages. The authors have attempted to evaluate the techniques by using a rating system of stars, similar to the system used by the AA for grading hotels, and have given after each definition references to books which explain the techniques more fully. *The director's guide to management technique* is discussed in the section on handbooks on p. 134.

Dictionaries and reference works on finance and accounting are well covered by Dr. A. Hopwood in Chapter 12. They can be supplemented by two small publications issued by professional bodies which are accepted for their authority— *Terms used in published accounts of limited companies* (Institute of Chartered Accountants, 1966) and *Terminology of cost accountancy* (Institute of Cost and Works Accountants, 1974). Another short but important list is the *European Federation of Financial Analysts Societies, Study Group on Terminology, List of Definitions.* It gives, for six European countries, including the UK, explanations of terms used in accountancy and investment analysis. This is a valuable list for all concerned with the harmonisation of European accounting practices.

Explanations of words and terms used in personnel management are included in the general management dictionaries mentioned above, but there are a few more specialised dictionaries which can be helpful. The most recent is *Encyclopaedia of personnel management,* edited by D. Torrington (Gower Press, 1974), which covers industrial relations, labour law, personnel administration, remuneration, training and welfare. *Dictionary on personnel and guidance terms,* by W. E. Hopke (J. G. Ferguson Publishing Co., Chicago, 1968), is a useful American reference work with a bias towards counselling and guidance. Much smaller and more specific but in many ways more essential for personnel departments is the Department of Employment's short *Glossary of training terms* (2nd ed., HMSO, 1971), which clarifies the meaning of about 250 terms used in industrial training. The definitions represent a consensus of views and have been widely used in practice.

The British Standards Institution has published several Standards which are, in effect, authoritative lists of terms which have been discussed and agreed by subject specialists. *Glossary of terms used in project network analysis* (B.S. 4335:1968), *Glossary of terms used in work study* (B.S. 3138:1969) are two examples. Others are listed in the *British Standards Yearbook.*

HANDBOOKS

It is difficult to define handbooks with any precision, because they are publications which fall somewhere between encyclopaedias and textbooks. They aim to provide surveys of subject fields so that users can refer to them for explanations of facts, principles and methods. Although the surveys are usually introductory, they presuppose some background knowledge of the subject, and the person using this kind of reference book does so frequently with the intention of refreshing his memory or getting a broad understanding of the topic. Management and business handbooks therefore provide comprehensive coverage of the main subject field by means of a series of articles, chapters or mini-textbooks on the various sub-divisions of the subject. This approach means that handbooks are liable to become out of date rather quickly unless new editions are published at intervals.

The Kluwer–Harrap *Handbook for managers,* edited by B. Folkertsma, which is jointly published by the Kluwer Publishing Co. of Amsterdam and George G. Harrap, the British publisher, has overcome some of the problems of comprehensiveness versus up-to-dateness by appearing in loose-leaf form—a form of publication which did not, as has been mistakenly supposed, originate with Adam! The instalments of pages were first published in 1972 and are now being issued at regular intervals until the whole work is complete in three volumes, when up-dating will continue. The work is aimed at practising managers who want to brush up or extend their over-all knowledge of management and at students of management, and covers the basic principles besides showing the inter-relationship of management problems. It consists of a selection of articles and writings taken from previously published management literature together with other contributions specially written for the *Handbook.* The subject is divided into eight main parts, each part being further subdivided in a helpful breakdown into sub-sections of main subjects. The index provides the point of entry needed when reference has to be made to a specific topic. The *Handbook,* in fact, provides a valuable over-all picture of management principles, practices and ideas. It is an essential reference work both for individual managers and for libraries.

A Handbook of management, edited by Thomas Kempner (Weidenfeld and Nicolson, 1971), has a different approach. Like the Kluwer–Harrap *Handbook,* it is aimed at practising managers and students and is intended 'to help managers survive in an increasingly complex and jargon-obsessed society'. Thus it is a handy one-volume reference book covering the main concepts and ideas which underpin management and is divided into 11 main subject areas. A synoptic index to each main subject lists the whole range of topics which fall within the subject and gives cross-references between topics. Every topic either has a cross-reference to another related topic which will extend the reader's understanding of it or has a brief list of references to relevant books. Together these two useful reference books provide an immense amount of valuable information across the whole field of management.

Two other useful British publications are the *Company administration handbook* (2nd ed., Gower Press, 1972) and the *Director's guide to management techniques,* edited by D. Lock and G. Taverner (Directors Bookshelf, 2nd ed., Gower Press, 1972). The former is virtually a series of articles on various aspects of company administration, law, finance, accounting practices, taxation, commercial functions and the management of physical assets. The book suffers from the fact that it lacks cohesiveness and appears to have been put together too quickly without that stamp of authority which is so essential to a reference book. The *Director's guide* consists of 21 articles on various management techniques used in finance, marketing, production, data-processing and industrial relations, together with a useful glossary of management terms and, in the first edition, a register of management consultants and advisory organisations. The register was rapidly revised and expanded into *Register of management consultants and advisory services to industry* (Directors Bookshelf, Gower Press, 1972).

American publishers have for many years been providing a whole selection of excellent large handbooks on various aspects of management, but some of these have now been superseded, for British managers, by the publications mentioned above. The sheer physical weight of some American handbooks must surely deter busy managers from using them. But undoubtedly they do provide a massive amount of potentially useful information within their covers. Only two need be mentioned here and they are well known to users of management libraries and literature. The first is *J. K. Lasser's Business management handbook* (McGraw-Hill), which first appeared in 1952 and has now reached the third edition. It consists of 21 chapters written by American specialists who with their experience of business practice provide valuable guidance to others who need to understand the complexities of running a modern business. *Handbook of business administration,* edited by H. B. Maynard in 3 volumes (McGraw-Hill, 1974), covers a much broader field and is almost 'encyclopaedic' in its comprehensiveness. It is a valuable work of reference and is essential for business libraries.

DIRECTORIES

Directories are, as the word implies, signposts to something or other—

organisations, people, areas of knowledge, places. They must therefore be up to date, like a telephone directory, and they must be accurate, like a map. Provided they are both these things and they give *useful* information, then they are essential. Without directories we would be left in a sorry state of confusion in today's complex society. Any good public library is always well stocked with these invaluable reference works; but unfortunately there are comparatively few people who really understand how to make effective use of them. Using reference books of this kind should be a skill to be taught to children at school.

Source Directory (Predicasts Inc.), which has previously been mentioned in Chapter 5, is an important new publication from the well-known Predicasts company, which has done so much to provide guides, indexes and directories to sources of business information. Although strongly weighted towards American publications, it lists sources of information in newspapers, trade journals, government publications, directories and monographs under subjects and geographical regions, and alphabetically by titles. It also includes a selection by Predicasts Inc. of the 100 titles considered to be essential to a business library. The *Source Directory,* with its comprehensive coverage and continuous updating policy, is a necessary reference work in every business library.

The outstanding guide to British directories is G. P. Henderson's *Current British Directories,* edited by I. G. Anderson. (7th ed., CBD Research Ltd, Beckenham, Kent, 1973-4). It is designed to assist in any search for information involving the use of directories or lists and it is being continually updated and re-issued. No library can afford to be without it and no business organisation, except the very smallest, can be using published sources of information effectively if it does not possess at least one copy of *CBD*—for marketing departments it is a vital piece of equipment. Part 1 lists regional, telephone and local directories. Part 2 lists specialised directories of industries, trades, professions, membership lists of associations and year-books containing directory-type information. The index is the key to this store of information.

Having described '*Henderson*' it is almost superfluous to mention other directories individually, but a few which must be available in business organisations need to be included here, because it is easy to forget how to find certain information unless one is constantly reminded of the sources which are available to us.

First there is another essential guide-book from the same fertile CBD Research stable—*Directory of British Associations,* edited by G.P. and S. P. A. Henderson (CBD Research Ltd, Beckenham, Kent). It is a regularly updated guide to the activities and publications of trade associations, scientific and technical societies, professional and learned societies, research organisations, chambers of commerce, trade unions, and cultural, sports and welfare organisations in the UK and Ireland.

Other directories are obviously necessary for both general and specialised purposes. *Industrial Research in Britain* (7th ed., Francis Hodgson, 1972) was first published 25 years ago and is now a standard reference work. *Financial Times International Business Yearbook* (Financial Times, Business Enterprises Division), first appeared in 1973, but is now well known as a valuable source of information for facts and figures on 52 of the principal trading countries of the world. It provides much useful information on the leading companies in these countries. Similar in purpose but much more comprehensive is *The Director's Guide to Europe* (Directors Bookshelf, Gower Press, 1973), which has the subtitle 'a companion for the businessman visiting and trading with Europe'. It contains five introductory general articles on Europe and the EEC but is mainly a country-by-country guide supplying useful business and economics information. More specialised, newer and therefore not widely known yet is *European Directory of Economic and Corporate Planning 1973-74* (Gower Economic Publications). It provides information on UK and European organisations of all kinds concerned with economic and corporate planning, and also lists of journals, seminars, courses and even some selected articles from periodicals on this subject area.

Enough has been said to indicate the rich information resources available to anybody with a nose for finding facts and data. For other directories the best advice to follow is to buy Henderson's *Current British Directories,* identify relevant publications from it, look at them in a good public library and then purchase the most important ones for everyday use in offices and company libraries. For American directories one of the best guides is the *Guide to American Directories,* by Bernard Klein (B. Klein and Co., New York) which gives information about the major business directories of the United States covering all industrial, professional and mercantile categories.

BIBLIOGRAPHIES

Beloved by librarians, utilised by researchers, flirted with by students and unfortunately often ignored by managers, bibliographies serve us well. They range in size from massive multi-volume compilations down to short lists for 'further reading' which are appended to articles in periodicals, often to make them look 'respectable', or in another form as footnotes to books. There are many forms of bibliographies—some are confined entirely to books, others include articles in periodicals while others merely list the items by title or author. Some are very selective in the items listed; others try to be comprehensive. Some arrange everything alphabetically; others carefully divide the subject into sections. A library catalogue is a bibliography especially when it is published in book form or printed out from a computer store. But above all a bibliography must be accurate; otherwise it will go on misleading everybody who uses it.

As more and more books are published each year, the task of recording them, which is in fact the art of bibliography, grows increasingly more formidable. But most countries have their own national bibliographies which record all books published in the country. Attempts have been made to achieve the impossible task of compiling a universal bibliography, and in 1895 the Institut International de Bibliographie was founded at Brussels with the object of creating a world bibliography. It optimistically began by cutting up and assembling the entries taken from the largest available library catalogues—by the end of 1928 it had collected 13 738 533 entries; but the effort was doomed to failure because the bibliography was also intended to include all articles from all periodicals.

The need for national bibliographical services, on the other hand, is beyond dispute. Despite the ever-growing number of publications issued annually—there were 34 374 new books and reprints published in the UK in 1973—the need to record them is obvious. Without accurate and comprehensive records we would rapidly decline into complete biblio-graphical chaos. Yet it is less than 25 years since the Council of the British National Bibliography was set up to produce a continuing record of all British books being published. The *British National Bibliography* first appeared in 1950—its birth was hailed with enthusiasm by the library profession. It is issued weekly and cumulated quarterly and contains details of all books which all publishers have, under the Copyright Act, deposited at the Copyright Office in the British Museum. The books are listed in classified order by the Dewey Decimal Classification, with an author, title and subject index. The details given for each book are in the form of a complete catalogue entry; and as the *BNB* service includes the issuing of catalogue cards, many libraries prefer to purchase these cards and thereby save much of their own cataloguing costs. The *BNB* is now under the direction of the newly founded British Library, and considerable advances have been made during the past few years in recording all the bibliographical information on computer tape and issuing the tapes to some of the largest libraries. These tapes, known as MARC tapes, include details of all English-language publications, because the work of preparing them is shared with the Library of Congress in America. In fact the MARC tapes were first developed in the Library of Congress at Washington after a long period of experimentation. The advantages of this fine bibliographical service are likely to increase still further in the near future as computers are used increasingly for bibliographical control.

The annual volumes of the *BNB* are the main tools available at present for finding information about published books, including management and business books. But there are other similar bibliographies to supplement them— *Whitaker's Cumulative Booklist*, started as a weekly list of British books, which first appeared in *The Bookseller* in 1909, is the best-known. Unlike the *BNB*, it is not compiled from the books themselves but from publishers' announcements. It is very comprehensive and is the main list used by the book trade. A complete list of all currently available British books is *British Books in Print: the reference catalogue of current literature* (J. Whitaker and Son).

More comprehensive still is the great American publication *Cumulative Book Index* (H. W. Wilson Co.), which records all English-language books wherever they are published. *Books in Print* and *Subject Guide to Books in Print*, both of which are published by the R. R. Bowker Co. of New York, are complementary to *British Books in Print*. The American equivalent to our *BNB* is the *National Union Catalog*, which is published by the Library of Congress in Washington, but it goes further and covers the holdings of about 600 large American libraries.

The English language has therefore great bibliographical riches and it is comparatively easy to find information about individual publications. Many other countries also publish their own national bibliographies, so the nineteenth century dream of the founders of the Institut International de Bibliographie could come true. If all the national bibliographies were truly comprehensive and if their information could be stored in a computer and kept up to date, we could, provided the system worked, achieve complete bibliographical bliss!

But we are concerned with the literature of management and so the *BNB* and other national bibliographies are important to us for the wide coverage they give, but we also have more specific subject bibliographies to serve us. *Business Books in Print* (R. R. Bowker Co., New York) is the largest and most recent. It is a very comprehensive computer-produced list covering business, finance and the economic system and is an essential bibliography for all business libraries.

Most users of management and business libraries, however, prefer to ask librarians for information and it is therefore the librarians who are the most avid users of bibliographies. Librarians also have naturally been most aware of the need for bibliographical control over the literature and they have been responsible for compiling a large proportion of the bibliographies in existence. Many librarians rightly regard it as part of their duty to compile bibliographies and lists of all kinds, and within the subject area of management they are actively engaged in this kind of work on behalf of their library users. For example, the library of the British Institute of Management compiles and issues a valuable series of reading lists covering about 170 specific subjects concerned with management and business, while the useful, *Basic library of management* (BIM, 1974) lists titles of selected books which are considered to be important in this subject. The library of the London Business School issues a series of *Sources of Information* which are mini-guides to finding information on selected business topics and include short lists of books and articles. Manchester Business School Library issues short bibliographies and reading lists on topics which are important to the work of the School. Other business school libraries in the UK, America and Europe, the commercial departments of the larger public libraries and some of the more specialised business and professional libraries are actively engaged in similar work. Manchester Commercial Library, for example, has issued a whole string of bibliographies, guides and notes designed to help people find business information.

American librarians working in this subject field have been particularly active in compiling and publishing bibliographies of all kinds. The Baker Library at Harvard Business School has published useful bibliographies on *Business literature* (1968), *Selected business reference sources* (1965), *Corporate and business finance* (1964) and *Business forecasting* (1970), in addition to the *Core Collection: an author and subject guide*, which has been referred to in Chapter 2, and of course there are also the well-known *Intercollegiate Bibliographies* of case studies which are regularly published by the Intercollegiate Case Clearing House at Harvard. But the greatest of all the Harvard bibliographies is the *Author-Title and Subject Catalogs of the Baker Library* (G. K. Hall and Co., 1971) in 22 volumes. It is a complete record of nearly 450 000 books held in the library and is the most comprehensive published bibliography of management and business literature. It is in fact a reproduction in book form of the 600 000 cards contained in this great library's card catalogue at the Harvard Business School. As a permanent record of the literature it will remain as a great bibliographical achievement and an essential tool for scholars. Other business school librarians at California, Cornell and elsewhere have been equally active in bibliographical work and have compiled numerous lists which help people to find their way through the tangled undergrowth of literature.

Of the many other general bibliographies of management which have been published in addition to those already mentioned, the following three examples must suffice to indicate the resources available. *Selective management bibliography*, by Georges Sandeau (Gower Press, 1975), is an important new reference work compiled by the Librarian of INSEAD, the international business school at Fontainebleau. It gives full details of over 5000 books and articles in English, French and German which have been selected by the author for their significance. This bibliography, with its comprehensive indexes and subject arrangement based on the *London Classification of Business Studies*, will be a valuable guide to the literature for many years to come. Important also, because it is continually updated, is the *Anbar Management Services Bibliography*, which is part of the Anbar Documentation Service. It is issued three times a year and cumulated annually; it lists books, pamphlets and films which have been reviewed in management periodicals. *Readers' guide to books on management* (Library Association, County Libraries Group, 1971) is a very handy and well-selected list covering all aspects of management.

Through all these bibliographies, together with the three guide-books by Johnson, Bakewell and Wilson mentioned at the beginning of this chapter, the extent of the literature available is revealed. By using them research workers can conduct literature searches, and the answers to many questions can be supplied.

We have been concerned here only with bibliographies covering the whole area of management and business, but many other important subject bibliographies are available—a few have been mentioned in Part 3 of this book in the chapters surveying the subject literature. Others, such as the numerous specialised bibliographies published by the American Marketing Association, can be traced through the guide-books cited at the beginning of this chapter. The *International bibliography of marketing and distribution*, by G. Sandeau (Staples Press, 1972), now in its fourth edition, is particularly important—it includes many European books and articles and is arranged in a helpful classified subject order. The Institute of Personnel Management is currently publishing *IPM Bibliography* in six parts. Part 1, which covers management and the enterprise, was issued in 1973 and Part II, on manpower studies, in 1974. This is a selective annotated bibliography covering a representative sample of the literature. It is an important list and provides a valuable guide to significant books.

International business is another important subject area which has received considerable attention, particularly from American bibliographers. Much of the earlier literature is listed in the very comprehensive *Bibliography of international business*, by C. F. Stewart and G. B. Simmons (Columbia University Press, 1964). This is updated by *Multinational corporation–nation, state interaction: an annotated bibliography*, edited by D. Burtis and others (Foreign Policy Research Institute, Philadelphia, 1971), which is an authoritative and extensive listing of publications concerned with this very wide subject field. More generally useful, however, is the quarterly *International Executive* (Foundation for the Advancement of International Business Administration), which scans the current literature very effectively. This valuable abstracting publication is discussed in more detail in Chapter 5.

To complete this brief survey of bibliographies and to guide us through even wider fields we are blessed with publications which are bibliographies of bibliographies—listings which are twice removed from the originals but yet are essential signposts to the signposts through the jungle. Theodore Besterman's *World Bibliography of Bibliographies* (4th ed., Societas Bibliographica, Lausanne, 1965–6) is published in 5 volumes and is the most comprehensive list of this kind—it gives details of over 80 000 bibliographies arranged by subjects. For current items there is the *Bibliographic Index* (H. W. Wilson Co.), which is published at regular intervals and cumulated annually—it lists bibliographies published in books and peridocials. But these publications, valuable though they are, can only be of occasional use for tracing management bibliographies. Short subject lists are usually more practical for most library users if they are sufficiently specific. For example, there is the typescript *Index of Bibliographies* (Sources of Information No. 13, London Business School Library, 1972)— it lists over 200 bibliographies concerned with management and business. Or *Sources of Business Information: a select list of bibliographies of business* (Business Bibliographies 3, Manchester Public Libraries, 1967), which is a very useful annotated list.

CONCLUSION

Finally, it is worth remembering that because all the reference works mentioned in this chapter have been produced in order to answer questions or to indicate the way to find information, they are tools designed for particular purposes. As such, it is essential to learn how to use them, or at least to know which ones are relevant to you, the searcher for information. Taste them and make friends with those that suit your palate. Without them we would be left floundering hopelessly in the mounting flood of publications which pours from the world's printing presses.

PART 2

Business information in three different forms

8

Research in Progress and Unpublished Material

John Fletcher

The term 'research' covers a wide range of levels of activity from a master's term project to a programme lasting several years and employing numbers of high-level academics and assistants. The results may similarly vary from a short note in a journal to a series of volumes of data and analysis. In this chapter we are concerned with research in progress and the unpublished or semi-published results of research. Research work reported in conventionally published forms, in books or journal articles, is dealt with elsewhere.

The location of the research, combined with the source of its funds, often affects the way in which results are made publicly available. Academic institutions, such as universities and colleges, with schools of business studies, are probably the most prolific research centres, but many independent research institutes and government departments carry out large programmes of research, much of which can be of interest to students and practitioners of management. A great deal of 'management' research is carried out by private firms and consultants, but this is usually to some degree confidential and not available outside the company or the client. In general, the results of research carried out in universities and independent institutes will be made available to a wider audience, although even here the method of funding the project or the confidential nature of some of the information used may restrict the circulation of results. A smaller proportion of research carried out in government departments will be publicly released, although there are indications that in both the UK and the USA research work carried out for government commissions and advisory bodies is increasingly being made public.

RESEARCH IN PROGRESS

The 'invisible college' or 'old boy network' is as important a means of communication between researchers in management studies as in other subjects. A major source of information about who is researching into what is the casual meeting at a conference, the mutual acquaintance and the mobile research assistant. There are, however, a few published sources of information on research projects in progress. For the UK there is the annual *Scientific Research in British Universities and Colleges*, prepared by the Department of Education and Science and published by HMSO. Volume 3 is subtitled *The Social Sciences* and under broad subject headings (the most fruitful heading for management subjects is Industrial Administration) research projects are listed under institutions alphabetically arranged with separate sequences for universities/colleges and other research organisations. Information given includes the name of the researcher, a brief description of the project and, in some cases, dates, and there are indexes of personal names and specific subjects.

Business Horizons contains notes on research in progress on management subjects under the heading Research Clearinghouse, and this appears to be the only continuing up-to-date list covering all aspects of management research in the USA. *Journal of Business* of the University of Chicago includes in its spring and autumn issues a Register of Current Research, which gives 'details of new, on-going and completed research projects that relate directly to the measurement and improvement of the financial performance and management of firms or that relate to the environment . . . which conditions or constrains their financial behaviour'. Coverage is thus narrower than it is in the two sources mentioned but over 200 entries had been made by early 1973, giving brief title, researchers, starting and predicted completion dates, and publications.

In the industrial relations area *Industrial and Labor Relations Review* contains in each quarterly issue a section of Research Notes of varying length giving descriptions of work being carried out in various industrial relations institutes throughout the world; these are chiefly university-based but research under way in government departments is also noted.

Volumes 1 and 2 (1967 and 1968) of the *British Journal of Marketing* contained a Register of Current Research (in marketing) but this was not continued. Other possible fruitful sources of information are lists of grants awarded for research which give notes on the aims of the project being funded. The (British) Social Science Research Council has just published the first edition of a new annual *Research Supported by the Social Science Research Council, 1971-72*, which includes a detailed subject index and an author index. The *SSRC Newsletter* will keep the information up to date, and also includes grants given by other similar bodies in the United Kingdom. The Notes section of *Journal of Business* is also worth noting in this context.

There are three major published sources of information about research institutes. World-wide coverage, but little detail, is given in *World of Learning* (Europa Publications, annual). The heading Learned Societies and Research Institutes should be checked, and Universities and Colleges for organisations attached to educational institutions: each chapter is devoted to one country. *Research Centers' Directory* (Gale Research) now includes Canada as well as the USA, and with smaller geographical coverage than *World of Learning* can give more detail of the aims, functions and organisation of the institutes listed. *Social sciences research and industry*, edited by A. T. M. Wilson and others (Harrap, 1971), gives brief notes on British organisations concerned with research of interest to industry and commerce, including universities, research institutes, government departments and private firms and consultants.

RESEARCH REPORTS

The results of research may be made public in many forms, the most common being monographs, journal articles and conference papers. But increasingly there is developing in management studies a report literature which is not published through the conventional commercial channels. These reports may be to the body funding the research or mimeographed papers circulated to known colleagues. Finally, there is the increasing quantity of research being carried out for postgraduate degrees and reported initially, and in many cases only, in the student's dissertation or thesis.

Reports to funding bodies which are publicly available may be traced through several publications. Probably the largest supplier of research grants is the US government and its agencies, and their research reports are listed in *Government Reports Announcements,* issued by the National Technical Information Service of the US Department of Commerce. This is a semi-monthly publication giving short abstracts of reports under broad subjects with sub-divisions; Field 5: Behavioral and Social Sciences covers most reports of interest in management studies. Annual and semi-monthly indexes (entitled *Government Reports Index*) list the reports under personal and corporate authors, by subject, and by report and contract number. Most reports are, of course, on scientific or technical subjects, but there is a large body of management and behavioural science research being carried out in both government and independent institutions funded by Federal agencies. The National Technical Information Service also provides a *Fast Announcement Service* listing new reports in broad subject areas in advance of the appearance of the fuller abstracts in *Government Reports Announcements. Management Practice and Research,* also published weekly by the NTIS, gives abstracts of government research reports of particular interest to management practitioners. Other similar publications in the same series cover computers, control and information theory, environment pollution and control, and transportation.

One American institute particularly concerned with research is the Rand Corporation, which provides, in *Selected Rand Abstracts* (Vol. 1, 1946-62, thereafter quarterly, cumulating annually), short abstracts of reports on its research projects. The abstracts are indexed by author and by subject.

In the UK the British Library Lending Division obtains copies for loan of much research report material. Again most is on technical subjects but the new acquisitions listed in the monthly *BLL Announcements Bulletin* under the rather broad heading Behavioural and Social Sciences and Humanities include many reports of interest to students of management subjects. The sources of the reports range from universities, government and independent research institutes to private firms. All the reports listed in the *Bulletin*, in the American *Government Reports Announcements* and in *Selected Rand Abstracts*, noted above, are available for loan from the BLL.

In a narrower subject field the Marketing Abstracts section of the *Journal of Marketing* includes abstracts of unpublished and semi-published research reports from government and private organisations.

THESES

The term 'thesis', or 'dissertation', can be applied to the results of a variety of research from a term paper to the end-product of several years' work, but here we are concerned only with papers written in partial or complete fulfilment of the requirements of a master's or doctor's degree. Theses in management subjects sometimes suffer from the problem of confidentiality: firms or other organisations make available to students confidential data on the understanding that they are not made freely public. In so far as the finished thesis contains such data, the university may have to restrict its circulation, but apart from this all but a few universities are prepared to lend their accepted theses to interested researchers, and in many cases will provide microform or full-size copies for sale.

The largest, regular, up-to-date list of theses is *American Doctoral Dissertations,* an annual publication of University Microfilms compiled for the Association of Research Libraries, which aims to list all doctoral dissertations accepted in American and Canadian universities. Theses are listed under broad subjects by university; an author index is provided; and there are notes on the availability of the theses.

Dissertation Abstracts International is a monthly publication giving lengthy abstracts of doctoral dissertations accepted in certain American universities (the *International* was added to the title in 1970, when some Canadian and European theses were first included). Although less comprehensive than *American Doctoral Dissertations*, the abstracts are useful, as are the detailed indexes. All theses listed in *Dissertation Abstracts International* are available as xerographic or microfilm copy from the publishers, University Microfilms. Many universities, however, prefer to supply copies of their own dissertations for sale themselves (Harvard Business School is an important example) and their theses are not included in *Dissertation Abstracts International.*

The abstracts are arranged under broad subjects, and both section A (*The Humanities and Social Sciences*) and section B (*The Sciences and Engineering*) need to be checked for management topics; section A includes Accounting, Business Administration, and Commerce, Business (as a subdivision of Economics), while section B includes Computer Science, Data Processing, Hospital Management, Industrial Engineering, Industrial Psychology and Statistics. Keyword subject indexes (not the most efficient of indexing methods) and author indexes appear in each issue, and cumulations are published annually. The *Dissertation Abstracts International Retrospective Index* covers Volumes 1 to 29 (1938 to 1968/69) by author and by subject in 10 volumes. Once more the wide spread of business studies topics makes it necessary to use several of the volumes to ensure complete subject coverage. Since 1970 the British Library Lending Division has bought all microfilmed theses listed in *Dissertation Abstracts International* and makes them available for loan.

There are no equivalent services abstracting and producing copies of theses for other countries, but there are usually fairly comprehensive lists of doctoral theses for most developed countries; the Swiss *Jahresverzeichnis der Schweizerischen Hochschuleschriften* is typical, listing theses by university and degree with subject/title and author indexes. For the UK there is the *Aslib Index to Theses Accepted for Higher Degrees in the Universities of Great Britain and Ireland and the Council for National Academic Awards*, an annual listing master's and doctor's theses in broad subjects with an author index. Most management subjects will be found subsumed to Economics under headings such as Industry, Business Finance and Marketing. There are notes in each volume on the availability of theses for loan and/or copying from each university. Within its geographical coverage, the *Aslib Index* aims to be comprehensive, but in spite of providing neither abstracts nor detailed subject indexes, publication of each volume is almost 2 years after the end of the academic year covered.

Many universities list their theses in their course prospectuses (Harvard Business School, for example) or in separate pamphlets or books (Leeds and Oxford Universities), and these are also useful in that they indicate the range of subjects being studied. *American Doctoral Dissertations* contains a list of American universities issuing lists of their own theses, but it should be noted that some of these include research proposals as well as accepted theses. Some postgraduate thesis proposals are also included in *Scientific Research in British Universities*, noted above.

A few academic journals in management subjects include lists or abstracts of accepted theses on their subjects, and a few examples will suffice to show the kind of coverage provided. The December (September until 1972) issue of *American Economic Review* includes an excellent section of abstracts of doctoral dissertations accepted in American universities, arranged in broad subject areas within economics. The *Economic Journal* began in the March 1973 issue a similar article for British theses. The January issue of *Journal of Business* of the University of Chicago has a list of doctoral dissertations accepted in the previous academic year in American universities. These are on all aspects of business studies, and are arranged in 17 subject groups. *Journal of Finance* contains a few long abstracts of American doctoral dissertations on financial topics.

WORKING PAPERS

The term 'working paper' used here refers to that type of semi-published paper issued often in university departmental series, usually typescript mimeographed and then made available to a select mailing list of individuals and institutions known to be interested in the subject area. They may be variously termed seminar papers, discussion papers, research reports or simply papers; they are the second drafts of potential journal articles (the first having been circulated much less widely) or papers given to seminars or conferences. The aim of circulating them is to have them examined and criticised by interested and knowledgeable colleagues with a view to eliciting comment before submitting the final draft to a journal for publication.

Working papers are an important feature of the literature of management, because they provide the first publicly available script of a proposed publication. In general, the delay in publication in management journals is shorter, and the supply of manuscripts closer to the demand for them, than in, say, economics, where working papers are a considerable and increasingly important portion of the literature. Most working papers are subsequently published conventionally, although many remain available only in this mimeographed form. Often citation of a working paper is allowed only with the permission of the author, but this form of semi-publication is being increasingly used, and cited, especially in other working papers, so that the problems of access are becoming acute.

Many papers are issued in series sponsored by the department or institute employing the authors, although some are obtainable only from the authors personally. So far there are no comprehensive lists of working papers, so that knowledge of their existence is still a problem. *Public Affairs Information Service Bulletin* includes a few, as does the *BLL Announcements Bulletin.* The Baker Library of Harvard University issues a list entitled *Working Papers in Baker Library: a quarterly checklist*, but these are all selective, and so fas as the present author is aware there are no comprehensive or published lists of working papers.

In an attempt to overcome this deficiency, the Library of the University of Warwick has been attempting to make as comprehensive a collection as possible of working papers in economics and business studies subjects. In 1972 the Social Science Research Council gave the Library a 1-year grant to bring the project to fruition, and put it on a sound and more permanent basis. With the willing co-operation of the originating authors and their institutions, Warwick University Library now receives a very wide range of working papers from all over the world, and these are indexed by author, by subject and by series. Lists of new arrivals at Warwick are sent each week for inclusion in *Contents of Recent Economics Journals* (published by HMSO, London) and *Contents Pages in Management* (Manchester Business School), and non-British papers are then lent, through their libraries, to interested researchers in the UK.

From 1973 Transmedia Publishing Co. (a member of the Oceana Group of Dobbs Ferry, New York), in conjunction with the University of Warwick Library, began publication of a new double service in economics documentation: first, a quarterly *Economics Working Papers Bibliography* indexing the papers by author, subject and series, with the fourth issue each year being an annual cumulation; the second service comprises the supply of microfilm of the original working papers where permission has been given for this to be done. The *Bibliography* included over 1500 papers, and the microfilm service over 1000 papers in 1974.

Although the weekly listing and the loan service include working papers on management subjects, the new published services cover only economics topics: if the venture is commercially viable, it is hoped to begin a similar, though smaller, because there are fewer papers, service for business studies.

The range of subjects of interest to researchers in management studies is wide, but there are already well-established and often large series of working papers in these subject areas. Not surprisingly, most emanate from American and European business schools and university departments. All aspects of management are covered by the discussion papers of the Wharton School of Finance and Commerce of the University of Pensylvania; the working papers of the Alfred P. Sloan School of Management of Massachusetts Institute of Technology; HBS working papers from Harvard Business School; the Institute papers of Purdue University's Institute for Research in the Behavioural, Economic and Management Sciences; and the working papers series from the Graduate School of Business Administration at New York University.

European management schools are, in general, younger than their American counterparts, but already there are important working papers series from INSEAD (European Institute of Business Administration, research papers series), European Institute for Advanced Studies in Management (working papers) and the International Institute for Management (preprint series).

Some series emanate from departments with more limited subject interests, and there are some very useful papers among the technical reports of the Operations Research Center of MIT, the technical reports of the Department of Operations Research at Case Western Reserve University, and the closely allied mimeo series of the Institute of Statistics at the University of North Carolina, and the technical reports of the University of Wisconsin's Department of Statistics.

There are few series in marketing or financial management, but the following are worth mentioning: working papers of the Marketing Science Institute, and of the Research Program in Marketing at the University of California at Berkeley; the Rodney L. White Center for Financial Research at the University of Pennsylvania also produces a series of working papers.

CONCLUSION

This is a very difficult 'grey area' of literature where there is probably an increasing amount of useful material written, and usually available if one can find out about it: it is difficult for both the researcher and his librarian, because the guides and lists are rare, and incomplete. Science subjects have learned to control their report literature reasonably well after many years of trouble. It is to be hoped that, as it grows, the much smaller body of management reports literature will be even more successfully tamed.

9

Statistical Publications for Business and Management

Joan M. Harvey

For a long time statistics have been collected and used by central government in connection with the administration of the country. First, population and vital statistics; later, statistics of foreign trade; much later, statistics of income, labour and production: but from 1946 onwards there has been an ever-increasing volume and variety of quantitative data. Only comparatively recently have management and business begun to make use of this valuable material as a basis for decision-making, partly because of the small size of the average business and partly because the statistics were collected solely for government purposes with no thought given to collecting and analysing information in a way more suitable to other possible users.

Nowadays government departments are still the main collectors of statistics but there is much more concern for the needs of other users of the data. Traditionally, each government department collected the data it needed, sometimes through organisations such as trade associations, and in the UK the Central Statistical Office has since 1946 acted as a co-ordinating body. Now, as part of a programme to reorganise government statistics along more centralised and integrated lines, the Business Statistics Office (BSO) and the Office of Population Censuses and Surveys (OPCS) have been set up, and these two agencies, together with the Central Statistical Office and the statistics divisions of individual government departments, constitute the Government Statistical Service.

The Business Statistics Office, created in 1969 out of the Board of Trade's Census Office, is the principal government agency for the collection of statistics from business firms. It has the responsibility for the improvement of both long-term statistics designed to throw light on the structure of the economy and short-term enquiries designed to show how the economy is currently moving; also to develop a unified central register of business as the basis for handling nearly all business statistical enquiries on behalf of other government departments. The Office has used a computer in its work for some considerable time and one of its long-term objectives is to maintain data banks of business statistics.

The Office of Population Censuses and Surveys was set up in May 1970 when the General Register Office and the Government Social Survey were brought together as one department responsible for vital statistics, demographic statistics, the census of population, medical statistics and social surveys on a very wide range of subjects. Through the censuses and surveys it is responsible for the collection of most government statistics relating to persons and households.

More statistical information is available for some subjects than for others. Little was available on finance and banking in the United Kingdom until after the Radcliffe Committee on the *Working of the monetary system* reported in 1959 (Cmnd 827); fewer data are available about certain industries and commodities than about others, mainly because few firms are involved and the terms of the *Statistics of Trade Act 1947* ensures the confidentiality of the business of individual firms.

In the realm of management and business, statistics can provide estimates or comparisons on which decisions can be made. They cannot give the complete solution to problems but they can deal with the measurable aspects of many problems; although for statistics to be used satisfactorily, their limitations must be understood. Most statistics are collected by the medium of forms or questionnaires: for example, heads of households complete census of population forms, industrial firms complete forms concerning production, sales, etc., exporters and importers complete forms for Customs and Excise departments before goods can be exported or imported, and errors can be made at this stage. They can also be made in the processing of the data collected, but in the main the faults arise through misunderstanding or misinterpretation of the data by users. It is important that the users, whether primary or secondary users, know just how the data for a particular table were collected and analysed, what was included and what was omitted. Firms with under a certain number of employees may be omitted from tables of production or employment statistics; and certain industries may, for one reason or another, be omitted from more general tables. In regular tables the content or classification may change at some time; and errors or later information may mean that some regular tables (trade statistics, for instance) are corrected in the cumulated figures published in a later issue. The new base year for index numbers will mean that one cannot use earlier index numbers in the same context. Figures may be rounded up or rounded down in a table or series of tables; and if these figures are added together, they can result in a very inaccurate figure. Misinterpretations can be avoided if care is taken to read the explanatory matter which statisticians usually take trouble to provide in an effort to overcome these dangers, and if care is also taken to check on table headings, footnotes, etc.

Forecasts must be treated with caution, particularly if compiled some time previously, because they can be falsified by unforeseen circumstances, such as political or economic crises. Time series are valuable and are often amended to allow for seasonal or other variations. Charts and histograms, while perhaps not always so accurate, are often quicker to understand than statistical tables, the salient features of comparisons or trends being immediately apparent.

Classification schemes for industries and commodities are invaluable for locating the required tables or figures in many statistical publications. In the UK the *Standard Industrial Classification* (HMSO), a classification of industries, is used for the compilation of the censuses of production, distribution and population and by the Department of Employment, and this enables data in the various publications to be compared more easily. An international equivalent is the *International Standard Industrial Classification of All Economic Activities*, compiled by the United Nations Statistical Office. For external trade statistics HM Customs and Excise *Tariff* (HMSO) is used for classifying commodities, and this classification is correlated with the *Brussels Tariff Nomenclature*, used in the European Economic Communities and some other European countries, and the United Nations' *Standard International Trade Classification, revised*, used by a number of countries and by all countries when reporting external trade statistics to the United Nations.

GUIDES TO STATISTICAL PUBLICATIONS

There is nothing today to compare with the annual *Guide to Current Official Statistics*, published by HMSO from 1922 to 1938, although, with the much larger number and variety of official UK statistics now available and the increased use of published statistics, the need is correspondingly greater than it was. However, the problem is being tackled both by the Central Statistical Office and by the Committee of Librarians and Statisticians and it is hoped that at least one comprehensive guide of some kind will emerge in due course. In the meantime there is the Central Statistical Office's *List of principal statistical series and publications* (rev. ed., HMSO, 1974), which not only lists the main titles but also gives brief commentaries on their nature and coverage, and is updated in the quarterly *Statistical News: developments in British official statistics* (HMSO) as important new statistical titles appear or the content of existing titles changes. *Sources of statistics* (2nd ed., Clive Bingley and Linnet Books 1971), by Joan M. Harvey, is a guide which describes the principal sources of statistics in the UK and USA, and of the main international organisations. *American Statistics Index* (US

Congressional Information Service) is a comprehensive quarterly guide and index to the statistical publications of the United States Government, and *Statistics sources,* edited by Paul Wasserman and Joanne Paskar (4th ed., Gale Research, 1974) is a subject guide to mainly US statistical data.

There are also a number of guides, mainly written by lecturers in economics and statistics, for students and others who need to interpret British economic statistics, and they follow the general pattern of chapters dealing with each of the major fields, describing what information is available, how it is compiled and how it can be used. For many years the most important work of this kind was Ely Devon's *An introduction to British economic statistics* (rev. ed., CUP, 1961), but more recent, and so more up-to-date, are F. M. M. Lewes' *Statistics of the British economy* (Unwin, 1967), A. R. Ilersic's *Statistics* (13th ed., HFL (Publishers) Ltd, 1964), Bernard Edward's *Sources of economic and business statistics* (Heinemann, 1972), and L. R. Connor and A. J. H. Morrell's *Statistics in theory and practice* (6th ed., Pitman, 1972).

The first volumes of a new series of authoritative reviews of various areas of UK statistics were issued in 1974 published by Heinemann for the Royal Statistical Society and the Social Science Research Council, to update the valuable series edited by M. G. Kendall and published in the 1950s in the *Journal of the Royal Statistical Society* and subsequently in book form as *The sources and nature of the statistics of the United Kingdom* (Oliver and Boyd, 1952/57).

Designed particularly for the use of market researchers are the four volumes of Joan M. Harvey's *Statistics: sources for market research* (CBD Research Ltd and Gale Research Ltd), which describe statistical publications and organisations useful for market research throughout the world, the volume covering Europe including the UK. Other guides on more specific subjects are referred to later in this chapter, but a useful source of information on statistical publications of trade and other associations is the *Directory of British Associations* and the *Directory of European Associations* (also CBD Research Ltd and Gale Research Ltd).

GUIDES TO STATISTICAL METHOD

Some of the titles mentioned above are textbooks as well as literature guides, but the following are simply textbooks. There are, in fact, many textbooks on statistical theory and method, including the well-known *An introduction to the theory of statistics,* by G. U. Yule and M. G. Kendall (14th ed., Griffin, 1950), designed for students of statistics and other subjects in which statistics are employed, and the three-volume *The advanced theory of statistics,* by M. G. Kendall and A. Stuart (Griffin, Vol. I: Distribution theory, 3rd ed., 1969. Vol. II: Inference and relationship, 3rd ed., 1973. Vol. III: Design and analysis, and time-series, 2nd ed., 1968), intended as a work of reference for statisticians concerned with theoretical and applied statistics. *Applied general statistics*, by Frederick E. Croxton, Dudley J. Cowden and Sidney Klein (3rd ed., Prentice-Hall and Pitman, 1968) is particularly useful for its chapters on time series and index numbers, and *Introduction to the theory of statistics*, by Alexander M. Mood and Franklin A. Graybill (2nd ed., McGraw-Hill, 1963) is a good introduction to mathematical statistics. *Teach yourself statistics*, by Richard Goodman (EUP, 1957), concentrates on fundamentals and aims to help those who have to teach themselves some of the fundamental ideas and mathematics necessary to understand statistics; and the popular Pelican paperback *Facts from figures*, by M. J. Moroney (rev. ed., Penguin, 1964), is an introduction to the subject intended mainly for those whose work calls for a general knowledge of statistical techniques in the industrial and research world, ranging from purely descriptive statistics to probability theory, the design of sampling schemes and production quality control, but does not include the making of index numbers or forecasting. While really intended for students reading for an honours degree in economics, R. J. Nicholson's *Economic statistics and economic problems* (McGraw-Hill, 1969) shows how available statistical material can be used to investigate economic problems rather than to teach formal statistical methods for economists or to describe sources of economic statistics.

As with statistical theory and method, there is not space in this chapter to mention all the books, mainly textbooks for students again, dealing with management and business statistics, and the reader may, in fact, find other titles than those mentioned here more to his taste. Economics applied to the problems of the firm are dealt with in *Business economics and statistics*, by A. J. Merrett and G. Bannock (Hutchinson, 1962); *Statistics for business studies*, by Derek Gregory and Harold Ward (McGraw-Hill, 1967), is written in an easy style for those interested in statistics rather than having to study them; *Statistical methods for business decisions*, by Charles T. Clark and Lawrence L. Schkade (South-Western Publishing Co. and Edward Arnold, 1969), is oriented towards the digital computer; *Modern business statistics*, by John E. Freund and Frank J. Williams. (2nd ed., Prentice-Hall and Pitman, 1970), claims to be for the future businessmen; and *Statistical methods in management*, by Tom Cass (Cassell, 1969), aims to provide the introduction to statistical methods needed in management services departments for work study, O & M, operational research and computer services. More specialised are *Elements of statistics for market research*, by Pierre Weber (Crosby Lockwood), and *Statistical techniques for market research*, by Robert Ferber (McGraw-Hill, 1949). Sampling techniques are explained in *Sampling methods for censuses and surveys*, by F. Yates (3rd ed., Griffin, 1960), a widely known book written for those with little previous training in mathematical statistics, and *Some theory of sampling*, by W. G. Deming (Dover, 1966).

In the foreword to *An introduction to business forecasting* (Institute of Cost and Works Accountants, 1960) it is stated that 'the techniques of business forecasting have been developed to give a logical and comprehensive means of providing management with information to determine the most advantageous plans which can be made within the anticipated resources of the business' and this small volume of 42 pages compiled by the Institute briefly and clearly describes the technique. *Business forecasting*, by Elmer Bratt (McGraw-Hill, 1958), is a much more detailed guide to forecasting practices and achievements, and *Business economics*, by James Bates and J. R. Parkinson (2nd ed., Blackwell, 1969), has a useful chapter on planning, forecasting and control which includes methods of forecasting and errors involved.

A definitive work on index numbers is Irving Fisher's *The making of index numbers* (3rd ed., Houghton Mifflin, 1927; reprinted by Kelley, 1967), and a more recent work on the subject is W. R. Crow's *Index numbers: theory and applications* (Macdonald and Evans, 1965).

Two useful dictionaries of statistical terms are M. G. Kendall and W. R. Buckland's *A dictionary of statistical terms* (3rd ed., Oliver and Boyd for the International Statistical Institute, 1971) and John E. Freund and Frank J. Williams' *Dictionary/outline of basic statistics* (McGraw-Hill, 1966). A comprehensive survey of international and national systems of weights and measures and unit weights for a variety of different commodities is given in the United Nations' *World weights and measures* (1966).

STATISTICAL SERIALS AND MONOGRAPHS

General Compilations

General compilations carrying summary statistics on a wide range of subjects are useful when not much detail is required. The tables usually include a run of several months, quarters, or years of earlier figures so enabling trends to be noted. The Central Statistical Office's *Annual Abstract of Statistics* (HMSO), supplemented by the *Monthly Digest of Statistics*, contains a wealth of information relating to the UK, while the annual *Abstract of Regional Statistics* (HMSO), the Scottish Statistical Office's annual *Scottish Abstract of Statistics* (HMSO), the Welsh Office's annual *Digest of Welsh Statistics* (HMSO) and the twice-yearly *Digest of Statistics, Northern Ireland* (HMSO, Belfast), compiled by the Economic Section of the Cabinet Office at Belfast, contain such information as is available on a regional basis.

The British economy: key statistics (Times Newspapers Ltd) contains over 200 tables of economic and social background information on the long-term development of the economy and this, issued annually, is supplemented by data in the quarterly *Bulletin of the London and Cambridge Economic Service*, now published first in *The Times* newspaper and later in booklet form. The Central Statistical Office's monthly *Economic Trends* (HMSO) and annual *Social Trends* (HMSO) and the National Institute for Economic and Social Research's *National Institute Economic Review* all contain statistical tables and graphs showing trends and can be used as a basis for forecasting. *Economic Trends* includes data on employment, output, consumption, prices, trade and finance; *Social Trends* includes data on employment, leisure, personal income and expenditure, education and housing; and the *National Institute Economic Review* includes data on gross domestic product, industrial production, the labour market, productivity, prices, incomes, consumer expenditure and retail sales, finance, and foreign trade as well as gross national product and industrial production for selected countries overseas for comparison. For general historical statistics there is B. R. Mitchell and P. Deane's *Abstract of British historical statistics* (CUP, 1962), which includes information up to about 1938, and its supplement *Second abstract of British historical statistics*, by B. R. Mitchell and H. G. Jones (CUP, 1971). Similar compilations of the United States are the Bureau of the Census's *Statistical Abstract of the United States* (US Government Printing Office), which includes both national and state statistics, the annual *Economic Report of the President to the Congress* (US Government Printing Office), the Council of Economic Advisers' monthly *Economic Indicators* (US Government Printing Office) and the Office of. Management and Budget's new annual *Social Indicators* (US Government Printing Office). Historical statistics are published in two supplements to the *Statistical Abstract . . ., Historical Statistics . . ., to 1957* and *Historical Statistics . . . continuation to 1962 . . .*

Practically every country in the world collects, analyses and publishes more or less the same kind of statistical data in more or less the same amount of detail. International or intergovernmental organisations such as the United Nations (UN), the European Economic Community (EEC), and the Organisation for Economic Co-operation and Development (OECD) collect statistical data from member countries, often in a somewhat different form from that published in the countries themselves because of the need for the data published internationally to be comparative nationally so far as is possible. The most important international statistical publications of a general nature are the United Nations' *Statistical Yearbook* and *Monthly Bulletin of Statistics*, with data from all countries reporting to the United Nations, and UNESCO's *Statistical Yearbook*, which is limited to more social data than the former titles. For information on countries which are members of OECD there is the monthly *Main Economic Indicators*, indicating recent economic developments in those countries, and for the countries, which are members of the EEC there is the annual *Basic Statistics of the Community* and the monthly *General Statistical Bulletin.*

Population

The base source of statistics of population is, of course, the decennial census of population, taken for England and Wales by the Office of Population. Censuses and Surveys, for Scotland by the General Register Office, Scotland, and for Northern Ireland by the General Register Office, Northern Ireland. *Guides to official sources, No. 2: census reports of Great Britain, 1801–1931* (HMSO, 1951), compiled by the Interdepartmental Committee on Social and Economic Research, is valuable for describing the earlier census reports and it is understood that this guide is being revised and updated to 1966 by the OPCS. Another useful work in this field is Bernard Benjamin's *Population census* (Heinemann for SSRC, 1970), which explains the practices and problems of taking population censuses in Britain. Each office collects and analyses the data in a slightly different form, but there is now more co-ordination than there used to be and some of the volumes published cover Great Britain as a whole, while others are devoted to each of the three separate areas, and there are also detailed volumes for each county. The latest census was taken in 1971 and is currently being published by HMSO. A sample census was taken for the first time in 1966, but it is not yet known whether this will be a regular practice in between the full censuses. More up-to-date estimates of population are published in the *Statistical Review of England and Wales* (HMSO), *Annual Estimates of the Population of England and Wales and of Local Authority Areas* (HMSO), *Quarterly Return for England and Wales* (HMSO), equivalent publications for Scotland and Northern Ireland, and the more general statistical compilations. In 1971 a new annual publication, *Population Projections* (HMSO), was introduced by the OPCS with information previously summarised in the *Annual Abstract of Statistics.* Prepared by the Government Actuary, each issue covers 40 years and includes for each county and the UK as a whole estimates of the basic population by sex and age, marital condition, mortality, births and migration.

The latest population census for the US was taken in 1970 by the Bureau of the Census and is being published by the Government Printing Office, and the Bureau's series of *Current Population Reports* (US Government Printing Office) includes more up-to-date information on a variety of subjects concerned with population.

Internationally, the Statistical Office of the United Nations, apart from including statistics of population in the *Statistical Yearbook* and *Monthly Bulletin of Statistics*, issues a *Demographic Yearbook* which covers about 200 geographical areas of the world and statistical data on all aspects of demography, some of the tables being updated by the quarterly *Population and Vital Statistics Report* of the World Health Organisation. Population forecasts for the world are given in *Growth of the world's urban and rural population, 1920–2000* (UN) and for part of the world in *Demographic trends, 1965–1980, in Western Europe and North America* (OECD).

National Accounts, Finance and Business Statistics

The most important publication in this field in the UK is the 'blue book', *National Income and Expenditure* (HMSO), compiled annually by the Central Statistical Office, which contains data on the British economy, including gross national product, national expenditure, personal income and expenditure, taxation, capital formation, etc. A detailed description of the basis and methods used in the calculation of the data published in the book is given in *National accounts statistics: sources and methods* (HMSO, 1968). A white paper, *Preliminary estimates of national income and balance of payments* (HMSO), is published several months earlier than the 'blue book', at the time of the Budget, and quarterly estimates of the main national accounts tables appear in *Economic Trends* and the *Monthly Digest of Statistics*. A number of government publications relating to the national finances are issued throughout the year from the *Civil Estimates* to *National Income and Expenditure*, and the pattern is described briefly in Joan M. Harvey's *Sources of statistics*. Local government finance statistics are described in W. Barker's *Local government statistics* (Institution of Municipal Treasurers and Accountants, 1965).

As has already been mentioned, the Radcliffe Committee was instrumental in the introduction of two valuable publications dealing with financial statistics, the Central Statistical Office's monthly *Financial Statistics* (HMSO) and the *Bank of England Quarterly Bulletin* (the Bank), the former containing the key monetary and banking statistics of the UK and the latter mainly confined to banking statistics. The US Federal Reserve System's monthly *Federal Reserve Bulletin* (Federal Reserve Service) is the standard source of statistics dealing with money and banking in the United States.

On an international basis, the United Nations publishes a *Yearbook of National Accounts Statistics*, OECD issues *National Accounts of OECD Countries*, and the EEC has an annual supplement, *National Accounts*, to the *General Statistical Bulletin*. The International Monetary Fund publishes the monthly *International Financial Statistics*, which includes both international and national monetary and banking statistics, and OECD issues *OECD Financial Statistics* twice a year, with comparative information on financial markets for most countries.

Statistics of new UK company registrations are given monthly in the

Departments of Trade, Industry and Prices and Consumer Protection's journal *Trade and Industry* (HMSO), more detailed information on companies as a whole being in the *Business Monitor: miscellaneous series, M3: Company finance*, which includes an analysis of large companies, and *M7: Acquisitions and mergers of companies*. Less detailed information is also included in *Financial Statistics*, the *Bank of England Quarterly Bulletin*, the *Monthly Digest of Statistics* and the *Annual Abstract of Statistics*, but data about individual companies can be found only in the annual reports of the companies, in the card services provided by such organisations as Extel Statistical Services Ltd and Moodies' British Company Service, and in reference books such as the *Stock Exchange Official Yearbook*.

The Times 1000: leading companies in Britain and overseas (Times Newspapers Ltd) is the best source of company ranking, listing the top UK companies and the leading European companies, and including many smaller lists of more specialised and usually financial companies and other institutions. Company ranking in particular industries is often published in the trade or professional press devoted to the industry. Apart from *The Times 1000* . . ., the most important US and international listings are published by the American magazine *Fortune*.

Company investment statistics are published in *Statistics Relating to Securities Quoted on the London Stock Exchange* and *Interest and Dividends upon Securities Quoted on the Stock Exchange*, both issued annually by the London Stock Exchange. Indexes of general movements in security prices are published in newspapers and in economic and financial journals, and include the FT actuaries share index in the *Financial Times* and *The Times* stock exchange indices in *The Times*.

Personnel

The main source of UK employment and unemployment statistics is the Department of Employment, so that the most detailed data is published in the *Department of Employment Gazette*, some information also being published in the *Monthly Digest of Statistics* and subsequently in *British Labour Statistics: yearbook* (HMSO), the *Annual Abstract of Statistics*, *Social Trends* and the *Abstract of Regional Statistics*. The University Grants Committee compiles an annual *First Employment of University Graduates* (HMSO), and there are, of course, employment statistics included in the annual reports and statistical volumes devoted to individual industries, referred to on pp. 164–165.

Earnings of manual workers are given in the Department of Employment's publications mentioned above, and the department now undertakes an annual sample survey of the earnings of manual and non-manual employees in all industries and service trades in the UK, average earnings being analysed by industry, occupation, etc. Preliminary results of the survey are published in the gazette and full results later in *New Earnings Survey* (HMSO). The Institute of Office Management publishes in alternate years *Clerical Salaries Analysis*, which compares wage increases of clerical workers with cost of living increases, and the Incomes Data Service publishes information on wages, negotiations and income policy in *Incomes Data*. Some data on the distribution of personal incomes by range of income, analysed geographically, are included in the annual *Inland Revenue Statistics* (HMSO), and quarterly data on personal income are published in *Economic Trends*, *Financial Statistics* and the *Monthly Digest of Statistics*. The US Bureau of Labor Statistics' *Monthly Labor Review* (US Government Printing Office) is the most important US publication in this field, with current data on employment, earnings of workers, consumer price index, wholesale prices, etc.

Internationally, the International Labour Office issues a *Yearbook of Labour Statistics* and a quarterly *Bulletin of Labour Statistics*, with a monthly updating supplement. The OECD publishes annually *Labour Force Statistics*, the latest issue covering the years 1960 to 1971; published *Statistics of the occupational and educational structure of the labour force in 53 countries* in 1969; and includes labour statistics in *Main Economic Indicators*. The EEC occasionally devotes an issue of *Social Statistics* to employment, wages and salaries, and also includes this kind of information in the *General Statistical Bulletin*. The United Nations' *Monthly Bulletin of Statistics* includes, twice a year, a useful table of retail price comparisons to determine salary differentials of United Nations officials, and Associated Industrial Consultants Ltd publishes *International salaries and fringe benefits*, with information for about eight countries, not necessarily the same ones in each edition.

Production

The Ministry of Agriculture, Fisheries and Food's *Agricultural and food statistics: a guide to official sources* (HMSO, 1969), complemented by the National Economic Development Office's *Food statistics: a guide to the major official and unofficial United Kingdom sources* (NEDO, 1969), are the main guides to statistics of agriculture, fisheries and food. The most important publications in this field are the annual *Agricultural Statistics, United Kingdom* (HMSO) and the separate publications with much the same title covering England and Wales, Scotland and Northern Ireland, which have more geographical detail; *Sea fisheries statistical tables* (HMSO) and similar titles covering Scotland and Northern Ireland; and the *Business Monitor: production series* (HMSO), which includes issues on production statistics for some manufactured foods. US publications include the Department of Agriculture's annual *Agricultural Statistics*

Statistical Publications

(US Government Printing Office), the Department of the Interior's Bureau of Commercial Fisheries' *Fishery Statistics of the United States*, and *Commodity Yearbook* (Commodity Research Bureau). Internationally, the publications of the United Nations Food and Agriculture Organisation (FAO), *Production Yearbook* and *Monthly Bulletin of Agricultural Economics and Statistics*, are important, and both OECD and EEC issue statistical publications on agriculture, while the Commonwealth Secretariat has a sizeable publishing programme on world production, trade, consumption and prices of certain crops.

Detailed censuse of industrial production for the UK were taken every few years from 1907 to 1968, very much less detailed censuses, useful for showing current trends, being taken in intervening years. These earlier censuses up to and including 1958 are described in the Interdepartmental Committee on Social and Economic Research's *Guides to official sources, no. 6: censuses of production* (HMSO, 1961). *Reports of the 1968 Census of Production* (HMSO, 1970–74) is published in 171 parts, including a description of the census, reports for individual industries, an index of products, a directory of business industries covered by the census and summary tables. From 1970 most of the information (total purchases and sales, stocks, capital expenditure, employment and wages in establishments engaged in manufacturing, mining and quarrying, electricity, gas and water supply) is being collected annually and again published in a number of parts as the information becomes available, and will now be in the *Business Monitor: census series*. Supplementary enquiries are to be made at longer intervals. *Input–output statistics* (HMSO) have so far been based mainly on the results of the censuses of production for 1954, 1963 and 1968.

Statistics of production (and sometimes also of exports from and sales in the UK) in individual industries are published in the *Business Monitor: production series*, of which there are now nearly 100 and will soon be increased to 165 titles, mostly issued quarterly but a few issued monthly. Less detailed data are published in the *Annual Abstract of Statistics*, the *Abstract of Regional Statistics*, the *Monthly Digest of Statistics* and *Trade and Industry*. The index of industrial production is published monthly in the *Monthly Digest of Statistics* and *Economic Trends*, both unadjusted and seasonally adjusted index numbers for production in manufacturing industries being given, the seasonally adjusted tables also appearing in *Trade and Industry* once a month. The index is explained in *Index of industrial production and other output measures* (HMSO, 1970). The US Bureau of the Census conducts a *Census of Manufactures* (US Government Printing Office) at regular intervals and the information is updated between censuses by the annual *US Industrial Outlook* (US Government Printing Office), while more current data are published in a series of *Current Industrial Reports* (US Government Printing Office), issued either quarterly or monthly.

Detailed statistics for individual industries are often published in more specialised publications, such as the Department of Energy's annual *Digest of United Kingdom Energy Statistics* (HMSO), the annual reports of nationalised industries, the Institute of Petroleum's *UK Petroleum Industry Statistics,* the National Economic Development Office's *Annual Statistical Survey of the Electronics Industry* (HMSO), *The mechanical engineering industry—a digest of statistical information, 1971* (NEDO) and annual *Motor Industry Statistics* (NEDO). There is also a monthly *Business Monitor: miscellaneous series: motor vehicle registration,* and statistics of all kinds concerning the motor industry are given in detail in the Society of Motor Manufacturers and Traders' annual *Motor Industry of Great Britain* and *Monthly Statistical Review.* Examples of other trade and research associations' statistical publications include the Scientific Instrument Manufacturers' Association of Great Britain's annual *Statistics of the Instrument Industry,* the Furniture Industry Research Association's *Economic Review for the Furniture Industry,* the British Footwear Manufacturers' Federation's *Footwear Industry Statistical Review,* and the Iron and Steel Statistics Bureau's *Iron and Steel Industry: annual statistics* and *Iron and Steel Industry: monthly statistics.* Most of these publications have data on production, sales, foreign trade, employment, finance, etc.

Most official information about prices is given in the form of index numbers, except for agricultural products given in the publications of agricultural statistics already referred to. There is an annual article on prices in *Trade and Industry* and a table in the *Annual Abstract of Statistics* which gives average wholesale prices for certain imported commodities. When issued at all, the current wholesale prices of individual commodities are usually to be found in journals related to the industry or trade concerned, such as the *Public Ledger, Metal Bulletin,* etc. Index numbers of wholesale prices are given monthly in *Trade and Industry* and the *Monthly Digest of Statistics* and annually in the *Annual Abstract of Statistics.* International wholesale price indexes are published in *International Financial Statistics* and the United Nations' *Statistical Yearbook* and *Monthly Bulletin of Statistics.*

The United Nations' Statistical Office compiles an important two-volume work, *The growth of world industry.* Published every two or three years it shows internationally comparable data on industry in about 100 countries, with national data on gross national product, production indexes characteristics, etc., in one volume and international data in the other. The EEC issues a quarterly and annual *Industrial Statistics,* containing index numbers of industrial production and production statistics for the Common Market countries. OECD includes industrial statistics in *Main Economic Indicators* but its more important contribution in this field is the annual volumes devoted to individual industries, such as *The Chemical Industry, The Iron and Steel Industry, The Non-ferrous Metals Industry, The Pulp and Paper Industry, The Textile Industry, The Cement Industry* and *The Hides, Skins and Footwear Industry.* These volumes are mainly, but not entirely, concerned with industry in the OECD member countries and cover supply and demand, raw materials situation, employment, investment and prices, as well as production and trade. Also for individual industries, there are important volumes, usually annual, issued by a variety of organisations, such as the Institute of Geological Science's *Statistical Summary of the Mineral Industry: world production, exports and imports* (HMSO), *Metal Bulletin Handbook* (Metal Bulletin Ltd), *World Metal Statistics* (World Bureau of Metal Statistics), *Quarterly Statistical Review* (Textile Statistics Bureau), *International Cotton Industry Statistics* (Federation of Cotton and Allied Textile Industries), the Society of Motor Manufacturers and Traders' *Motor Industry of Great Britain,* which, despite its title, has international coverage, *World Automotive Market* (Automobile International), *World Energy Supplies* (United Nations' Statistical Office), *BP Statistical Review of the World Oil Industry* (British Petroleum Co. Ltd) and *Oil: world statistics* (Institute of Petroleum).

Marketing

Two important publications of the Institute of Marketing, both edited by E. B. Groves, are *Basic economic planning data* (3rd ed., 1970/71), which makes available and comparable in a simple format all the statistics necessary for the location and appraisal of area markets in the UK, such as population, employees, incomes, retail spending, car density, and rateable values by regions, counties and, for some of the information, the major cities; and *Basic sales grid—UK: research and compilation* (2nd ed., 1970/71), which is based on a geographical grid system, dividing the UK into approximately 600 economically significant areas. The *IPC Marketing Manual of the United Kingdom* (International Publishing Corporations Ltd, 4th ed., 1974), edited by R. A. Critchley, is another useful publication which aims to bring together basic planning data for market research. Divided into three sections, it contains basic statistics showing social and economic trends, summary information on markets for over 90 product fields, expenditure and other information on media and advertising. The results of market surveys carried out by newspapers and journals are often published and when current can be a useful source of marketing information.

Until comparatively recently, statistics of internal trade scarcely existed but the situation has improved. In 1970 the National Economic Development Office produced a useful publication, *Distributive-trade statistics: a guide to official sources* (HMSO), to assist the searcher to identify suitable UK publications, but this is already somewhat out of date. A *Census of Distribution and other Services* (HMSO) is taken every 5 years, but only every 10 years is this done in detail, the intermediate censuses being sample enquiries. Only the first of these censuses, for 1950, covered the wholesale trade as well as retail and service trades. The census for 1971 covered retail trades and service trades such as hairdressing, laundering and drycleaning, pawnbroking, footwear repairing, check trading, and the installation, maintenance, hire and repair of consumer goods such as radios and television sets. The wholesale trade, motor trades, and hotel and catering industry are the subject of large-scale quinquennial enquiries concerning sales, stocks, capital expenditure, etc., the results of which are now published in *Trade and Industry* and were previously published in its forerunner, the *Board of Trade Journal.* The *Business Monitor: service and distributive series* includes monthly titles with data on food shops (SD1), clothing and furniture shops (SD2), durable goods shops (SD3), miscellaneous non-food shops (SD4), catering trades (SD5), and instalment credit business of retailers (SD8). Less detailed data on these topics are published in *Trade and Industry*, the *Monthly Digest of Statistics* and the *Annual Abstract of Statistics.* The only internal trade statistics issued on an international basis are those included in the general compilations of the United Nations, OECD, EEC, etc.

The most important source of UK foreign trade statistics is the monthly *Overseas Trade Statistics of the United Kingdom* (HMSO), which contains statistics for the month and cumulated figures for the year up to and including that month of visible trade arranged initially in order of commodities, subdivided by countries of origin in the case of imports and destination in the case of exports. Because the figures are cumulated each month, the December issue has statistics for the whole year. However, a more detailed five-volume *Annual Statement of the Overseas Trade of the United Kingdom* is published later, with separate volumes of summary tables, exports and re-exports, imports and re-imports, trade by countries and trade by ports. Foreign trade statistics are also given, but in very much less detail, in *Trade and Industry*, the *Monthly Digest of Statistics*, *Economic Trends*, some of the *Business Monitor: production series*, the *Annual Abstract of Statistics*, and some of the publications devoted to particular industries referred to earlier in the section on production statistics. As with many government departments collecting and analysing statistics, HM Customs and Excise uses a computer and it is possible to obtain for a small charge from the Bill of Entry Section of the Statistical Office of HM Customs and Excise (27 Victoria Avenue, Southend-on-Sea, Essex) regular or *ad hoc* tabulations showing the trade of a particular commodity listed in HM Customs and Excise's *Guide to the classification for overseas trade statistics* (HMSO). The main source of US internal trade is the 5-yearly *Census of Business* (US Government Printing Office) of the Bureau of the Census. The Bureau also issues a series of regular foreign trade statistics under the over-all title of *US Foreign Trade* (US Government

Printing Office), the contents of each title in the series being described in its annual *Guide to Foreign Trade Statistics* (US Government Printing Office).

The United Nations Statistical Office collects quarterly or annual statistics of external trade from reporting member countries and publishes them as received in *Commodity Trade Statistics*, arranged initially in order of countries, subdivided by commodities, and subdivided again by countries of origin or destination, making the computer tapes available later to Walker and Co., of New York, who publish *World Trade Annual. World Trade Annual* consists of five main volumes showing the trade of 24 principal industrialised countries (Vol. 1—food, beverages, crude inedible materials, mineral and vegetable oils and fats; Vol. 2—fuels, lubricants, chemicals; Vol. 3—manufactured goods; Vol. 4—miscellaneous manufactured articles; Vol. 5—machinery and transport equipment, etc.) and five supplementary volumes on the trade of the industrialised countries with Eastern Europe and the developing countries, each volume dealing with a particular geographical area. The United Nations also issues a more general *Yearbook of International Trade Statistics*, which is useful for indicating trends in international trade. OECD publishes a series of *Foreign Trade Statistics*, consisting of *Series A: overall trade by countries,* issued quarterly with monthly updating supplements; *Series B: trade by commodities, analytical abstracts*, issued quarterly; and *Series C: trade by commodities, market summaries*, issued half-yearly. EEC issues quarterly detailed analytical tables of foreign trade, *Commerce Extérieur: tableaux analytiques (NIMEXE)*, and also a less detailed monthly, *Commerce Extérieur: statistiques mensuelles.*

Both the Institute of Practitioners in Advertising and the Advertisers' Association collect statistics but publish very little. The main publications containing advertising statistics are the monthly *ASR (Advertising Statistical Review)* (Legion Information Services Ltd); *British Rate and Data* (Audit Bureau of Circulation), which has a supplement, *ABC: the half-yearly circulation review*; and *MEAL Monthly Digest* (Media Expenditure Analysis Ltd).

Some retail prices of foodstuffs in the UK, derived from prices collected for the general index of retail prices, are given in the *Department of Employment Gazette* each month, and retail price indexes are also published in the gazette, the *Monthly Digest of Statistics*, the *Annual Abstract of Statistics* and *Social Trends*. The index of retail prices is often referred to as the cost of living index, but the old cost of living index, devised in 1914 and discontinued in 1947, covered only the necessities of life, whereas the index of retail prices covers all normal items of expenditure on retail goods and services. The current index is explained in the Department of Employment's *Method of construction and calculation of the index of retail prices* (4th ed., HMSO, 1967). The Cost of Living

Advisory Committee, set up to decide the pattern of the index, recommended in its interim report (Cmd 8328) that an enquiry should take place into the pattern of expenditure of private households as a source for the weighting pattern of the index of retail prices, as a result of which the first household expenditure survey was taken. Now taken annually by the Department of Employment, the *Family Expenditure Survey* (HMSO) includes household expenditure tables by income and composition of the household, by administrative area and by occupation of the head of the household. There is also the Ministry of Agriculture, Fisheries and Food's annual *Household Food Consumption and Expenditure* (HMSO), and the Office of Population Censuses and Surveys have now published the first *General Household Survey* for the year 1970 (HMSO, 1973). Quarterly estimated statistics of consumers' expenditure, based on a wide variety of sources, including retail sales, the national food survey and the family expenditure survey, are published in *Economic Trends* and the *Monthly Digest of Statistics*.

Internationally, retail price indexes are included in the monthly *International Financial Statistics*, the *Yearbook of Labour Statistics*, the *Bulletin of Labour Statistics* and the United Nations' *Statistical Yearbook and Monthly Bulletin of Statistics*.

COLLECTIONS OF STATISTICAL PUBLICATIONS AND STATISTICS

Good collections of the statistical publications of a country, particularly government publications, together with the general statistical abstracts or yearbooks of a selection of other countries and the more important statistical publications of international organisations, can usually be found in the reference departments of the larger public libraries, and the more important general titles of the home country are taken by the smaller public libraries. Some university libraries take all the government publications of their country, while others have a more selective acquisitions policy. However, collections in universities and other academic institutions are not always easily accessible to those outside such institutions, although the current trend is in this direction. For instance, Warwick University Library is building up a collection of both British and foreign statistical publications and offers a service to businessmen and others outside the university. National libraries usually collect all their own country's official publications and much foreign material. For instance, the State Paper Room at the British Library, Reference Division, housed in the British Museum, collects both British and foreign official publications, although owing to shortage of space the foreign material is not always immediately available to the reader. The Department of Industry's Statistics and Market Intelligence Library has a good collection of British published statistics and is, in fact, designated the statistics library for all government departments, but it is even more important for its collection of national statistical publications of other countries and international statistical publications.

A few years ago what is now the Committee of Librarians and Statisticians surveyed the position regarding the availability in the UK of statistical publications, and have produced *A Union list of statistical serials in British libraries* (Library Association, 1972) and *Economic statistics collections: a directory of research resources in the United Kingdom for business, industry and public affairs* (Library Association, 1970). The union list includes statistical serials compiled by UK government departments, international organisations such as the United Nations, OECD and EEC, and non-official organisations, which are arranged alphabetically by title with locations and their holdings listed under each title; a subject index allows for a subject approach to the union list. The directory lists organisations, excluding the large formally organised libraries containing statistical material, which hold collections of economic statistics, and, because of its geographical arrangement of libraries, it can be a useful means of locating a local or reasonably accessible source of statistical information on a required subject.

Unpublished statistical information is often available from the government departments which collect it and sometimes from the trade associations and other organisations. Much depends on the confidentiality of the material, but reasons for not publishing all the detail available may simply be the high cost involved or the lack of demand for the information. One can only suggest that when such unpublished data are required the most likely organisation to have collected it be approached. Government departments involved in the collection and processing of statistics have for some time been aided by computers; when this is the case, it is often possible for a program to be devised to produce from the basic data information in a different pattern or form from that given in the published tables as well as more detail. The trend seems to be that more and more of the computer-processed data will be retained for longer periods by the processing organisation, official or non-official, and that data banks will be accumulated. One data bank which has been in existence since 1967 is the Social Science Research Council's data bank, now called the SSRC Survey Archive, at the University of Essex, which was set up to help social scientists, accepting data from social and other surveys carried out by central government, local government, market research organisations and other organisations.

SOME WAYS IN WHICH PUBLISHED STATISTICS CAN BE USED

At home there is the need to watch trends in demand for the product, and to know what the total home market is so that an assessment can be made as to whether the firm is maintaining its share. For the majority of industries, useful information on production, manufacturers' sales or deliveries, imports and exports can be found in the appropriate quarterly, sometimes monthly publication, *Business Monitor: production series.* P 48, for example, includes data on manufacturers' sales, imports and exports of cameras (*Figures 9.1 and 9.2*). Much less detail is to be found regarding retail sales, as can be seen in *Business Monitor: service and distributive series*, where sales of cameras are included in the group 'Chemists, photographic dealers' (*Figure 9.3*), although these index numbers can be useful to show trends.

Similarly, firms which export need to be aware of trends in export trade as well as international trade and the trade of individual countries overseas. Some information on the UK export trade of individual products is given in the *Business Monitor: production series* (*Figure 9.2*), but more detailed breakdowns are published in the monthly *Overseas Trade Statistics* and the *Annual Statement of the Trade of the United Kingdom.* The monthly figures (*Figure 9.4*) are much less detailed than those in the *Annual Statement . . .* (*Figure 9.5*), which are issued at a much later date. However, it is possible to obtain the more detailed breakdown on a monthly basis from the Bill of Entry Service of HM Customs and Excise (see p. 167) in the form of photocopies of computer print-out.

Published statistics are one of several sources of market research into retail trade in a particular area and can be based on the relevant distribution statistics, such as the detailed *Report on the census of distribution and other services.* Taken only once every 10 years and including data for the country as a whole, for regions and for large towns by kind of business (*Figure 9.6*), the census results can be used as bench-marks and updated, if only by estimated figures, by the trends shown in the less detailed census taken 5 years later and by the *Business Monitor: service and distributive series* (*Figure 9.3*), which indicates the percentage increases or decreases for the country as a whole.

Profit from facts, a booklet issued by the UK Government Statistical Office and available free from the Central Statistical Office, contains a number of case studies indicating some of the various ways in which official statistics can be used, and is a valuable practical guide for those who have little experience of the uses to which published statistics can be put.

Both official and non-official statistics can be utilised in a surprising number of individual ways to suit particular needs, and a knowledge of what statistical data exist is very often the first step towards the compilation of important factual data.

1 SALES OF PHOTOGRAPHIC AND DOCUMENT COPYING EQUIPMENT BY UK MANUFACTURERS (a)

	1972	4th Qtr 1971	1st Qtr 1972	2nd Qtr 1972	3rd Qtr 1972R	4th Qtr 1972P
	£ thous	£ thous	£ thous	£ thous	£ thous	£ thous
Still cameras and projectors	6,913	1,216	1,448	1,830	1,765	1,870
Cinematographic Cameras and projectors	1,029	421	434	255	210	130
Other photographic and cinematographic equipment (including document copying machines and microfilm equipment but excluding lenses, chemicals and sensitized materials)	60,120	16,191	14,709	13,270	14,820	17,321
Unclassified sales and work done	766	187	180	206	182	198
TOTAL SALES OF PRINCIPAL PRODUCTS OF THE PHOTOGRAPHIC AND DOCUMENT COPYING EQUIPMENT INDUSTRY (MLH 351) AND WORK DONE	68,828	18,015	16,771	15,561	16,977	19,519
Less sales (included above) of principal products of MLH 351 by establishments classified to other industries	8,140	1,421	1,254	1,867	2,450	2,569
Plus sales by establishments classified to MLH 351 of principal products of other industries	1,582	874	432	320	458	372
Plus services rendered	216	21	99	34	76	7
Plus sales of merchanted goods	2,015	532	463	441	460	651
TOTAL SALES AND WORK DONE BY ESTABLISHMENTS CLASSIFIED TO THE PHOTOGRAPHIC AND DOCUMENT COPYING EQUIPMENT INDUSTRY (MLH 351)	64,501	18,021	16,511	14,489	15,521	17,980

(a) Please see note on coverage in introduction

Values are net selling values: purchase tax, trade discounts and commissions are excluded

Sales are deliveries on sale for home and abroad: forward sales are excluded.

Figure 9.1

2a IMPORTS AND EXPORTS OF PHOTOGRAPHIC AND DOCUMENT COPYING EQUIPMENT (a)

	1972	4th Qtr 1971	1st Qtr 1972	2nd Qtr 1972	3rd Qtr 1972	4th Qtr 1972
	£ thous	£ thous	£ thous	£ thous	£ thous	£ thous
Imports (cif)	(c)					
Still cameras and projectors	13,564	2,073	2,776	3,273	3,916	3,575
Cinematographic cameras and projectors	7,099	1,399	1,309	1,929	1,795	2,036
Other photographic and cinematographic equipment (including document copying machines and microfilm equipment but excluding lenses, chemicals and sensitized materials)	31,548	5,457	6,296	7,000	8,183	10,204
Total	52,211	8,929	10,381	12,202	13,894	15,815

Exports (fob)(c)						
Still cameras and projectors	12,617	2,942	2,729	3,247	2,439	3,984
Cinematographic cameras and projectors	1,773	587	638	410	317	386
Other photographic and cinematographic equipment (including document copying machines and microfilm equipment but excluding lenses, chemicals and sensitized materials)	59,576	18,271	15,962	14,026	11,727	17,983
Total	73,966	21,800	19,329	17,683	14,483	22,353

(a) The relationship between the sales and overseas trade headings is shown in table 2b

(b) These figures include re-exports in addition to exports of UK-produced goods.

(c) Annual totals include periodic revisions and are not strictly comparable to the quarterly breakdown.

Source: Overseas Trade Statistics

Figure 9.2

VALUE OF RETAIL SALES (AT CURRENT PRICES)

ANALYSIS BY DETAILED KINDS OF BUSINESS AND FORM OF ORGANISATION

1966 = 100

Index numbers of values of sales per week, and percentage increase on a year earlier

KIND OF BUSINESS (Sales in 1966)		Year	1st Qtr	2nd Qtr	3rd Qtr	4th Qtr	Jan.	Feb.	Mar.*	Apr.	May	June*	July	Aug.	Sept.*	Oct.	Nov.	Dec.*
MISCELLANEOUS NON-FOOD SHOPS																		
Miscellaneous non-food shops Total (£2,570 million)	1969	113	99	109	113	131	96	96	103	107	111	109	114*	114	111	112	117	157
	1970	120	104	115	120	141	100	102	109	112	116	117	123	122	117	119	126	170
	1971	129	110	124	130	154	106	107	115	122	125	125	132	130	127	129	137	188
	1972	144	123	134	143	175	118	119	130	128	135	138	145	144	141	146	153	217
	1970	7	6	6	8	8	5	7	6	5	5	8	8	7	6	7	7	7
	1971	8	5	8	8	9	5	5	5	9	8	7	8	7	9	9	9	10
	1972	11	12	8	10	14	11	11	13	5	8	10	10	10	11	13	12	15
Confectioners, tobacconists, newsagents Total (£1,040 million)	1969	112	103	109	112	123	101	102	106	111	108	109	112*	112	111	114	116	135
	1970	119	111	116	119	129	107	109	117	114	116	118	120	121	116	120	123	141
	1971	125	113	123	127	137	110	112	117	122	122	124	129	128	126	127	129	152
	1972	136	125	130	137	151	120	121	133	125	133	133	137	136	137	138	141	168
	1970	6	8	7	6	6	6	7	10	3	7	9	7	8	4	6	6	5
	1971	5	2	6	7	6	3	3	1	7	5	5	7	6	9	5	5	7
	1972	8	10	6	7	10	9	8	13	2	8	7	6	7	9	9	9	11
Independents (£889 million)	1969	111	103	109	111	121	101	101	105	110	108	109	112*	112	110	113	115	131
	1970	118	110	115	118	127	106	107	115	113	115	118	120	120	115	120	122	137
	1971	125	112	123	128	136	108	111	116	121	123	125	128	129	126	127	128	149
	1972	135	124	130	137	148	118	120	131	124	133	133	136	137	137	138	140	164
	1970	6	7	6	6	5	5	6	9	2	6	8	7	7	5	6	6	5
	1971	6	2	7	8	7	2	4	1	7	7	6	7	8	10	6	5	8
	1972	8	10	6	7	9	9	8	13	3	8	7	6	6	9	9	9	10
Multiples (£151 million)	1969	116	108	109	114	134	106	105	113	114	108	106	111*	114	117	120	122	154
	1970	127	120	120	123	142	115	118	127	120	121	120	124	126	121	125	130	165
	1971	129	121	126	126	146	121	119	123	129	120	120	131	124	124	128	134	169
	1972	142	134	131	138	164	130	130	142	131	131	130	140	135	138	142	149	193
	1970	9	11	10	8	6	8	13	13	5	11	13	12	10	4	4	7	7
	1971	3	2	2	2	3	5	1	-3	8	-	-	6	-1	3	2	3	3
	1972	10	11	6	8	12	7	9	15	1	9	9	7	9	11	11	11	14
Booksellers, stationers Independents (£80 million)	1969	121	110	100	114	158	112	106	113	99	99	100	107*	110	122	137	144	187
	1970	132	118	112	124	173	118	118	119	118	109	111	121	116	132	144	158	207
	1971	147	125	126	138	199	128	114	130	124	125	128	131	133	157	166	179	243
	1972	164	145	140	153	220	150	137	147	137	141	141	152	150	184	184	197	268
	1970	9	7	13	8	9	6	12	5	19	10	11	13	10	8	5	10	11
	1971	12	5	11	11	16	9	-4	10	5	15	16	8	15	15	15	13	17
	1972	12	16	11	11	10	17	20	13	10	13	10	16	13	7	11	10	10
Chemists, photographic goods dealers Total (b) (£353 million)	1969	114	95	110	119	132	96	93	97	103	109	116	125*	123	110	107	111	168
	1970	122	99	117	128	145	99	98	100	104	117	127	134	133	117	117	122	185
	1971	139	110	132	145	168	109	107	113	120	134	139	156	147	136	134	140	218
	1972	157	125	143	162	198	125	120	128	129	145	153	172	166	154	154	163	262
	1970	7	4	7	8	10	3	5	3	1	8	10	7	8	5	10	10	11
	1971	13	11	13	16	16	10	9	12	15	15	9	17	10	15	15	15	17
	1972	13	14	9	12	18	15	12	14	8	8	10	11	13	11	15	16	20

(b) These index figures do not reflect chemists' receipts under the National Health Service, which are as far as possible excluded by contributors in their returns.

175

Index numbers of values of sales per week, and percentage increase on a year earlier
1966 = 100

KIND OF BUSINESS (Sales in 1966)		Year	1st Qtr	2nd Qtr	3rd Qtr	4th Qtr	Jan.	Feb.	Mar.*	Apr.	May	June*	July	Aug.	Sept.*	Oct.	Nov.	Dec.*
Miscellaneous non-food shops (continued)																		
Chemists, photographic goods dealers (continued)																		
Independents (£187 million)	1969	110	93	109	118	113	93	91	93	102	1C7	116	124	123	109	106	100	143
	1970	116	95	116	126	126	97	94	95	101	116	128	133	133	115	113	105	151
	1971	129	102	128	141	143	101	99	105	114	131	138	152	145	129	127	118	176
	1972	141	114	136	152	161	115	107	117	121	135	147	165	157	137	143	132	200
	1970	6	3	7	7	11	4	3	2	-	8	11	7	8	5	7	5	5
	1971	11	7	10	12	13	4	5	10	12	13	7	15	9	12	12	12	17
	1972	9	12	6	8	13	13	10	12	7	4	7	8	6	6	13	12	14
Jewellers Total (£124 million)	1969	115	96	98	107	160	93	93	99	94	59	101	106*	110	104	105	122	235
	1970	121	92	101	115	175	91	92	94	97	100	105	117	120	109	108	132	265
	1971	128	95	108	121	188	94	90	101	100	106	114	119	124	119	117	134	289
	1972	154	105	123	146	248	104	97	112	112	121	132	144	150	145	144	175	377
	1970	5	-3	3	8	11	-2	-1	-6	3	1	4	10	9	4	2	8	13
	1971	6	3	7	5	7	3	-3	8	4	6	9	1	5	9	9	2	9
	1972	20	10	14	21	29	10	8	12	12	14	16	21	20	21	23	30	30
Independents (£93 million)	1969	114	96	99	105	155	96	95	97	95	99	102	106*	109	103	102	120	225
	1970	117	91	100	112	167	92	92	89	97	99	104	115	118	105	104	128	247
	1971	124	94	106	119	178	94	87	98	98	105	113	116	124	117	114	130	270
	1972	148	103	120	142	228	104	96	109	110	119	130	140	146	139	139	169	346
	1970	3	-5	1	6	3	-4	-3	-8	2	-1	1	9	8	2	2	7	10
	1971	6	3	6	6	7	3	-5	10	2	6	9	2	5	11	9	1	9
	1972	19	11	14	19	28	10	11	11	11	14	15	20	18	19	22	30	28
Multiples (£31 million)	1969	120	95	96	111	170	85	90	107	92	99	98	109*	114	110	114	131	265
	1970	132	96	104	124	200	88	93	106	97	103	109	126	127	121	118	143	316
	1971	139	100	112	127	208	93	97	109	106	111	119	126	127	127	126	147	346
	1972	171	109	129	159	283	103	98	123	120	126	139	156	160	160	159	193	469
	1970	10	1	8	12	14	3	4	-1	6	5	11	15	11	10	4	9	19
	1971	6	4	8	2	7	6	-	3	9	7	9	9	5	5	7	3	9
	1972	23	9	15	25	28	11	1	13	14	14	17	24	26	26	26	31	35
Leather goods, sports goods, toys and fancy goods shops Total (£130 million)	1969	112	78	97	118	155	82	71	81	92	97	101	120*	127	108	105	121	223
	1970	121	85	104	128	169	84	80	89	98	106	108	136	135	117	112	129	241
	1971	131	91	114	138	181	92	85	96	110	113	119	146	146	126	122	137	258
	1972	149	100	126	157	211	103	94	104	115	124	136	164	164	145	143	158	308
	1970	8	8	8	9	7	2	10	10	7	9	7	13	6	6	6	6	8
	1971	8	8	10	8	7	10	6	8	13	7	10	7	8	7	9	7	7
	1972	14	10	10	14	18	12	10	8	5	9	14	13	13	15	17	15	19

Figure 9.3

S.I.T.C.(R) 861.31   TABLE VI - EXPORTS   S.I.T.C.(R) 861.71

SECTION 8	DECEMBER 1972		TWELVE MONTHS ENDED DECEMBER 1972	
	QTY.	VALUE £ THOUS.	QTY.	VALUE £ THOUS.
861.3 BINOCULARS, MICROSCOPES, & OTHER OPTICAL INSTRUMENTS VAL	...	789	...	8,292
861.31 REFRACTING TELESCOPES (MONOCULAR & BINOCULAR) PRISMATIC OR NOT VAL	...	9	...	174
COMMONWEALTH VAL	...	5	...	75
EEC VAL	...	0	...	28
EFTA VAL	...	2	...	13
861.32 ASTRONOMICAL INSTRUMENTS & MOUNTINGS THEREFOR, BUT NOT INC INSTRUMENTS FOR RADIO-ASTRONOMY VAL	...	23	...	72
COMMONWEALTH VAL	...	3	...	13
EEC VAL	...	18	...	21
EFTA VAL	...	--	...	1
NETHERLANDS VAL	...	--	...	---
861.33 MICROSCOPES & DIFFRACTION APPARATUS, ELECTRON & PROTON VAL	...	147	...	2,901
COMMONWEALTH VAL	...	22	...	298
EEC VAL	...	55	...	518
EFTA VAL	...	2	...	218
GERMANY:WESTERN VAL	...	37	...	314
ITALY VAL	...	0	...	22
U.S. OF AMERICA VAL	...	12	...	1,254
861.34 COMPOUND OPTICAL MICROSCOPES ETC VAL	...	11	...	329
COMMONWEALTH VAL	...	3	...	66
EEC VAL	...	2	...	61
EFTA VAL	...	0	...	20
861.39 OPTICAL APPLIANCES & INSTRUMENTS NES VAL	...	599	...	4,815
COMMONWEALTH VAL	...	19	...	258
EEC VAL	...	22	...	495
EFTA VAL	...	60	...	376
GERMANY:WESTERN VAL	...	8	...	267

SECTION 8	DECEMBER 1972		TWELVE MONTHS ENDED DECEMBER 1972	
	QTY.	VALUE £ THOUS.	QTY.	VALUE £ THOUS.
COMMONWEALTH VAL	...	55	...	432
EEC VAL	...	48	...	412
EFTA VAL	...	22	...	317
SWITZERLAND VAL	...	1	...	77
GERMANY:WESTERN VAL	...	20	...	135
SOVIET UNION VAL	...	0	...	18
CANADA VAL	...	1	...	68
U.S. OF AMERICA VAL	...	14	...	424
861.6 PHOTO & CINE APPARATUS & EQUIPMENT (EXC CAMERAS, FLASHLIGHT APP, PROJECTORS, SOUND RECORDERS & REPRODUCERS) VAL	...	6,173	...	59,175
861.61 IMAGE PROJECTORS (OTHER THAN CINEMATOGRAPHIC), ETC VAL	...	66	...	706
COMMONWEALTH VAL	...	11	...	98
EEC VAL	...	11	...	219
EFTA VAL	...	13	...	128
CANADA VAL	...	0	...	21
861.69 PHOTOGRAPHIC EQUIPMENT, NES VAL	...	6,107	...	58,467
COMMONWEALTH VAL	...	164	...	2,935
EEC VAL	...	4,382	...	36,343
EFTA VAL	...	863	...	8,853
FINLAND VAL	...	38	...	960
SWEDEN VAL	...	261	...	3,158
NORWAY VAL	...	106	...	719
DENMARK VAL	...	228	...	1,467
SWITZERLAND VAL	...	71	...	1,319
PORTUGAL VAL	...	33	...	331
GERMANY:WESTERN VAL	...	129	...	1,643
NETHERLANDS VAL	...	4,068	...	31,655
BELGIUM VAL	...	28	...	610
FRANCE VAL	...	120	...	1,658
ITALY VAL	...	36	...	778
YUGOSLAVIA VAL	...	20	...	470
SPAIN VAL	...	52	...	594
IRISH REPUBLIC VAL	...	96	...	077
REP.OF S.AFRICA VAL	...	77	...	740
AUSTRALIA VAL	...	72	...	1,666
CANADA VAL	...	10	...	279
U.S. OF AMERICA VAL	...	59	...	1,623

Figure 9.4 (rotated table). Trade statistics by country — values (VAL) in two columns per panel.

Left panel (column totals: 1,198 | 12,634)

	VAL	VAL
COMMONWEALTH	213	2,386
EEC	377	3,755
EFTA	238	2,100
FINLAND	17	85
SWEDEN	49	509
NORWAY	25	280
DENMARK	26	227
SWITZERLAND	45	509
PORTUGAL		80
AUSTRIA	3	390
GERMANY:WESTERN	69	444
NETHERLANDS	54	2,387
BELGIUM	263	217
FRANCE	19	389
ITALY	36	319
YUGOSLAVIA	—	8
SPAIN	33	331
CANARY ISLANDS	7	7
IRISH REPUBLIC	23	255
SOVIET UNION	—	26
POLAND	—	36
GERMANY:EASTERN	—	6
HUNGARY	0	34
CZECHOSLOVAKIA	—	53
BULGARIA	—	15
ROMANIA	—	9
KENYA	3	3
REP.OF S.AFRICA	29	209
ISRAEL	1	28
IRAN	1	6
MALAYSIA	2	44
SINGAPORE	32	67
HONG KONG	111	72
JAPAN	65	825
AUSTRALIA	23	733
NEW ZEALAND	70	62
CANADA	127	1,239
U.S. OF AMERICA	0	1,851
BRAZIL		122

061.5 CINEMATOGRAPHIC CAMERAS, PROJECTORS, SOUND RECORDERS & SOUND REPRODUCERS   VAL ... 169 | 2,154

Right panel (column totals: 1,812 | 22,880)

	VAL	VAL
COMMONWEALTH	345	4,649
EEC	525	6,992
EFTA	335	3,101
FINLAND	41	256
SWEDEN	135	1,005
NORWAY	33	339
DENMARK	40	601
SWITZERLAND	35	434
GERMANY:WESTERN	163	1,727
NETHERLANDS	51	1,105
BELGIUM	47	530
FRANCE	140	2,202
ITALY	125	1,337
GREECE	9	104
SPAIN	62	559
IRISH REPUBLIC	82	591
SOVIET UNION	25	100
LIBYA	9	153
EGYPT	1	568
NIGERIA	43	732
UGANDA	6	97
KENYA	16	117
ZAMBIA	17	201
REP.OF S.AFRICA	31	652
ISRAEL	22	208
SAUDI ARABIA	7	87
IRAQ	16	173
IRAN	25	213
MALAYSIA	25	224
JAPAN	89	369
AUSTRALIA	17	1,045
NEW ZEALAND	61	252
CANADA	141	669
U.S. OF AMERICA	—	2,702
CUBA		60
VENEZUELA	11	146
BRAZIL	12	209
ARGENTINE REP.	5	93

Figure 9.4

861 21   TABLE I—EXPORTS

HEADINGS AND COUNTRIES TO WHICH CONSIGNED	1971	
	QUANTITIES	VALUE
861.21 Frames & mountings, & parts thereof, for spectacles, pince-nez etc.		
90030018 FRAMES & MOUNT-INGS, & PARTS THEREOF, FOR SPECTACLES, PINCE-NEZ, LORGNETTES, GOGGLES & THE LIKE		£
U.S.of America		106,558
Other Countries		242,416
TOTAL		348,974
861.22 Spectacles, pince-nez etc.		
90040005 SPECTACLES, PINCE-NEZ; LORGNETTES, GOGGLES & THE LIKE, CORRECTIVE, PRO-TECTIVE OR OTHER		
Irish Republic		91,606
Other Countries		397,269
TOTAL		488,875
861.31 Refracting telescopes (monocular & binocular) prismatic or not		
90050017 RETRACTING TELES-COPES (MONOCULAR & BINOCU-LAR), PRISMATIC OR NOT		
TOTAL		113,263
861.32 Astronomical instruments & mountings therefor, but not inc instruments for radio-astronomy		
90060004 ASTRONOMICAL IN-STRUMENTS & MOUNTINGS (EG TELESCOPES & TRANSIT INSTRU-MENTS), O/T FOR RADIO-ASTRONOMY		
Netherlands		202,046
Other Countries		50,952
TOTAL		252,998
861.33 Microscopes & diffraction apparatus, electron & proton		
90110005 MICROSCOPES & DIFFRACTION APPARATUS, ELECTRON & PROTON		
Sweden		94,963
Switzerland		62,848
Germany: Western		358,988
Netherlands		52,826
Belgium		71,910
France		108,214
Italy		191,814
Soviet Union		162,361
Rep. of S. Africa		67,482
Australia		61,049
Canada		79,110
U.S. of America		1,105,168
Other Countries		219,204
TOTAL		2,635,937
861.34 Compound optical micros-copes etc		
90120017 MICRO-MANIPULA-TORS WHETHER OR NOT PRO-VIDED WITH MEANS FOR PHOTO-GRAPHING OR PROJECTING THE IMAGE		
TOTAL		16,991

Figure 9.5. Annual statement of the trade of the United Kingdom, 1971, Vol. III

OF MERCHANDISE

HEADINGS AND COUNTRIES TO WHICH CONSIGNED	1971	
	QUANTITIES	VALUE
90120095 COMPOUND OPTICAL MICROSCOPES WITH OR WITH-OUT MEANS FOR PHO OR PRO-JECTING THE IMAGE, O/T MICRO-MANIPULATORS		£
U.S. of America		53,882
Other Countries		286,460
TOTAL		340,342
861.39 Optical appliances & instruments NES		
90130004 SPOTLIGHTS (NON-FOCUSING) & SEARCHLIGHTS		
TOTAL		178,069
90130125 ALL OTHER OPTICAL APPLIANCES & INSTRUMENTS (EXC LIGHTING APPLIANCES), NES, O/T SPOTLIGHTS & SEARCH-LIGHTS		
Germany: Western		119,083
Netherlands		90,119
Libya		86,816
Iran		176,534
India		60,631
U.S. of America		97,245
Other Countries		521,292
TOTAL		1,151,720
861.4 Photographic cameras (other than cinematographic) & flashlight apparatus		
90070009 PHOTOGRAPHIC CAMERAS OF FIXED FOCUS WITH SINGLE SIMPLE LENS, EXC FOLDING CAMERAS FOR 35 MM FILM OR LESS	NO	
Sweden	24,375	69,069
Switzerland	39,851	68,359
Netherlands	97,136	136,897
Rep. of S. Africa	29,260	68,541
Japan	55,300	122,537
Canada	30,517	56,449
Other Countries	204,133	367,247
TOTAL	480,572	889,099
90070062 PHOTOGRAPHIC CAMERAS OF FIXED FOCUS WITH SINGLE SIMPLE LENS, EXC FOLDING CAMERAS—FOR FILM OVER 35 MM	NO	
Netherlands	50,559	55,659
Canada	19,358	79,754
Other Countries	37,144	99,307
TOTAL	107,061	234,720
90070201 PHOTOGRAPHIC CAMERAS, OF FIXED FOCUS WITH SINGLE SIMPLE LENS, EXC FOLDING CAMERAS—PARTS & ACCESSORIES		
France		63,837
Italy		61,794
Spain		57,797
Australia		148,928
Canada		69,370
U.S. of America		186,722
Brazil		80,759
Other Countries		301,288
TOTAL		970,495

Figure 9.5. Annual statement of the trade of the United Kingdom, 1971, Vol. III

TABLE 1—EXPORTS

HEADINGS AND COUNTRIES TO WHICH CONSIGNED	1971	
	QUANTITIES	VALUE
90070347 PHOTOGRAPHIC CAMERAS INC FOLDING (O/T FIXED FOCUS WITH A SINGLE SIMPLE LENS)—FOR FILM OF 35 MM OR LESS	NO	£
Sweden	84,343	315,065
Norway	27,544	117,997
Denmark	23,118	96,965
Switzerland	72,555	322,758
Austria	25,770	124,711
Germany: Western	1,408	100,250
France	755	75,044
Rep. of S. Africa	54,463	195,332
Other Countries	77,657	584,481
TOTAL	367,613	1,932,603
90070468 PHOTOGRAPHIC CAMERAS INC FOLDING (O/T FIXED FOCUS WITH A SINGLE SIMPLE LENS)—FOR FILM OVER 35 MM	NO	
Finland	64	177,497
Sweden	1,718	134,878
Denmark	22	123,036
Germany: Western	1,536	430,584
Netherlands	357,378	2,194,156
Belgium	22	141,556
France	325	74,748
Irish Republic	934	56,530
Japan	26,155	329,006
Australia	60,961	375,986
Canada	23,945	156,909
U.S. of America	5,998	380,758
Other Countries	9,918	470,388
TOTAL	488,976	5,046,032
90070607 PHOTOGRAPHIC CAMERAS INC FOLDING (O/T FIXED FOCUS WITH A SINGLE SIMPLE LENS)—PARTS & ACCESSORIES		
Germany: Western		68,800
Australia		179,139
U.S. of America		111,797
Brazil		69,450
Other Countries		362,290
TOTAL		791,476
90070728 PHOTOGRAPHIC FLASHLIGHT APPARATUS		
TOTAL		172,961
90070863 PHOTO-COPYING APPARATUS (NOT CONTACT TYPE)	NO	
Finland	533	523,794
Sweden	3,376	3,272,687
Norway	336	443,042
Denmark	1,111	1,282,090
Switzerland	1,372	1,409,649
Portugal	160	102,450
Austria	638	717,656
Germany: Western	574	372,227
Netherlands	8,668	14,830,369
Belgium	226	162,295
France	178	114,778
Yugoslavia	565	527,565
Spain	167	385,372
Canary Islands	132	108,966
Irish Republic	440	351,294
Soviet Union	695	1,599,550
Poland	74	175,601
Germany: Eastern	101	134,815
Hungary	91	131,238
Czechoslovakia	81	186,894
Bulgaria	78	126,653
Rumania	321	315,606
Uganda	103	102,711
Kenya	170	180,855
Rep. of S. Africa	1,457	1,031,135
Iran	172	139,637

Figure 9.5. Annual statement of the trade of the United Kingdom, 1971, Vol. III

HEADINGS AND COUNTRIES TO WHICH CONSIGNED	1971	
	QUANTITIES	VALUE
	NO	£
Singapore	147	138,171
Hong Kong	142	132,743
Japan	253	259,781
Australia	1,499	2,370,320
New Zealand	477	661,157
Other Countries	374	257,942
TOTAL	24,711	32,539,043

90070991   PARTS & ACCES-
SORIES FOR PHOTO-COPYING
APPARATUS (NOT CONTACT
TYPE)

Sweden		1,226,779
Denmark		104,496
Switzerland		411,572
Austria		218,545
Germany: Western		919,117
Netherlands		12,901,262
Belgium		344,464
France		1,017,137
Italy		408,825
Spain		322,987
Irish Republic		57,957
Soviet Union		364,972
Poland		54,998
Rep. of S. Africa		325,043
Israel		106,490
Japan		280,675
Australia		1,071,812
New Zealand		165,160
U.S. of America		96,156
Other Countries		502,514
TOTAL		20,900,961

90071125   TRIPODS, OTHER
STANDS & PISTOL GRIPS FOR
PHOTOGRAPHIC CAMERAS,
FLASHLIGHT & PHOTO-COPY-
ING APPARATUS

TOTAL		10,849

861.5   Cinematographic cameras,
projectors, sound recorders &
sound reproducers

90080003   TRIPODS/STANDS/
PISTOL GRIPS FOR SOUND RE-
CORDERS & REPRODUCERS CIN
CAMERAS & PROJECTORS (NOT
FOR FILM EDITING)

TOTAL		39,794

90080099   CINEMATOGRAPHIC
PROJECTORS

	NO	
TOTAL	7,200	296,286

90080220   PARTS & ACCES-
SORIES FOR CINEMATOGRAPHIC
PROJECTORS

TOTAL		247,267

90080366   CINEMATOGRAPHIC
SOUND REPRODUCERS (PHOTO-
ELECTRIC)

	NO	
TOTAL	406	49,271

90080494   PARTS & ACCES-
SORIES FOR CINEMATOGRAPHIC
SOUND REPRODUCERS (PHOTO-
ELECTRIC)

TOTAL		36,169

Figure 9.5. Annual statement of the trade of the United Kingdom, 1971, Vol. III

TABLE 2 - TOWNS WITH POPULATION OF 200,000 OR MORE, 1961
Establishments by form of organisation and by kind of business: returns received (a)

NUMBER, TURNOVER AND PERSONS ENGAGED

NORTH MIDLAND REGION

LEICESTER — Population 273,298

Kind of business	All establishments				Establishments in the town as a whole							
					Co-operative societies and Multiple organisations				Independent organisations			
	Establishments	Turnover	Persons engaged		Establishments	Turnover	Persons engaged		Establishments	Turnover	Persons engaged	
			Full-time	Part-time			Full-time	Part-time			Full-time	Part-time
	Number	£'000	Number	Number	Number	£'000	Number	Number	Number	£'000	Number	Number
TOTAL RETAIL TRADE	3,842	64,423	12,707	5,272	821	33,757	5,892	2,234	3,021	30,667	6,815	3,038
Grocers and provision dealers	865	14,032	2,323	684	179	7,850	1,169	218	686	6,182	1,154	466
Other food retailers	926	13,546	2,668	818	267	7,169	1,372	276	659	6,377	1,296	542
Dairymen	12	3,653	708	13	*	*	*	*	*	*	*	*
Butchers	305	3,702	718	155	81	1,123	225	22	224	2,579	493	133
Fishmongers, poulterers	57	627	125	45	10	220	40	19	47	407	85	26
Greengrocers, fruiterers (including those selling fish)	369	2,256	486	266	72	290	57	33	297	1,966	429	233
Bread and flour confectioners	80	1,856	448	239	49	1,360	306	147	31	497	142	92
Off-licences	98	1,371	160	82	49	809	81	47	49	561	79	35
Other food shops	5	81	23	18	*	*	*	*	*	*	*	*
Confectioners, tobacconists, newsagents	374	3,788	607	860	38	626	59	167	336	3,161	548	693
Clothing and footwear shops	724	11,956	2,192	1,057	184	7,467	1,025	566	540	4,489	1,167	491
Boot and shoe shops	111	1,638	313	196	55	1,319	231	143	56	319	82	53
Men's and boys' wear shops	91	2,287	396	141	37	1,413	203	82	54	874	193	59

Radio and/or electrical goods shops	117	2,285	509	89	26	1,019	192	29	91	1,266	317	60
Cycle and perambulator shops (including cycle and radio shops)	48	314	76	28	–	–	–	–	48	314	76	28
Ironmongers, hardware shops	175	2,052	487	173	22	315	75	25	153	1,736	412	148
Other non-food retailers	**429**	**4,806**	**1,165**	**527**	**68**	**1,962**	**433**	**185**	**361**	**2,845**	**732**	**342**
Booksellers, stationers	44	462	132	57	7	308	75	25	37	154	57	32
Chemists, photographic dealers	114	2,341	504	245	27	1,159	250	140	87	1,181	254	105
Jewellery, leather and sports goods shops	156	1,476	361	149	21	409	88	15	135	1,068	273	134
Other non-food shops	115	528	168	76	13	86	20	5	102	442	148	71
General stores	**21**	**8,297**	**1,977**	**872**	**11**	**6,088**	**1,355**	**725**	**10**	**2,209**	**642**	**187**
Department stores	6	5,881	1,490	512	*	*	*	*	*	*	*	*
Variety stores	*	*	*	*	*	*	*	*	–	–	–	–
Other general stores	*	*	*	*	5	460	117	2	*	*	*	*
SERVICE TRADES												
Hairdressers	**299**	**754**	**878**	**142**	–	–	–	–	**299**	**734**	**878**	**142**
Boot and shoe repairers	**60**	**98**	**83**	**23**	*	*	*	*	*	*	*	*

Figure 9.6

10

The Importance of Company Information

G. P. Henderson

NB: Variations in company law between one country and another, and in the USA between one state and another, are such that much of this chapter could be written in a separate version for each country or state; the chapter as it stands is intended primarily for the British reader, but the general principles of company information work described are the same in nearly all market-economy countries.

From earliest childhood we are all accustomed to assess people. We notice automatically a man's physique, age, clothes, speech, manners and mannerisms, and from these clues form an opinion of his character; and this opinion will determine and condition all our dealings with him. Fortunes have been won or lost through ability or failure to judge character.

Nowadays a very large proportion of commerce and industry throughout the world is in the hands of corporations—'persons' existing only as legal fictions, so aptly termed by the French 'sociétés anonymes'. Corporations are as varied as human beings—rich or poor, efficient or incompetent, beneficial or parasitic, friendly or hostile, generous or mean. In our dealings with them we need to be able to assess their characters.

Since we cannot see a company's face or hear its voice, we must learn to apply techniques other than those we use in assessing people. This chapter discusses the various situations in which assessments need to be made, the categories of information which contribute to a company profile, and the reasons for some of the difficulties encountered when one seeks to obtain information about business enterprises, however constituted. The next chapter outlines the principal sources from which data about companies can be obtained.

SITUATIONS IN WHICH INFORMATION IS NEEDED

The need for information about companies may arise in any of the following operations: (1) investing in a company, (2) taking over or merging with another company, (3) selling to a company, (4) buying from a company, (5) studying one's competitors, (6) conducting industrial marketing research, (7) conducting research into the effects of specific industrial or commercial activities upon society or upon the environment. This list is by no means exhaustive: few sensible applicants for employment will attend for an interview without making some preliminary enquiries about their prospective employer and companies seeking to become members of trade associations are subject to careful scrutiny by the existing members. But the seven headings above represent the most important activities in which extensive information is regularly sought; they are discussed more fully in the following paragraphs.

Investment

The most widespread situation involving the requirement of extensive information about a company arises when a decision is to be taken to invest money in it.

No serious investor buys shares without assessing the known facts which indicate a company's stability and potential; the investor will want to know who manages the company, what products it makes or what services it provides, whether it has grown consistently over recent years and has paid good dividends, and—a factor that usually reflects the judgement of the majority of other investors—the price at which its shares have been quoted on the Stock Exchange. The Companies Acts have been devised very largely for the purpose of protecting the public from being misled into investing money in speculative or fraudulent enterprises, and it is largely in recognition of the special information requirements of the investor that the Acts provide for so much data about public companies to be made available.

Take-over

The take-over or merger operation is really an extension of the investment situation. The investor buys shares in a company primarily with the object of financial benefit from either dividends or capital gains, and, in general, uses his voice in the company's affairs only to safeguard his investment. In the take-over situation a company seeks to acquire a major slice of another company's capital stock, with a view to obtaining a controlling interest in its affairs. Such an operation may be carried out for a variety of motives, from killing a competitor to securing the resources of important supplies. The need for the purchaser to obtain the most detailed possible information about the acquired company is obvious.

Selling

The selling of goods or services on credit is a situation in which the vendor needs the answer to one vital question: Can and will the purchaser pay? The question may, in fact, be more complex than simply whether or not the purchaser has immediate cash resources: for example, his record as a prompt or slow payer may be of vital interest to a vendor who himself has important commitments to *his* suppliers. The willingness of a vendor to extend credit is often an important factor in establishing good business relations with his market, in which case risks must inevitably be taken, but they should always be informed risks; hence the constant requirement throughout the business world of credit information about all types of customers, including companies.

Purchasing

In the converse of the selling situation, information about the supplier of goods or services is of great importance to the purchaser. This information may be no more complex than that needed to determine which of a number of alternative suppliers can provide the required item of the right quality, at the right time, at the right price and on the right terms. But in reaching major purchasing decisions it will be necessary to know a great deal more: Is it reasonable to expect that the supplying company will still be in business when the need arises for servicing and spares? Does the supplying company constantly change its products, leaving purchasers with 'white elephants' on their hands? Has the supplying company a good record of honouring obligations under contracts and guarantees, or is it notorious for evading them on legal technicalities? Has the company a reputation for producing goods that are reliable? Does its spending on research and development justify confidence that its products are the best that modern technology can offer?

Industrial marketing research

Industrial marketing research is an activity requiring extensive information about the companies that form the market to be studied. Initially, the researcher will need to identify the companies which use the product under investigation, or have a potential use for it; and from this list he will have to discover which companies are the largest consumers, whether their requirement is increasing or diminishing, who their present suppliers are, and as much additional relevant information about their operations as possible. From there on further fact-finding will normally be conducted by interview or questionnaire, in the knowledge that the companies approached will (a) be important and (b) have an interest in prospective improvement in the supply of an important raw material or component vital to their production.

Competitors

Every business enterprise keeps careful watch on its competitors. In its simplest form this may be done by the trader who walks the high street or market-place and notes the goods offered and prices charged by his neighbours. In a more complex organisation a whole department may be charged with the task of acquiring and interpreting all available data about existing and potential competitors, and using all legitimate means to forecast their moves and motives.

The word 'legitimate' in this context needs to be emphasised. The advantages that can accrue to a company from possession of inside knowledge of a competitor's affairs are such that 'industrial espionage' has become an ominous activity both among competitors of the same nationality and on an international scale; the methods used, even if sometimes technically legal, are undoubtedly unethical; and, being far removed from the normal concepts of documentation, are outside the scope of this chapter.

Social responsibility

Until recently it was generally accepted that a company's sole responsibility was to produce a profit and ensure a dividend for its shareholders. Social changes during the past few decades have produced a very different situation; in the thalidomide case and in the matter of low-paid employees of associates and subsidiaries of British companies operating in South Africa, the consciences of shareholders have been profoundly disturbed. Questions of pollution, monopoly, health hazards, safety, conditions of employment, quality of products and many other factors are facets of the concept of the social responsibility of companies. Much has been done by legislation to curb the damaging or destructive actions of irresponsible companies; but there are still many loopholes, and it is these that are now being watched much more vigilantly by shareholders, by consumer protection organisations, and by the public at large. Hence, a new information problem has arisen: that of obtaining, as early as possible, evidence of how a company's activities may be actually or potentially damaging to the general public interest. The organisation of such information is in its infancy; but as the concept of social responsibility takes root and develops, it is certain that the collection and codification of data on hazardous or damaging activities will gather force.

Why information about companies may be hard to find

Anyone whose knowledge of company documentation is limited to the perusal of glossy reports and voluminous 'public relations' output of the more extrovert corporations may well wonder why so much importance is attached to the problem of finding information about companies. Even if all companies produced extensive reports abounding in illustrations and ideograms, there would still be problems — all too often the required fact has been deliberately omitted from the published data or has to be deduced from trend indicators requiring retrospective analysis of a company's operations.

In practice the situation is very different. All limited companies in the UK are obliged, by law, to publish by means of regular returns to the Registrar of Companies certain facts about themselves as indicated below; but (apart from duly authorised investigations by government, e.g. in the case of suspected fraud) no company can be compelled to reveal more information about itself than the law prescribes. Therefore it is not unusual to encounter a private company about which the only discoverable facts are its registration number and date of incorporation; its authorised and subscribed capital; the names of its shareholders, directors and secretary: the address of its registered office; and the original purpose for which it was formed. If it has been in existence for 18 months or longer, there should also be an annual return on the file, containing, *inter alia*, a balance sheet and a profit and loss account, but there are companies which, through inefficiency or for specific motives, delay the submission of returns for inordinate lengths of time, with small risk of detection or penalty. (Improvements in the system of control at Companies House will ultimately remedy this situation.)

The enquirer whose information about a company is limited to the address of its registered office may decide to pay it a visit; there he may, upon payment of nominal statutory fees, inspect the Register of Members and the Register of Directors' Shareholdings; unless he is a shareholder himself, or a creditor, he is not entitled to any further information. If the registered office is, as frequently happens, at the premises of a firm of accountants, the enquirer at this point lacks even such a basic item as the trading address (if any) of the company. The above is an extreme example; far more common is the case of the company which may give the appearance of being communicative but, possibly for quite legitimate reasons, contrives to suppress or disguise information about certain aspects of its operations. In Great Britain we are accustomed to an exceptionally high standard of accountancy and a notable degree of uniformity in the computation of figures for inclusion in company accounts; but in other countries, including several in continental Europe, bases of computation are less stringently standardised and controlled, and the elucidation of accurate and truly comparable data can consequently be much more difficult.

The difficulties envisaged in the preceding paragraphs will be encountered in the search for information about companies which are acting strictly within the law. But the researcher should also be aware of the possibility of companies attempting to conceal illegal operations by the distortion or suppression of information; such attempts may range from such blatant malpractices as trading without being duly registered, or neglect to file proper returns, to the deliberate publication of false information. Further afield it is not unknown for political considerations to interpose an impenetrable barrier: it has been reported that in one Latin American country trading results of certain companies are suppressed at the behest of the government.

FACTORS IN A COMPANY PROFILE

This chapter has dealt with the various situations in which information may be sought about companies, and has outlined some of the difficulties that may be encountered in obtaining information. In conclusion, this section sets out the heads of information requisite for a complete company profile; for anyone in possession of all the facts indicated on this check-list, the only source of further information will be an interview with the company's chairman, or—by no means an unusual ploy—a quiet beer with its janitor!

Management. The age, experience, qualifications and other appointments of the directors and executives; their holdings of shares in the company; their remuneration, and any service contracts relating to their employment. The quality and efficiency of the work force at all levels, its conditions of employment, and its relations with top management.

Finance. The capital structure of the company. Its fixed and liquid assets—property, plant and machinery, cash, stock-in-trade, goodwill and investments; holdings of shares—especially controlling interests—in other companies. Any mortgages or other charges on its property. Its performance record—profits earned, dividends paid and, if a public company, the quoted prices of its shares on the Stock Exchange.

Operations. What products does the company manufacture, or what services does it provide? Are they diversified or does the company depend entirely on a single 'line'? Are its products protected by patents? Has it licensed production rights to manufacturers overseas? Does it manufacture other companies' products under licence? Does it market goods under a brand name? What does it spend on research and development, on market research, on advertising? How is its sales force organised? Has it subsidiaries, sales offices or accredited agents overseas? What is its share of the home and world markets for its products?

Social responsibility. Are any of the company's activities, products, by-products or effluents likely to give rise to public reaction through causing social injustice, pollution of the environment or other damaging side-effects?

In the next chapter we will examine the published information sources that are available.

11

Sources of Company Information

G. P. Henderson

NB: Variations in company law between one country and another, and in the USA between one state and another, are such that certain paragraphs in this chapter could be written in a separate version for each country or state; the chapter as it stands is intended primarily for the British reader, but the general principles of company information work described are the same in nearly all market-economy countries.

Information about business enterprises is derived from three basic categories of source material: (1) information which an enterprise is obliged by law to make available to the public; (2) information which an enterprise supplies voluntarily about itself; and (3) information supplied by those who have been in contact with the company, e.g. its creditors.

In practice, categories (2) and (3) are generally blended with information from each of the others to produce a composite picture of an enterprise.

Each category will be considered in turn in this chapter. Reference will frequently be made to *European companies: a guide to sources of information* (CBD Research Ltd, Beckenham), which lists and describes in much detail all types of sources for information on business enterprises throughout Europe.

STATUTORY INFORMATION

The law of every European country and of most other countries throughout the world provides that some, if not all, forms of business enterprise shall be registered with a prescribed authority and that the register—and in most cases the files relating to specific companies—shall be available for public inspection. Between one country and another there are several variables: the range of business organisations for which registration is obligatory, the extent of the information required to be lodged in the official files, the extent to which such information is made accessible either to personal callers or through publication in the government gazette. There are also numerous differences in the facilities provided by registrars for communicating data to non-personal enquirers (for details see *European companies*).

Great Britain

In the UK the *Companies Act* provides that every limited company shall publish various documents by delivering copies to the Registrar of Companies (Companies House*, 55–71 City Road, London EC1, for companies in England and Wales; there are separate registries in Edinburgh and Belfast for Scottish and Northern Ireland companies, respectively). The most important of these documents are:

Memorandum and Articles of Association
Notice of situation of registered office
Particulars of directors and secretary
Annual return giving, *inter alia*, names and addresses of members, with details of their shareholdings; names and addresses of directors, with particulars of other directorships; balance sheet and profit and loss account; amount of debts secured by mortgages and charges on the company's property
Interim notices of changes in the registered particulars relating to the company.

The above-named documents are placed in the company's file at Companies House, where they can be examined by anyone on payment of a statutory fee of 5p per file. Additionally, the Register of members, the Register of directors' shareholdings and the Register of any charges on the company's property must be kept available for public inspection at the company's registered office.

Public companies are required to publish considerably more information than private companies; for example, the balance sheet and accounts of a public company must include:

Number of persons employed
Identity and location of subsidiaries
Identity and location of the companies in which the company has shares

---

*Companies House: At the time of writing, the Register of Companies is in process of being transferred to Cardiff; when the move has been completed, copies of company documents will be available at Companies House, London, in the form of microfilm and microfiche; persons wishing to examine the original files will have to visit the new office in Cardiff.

Certain information about directors' remuneration

Particulars of salaries of employees receiving more than £10 000 per annum.

Furthermore, whenever a public company invites public subscription, either by sale of shares or by issue of debenture stock, it must prepare and publish a prospectus—a document containing detailed information about everything of importance to potential investors—specifically including all known facts which may be either propitious or unpropitious to the future of the company.

All limited companies are obliged by law to circulate accounts, balance sheets and associated documents to shareholders prior to the AGM; in the case of public companies these 'annual reports' often contain a considerable amount of information additional to that prescribed by law.

Enterprises operating under business names

The *Registration of Business Names Act 1916* provides for the registration of particulars relating to any business conducted by an individual or partnership (which may be a partnership either of individual persons or of corporations) operating under a name other than his, her or their personal names, or a company trading under a name other than its own. The information recorded by the Registrar of Business Names includes the business name; the general nature of the business; the principal place of business; the name, nationality, address and any other occupation of any individual or partner (or name and address of registered office if a company); and the date of commencement of the business. This information is available to the public on payment of a search fee of 5p for each business name. The Register of Business Names is housed at Companies House in London.

Overseas companies

It is not generally known that files relating to 'overseas companies' having a place of business in Great Britain are available for public inspection at Companies House. The documents filed must include:

A certified copy of the company's constitution or articles (with translation if the original is not in English)

List of names of the directors and secretary

Particulars of one or more persons resident in the UK authorised to accept notices

Balance sheet and profit and loss account in a form similar to those required from British companies.

New companies

The Registrar of Companies publishes (in the form of a microfiche supplement to the *London Gazette*) a list of documents received, specifying date, type of document, name and registered number of the company *only*. Information relating to new companies (usually comprising name, registration number, names of directors or subscribers and address of registered office) is obtainable in a service provided by Jordan and Sons Ltd, London; a cumulative index to this service is compiled on a co-operative basis by the commercial departments of the major public libraries.

Ireland

The practice for the registration of companies in Ireland follows closely that of Great Britain; company files are available for inspection at Dublin Castle.

Continental Europe

As indicated earlier, the laws of most European countries provide for public inspection of statutory documents relating to business enterprises; owing to variations between one country and another, it is difficult to generalise, but the main differences between continental and British practices are as follows:

1. Companies are registered with a regional or local office—for example, the Tribunal de Commerce of the departement in France, or the Kamer van Koophandel en Industrie of the city or province in the Netherlands; in certain countries information is also centralised by means of either a duplicate set of records or an index, maintained in the capital, but this is not universal.

2. Not only companies have to register: in many countries (France for one) individuals and partnerships must file appropriate documents with their local commercial registry.

3. The texts of statutory documents are published either in full or in précis in the government gazette or a supplement thereto; the cost of such obligatory publication in the gazette is charged to the business concerned, a procedure which enables the price payable for copies of the gazette to be kept to a minimum—that for France, the *Bulletin Officiel des Annonces Commerciales*, which records formations, modifications and cessations of every business in France, costs the equivalent of about £6 for a year's subscription.

Facilities for providing copies or extracts from registered particulars of companies to either personal or postal applicants are provided by virtually all company registration authorities in Western Europe; some also provide information by telephone.

Outside Europe

With certain exceptions, countries outside Europe operate systems of company registration similar to those described above and provide for public access to relevant information. So far as Africa is concerned, the appropriate details relating to company documentation in each country are given in *Current African Directories* (CBD Research Ltd, Beckenham).

INFORMATION PROVIDED VOLUNTARILY BY COMPANIES

Virtually all publications which can be regarded as sources of company information—directories, financial year-books, investors' services, trade periodicals, etc.—contain a blend of details derived from statutory data and of information supplied voluntarily by the companies themselves; such voluntary information is communicated to publishers by means of interviews, questionnaires, advertisements, entries in directories and trade catalogues, and announcements to the press. Commercial publications carrying company information are, of course, subject to normal market forces, and it is this that governs the existence or lack of publications containing specific information.

Investors' services

The most extensive information published about companies is contained in services and publications designed primarily for the investor; public companies are compelled by law to publish more information than private companies, but they also usually regard the communication of adequate information as being a necessary function of their responsibility to shareholders; added to which the investor's thirst for information is such that highly sophisticated (and highly priced) services find a ready market.

Two closely similar 'card services' containing information on British quoted companies are available, issued, respectively, by Extel Statistical Services Ltd and by Moodies Services Ltd; both contain basic data (date of formation, address, names of directors, activities, capital, history, etc.); both provide extensive ranges of statistics over a number of years calculated to provide the investor with all the appropriate data for assessing performance and prospects; both operate on a basis of regular distribution of news and 'replacement' cards; and both are available on a selective basis—

a specific industry or market, or even nominated companies. The differences between the two services are essentially technical and are discussed at length in two articles by Michael F. Morley which appeared in *Accountancy* in April and November 1972. A card service relating to German companies is provided in *Das Spezial-Archiv der deutschen Wirtschaft* (Verlag Hoppenstedt, Darmstadt), and to French companies in *Les Notices SEF* (Société SEF-DAFSA, Paris). Hoppenstedt and SEF-DAFSA also collaborate to produce *Informations Internationales*, containing extensive data in French, German and English relating to about 800 major companies and their 15 000 subsidiaries. A service relating to about 300 major companies in continental Europe is provided by Extel Statistical Services Ltd. For further details of these and other services in Europe refer to *European Companies* (CBD Research Ltd).

Financial year-books

Handier to use and less expensive than card services, but suffering the disadvantages inherent in all annual publications, are the financial year-books. The *Stock Exchange Yearbook* brings together the essential financial data on companies (including many important foreign companies) quoted on the UK Stock Exchange; a comprehensive index provides a quick reference to the subsidiaries and associates of the companies included. Jane's *Major Companies of Europe* contains basic financial data on about 1000 important companies throughout Western Europe.

Comparable financial year-books are produced in the majority of major 'market economy' countries and some of the more important are listed in *Table 11.1*.

Informative directories

Although the amount of information published about quoted companies is massive, much information that is not of direct interest to the investor is omitted and has to be sought elsewhere. Moreover, quoted companies represent numerically only a small proportion of all business enterprises. There is therefore a need for directories which cast their net wider than quoted companies and which give information beyond the simple details of 'name, address and telephone number'.

A notable example is the *Kompass* series (covering most West European countries, and a growing number of countries outside Europe) giving, for a wide cross-section of industrial and commercial enterprises, addresses, office hours, names of directors and other executives, capital, number of employees and—frequently—products, trade names, factories

TABLE 11.1

Country	Title	Volumes	Coverage
Australia	*Jobson's Yearbook* (Jobson's Financial Services Pty. Ltd, Sydney)	1	Quoted companies of Australia and New Zealand; index of directors
Belgium	*Recueil Financier* (Ets. Emile Bruylant, Brussels)	4	Companies quoted in Belgium; index of directors
Canada	*Financial Post surveys* (Maclean-Hunter, Ltd, Toronto)	3	The three volumes cover, respectively, oil, mining and industrial companies quoted in Canada
France	*Annuaire Desfossés* (Sté DAFSA, Paris)	2	French quoted companies; index of directors
Germany	*Handbuch der Deutschen Aktiengesellschaften* (Verlag Hoppenstedt & Co., Darmstadt)	8	German quoted companies
India	*Kothari's Economic Guide & Investor's Yearbook* (Kothari & Sons, Madras)	1	Indian quoted companies
Italy	*Repertorio delle Società per Azioni* (Associazione fra le Società Italiane per Azioni, Rome)	3	Italian joint-stock companies whether quoted or not
	Il taccuino dell' azionista (SASIP, Milan)	1	Italian quoted companies
Netherlands	*Van Oss' Effectenboek* (NV Uitgeverij J. H. de Bussy, Amsterdam)	2	Dutch quoted companies
South Africa	*Beerman's Financial Yearbook* (Combined Publishers (Pty) Ltd, Johannesburg)	2	Quoted companies in South Africa, Rhodesia, Zambia and Malawi
Spain	*Anuario Financiero* (Editorial SOPEC, Madrid)	1	Spanish companies, both quoted and unquoted
Sweden	*Svenska Aktiebolag* (P. A. Norstedt, Stockholm)	1	Swedish joint-stock companies
USA	*Moody's Manuals* (Moody's Investors Service Inc., New York)	5	Mainly American quoted companies, but also some Canadian and foreign

and branches, subsidiaries, agents, etc.; selection of enterprises for inclusion is based on size and importance rather than legal form, and the series includes a total of 250 000 companies and firms in Europe alone. The

Dun and Bradstreet publications *Guide to Key British Enterprises* and *British Middle Market Directory* contain descriptions of some 21 000 companies and firms prominent in their fields in the UK; many entries contain a figure for sales turnover; both volumes have sections setting out the group affiliations of the companies listed.

A comparable range of 'informative directories' is published in each major country. Notable examples are *Thomas's Register* (USA) (Thomas Publishing Co, New York); *Handbuch der Grossunternehmen* (Germany) (Verlag Hoppenstedt, Darmstadt); *Nederlands ABC voor Handel en Industrie* (Netherlands) (ABC voor Handel en Industrie CV, Haarlem); *Annuaire de la Mécanique* (France), (Fédération & Associations des Industries Mécaniques, Paris); *Svensk Industrikalender* (Sweden), (PA Norstedt Förlag, Stockholm); *The Business Who's Who of Australia* (R. G. Riddell, Sydney); and the *Standard Trade Index of Japan* (Japanese Chamber of Commerce and Industry, Tokyo).

For companies within specific industries, or for certain specific items of information about companies, it is frequently necessary to refer to specialised directories relating to particular industries or trades; examples are the *Directory of Shipowners* (IPC Industrial Press, London), which lists the vessels owned by ship-owning companies, with their tonnage and capacity, and *Stores, shops and supermarkets retail directory* (Newman Books, London), which includes names of buyers and areas of sales floors of principal shops; several hundreds of equally valuable specialised sources are listed and described in *Current British Directories* (CBD Research Ltd).

There is also a growing range of specialised directories containing useful details of companies and offering either European or world-wide coverage of specific industries; examples are *Iron and Steel Works of the World* (Metal Bulletin Books, London), *Brauereien und Mälzereien in Europa* (Verlag Hoppenstedt, Darmstadt) and *Birkner−Europa: Handbuch der Hersteller und Verarbeiter von Zellstoff, Papier und Pappe* (Birkner Verlag, Hamburg). A point of interest about the last is that descriptions are in either German, English or French, whichever is the predominant business language of the country concerned.

Conventional directories

Although the searcher for company information generally requires the extensive data that can usually only be obtained from more elaborate sources, the importance of the conventional directory should never be forgotten. Reference, at the outset of an enquiry, to *Kelly's Manufacturers and Merchants* (with over 110 000 listings, it has by far the largest number of British enterprises contained in a single volume), or even to a telephone directory, may provide evidence of a spelling error, confirm a location, or determine the nature of a business — all factors which may be important when extending the search further afield. Directories of major cities, such as *Kelly's Post Office London Directory*, provide the additional facility of listing by streets; from these it is possible to identify a company's immediate neighbours in the same building, often a valuable clue in the search for a company's affiliations.

Das Deutsche Firmen-Alphabet (Deutsche Adressbuch Verlag, Darmstadt), which lists some 500 000 concerns in one alphabetical sequence, provides an immediate means of locating half-a-million German enterprises. Not all countries have such convenient general directories, and it is often necessary to resort to telephone or telex directories in order to check the location or identity of a company.

'League tables'

Within the past decade a new type of publication has been appearing in increasing numbers, namely the 'league table' listing the most important companies in a country or industry, or even in the world. Among the first of its kind was the *Fortune* directory of the 'top 1000' companies in the USA; in Britain *The Times 1000* lists leading UK industrial companies, ranked by turnover, also 300 European and shorter tables of US, Australian, Japanese, etc. 'Le Classement des 5000 premières sociétés françaises', tabulating the 500 top French companies by assets, profits and size, and the leading 5000 by turnover, is published by the journal *Entreprise*, which also frequently includes in its text pages smaller tables of German, British, Swiss and Belgian companies. *Top companies* (Financial Mail, Johannesburg) and *Die Grossen 500* (Droste Verlag, Düsseldorf), respectively, tabulate extensive details of the largest South African and German companies. An ambitious series initiated by A/S Økonomisk Literatur of Oslo has included tables of the 500 largest concerns in each of the Scandinavian countries. The Union Bank of Switzerland, Zurich, publishes annual tables of the largest companies of the world. A bibliography of company ranking lists has been published by Manchester Commercial Library.

Company relationship directories

Complex groups of companies, frequently international and often worldwide, have become permanent features on the business scene, and it becomes increasingly important to be able to identify the parents, associates and subsidiaries of a specific company. A number of publications have been devised to provide this information; among the first was the German *Wer gehört zu wem* (Commerzbank AG, Hamburg), closely followed by *Who owns whom* (O. W. Roskill, London); both contain alphabetical lists of companies with the names of their parent companies, followed by a list of parent companies with the names of their subsidiaries; similar in arrangement are *Who owns whom (Continental edition)*, *Who owns whom—Australia and Japan* and *Who owns whom—international subsidiaries of US companies*. In France, *Les Liaisons financières* (DAFSA, Paris), brings together in each entry the names of parent and grand-parent companies, and of daughter and grand-daughter companies of each company listed. More elaborate presentation of information about company relationships, including the percentage of stock held in one company by another, is provided by *Les Analyses de groupes* (France) (DAFSA, Paris) and by *Konzernein Schaubildern* (Germany) (Verlag Hoppenstedt, Darmstadt).

Directories of directors

In addition to the publications mentioned above, which are designed specifically to reveal company relationships, directories of directors frequently provide evidence—or at least clues—to such relationships. The *Directory of Directors* (Thomas Skinner Directories, Croydon) lists about 40 000 directors of major British public and private companies, giving the names of the companies with which each is associated; similar works are published in Germany—*Leitende Männer der Wirtschaft* (Verlag Hoppenstedt, Darmstadt); Austria—*Personen Compass* (Compass-Verlag, Vienna); and Italy—*Il Chi é? nella finanza italiana* (Casa Editrice Nuova Mercurio, Milano); while France has a loose-leaf 3-volume work *Administrateurs et dirigeants français des sociétés cotées en bourse* (Sté Générale de Presse, Paris). In the USA *Poor's Register of Directors and Executives* (Standard and Poors Corporation, New York) includes both an alphabetical list of some 34 000 corporations, with the names of their presidents, vice-presidents and directors, and an index to about 70 000 personal names mentioned.

For many centuries with no separate publication similar to the *Directory of Directors*, a means of identifying companies with which a director is associated is provided by a personal names index to the financial year-book; such indexes are to be found in *Svenska Aktiebolag* (Sweden) and in the *Recueil Financier* (Belgium).

The press

By far the most voluminous source of information about companies is undoubtedly the press: financial newspapers, 'city pages' of general news-papers, trade periodicals, investors' reviews and—often overlooked—local newspapers. News items include abstracts of annual reports and accounts, narratives of company meetings, news of appointments and resignations, news of acquisitions and mergers, awards of contracts, labour disputes, new products, sales promotions, opening of new factories, celebrations of jubilees or centenaries; the list is endless, but almost every item can help to build up the picture of a company as a living organism.

The *Financial Times* is generally acknowledged as one of the world's leading newspapers, and its contents will be familiar to most readers of this work. The nearest equivalent outside the UK is the *Wall Street Journal* (New York), which also has an international reputation and is the major source for news of American companies. In continental Europe there are a number of specialist financial dailies and weeklies, notably *Handelsblatt* (Düsseldorf), *L'Agence Economique et Financiére* (Paris), *l'Agence Nouvelle* (Paris), *La Vie Française* (Paris), *Il Globo* (Rome), *Il Sole—24 Ore* (Milan) and *Het Financieele Dagblad* (Amsterdam); company news is also an important feature of many general European newspapers, especially *Frankfurter Allgemeine Zeitung, Neue Zürcher Zeitung, Le Figaro* and *Le Monde.*

Apart from newspapers, there are, as indicated earlier, several other categories of serial publication which are valuable sources of company news and comment; obvious examples are the general weekly, fortnightly or monthly business periodicals such as The *Economist, Investors Chronicle* (London), *Burron's Weekly* (New York), *L'Entreprise* (Paris) and *Wirt schaftswoche* (Frankfurt /Main) News of companies operating in specific industries or trades can usually be found in specialist trade journals, which often contain regular lists of new companies within the industry and feature articles describing the achievements of individual companies.

For certain items of information it is important to know the specially published sources; for example, stock exchange prices, although usually listed in newspapers, are only technically 'official' if quoted from the official lists of the individual stock exchanges.

The major problem in attempting to use the various sources of company news is that of retrieval. Of the financial dailies, only the *Wall Street Journal* publishes an index; The *Financial Times* is indexed in great detail by its library and every assistance possible is given to readers in tracing news items that have been printed on specific companies.

In the UK the problem has to some extent been relieved by two services. *Research Index*, published fortnightly by Business Surveys Ltd, indexes company news items appearing in about 100 British newspapers and periodicals. McCarthy card services, for both quoted and unquoted companies, contain reproductions of extracts from press comments and news items on individual companies, taken from 20 leading newspapers; there is also a McCarthy European service and a McCarthy Australian service.

A world-wide index to company news appearing in about 600 (mainly English-language) journals is provided by *F & S Index International* (Predicasts, Cleveland, Ohio); its publishers are also responsible for *F & S Index of Corporations*, a similar index limited to items relating to US companies appearing in about 1000 mainly American journals.

INFORMATION SUPPLIED BY 'THIRD PARTIES'

This chapter has so far dealt with (1) information which a company is compelled by law to make public, and (2) information which it reveals voluntarily; it is, however, frequently necessary to obtain information from other sources when the readily available information is either inadequate or suspect. This applies particularly in the field of credit control; the information necessary to determine a company's creditworthiness is by no means always revealed by its published accounts. A number of organisations exist to supply information specifically for credit control purposes. Their modus operandi is to provide subscribers with reports about companies (or about other forms of business enterprises or individuals); these reports embody not only the basic statutory and published information but also 'credit ratings' —assessments of creditworthiness based on information obtained either from the company's suppliers or existing creditors or from others with a close knowledge of its affairs. It must be understood that an adverse credit rating is potentially a libel; consequently all information passing between status investigators and their subscribers must be strictly controlled to ensure confidentiality.

Among the best-known organisations in this field is Dun and Bradstreet; originating in the USA, it now also operates in Great Britain as well as in other European countries, and has units in many other parts of the world. To enable subscribers to check potential customer's credit ratings without the expense of making special enquiries, the company produces printed registers and marketing guides containing, *inter alia,* the credit ratings of a very large number of enterprises. Although confidential, these registers provide those who work in subscriber companies with a ready and up-to-date source for basic details of the enterprises listed, with the additional facility of being able to obtain special reports on companies not listed.

A number of long-established credit-reporting services exist in Europe, with extensive networks both on the continent and further afield. Important names are Bürgel, Creditreform, Schimmelpfeng (Germany); Wys Muller (Switzerland); Agence Française de Renseignements Commerciaux, André Piguet, Société Commerciale de Recouvrements Litigieux and Société Nationale de Renseignements Commerciaux (France); Dessilly, Eckel and Eurinform (Belgium); Blanc & Rosso, Euroinform and Kosmos (Italy).

The last-named provides subscribers with a nine-volume rating register of various sectors of manufacturing and distributive trades in Italy. For those outside credit control departments, the information gathered by credit-reporting agencies represents a large untapped reserve of information. Dun and Bradstreet recognised this potential and have used it as a basis for selecting companies for inclusion in their *Key British Enterprises* and *British Middle Market Directory*; through the medium of the computer, they have also made information about 200 000 companies accessible in a variety of selections and a variety of physical forms in *Dun's Market Identifiers*. There can be little doubt that in time other credit-reporting agencies will follow this example.

Most of the important credit-reporting services in Europe (including Great Britain) are listed in *European Companies*, with details of any special service provided, and of the languages used for correspondence.

General points

Libraries

Comparatively few businesses can afford to buy all the published sources necessary for answering problems that require information about com panies; and even those who possess extensive libraries have frequently to use other resources. It is therefore important to know where collections of directories, financial journals and other material are accessible. Although commercial reference services have been provided in the UK by many large public libraries for well over half-a-century (and in Manchester and the City of London for very much longer), the extent of their resources is fully realised by only a very small section of the business community; even fewer appreciate the degree of expertise and resourcefulness possessed by the staff of these libraries and the facilities available for obtaining material and answers which may not be immediately obtainable. The City Business Library and the Commercial Library at Manchester both have stocks of several thousand directories and financial year-books covering all parts of the world; numerous card services such as Moodies, Extel, Informations Internationales, McCarthy, ExTract; current issues of several hundred newspapers and trade periodicals, backed by files commensurate with known or expected demand; a large range of annual reports of major British and overseas companies; special indexes, news cuttings and much other material. Both libraries are staffed by librarians who possess specialised experience in dealing with business enquiries.

Many other large city libraries, such as Glasgow, Nottingham, Sheffield and Birmingham, have extensive commercial departments with ample resources for answering the majority of company information enquiries;

and the reference libraries of many smaller cities and towns are also
well equipped to answer business enquiries. Another source for information
about companies overseas is the Statistics and Marketing Intelligence
Library of the Department of Trade and Industry, which possesses a
large range of directories for all parts of the world; like the city libraries,
this Library is open to the public without formality. It is important to
remember the resources of information possessed by the major chambers
of commerce, although their services are, technically at least, restricted
to members. London and Birmingham Chambers, for example, both have
large collections of British and foreign directories and a considerable number
of trade journals; the latter include the journals of overseas Chambers
of commerce, which often contain details of newly formed companies
in their areas. People working in large companies are frequently unaware
that their employers are members of a Chamber, or even if they do,
tend to forget that the Chamber can help them with company information
problems. Very large resources of trade periodical files are accessible in
the National Library of Science and Invention and through the British
Lending Library.

Cost of reference books and services

For many purposes it is important to have a copy of the appropriate
source of information in one's own office or company library, rather
than to borrow or use it in another place. For a specific task it may
be necessary to acquire material not previously considered essential. At
this point two difficulties may be encountered: (1) The item required may
be out of print, and therefore unobtainable until the next edition is produced
in 6 months, a year or even longer; many reference books, such as
the *Stock Exchange Year Book* and the *Bankers Almanac,* are very
expensive to produce, and publishers often prefer them to sell out within
a month or two of publication rather than have unsold stock destined
for the scrap paper merchant; hence, it is advisable, whenever planning
research for which specific material is required, to make certain that the
material is available and, if necessary, obtain or reserve copies well in
advance. The above remarks apply with double force when material is
required from overseas. (2) In the UK we are accustomed to low book
prices: at £15 the *Stock Exchange Year Book* is almost the cheapest
work of its kind in Europe; equivalent publications for the seven continental
countries of the EEC would cost, in 1973, a minimum of £430 to obtain;
more specialised and more sophisticated material from overseas is pro-
gressively more expensive, up to a subscription of Fr 42 000 per annum
(about £4250) for *Les Fiches Synthétiques DAFSA* (covering 600 French
and 300 other European companies). Such prices can have a noticeable

effect on even a generous research budget, and preliminary enquiries should always be made, before placing orders.

Language problems

In any enquiry relating to companies outside the UK the searcher must be prepared to use material in the language of the company's country of domicile. This even applies to countries where English is spoken but where the terminology of company structure, finance and accountancy may be different from that used in the UK—e.g. what we call a 'private company' is a 'proprietary company' in Australia and New Zealand. Those who are likely to be engaged in deep research into companies in a foreign country will be well advised to study the company law of that country and also to seek advice from someone familiar with its practices and terminology. For others whose searches are less detailed and more widespread here are three suggestions.

1. *European Companies* includes, for each country, brief notes on the various forms of business enterprise, and provides references to sources of more detailed information—often in English. This enables the searcher at least to distinguish between a joint-stock company and a simple partnership in the country concerned, and thereby to assess the likelihood or otherwise of finding extensive published information. Similar notes on legal forms of enterprises in the various countries of Africa are given in *Current African Directories*.

2. There is a growing number of manuals and services relating to companies in Europe, published either entirely in English or with English as one of the text languages. Examples of the former are *Jane's Major Companies of Europe* and the *Extel Companies Service*. *Informations Internationales* is completely trilingual (English, French and German), while most volumes of the *Kompass* series have indexes and headings in five languages including English. Many important international specialised directories are published in English, either in Britain (e.g. *Non-ferrous metals works of the world)* or in the USA (e.g. *Chemical guide to Europe);* and a number of such directories published on the continent are multilingual (e.g. *Brauereien und Mälzereien in Europa,* and *Birkner*), while some appear entirely in English (e.g. *Handbook of the Northern wood industry).*

3. *European Companies* includes a series of glossaries, into and out of English, of the terms most often occurring in company profiles and balance sheets throughout Europe; the purpose of these glossaries is to enable the English-speaking user, faced with company descriptions in Danish, German, Italian, etc., to identify, say, the names of directors, the turnover, gross profit and latest dividends of any company; the terms

are the ones that actually appear as column or paragraph headings in financial year-books and services, and include many interpretations which are not to be found in any but the most highly specialised dictionaries. For more extensive and detailed study of company descriptions the searcher will need a good working knowledge of the languages concerned and will generally need to supplement his vocabulary from one of the special dictionaries of business and financial terms, such as:

Kettridge: *French-English and English-French dictionary of commercial and financial terms* (Routledge and Kegan Paul, London)

Horn: *Glossary of financial terms in English/American, French, Spanish, German* (Elsevier, Amsterdam)

Thole: *Elsevier's Lexicon of Stock-market terms* (Elsevier, Amsterdam)

Eichborn: *Business dictionary, English-German, German-English* (Prentice-Hall)

Understanding the data

Many information workers who are called upon to seek out information on companies find that they can do so more efficiently if they acquire a better understanding of the data they discover. For those who wish to acquire such knowledge recommended reading is *Understanding company financial statements*, by R. H. Parker (Penguin Books Ltd, Harmondsworth), which is aimed specifically at the general reader. Relevant information relating to European companies is given in *Companies in the Common Market*, by R. R. Pennington (Oyez Publications, London) and in *Accounting principles and practices in European countries*, by Price Waterhouse and Co. (Institute of Chartered Accountants, London); *French Company Law*, published in August 1974, is the first title in the 'European Commercial Law Library' (Oyez Publications, London) which will eventually cover all countries of the EEC. For those who require explanations of stock market procedures much important information is available in the *European stock exchange handbook* (Noyes Data Corporation, New York) and in *The principal stock exchanges of the world*, edited by D. E. Spray (International Economic Publishers, Washington).

Apart from published accounts, it is often necessary to interpret clues which may indicate the standing of enterprises for which no recent accounts are available. The experienced searcher will be able to draw conclusions about a company from what is missing from its file at Companies House (e.g. if no annual return has been filed for the past 3 years). Likewise, managements which fail to take advantage of the opportunity to have information about their companies published as free editorial matter in relevant directories reveal much about themselves by that very omission.

Accountancy practices

The material described in this chapter includes a great many costly publications and services, and the reader might assume that, equipped with those of his choice, he would be able, for example, to draw accurate comparisons between the performances of companies in various industries throughout Europe or even the world. This is not the place to attempt an essay on the variations in accountancy practices between one country and another, but the reader should be warned that such variations do exist. The European Federation of Financial Analysts Societies has devised a 'Méthode Européenne' which enables comparable sets of accounts to be calculated from the published accounts of any company in Europe; this system has been adopted for the data included in *Les Fiches Synthétiques DAFSA*. Work is also being done on the standardisation of company law throughout Europe, but by its very nature this will certainly be a slow process. Some degree of standardisation will eventually come, but meanwhile the international comparison of company performance is essentially a task for experts.

PART 3

Subject surveys of the literature

12

Corporate Finance and Management Accounting

Anthony G. Hopwood

Recent decades have seen a growing awareness of the significant role which an active finance and accounting function can play in the management of all industrial and commercial organisations. Although many senior managers may still regard themselves as being in business merely to manufacture and market their products and services, without adequate finance and financial information the very survival of the organisation can be jeopardised. And just in case anyone has any lingering doubts, recurrent crises such as the Rolls-Royce affair serve to continually emphasise their vital importance. Perhaps even more significantly, however, many firms have increasingly realised that the finance and accounting function is quite capable of being a creative business activity in its own right which can make a unique contribution to a company's success.

Financial decision-making concerns all aspects of a company's operations where flows of funds are involved. The purchase of raw materials raises problems of policies towards creditors, and when they are stored prior to use, funds can easily be tied up for long periods of time without earning any return. During the production, marketing and distribution processes, there is a need for all expenditures to be kept under continuous review. And at the point of sale the finance function has at least some say in the company's pricing strategy and is certainly concerned with policies for collecting debts and ensuring that the timing of the cash inflows and outflows ensures the company's continued financial viability.

But the management of a company's financial affairs is as much concerned with planning the future growth of the enterprise and obtaining appropriate sources of new funds as it is with the effective use of the funds already employed. Since financial resources are inevitably scarce, a strategy for corporate growth requires a detailed understanding of the available sources of finance, both internal and external to the organisation, and the means for effectively deploying them for maximum financial advantage. If management could make its resource commitments under conditions of perfect knowledge, their deployment would be a simple, if not minor, administrative problem. But the situation is never so easy. Resources have to be allocated between alternative uses without complete assurance of the benefits to be derived from each. The financial task must therefore include an assessment of the full range of risks associated with the alternatives and the selection of both a portfolio of projects which reflects management's attitudes towards risk and a complementary structure of financial resources.

So thoroughly interconnected with all aspects of the management task, a financial perspective provides one vital, even though partial, way of representing and understanding the over-all activities of the enterprise. But such a representation and the subsequent decisions, whether strictly financial or not, which may be based upon it, require a regular flow of relevant and timely information. The accounting system has traditionally been the most important formal source of such information in most organisations.

Accounting is a system for collecting, summarising, analysing and reporting in monetary terms information on the economic activities of an organisation. At one level the accountant is concerned with reporting on the financial performance of the total enterprise and its component units. But in addition, he also has the potential of playing a vital role in supplying all levels of management with information which can help them improve the organisation's longer-term effectiveness. In this latter capacity the accountant should be concerned with forecasting the financial consequences of alternative courses of action and helping to process the information so as to arrive at an acceptable, if not optimal, choice. Then, once the decisions have been made, he can not only help in communicating the plans to the managers responsible for their administration, but also try to focus managerial attention by monitoring the actual results against the expectations inherent in the plans. However, the very significance of accounting information has been responsible for a number of major problems in many business information systems. In order to satisfy their legal responsibilities, accountants have had to process their data in certain precise ways, and the pressures for greater precision and technical rigour quite rightly continue to grow. But despite their rather specific orientation, many of the technical aspects of financial and stewardship accounting have unnecessarily crept into the information systems which the accountant has designed for managers; and in focusing on what has been done rather than on what needs to be done, the reports have often been more useful for accountants wishing to control managers than for managers wishing to increase the effectiveness of their own decisions.

Such difficulties are beginning to induce a major reappraisal of the means of designing management information systems. As discussed in such works as S. C. Blumenthal's *Management information systems—a framework for planning and development* (Prentice-Hall, 1969) and J. Galbraith's *Designing complex organisations* (Addison-Wesley, 1973), the task is no longer seen as the almost exclusive province of the accountant. Originally in governmental organisations and later in industrial concerns, economists and mathematicians have demonstrated their ability to contribute new insights and advances. Computer specialists have shown the potential of their high-speed information processors and organisation theorists have started to place the task in a wider perspective. But even among accountants management accounting is now developing into a distinct area of activity which draws on the perspectives and understandings of other management disciplines. It is no longer seen as a mere reckoning of past events but as a more creative application of an expanding accounting knowledge to the purpose of assisting management decision-making. The literature of corporate finance and management accounting is growing rapidly. The following review primarily focuses on English language literature although some occasional references are made to continental European sources.

HISTORICAL PERSPECTIVE

After being exposed to a continuous stream of what are seemingly the latest fads and fashions in accounting and financial practice, it is often refreshing to discover the long and distinguished history of so many of them. After studying the development of cost accounting, Solomons* observed that '. . . if there is one conclusion to be drawn . . ., it is that there is remarkably little in modern costing which our fathers did not know . . .'.

The best short survey of the development of management accounting procedures is given in *Studies in cost analysis,* edited by D. Solomons (2nd ed., Sweet and Maxwell, 1968). More detailed discussions are contained in S. P. Garner's *Evolution of cost accounting to 1925* (University of Alabama Press, 1954), A. C. Littleton's *Accounting evolution to 1900* (American Institute Publishing Company, 1933) and J. O. Winjum's *The role of accounting in the economic development of England: 1500–1750* (Centre for International Education and Research in Accounting, 1972). *In Management accounting: an historical perspective* (Macmillan,

*D. Solomons, 'The Historical Development of Costing' *Studies in Cost Analysis,* edited by D. Solomons, 48 (2nd ed., Sweet and Maxwell, 1968).

1969) R. H. Parker gives a fascinating discussion of the development of discounted cash flow techniques, the break-even chart and cost concepts for decision-making, and includes an extremely comprehensive bibliography of the history of accounting. The history of direct or marginal costing is adequately dealt with in C. Weber's well-documented *The evolution of direct costing* (Centre for International Education and Research in Accounting, 1966) and the development of standard costing is discussed in E. M. Sowell's *The evolution of the theories and techniques of standard costs* (University of Alabama Press, 1973). Rather than merely trying to document the history of the various procedures, however, S. Pollard in *The genesis of modern management* (Edward Arnold, 1965) has also attempted to provide an analysis of the factors influencing their acceptance and use. Many of his conclusions are refreshingly germane to the present day.

GENERAL SURVEYS

Management Accounting

The number of introductory textbooks in any field must be one of the best indicators of the extent of its educational institutionalisation. In the UK, accounting, at least, through its vast legions of articled clerks and industrial trainees has a very long history of institutionalisation. The number of textbooks and introductory works available to any reader is correspondingly large. Most of them until fairly recently, however, were carefully written to serve the interests of the hoards of youthful examinees. Stressing the fine details of all the techniques and catering for all the usual examiner's quirks, they do little to provide an understanding of the underlying philosophies, organisational purposes and managerial relevance. A quick and uncritical reading of most of them conveys the impression that accounting is an exact, mechanical discipline, devoid of controversy and debate. Nothing could be further from the truth. Boulding put it so well when he commented: *

> Even such an apparently rational activity as accounting turns out upon examination to have large elements of ritual within it; the basic problems of the accountant are fundamentally insoluble, as they involve information about the future that is not accessible to him. A great deal of accounting technique, therefore, is an attempt to ensure that all accountants will come out with the same answer, whether it is the right answer or not.

Any reader entering the field afresh, and perhaps others as well, should therefore proceed with great care.

*K. Boulding, *Conflict and defense*, 95 (Harper and Row, 1963).

The old British school of management accounting texts is represented by such works as J. Batty's *Management accountancy* (3rd ed., Macdonald and Evans, 1970), W. W. Bigg's *Cost accounts* (8th ed., Macdonald and Evans 1970) and W. M. Harper's *Cost accountancy* (Macdonald and Evans, 1967). There are many others. H. C. Edey's *Business budgets and accounts* (3rd ed., Hutchinson, 1966) attempted to provide a more managerial perspective and is a useful work for the novice. However, it was not until R. I. Tricker's *The accountant in management* (Batsford, 1967) and particularly J. Sizer's inexpensive *An insight· into management accounting* (Penguin, 1969) that anything like an adequate introduction to the subject was available in the British Isles. There have since been a number of followers. With accounting education both less dominated by traditional professional concerns and more closely related to the universities in the USA and Australia, their texts have been far more questioning and management-oriented. There have also been far more of them! A legion of authors have followed the pioneering approaches outlined in C. T. Devine's *Cost accounting and analysis* (Macmillan, 1950) and W. J. Vatter's *Management accounting* (Prentice-Hall, 1950), and the potential reader will certainly be confused by their number if not dismayed by their cost. However, R. N. Anthony's *Management accounting: text and cases* (4th ed., Irwin, 1970), J. Dearden's *Cost accounting and financial control systems* (Addison-Wesley, 1973), M. J. Gordon and G. Shillinglaw's *Accounting: a management approach* (4th ed., Irwin, 1969), C. T. Horngren's *Accounting for management control: an introduction,* (2nd ed., Prentice-Hall, 1970), C. T. Horngren's *Cost accounting: a managerial emphasis* (2nd ed., Prentice-Hall, 1967) and G. Shillinglaw's *Cost accounting: analysis and control* (revised ed., Irwin, 1967) are among the most widely used and respected texts. The Australian R. Mathews's *Accounting for economists* (Cheshire, Melbourne, 1962) is well grounded in economic theory.

More integrated approaches to management accounting which attempt to comment on the implications of recent advances in operational research and the behavioural sciences are provided by N. Dopuch, J. G. Birnberg and J. Demski's *Cost accounting: accounting data for management's decisions* (2nd ed., Harcourt, Brace and World, 1974) and L. R. Amey and D. A. Egginton's *Management accounting: a conceptual approach* (Longman, 1973). Accounting has, in fact, been described as a peculiarly parasitic discipline. Economics has certainly provided a major influence on current thinking. Such concepts as cost, income and capital, if not the procedures of current practice, are grounded in classical economic theory, as is illustrated by the works included in the collection edited by Solomon which is mentioned above (p. 213), and such works as J. M. Clark's pioneering *Studies in the economics of overhead costs* (University of Chicago Press, 1923). And one of the main forces behind current research in management accounting is the desire to provide an integration with the perspectives of mathematics and the behavioural sciences.

An insight into these endeavours is given in the seminar proceedings reported in C. P. Bonini, R. K. Jaedicke and H. M. Wagner's *Management controls: new directions in basic research* (Wiley, 1964), N. Dopuch and L. Revsine's *Accounting research 1960–1970: a critical evaluation* (Centre for International Education and Research in Accounting, 1973) and *Accounting in perspective: contributions to accounting thought by other disciplines* (South-Western Publishing Co., 1971), edited by R. R. Sterling and W. F. Bentz. More particularly, R. Mattessich's *Accounting and analytical methods* (Irwin, 1964) and T. M. Williams and C. H. Griffin's *The mathematical dimension of accountancy* (South-Western Publishing Co., 1964) provide general surveys of the mathematical interface, while J. L. Livingstone's *Management planning and control: mathematical models* (McGraw-Hill, 1970) provides a comprehensive survey and B. V. Carsberg's *An introduction to mathematical programming for accountants* (Allen and Unwin, 1969) a more particular discussion of specific applications. The role of the computer is discussed in T. W. McRae's *The impact of computers on accounting* (Wiley, 1964) and R. Mace's *Management information and the computer* (Accountancy Age Books, 1974). The concern with the behavioural interface is more recent but collections of the available writings are included in W. J. Bruns and D. T. DeCoster's *Accounting and its behavioural implications* (McGraw-Hill, 1969) and M. Schiff and A. Y. Lewin's *Behavioural aspects of accounting* (Prentice-Hall, 1974). More detailed introductions to the potential of a behavioural perspective are given in E. H. Caplan's *Management accounting and behavioural science* (Addison-Wesley, 1971) and A. G. Hopwood's *Accounting and human behaviour* (Accountancy Age Books, 1974). A partial bibliography is contained in the American Accounting Association's 'Report of the Committee on the Behavioral Science Content of the Accounting Curriculum' which is printed in the Supplement of Volume 46 (1971) of *The Accounting Review.**

For the person wanting to investigate a series of more particular subjects, accounting is well served by encyclopaedias and handbooks. The four-volume *Accountant's encyclopaedia* (Prentice-Hall, 1962) seeks to cover all aspects of accounting, while the *Encyclopaedia of accounting systems* (Prentice-Hall, 1956), edited by R. I. Williams and L. Doris, the *Encyclopaedia of accounting forms and reports* (Prentice-Hall, 1964), the *Encyclopaedia of cost accounting systems* (Prentice-Hall, 1965) and the *Handbook of accounting methods* (Van Nostrand, 1964), edited by J. K. Lasser, are sources of reference for gaining insights into the procedures

---

* A bibliography of the recent empirical research in accounting is given in 'Index of empirical research in accounting', by R. Ball *(Journal of Accounting Research,* **9,** Spring, 1-31, 1971).

appropriate for specific industries. R. Wixon's *Accountant's Handbook* (5th ed., Ronald Press, 1970) is a standard reference work on all aspects of financial and management accounting while the more theoretical issues are surveyed in *Modern Accounting Theory*, edited by M. Backer (Prentice-Hall, 1966) and *Handbook of Modern Accounting*, edited by S. Davidson (McGraw-Hill, 1971). Specifically management accounting topics are dealt with in *Accountant's Cost Handbook*, edited by R. I. Dickey (2nd ed., Ronald Press, 1960) *Management Services Handbook*, edited by H. De Vos (AICPA, 1964), *Industrial Accountant's Handbook,* edited by W. P. Fiske and J. A. Beckett (Prentice-Hall, 1954) and *Systems and Procedures: A Handbook for Business and Industry*, edited by V. Lazzaro (2nd ed., Prentice-Hall, 1968). At least some of the confusions of accounting terminology are clarified by E. Kohler's excellent *Dictionary for Accountants* (4th ed., Prentice-Hall, 1970) and *Terminology of management and financial accounting* (1974), published by the Institute of Cost and Management Accountants.

Corporate finance

The outsider might justifiably expect the literature of management accounting and corporate finance to be closely related. However, while the accountant in industry has been and still is responsible for the management of both spheres, writings on the two subjects have followed very different directions. Without the tremendous need for texts and treatises generated by professional and university examinations, the literature on finance has until recently been slight in comparison with its accounting sister. And what has been available has often tended to concentrate on listing and describing the alternative sources of finance and the institutional framework of the capital and money markets. The financial management of the enterprise as distinct from the characteristics of the financial environment has been comparatively neglected.

First in the USA, however, and more recently in the UK, a distinct and growing literature in the area of 'corporate finance has emerged in the last decade. Increasingly analytical in approach rather than merely descriptive of current practices and institutions, much of the recent literature has explicitly recognised financial management as an important area of economic activity. Many of the developments have been grounded in classical microeconomic theory and more recently in the sophisticated procedures of econometrics and operational research. In some cases this has resulted in a body of theory and evidence which many would see as far outside the bounds of practical application either now or in the foreseeable future. On the other hand, it is clear that the experiential and institutional understandings which, together with a few useful personal contacts, were sufficient for managing the financial affairs of a smaller concern are no longer adequate for dealing with the ever more complex problems of larger organisations. At least some of the new approaches have already gone some way towards demonstrating their potential, and while the ebbs and flows of intellectual and management fashions have certainly resulted in an unfortunate neglect of the dynamics of institutional activities, there are signs that this is now being corrected.

G. D. Newbould's *Business finance* (Harrap, 1970) and J. Freear's *Financing decisions in business* (Accountancy Age Books, 1973), provide useful and short general introductions to the economic, institutional and managerial aspects of the subject, and more detailed expositions of particular topics are contained in A. S. Jackson and F. C. Townsend's *Financial management* (Harrap, 1970) and R. C. Stapleton's *The theory of corporate finance* (Harrap, 1970). A comprehensive survey designed for the financial manager is given in J. M. Samuels and F. M. Wilkes's *Management of company finance* (Nelson, 1971). Among the many American texts, J. F. Weston's *The scope and methodology of finance* (Prentice-Hall, 1966) provides a useful introduction to the perspectives incorporated into many of the recent developments, while P. Hunt, C. M. Williams and G. Donaldson's *Basic business finance: text and cases* (4th ed., Irwin, 1971), B. J. Moore's *An introduction to the theory of finance* (Collier-Macmillan, 1968), J. C. Van Horne's *Fundamentals of financial management* (Prentice-Hall, 1971) and J. F. Weston and E. F. Brigham's *Essentials of management finance* (2nd ed., Holt, Rinehart and Winston, 1971) all provide general, but reasonably introductory, surveys of the whole field.

More advanced discussions of current theory, empirical studies, and financial practices and institutions are contained in J. C. Van Horne's *Financial management and policy* (Prentice-Hall, 1968) and J. F. Weston and E. F. Brigham's *Managerial finance,* (4th ed., Holt, Rinehart and Winston, 1972). S. H. Archer and C. A. D'Ambrosio's *The theory of business finance: a book of readings* (Macmillan, 1967), J. F. Weston and C. H. Wood's *The theory of business finance: advanced readings* (Wadsworth, 1967) and D. C. Van Horne's *Foundations for financial management: a book of readings* (Irwin, 1966) are excellent collections for providing an insight into the current state of knowledge in the area. A fairly comprehensive survey of the growing analytical content of financial thinking is given in A. A. Robichek and S. C. Myers's *Optimal financing decisions* (Prentice-Hall, 1965), and H. Bierman's *Financial policy decisions* (Macmillan, 1970) and J. Mao's *Quantitative analysis of financial decisions* (Macmillan, 1969) discuss the more mathematical developments. E. F. Fama and M. H. Miller's authoritative *The theory of finance* (Holt, Rhinehart and Winston, 1972) contains a much more advanced discussion of the modern theory of finance. Although there is little or no description of the institutional and organisational framework of the finance function, the role of the capital markets in facilitating the allocation of resources over time and the allocation of risks over investors is developed with vigour and clarity.

Unfortunately, G. P. E. Clarkson and B. J. Elliot's *Managing money and finance* (2nd ed., Gower Press, 1972) is almost the only book which manages successfully to convey the highly creative nature of the financial manager's task. Their treatment is undoubtedly partial but the book is so stimulating, perhaps even entertaining, that it is almost a little too easy for the reader unquestionably to accept its more controversial philosophy. Be that as it may, the book remains an excellent introduction for the novice.

For reference purposes, the standard work on financial practice is *Financial handbook,* edited by J. I. Bogen (4th ed., Ronald Press, 1964). The *Encyclopaedia of banking and finance,* (6th ed., Barkers Publishing Co., 1962) contains detailed definitions of financial terms and concepts and the four-volume *Corporate treasurer's and controller's encyclopaedia* (Prentice-Hall, 1958) contains a comprehensive guide to the tasks of the corporate financial officer. Regrettably, recent attempts to provide equivalent British works of reference have shown more regard for the economics of publishing than the value of the contents.

THE SPECIALISED LITERATURE OF CORPORATE FINANCE

Cash and working capital management

The writings on cash and working capital management have been produced at two very different levels. There is a descriptive literature which has been primarily concerned with the mechanics of cash flows, the utilisation of idle balances and the means for obtaining short-term loans. There has been a lot of attention devoted to minimum bank balances and the operation of the short-term securities and lending markets. In this area, describing what is done, the *Report of the committee on the working of the monetary system* (Cmnd 827, HMSO, 1959) remains an authoritative supplement to the discussions in such general texts as Clarkson and Elliott (see p. 219), and Samuels and Wilkes (see p. 218). At another level, a major portion of the academic writing on the subject has attempted to outline what should be done if the manager wants to follow a rational decision process. The problem has been seen in terms of viewing cash, for instance, as an inventory and applying mathematical modelling concepts developed for physical inventory decisions. An introduction to this approach is given in W. Beranek's *Working capital management* (Wadsworth, 1966) and a more detailed exposition of the analysis of cash and a comprehensive bibliography are contained in D. Orr's *Cash management and the demand for money* (Praeger, 1970).

However, between the descriptions of current practice and the rigorous mathematical insights, many of the pressures and uncertainties faced by the financial manager have been completely ignored. G. Donaldson's *Strategy for financial mobility* (Harvard University Press, 1969) gives a fascinating description of these difficulties and goes some way to developing a practical strategy.

External finance

A lively but informative account of the principal financial institutions is given in Capital city: London as a financial centre, by N. Macrae and F. Cairncross (Methuen, 1973), while a more detailed account of their economic and financial functions is contained in N. McCrae's *The London capital market* (Staples, 1957). A more critical introduction to the operation of the capital markets is provided in R. Spiegelberg's *The City: power without accountability* (Blond and Briggs, 1973). A much more comprehensive and analytical treatment is given in R. J. Briston's *The Stock Exchange and investment analysis* (Allen and Unwin, 1970). On the Stock Exchange itself, the authoritative *The book of the Stock Exchange,* by F. E. Armstrong (5th ed., Pitman, 1964), has now been supplemented by E. V. Morgan and W. A. Thomas's *The Stock Exchange: its history and functions* (2nd ed., Elek, 1970).

There are dangers, however, in only relying on historical and procedural outlines. That such descriptions fail to consider questions of efficiency and effect was emphasised by the controversial findings of A. J. Merrett, M. Howe and G. D. Newbould's *Equity issues and the London capital market* (Longmans, 1967) and G. D. Newbould's *Management and merger activity* (Guthstead, 1970). Unfortunately, so much of the more analytical literature is still confined to seemingly esoteric articles in the academic periodicals, but the financial manager should find R. A. Brealey's *An introduction to risk and return on common stocks* (MIT Press, 1969) and *Security prices in a competitive market* (MIT Press, 1971) excellent and highly readable guides to much of the recent literature in this area. At a more specialist level, the decades of research on finance and capital markets undertaken by the National Bureau of Economic Research is listed and expertly reviewed by J. Lintner in *Finance and capital markets* (Columbia University Press, 1972).

Investment appraisal

No financial procedure has attracted quite so much attention as the use of discounted cash flow techniques for the analysis of capital projects. An elementary guide to the subject is presented in the National Economic Development Council's *Investment appraisal* (HMSO, 1971). A. M. Alfred and J. B. Evans' *Appraisal of investment projects by discounted cash flow* (Chapman and Hall, 1965) is designed for the practitioner and pays particular attention to developing some useful short-cut methods. More thorough discussions are given in H. Bierman and S. Smidt's *The capital budgeting decision* (3rd ed., Collier-MacMillan, 1971), A. J. Merrett and A. Sykes's *The finance and analysis of capital projects* (2nd ed., Longmans, 1973), G. D. Quirin's *The capital expenditure decision* (Irwin, 1967) and B. Carsberg's *Analysis for investment decisions* (Accountancy Age Books, 1974). The significance of taxation in the decision is emphasised in G. H. Lawson and D. W. Windle's *Capital budgeting and the use of DCF criteria in a corporation tax regime* (Oliver and Boyd, 1967).

C. J. Hawkins and D. W. Pearce's *Capital investment appraisal* (Macmillan, 1971) gives a short introduction to the underlying theory while many of the pioneering articles on the subject are collected in *The management of corporate capital*, edited by E. Solomon (Free Press, 1959). Recent work on the techniques of investment appraisal has focused on the evaluation of projects whose returns are interrelated either through time or because of capital shortages, and the problems created by risk and uncertainty. F. S. Hillier's *The evaluation of risky inter-related investments* (North-Holland, 1969), H. Markowitz's *Portfolio selection: efficient diversification of investments* (Wiley, 1959) and H. M. Weingartner's *Mathematical programming and the analysis of capital budgeting problems* (Prentice-Hall, 1963) are major works dealing with the former topic, and much of this literature has been surveyed by H. M. Weingartner in 'Capital Budgeting of Inter-related Projects: Survey and Synthesis' (*Management Science,* **12**(7) 485-516, 1966). G. Salkin and J. Kornbluth provide a more elementary guide to much of this literature in *Linear programming in financial planning* (Accountancy Age Books, 1973). The treatment of uncertainty and risk has been discussed in D. E. Farrar's *The investment decision under uncertainty* (Prentice-Hall, 1962) and C. Jackson Grayson's *Decisions under uncertainty: drilling decisions by oil and gas operators* (Division of Research, Harvard Business School, 1960), while more practical guides are provided in D. B. Hertz's 'Risk Analysis in Capital Investment' *(Harvard Business Review,* **42**(1), 95–106 1964), W. C. House's *Sensitivity analysis in making capital investment decisions* (National Association of Accountants, 1968), C. Jackson Grayson's 'The Use of Statistical Techniques in Capital Budgeting' in *Financial research and management decisions,* edited by A. A. Robichek, 90–125 (Wiley, 1967), and E. C. Townsend's *Investment and uncertainty—a practical guide* (Oliver and Boyd, 1969).

No question in this area has raised more controversy than the determination of a firm's cost of capital and particularly how it is influenced by the capital structure. The debate on the subject, although seemingly without end, is important and both sides have amassed evidence supportive of their own position. The barest outlines of the arguments are reviewed in the text by Hawkins and Pearce (see p. 221) and a more comprehensive discussion is given in Robichek and Myers's monograph (see p. 218). Many of the important articles appear in the Archer and D'Ambrosio (p. 218) and Solomon (p. 221) collections.

The capital budgeting literature is comprehensively surveyed in 'Capital Budgeting—A Survey', by M. Bromwich (*Journal of Business Finance,* Autumn 2(3), 3–26, 1970), and 'A Survey of Capital Budgeting: Theory and Practice', by J. C. T. Mao (*Journal of Finance,* 25(2), 349–360, 1970). A more wide-ranging bibliography of related literature is contained in *Studies in budgeting,* edited by R. F. Byrne, A. Charnes, W. W. Cooper, O. A. Davis and D. Gilford (North-Holland, 1971). The large literature on replacement decisions at one end of the strategic spectrum and the financial aspects of mergers at the other end, are listed in B. Shore's *The equipment replacement aspects of capital budgeting: a bibliography* (Bureau of Business Research, University of Wisconsin, n.d.) and R. Sperry's *Mergers and acquisitions: a comprehensive bibliography* (Mergers and Acquisitions Inc., 1972).

Such descriptive studies as B. R. Williams and W. P. Scott's *Investment proposals and decisions* (Allen and Unwin, 1965) and P. Lorange's *Behavioural factors in capital budgeting* (Universitetsforlaget, 1972), have found, however, that the final financial evaluation of a series of alternative projects is only a part of the investment process. As J. L. Bower reports in *Managing the resource allocation process* (Division of Research, Harvard Business School, 1970), the early development of ideas and their marshalling through the appropriate lobbies, and the personal experience and ambitions of the managers, exert a vital influence on the final decision. Any scheme for controlling an investment programme therefore requires a much broader perspective than is inherent within a purely financial framework. As yet, however, such a perspective has to be developed, although what might be a preliminary outline is sketched in J. Morgan and M. Luck's *Managing capital investment: the total investment system* (Mantec Publications, 1973).

THE SPECIALISED LITERATURE OF MANAGEMENT ACCOUNTING

Management accounting remains a field in search of a conceptual framework. The probings reported in R. N. Anthony's *Planning and control systems: a framework for analysis* (Division of Research, Harvard Business School, 1965) remain at the conventional level. And although such efforts as are reported in J. C. Emery's *Organisational planning and control systems: theory and technology* (MacMillan, 1969), Y. Ijiri's

The foundations of accounting measurement: a mathematical, economic and behavioural inquiry (Prentice-Hall, 1967) and D. Ramstrom's *The efficiency of control strategies* (Almquist and Wiksell, Stockholm, 1967) offer a number of insights, they fail to provide the understandings which are necessary for the development of a more comprehensive information function. Yet, in the absence of such developments, accounting knowledge remains divided according to the techniques employed rather than the purpose served.

Costing

Rather than trying to satisfy merely the legal and professional requirements for external reporting, costing practice is increasingly concerned with providing information for decision and control within the enterprise. Many of these developments are based on perspectives drawn from economic theory, and the relevant theoretical framework is discussed and appraised in J. M. Buchanan's *Cost and choice* (Markham, 1969), J. M. Buchanan and G. S. Thirlby's *LSE essays on cost* (Weidenfeld and Nicholson, 1973) and *Studies in cost analysis*, edited by D. Solomons, (Sweet and Maxwell, 1968).

However, while economists have been concerned with developing the necessary theoretical perspectives, the means for their practical implementation have been the concern of the accountant and the statistician. The appropriate statistical methods and their problems are adequately discussed in J. Johnston's *Statistical cost analysis* (McGraw-Hill, 1960), while a useful introduction to accounting applications is given in the Institute of Cost and Management Accountants' *Report on marginal costing* (1961). A series of papers arguing the case both for and against marginal or direct costing are presented in *National Association of Accountants on direct costing: Selected Papers*, edited by R. P. Marple (Ronald Press, 1965).

Although some of the economist's cost concepts are gaining increasing acceptance, historical costs still remain the predominant basis for accounting. Yet now that inflation has become such a permanent feature of business life, the biases introduced into historical financial reports can be of real significance. Opinions on the desirability of adjusting the financial records for the effects of inflation remain divided. What is more, the means for adjustment are also subject to debate. The problem is, however, attracting greater attention and introductions are given in P. R. A. Kirkman's *Accounting under inflationary conditions* (George Allen and Unwin, 1974), *Readings in the concept and measurement of income*, edited by R. H. Parker and G. C. Harcourt (Cambridge University Press, 1969), and L. Revsine's, *Replacement cost accounting* (Prentice-Hall, 1973).

The significance of standard costing has resulted in a vast technical literature. J. Batty's *Standard costing* (3rd ed., Macdonald and Evans, 1970), G. Gillespie's *Standard and direct costing* (Prentice-Hall, 1962), J. B. Henrici's *Standard costs for manufacturing* (3rd ed., McGraw-Hill 1960) and W. Wright's *Direct standard costs for decision making and control* (McGraw-Hill, 1962) all give adequate descriptions of the procedures. However, although J. Batty's *Managerial standard costing* (Macdonald and Evans, 1970) attempts to provide some account of their managerial context and use, none of the accounting works adequately recognise the political nature of the standard setting process and the problems of interpreting variances in an uncertain environment. A fascinating discussion of the former problem is contained in W. F. White's *Money and motivation* (Harper and Row, 1955), while some attempts to deal with the question of uncertainty are reported in, 'Analysing the effectiveness of the traditional standard cost variance model', by J. S. Demski (*Management Accounting*, (N.A.A.) Oct., **49**(2) 9–19, 1967); 'An extension of standard cost variance analysis', by N. Dopuch, J. G. Birnberg and J. S. Demski, (*Accounting Review*, **42**(3) 526–536, 1967); and 'Standard Cost as a First Step to Probabilistic Control', by Z. S. Zannetos (*Accounting Review*, April, **39** (2), 296–304, 1964).

Budgeting

The procedures of budgeting are discussed at an introductory level in W. J. Vatter's concise *Operating budgets* (Wadsworth, 1969) and W. D. Knight and E. H. Weinwurm's *Managerial budgeting* (Planning Executives Institute, 1964). More technical discussions appear in J. A. Scott's, *Budgetary, control and standard costs* (6th ed., Pitman, 1970) and A. W. Willsmore's *Business budgets in practice* (5th ed., Pitman, 1973). Increasingly, however, it is being recognised that budgetary systems cannot be adequately viewed in isolation from their managerial context, and many recent texts on the subject have tried to stress the organisational problems involved in implementation and operation. J. Dearden's *Cost and budget analysis* (Prentice-Hall, 1962), J. B. Hickert and J. D. Wilson's *Business budgeting and control* (Ronald Press, 1967), W. Rautenstrauch and R. Villers's *Budgetary control* (2nd ed., Funk and Wagnalls, 1968) and G. A. Welsch's *Budgeting: profit and planning and control* (Prentice-Hall, 1964) are all illustrative of this approach. The literature of budgeting is comprehensively surveyed in the bibliography of J. Bergstrand, P. Gavatin A. Magnusson and L. Samuelson, *Budgetering—en litteraturoversikt* (Ekononiski Forskningsinstitutet, Stockholm, 1970).

C. Argyris's *The impact of buagets on people* (The School of Business and Public Adminstration, Cornell University, 1952) was the first study explicitly to recognise the significance of the human element in the budgetary process. Since this pioneering study, however, various other aspects of the process have been investigated in A. C. Stedry's *Budget control and cost behaviour* (Prentice-Hall, 1960), G. H. Hofstede's *The game of budget control* (Van Gorcum, 1967), R. B. Drew and K. P. Gee's *Management control and information* (Macmillan, 1973) and A. G. Hopwood's *An accounting system and managerial behaviour* (Saxon House, 1973). And although it is primarily concerned with the American Federal budgeting process, A. Wildavky's *The politics of the budgetary process* (Little, Brown, 1964) gives a fascinating description of the bargaining strategies.

Even at a technical level, however, increasing attention is being given to the inadequacies of conventional budgetary procedures. Their comparative inability to assist in the evaluation and control of such increasingly important policy costs as research and development, training and advertising has encouraged some accountants to explore the potential of the Programming–Planning–Budgeting procedures developed in the American defence and aerospace sectors during the 1950s and 1960s. R. F. J. Dewhurst's *Business cost–benefit analysis* (McGraw-Hill, 1972) attempts to survey their business applications. And at a more analytical level a number of academic authors have been concerned with utilising such operational research techniques as linear programming. Many of these studies are listed in 'An integrated evaluation system for budget forecasting and operating performance with a classified budgeting bibliography', by Y. Ijiri, J. C. Kinard and F. B. Putney, (*Journal of Accounting Research*, 6(1), 1–28, 1968)

Long-range planning

Viewed as an extension of the short-term budget, long-range planning was often seen as an accounting activity. Such a perspective, however, often failed even to consider the most important benefits of the planning process. Starting from the present, it often focused on identifying the constraints on the future which were inherent in current activities rather than trying to recognise the opportunities for change and advancement. As long-range planning started to deal with the more strategic factors inherent in change, however, it became increasingly more distant from the accountant's concerns.

The literature on the subject is immense and growing rapidly. P. J. Kettlewell's *A European bibliography of corporate planning, 1961–1971* (Long Range Planning, 1972) identified over 350 references and M. C. Branch's now rather dated *Selected references for corporate planning* (American Management Association, 1966) is illustrative of the even larger American literature. But many of the writings on the subject are either records of the meanderings of individual enterprises or rather crude procedural exhortations. So much of the literature is, in other words, devoid of focus or analytical content.

The majority of works on planning are overtly prescriptive, often incorporating check lists and general guides for action. J. Argenti's *Corporate planning: a practical guide* (George Allen and Unwin, 1968), E. P. Learned, C. R. Christensen, K. R. Andrews and W. D. Guth's *Business policy: text and cases* (Irwin, 1969) and E. K. Warren's *Long range planning: the executive viewpoint* (Prentice-Hall, 1966) are illustrative of this approach. They usually fail to confront the political nature of the planning process. Yet even the descriptive reports of how strategic planning has been done which appear in such works as J. K. Allen's *The corporate planner and his job* (Stanford Research Institute, 1962), *Long range planning for management*, edited by D. W. Ewing (Harper and Row, 1964), B. W. Scott's *Long range planning in american industry* (American Management Association, 1965) and *Managerial long range planning*, edited by G. A. Steiner (McGraw-Hill, 1963) all too frequently focus on the procedural mechanics. Although G. A. Steiner's *Top management planning* (Macmillan, 1969) is a comprehensive guide to the current state of the art, it suffers from the same problem.

The inadequacy of these viewpoints is now being realised but the development of a wider perspective is still in its early stages. H. I. Ansoff's *Corporate strategy* (Penguin Books, 1970) attempts to provide an analytical foundation and E. Rhenman's *Organisation theory for long range planning* (Wiley, 1973) the outlines for considering the organisational context. A more personal planning framework is given in D. N. Malcolm's *On learning to plan—and planning to learn* (Jossey-Bass, 1973). Progress, however, will depend on integrating these viewpoints with such understandings of the policy-making process as are reflected in C. E. Lindblom's *The intelligence of democracy* (The Free Press, 1965) and *The policy making process* (Prentice-Hall, 1968).

The measurement of performance

Performance measurement plays a significant role in the design of most management accounting systems. In part this is no doubt due to the fact that the perspectives of financial accounting were more readily transferable to questions of evaluation rather than decision. But it also reflects the growing pressures for establishing financial responsibilities within the enterprise. At lower levels in the organisation, the procedures of standard costing and budgeting provide the standard for comparison. At more senior levels, however, performance measurement raises many extremely difficult conceptual and practical problems. Indices need to be congruent with wider organisational purpose—although many in quite common use are not; organisational interdependencies have to be reflected through such accounting devices as transfer pricing; and the quantitative information has to be incorporated into a behavioural framework for viewing influence and control.

D. Solomon's *Divisional performance measurement and control* (Financial Executives Research Foundation, 1965) gives the most comprehensive guide to this growing literature and includes a useful bibliography. A more theoretical and often dissenting viewpoint is expressed in L. R. Amey's *The efficiency of business enterprises* (Allen and Unwin, 1969) and a general managerial view is provided in C. Tomkin's *Financial planning in divisionalised companies* (Accountancy Age Books, 1973). The fundamental problem of how to produce reports on the performance of interdependent activities is of concern to both financial and management accountants. Recent views on this subject are presented in M. Backer and W. B. MacFarland's *External reporting for segments of a business: a research study in management accounting* (National Association of Accountants, 1968), R. K. Mautz's *Financial reporting for diversified companies* (Financial Executive Research Foundation, 1968) and A. Rappaport and E. M. Lerner's *Segment reporting for managers and investors* (National Association of Accountants, 1972).

SOME PARTICULAR APPLICATIONS

So much of the corporate finance and management accounting literature is concerned with either the manufacturing activities of large industrial organisations or the over-all view. Their role in controlling such activities as marketing and personnel has been comparatively neglected and the literature on many other important areas of application is very small indeed. The smaller business on the one hand and the multinational corporation on the other hand present their own particular problems.

Marketing

It is paradoxical that while many of the most significant financial and accounting activities within any company start with the forecasts of market opportunities, sales volumes, prices and anticipated revenues, the explicit role of accounting and finance in the control of the marketing function itself has been neglected. Yet this is the case. Except for rather routine analyses of the who, what, where and when of sales, and some refinements of forecasting procedures, marketing managers have only rarely been provided with the type of financial information and advice which could help them to plan and control their own activities effectively.

Many of the problems associated with designing information systems for marketing, setting prices and analysing sales, cost and revenue data are discussed in such standard marketing texts as P. Kotler's *Marketing management: analysis, planning and control* (2nd ed., Prentice-Hall, 1972) and in V. P. Buell and C. Heyer's comprehensive *Handbook of modern marketing* (McGraw-Hill, 1970). A useful collection of relevant readings is also included in S. V. Smith, R. H. Brien and J. E. Stafford's *Readings in marketing information systems* (Houghton Mifflin, 1968). Until recently, however, there was no comprehensive discussion of the specifically accounting and financial aspects, since A. S. Johnson's *Marketing and financial control* (Pergamon Press, 1967) was little more than a rather traditional introduction to finance for the marketing manager. K. H. Schaffir and H. G. Trentin have now attempted to rectify this situation with their comprehensive and practical *Marketing information systems* (Amacon, 1973). R. M. S. Wilson's *Management controls in marketing* (Heinemann, 1973) and S. R. Goodman's *The marketing controller* (published by the author, 1972) now also provide brief introductions to the interface between accounting and marketing. Briefer, but useful, guides to the subject are contained in the American Accounting Association's 'Report of the Committee on Cost and Profitability Analysis for Marketing' *Accounting Review*, Suppl. 47, 575–615, 1972) and M. Hirst's somewhat more quantitative contribution to R. F. J. Dewhurst's *Business cost-benefit analysis* (McGraw-Hill, 1972).

Not too surprisingly, the specific problems of distribution costs and pricing have received more attention. The basic texts on the analysis of distribution costs remain J. B. Heckert and R. B. Miner's *Distribution costs* (2nd ed., Ronald Press, 1953) and D. R. Longman and M. Schiff's *Practical distribution cost analysis* (Irwin, 1955), although a general discussion is given in E. P. Hicks and A. Teasdale's more recent *Accounting for the distributive trades* (Intertext, 1970). The role of financial data in pricing is adequately and rather questioningly dealt with in D. C. Hague's *Pricing in business* (Allen and Unwin, 1971), while the more theoretical probings of the French electrical supply industry are interestingly discussed in *Marginal cost pricing in practice*, edited by J. R. Nelson (Prentice-Hall, 1964). The accountant, however, might appreciate the strong marketing orientation given to the subject in A. R. Oxenfeldt's *Pricing for marketing executives* (Wadsworth, 1961) or the more technical discussion in J. Arnold's *Pricing and output decisions* (Accountancy Age Books, 1973).

Personnel management

Personnel management might seem the most distant management function from finance and accounting. But with the increasing concern for financial efficiency there are even signs of change in this area. Trade unions are now experimenting with using financial information in wage claims* and rapidly rising costs of training have stimulated some thought on the means for evaluating and controlling them, as is discussed in D. Garbutt's *Training costs* (Gee, 1969). Somewhat paradoxically, the very same financial pressures have also resulted in a growing realisation of the dangers inherent in the inevitable partiality of existing. Increasingly both personnel managers and accountants are beginning to wonder whether the difficulties, if not impossibility, of quantifying human values result in a comparative neglect of their significance. At least, some consideration is now being given to including so-called 'human assets' in financial reports. The procedures are undoubtedly crude but they might be suggestive of future developments. This predominantly American literature is discussed in E. Flamholtz's *Human resource accounting* (Dickinson, 1974) and reviewed in the American Accounting Association's 'Report of the Committee on Human Resource Accounting' (*Accounting Review*, Suppl. 48, 169–185, 1973). The growing British interest in the topic is reflected in W. J. Giles and D. F. Robinson's *Human asset accounting* (1972), published jointly by the Institute of Personnel Management and the Institute of Cost and Management Accountants.

Small firms

While many of the general and more specialised books which have already been mentioned are relevant for the manager of the smaller business, only rarely do they give explicit recognition to the financial and accounting problems involved in managing the maller enterprise. Yet very often, although the needs of such firms can be great, they have neither the time nor the resources to devote to the more complex financial analyses. Of necessity, therefore, a thorough understanding and rather flexible use of the basic but still powerful approaches becomes all the more vital.

G. Ray and J. Smith's *Hardy Heating Co. Ltd* (BBC, 1968) provides a general and highly readable introduction to management accounting and financial decision making in the smaller firm. Based on the successful television series of the same name, it usefully illustrates many of the approaches by referring to the experiences of an engineering firm with 150 employees. R. W. Powell's *Profit by control: management controls for smaller companies* (1972) is another BBC publication which discusses

---

*The Transport and General Workers Union have published a number of these claims. A general discussion of the problems and benefits of providing financial information to employees and their unions is given in *Disclosure of information* (Commission on Industrial Relations, 1972).

the application of cash control, sales forecasting, costing, budgeting and planning, and financial reporting in the small firm.

On specifically accounting subjects, J. L. Gibson and W. W. Haynes's *Accounting in small business decisions* (University of Kentucky Press, 1963) describes many of the difficulties encountered in a sample of 100 firms and goes on to suggest feasible directions for improvement. The discussion is illustrated by numerous case examples. Clear, if somewhat conventional, procedural outlines are given in both F. Simmonds's *Financial Control for the small manufacturer* (Jordan, 1952) and J. W. Still's *A guide to managerial accounting in small companies* (Prentice-Hall, 1969), while the views of the Director of the Sheffield Centre for Innovation and Productivity are succintly presented in E. G. Wood's *Bigger profits for the smaller firm* (Business Books, 1972). The report of the Bolton Committee on *The problems of small firms* (HMSO, 1971) contains the most recent general survey of the financial and managerial difficulties faced by the small firm in the UK and the supplementary research reports numbers 4 and 5 prepared by the Economist's Advisory Group contain more detailed studies of external financing problems. The equivalent American experience is surveyed in *The financing of small business: a current assessment* (Collier-Macmillan, 1967), edited by I. Pfeffer.

Not too surprisingly, a lot of attention has been devoted to the particular problem of cash control in the smaller enterprise. J. C. Schabacker's *Cash planning in smaller manufacturing companies* (Small Business Administration, Washington DC, 1960) is perhaps the most comprehensive guide. On a broader front, the problems of designing parsimonious management information systems are discussed in the American Institute of Certified Public Accountants' Management Service Study, *Management information systems for the smaller business* (1969), while *Long range planning for small business*, by R. M. Haas *et al.* (Graduate School of Business, Indiana University, 1964) and 'Formulating strategy in smaller companies', by F. J. Gilmore (*Harvard Business Review;* May–June, **49**(3) 71–81, 1971) deal with more long-term considerations. Questions of pricing are discussed in W. W. Hayne's *Pricing decisions in small business* (University of Kentucky Press, 1962).

The multinational corporation

At the other end of the spectrum, a specific literature has developed on the accounting and financial problems faced by the large multinational corporations. General surveys are given in D. K. Eiteman and A. I. Stonehill's *Multinational business finance* (Addison-Wesley, 1973), J. F. Weston and B. W. Sage's *International managerial finance* (Irwin, 1972) and D. B. Zenoff and J. Zwick's *International financial management* (Prentice-Hall, 1969). However, the literature on such specialist topics as the international bond market, the Euro-dollar market and the financing of exports is huge and growing rapidly. All three of the general texts contain useful bibliographies, while a more comprehensive guide to the periodical literature is included in G. Dufey's *Financial management in the international corporation: an annotated bibliography* (Graduate School of Business, University of Michigan, 1971). A continuing review of the literature is published quarterly in *The International Executive.*

The particular problems of controlling international operations have received comparatively little consideration. R. J. Alsegg's *Control relationships between American corporations and their European subsidiaries* (American Management Association, 1971) attempted to describe the current state of the art. However, E. C. Bursk, J. Dearden, D. F. Hawkins and U. M. Longstreet's *Financial control of multinational operations* (Financial Executives Institute, 1971) remains the principal study to date and includes an extensive classified bibliography. At a more strategic level, *Multinational corporate planning* (Macmillan, 1966), edited by G. A. Steiner and W. M. Cannon, contains a number of case studies and discussions of the international planning environment, and Y. Aharoni's *The foreign investment decision* (Harvard University Press, 1966) is an insightful descriptive study of the investment process.

As the National Association of Accountants' *Management accounting problems in foreign operations* (Research Report No. 36, 1960) recognised, international operations also serve to multiply the difficulties involved in preparing and interpreting financial reports. Not only do accounting practices differ across countries, but the methods for translating remain controversial. G. G. Mueller's *International accounting* (Macmillan, 1967) and C. B. Berg, G. G. Mueller and L. W. Walker's *Readings in international accounting* (Houghton Mifflin, 1969) provide introductions to this area, while S. A. Zeff's *Forging accounting principles in five countries: a history and an analysis of trends* (Stipes Publishing Company, 1972) gives a discussion of the different approaches to formulating financial accounting standards. Current developments in Europe are discussed in *Business, finance and accounting in the EEC* (Saxon House, 1973), edited by A. T. McLean. The complexities of translation are clearly presented in S. R. Hepworth's *Reporting foreign operations* (University of Michigan Press, 1956) and R. MacDonald Parkinson's *Translation of foreign currencies* (Canadian Institute of Chartered Accountants, 1972), while shorter reviews of the alternative methods are given in the Zenoff and Zwick text (see p. 231) and in 'Accounting for exchange rate fluctuations', by K. R. Schwayder (*Accounting Review*, **47**(4), 747–760, 1972). The growing periodical literature on the international aspects of accounting is collected in K. W. Kubin and G. G. Mueller's *A bibliography of international accounting* (3rd ed., International Accounting Studies Institute, University of Washington, 1975), S. J. Gray's *Financial reporting in* *the EEC and the international economy: a selected bibliography* (International Centre for Research in Accounting, University of Lancaster, 1974) and the occasional *Forum on international accounting* (Bureau of Business Studies, Rider College, Trenton, New Jersey) surveys current developments.

THE PERIODICAL LITERATURE

The periodical literatures of both corporate finance and accounting are quite clearly divided into two groups—the professional and the academic. The long history of professional accounting has resulted in an extensive array of journals which not only serve as a medium for institutional announcements and news, but also attempt to keep their readers informed of current developments. The principal British ones are *Accountancy* and *The Accountants' Magazine*, both published monthly by the Institute of Chartered Accountants in England and Wales and the Scottish Institute of Chartered Accountants, respectively, and the weekly *Accountant.* The *Journal of Accountancy* is published monthly by the American Institute of Certified Public Accountants. *Management Accounting* is the name of monthly journals published by both the British Institute of Cost and Management Accountants (formerly *Cost Accountant*) and the American National Association of Accountants (formerly the *NAA Bulletin)*, and the American Institute's *Management Services* also contains the occasional useful article on this topic. In addition, a vast array of minor journals are published by national and local accountancy bodies and professional firms. Details of about 100 of these are given in R. R. Demarest's *Accounting information sources* (Gale Research Company, 1970), while information relevant for potential authors is included in R. J. Vargo's *The author's guide to accounting and financial reporting publications* (revised ed., College of William and Mary, 1971)*.

The *Financial Executive* (formerly the *Controller*), published monthly by the Financial Executive Institute in the USA, remains almost the only journal catering specifically for the financial manager as distinct from the accountant. In the UK the *Banker* is a not too close equivalent. The *Investment Analyst* and its American counterpart, the *Financial Analyst's Journal*, contain articles on financial analysis and the stock market, while *Mergers and Acquisitions: the journal of corporate venture* focuses on a more narrow range of subject material.

The *Accounting Review* and the *Journal of Accounting Research* are the most respected academic journals in accounting. The former is published quarterly by the American Accounting Association and it attempts to

---

*A useful review of the editorial policies of some accounting journals is given in 'Keeping current on new developments in accounting', by J. A. Weber (*International Journal of Accounting Education and Research*, Fall, 7, 115–123, 1971).

cover all aspects of the subject, while, since its inception in 1963, the latter journal has tended to emphasise the current frontiers of research. Since the unfortunate termination of *Accounting Research* in 1958, there was no British equivalent until the Institute of Chartered Accountants in England and Wales founded *Accounting and Business Research* in 1970. This journal has yet, however, to establish its reputation. *Abacus* is a scholarly Australian journal, and on international questions the *International Journal of Accounting Education and Research* (published by the Centre of the same name at the University of Illinois) and the *Journal UEC* (the official publication of the Union Europeene des Exports Comptables, Economique et Financiers) are useful sources of reference.

The *Journal of Finance* is the principal academic journal in its area. The more recent mathematical and statistical studies are often published in the *Journal of Financial and Quantitative Analysis*, and the *Journal of Financial Economics*, and important work by faculty and students of the University of Chicago Graduate School of Business frequently appears in the *Journal of Business*. The British *Journal of Business Finance*, which ceased publication in 1973, was replaced by the *Journal of Business Finance and Accounting* in 1974.

BIBLIOGRAPHIES AND INDEXES

Aiming to cover all literature published in the English language, including articles appearing in journals not specifically concerned with accounting and finance, *Accountants' index* (American Institute Publishing Company) is an invaluable bibliography listing items under author, subject and the title. The original volume (1921) covered books in print in 1912 and material published between 1913 and 1920, and supplementary volumes have been issued on a regular basis. Guides to the management accounting literature appear in J. E. Ross and R. G. Murdick's *An annotated bibliography of management information systems* (Association for Systems Management, 1970) and R. I. Tricker's *Management information systems: an annotated bibliography* (The General Educational Trust of the Institute of Chartered Accountants, 1969).

Articles appearing in the major accounting journals and a number of periodicals in related fields are listed by author and topic in the monthly *Accounting Articles* (Commerce Clearing House). Entries also include some workshops and books relating to accounting and management services. Abstracts of articles published in the English language, together with book reviews, are given in the quarterly *The Accountants' Digest*. And although confined to publications of the National Association of Accountants, their *Topical index* is a useful classified bibliography. The first volume covered 1920 to 1946, cumulative supplements appeared in 1952 and 1960, and annual supplements are published in *Management Accounting*.

R. R. Demarest's *Accounting information sources* (Gale Research Company, 1970) is an extremely comprehensive guide to the literature, associations and American federal agencies concerned with accounting. The earlier literature is listed in H. C. Bentley and R. S. Leonard's · *Bibliography of works on accounting by American authors*, Vol. 1, 1796–1900; Vol. II, 1901–1934 (H. C. Bentley, 1934–35), B. S. Yamey, H. C. Edey and H. W. Thomson's *Accounting in England and Scotland: 1543–1800, Double entry in exposition and practice* (Sweet and Maxwell, 1963) and J. Pryce-Jones and R. H. Parker's *Accounting in Scotland: a historical bibliography* (Institute of Chartered Accountants of Scotland, 1974). The extensive monograph, journal and reference collections of the Institute of Chartered Accountants of England and Wales are described and catalogued in *Current accounting literature* (1971 with periodic supplements).

The literature of corporate finance is succintly classified in G. Donaldson and C. Stubbs, *Corporate and business finance: a classified bibliography* (Baker Library, Harvard Business School, 1964). Much of the more recent analytical and empirical work is expertly surveyed in R. A. Brealey and C. Pyle's *Bibliography of finance and investment* (Paul Elek, 1973). More specialised bibliographies appear in European Federation of Financial Analysts Societies' *A concise bibliography for investment analysis in Europe* (1963), National Industrial Conference Board's *Bibliography on diversification and mergers* (1962), 'Bibliography of risks and rates of return for common stocks', by S. P. Pratt (*Financial Analysts Journal*, **24**, 151–166, 1968) and Society of Investment Analysts' *A bibliography for investment and economic analysis* (1965). The earlier literature is listed in M. Masui's *Bibliography of finance* (Kobe University of Commerce, 1935).

13

The Literature of Organisational Behaviour

John Child

WHAT IS ORGANISATIONAL BEHAVIOUR?

Organisational behaviour is the study of the structure and functioning of organisations and the behaviour of groups and individuals within them. It is concerned with the ways in which organisations cope with their environments, with the behaviour of departments and groups in those organisations, and with individuals in the context of their jobs and their relationships with other members of the organisation. What used to be called the study of 'human relations' was usually confined to the way people behaved in groups and the relations they had with their supervisors or managers. The modern approach contained in organisational behaviour appreciates that human relations at work have to be understood within a broader and more complex context in which the economic and social environment, trade unionism, conflicts of interest, technology, structures of authority and control, employees' expectations of rewards and conditions of work may all constitute relevant factors.

Organisational behaviour is an interdisciplinary science. It draws primarily upon the disciplines of psychology and sociology, but also upon social anthropology, political science, economics and aspects of production engineering. Its precursors are varied and include the earlier work of management and administrative theorists, investigations into organisation structure, small group and individual behaviour, research concerned with the impact of technology on modern work, and studies by economists interested in decision-making and other behaviour within the firm. However, it is precisely this division of a single area into so many different compartments that is so unhelpful to an understanding of organisational problems as a whole and that organisational behaviour seeks to move away from.

The concept of organisational behaviour has consequently been developed as a way of synthesising contributions from the various relevant disciplines into a unified science of individual, group and organisational activity. As well as attempting to synthesise as between disciplines, this approach also recognises that behaviour at these three levels is intimately interrelated and that its analysis should therefore be correspondingly integrated. This is one reason why the notion of organisations as open systems has become very popular, for this serves to emphasise the interdependence between different levels and segments within organisations, as well as between organisations as a whole and their environments.

The literature of organisational behaviour reflects the fact that it is a new concept applied to problems that have been with us for as long as organisations themselves. Much of the relevant literature adopts the perspectives of a single discipline, usually psychology or sociology — although some works do pursue a more integrative 'behavioural science' approach. Many of the writings directed towards practising managers and administrators are more concerned with popularising a particular technique or standard 'packaged' approach than with presenting a careful analysis of how problems arising in different circumstances will require their own particular solutions. A great deal of the available literature is also confined to individual issues which arise within the total field of organisational behaviour, and it will be necessary to categorise most of the selections from this literature according to a number of main topics.

Exactly how major topics are distinguished within an integrated approach such as that of organisational behaviour is a somewhat arbitrary matter. I have chosen to identify seven such topics.

The first is called work and the individual and is concerned with the motivation to work, rewards from work, careers, work and leisure, and the importance of differences in individuals' personalities and attributes for an appreciation of how they behave within organisations. The second topic is called working in groups and includes the study of group dynamics, the influence of group norms on people's behaviour and performance, the group as a source of social satisfactions, and so forth. The third topic is concerned with leadership style and social skills. It considers problems such as the choice of style in relation to different work situations and leaders' personalities.

With the first three topics we have moved from the individual to the group level of analysis. The next three topics all refer to the organisation as a whole. Topic four concentrates on the main processes which take place within organisations, such as securing information, decision-making, adjusting to change, conflict and playing politics. Topic five is concerned with organisation structure — that is, those elements of organisation which have some degree of regular form. These include the specialisation of jobs and departments, the hierarchy, the use of standard systems and procedures (including payment systems), delegation and mechanisms for maintaining co-ordination. The next topic, number six, looks at the relevance of prevailing contingencies for organisational structures and processes, contingencies created by an organisation's size, its environment and the nature of its technology.

A further contingency provided by the changing nature of the labour force is seen by many to lend the question of modifying traditional forms of organisation a particular urgency. The question of organisational change is not only of immediate practical importance, but also serves in many ways to remind one of the unity between the different topics just listed. For in studies of change it is possible to see just how organisations do behave like systems, in that changes in one area or level of activity have consequencies for other areas, which are often unforeseen by managers. The literature on the challenge of change constitutes my seventh and last topic.

Before offering a selection of literature on these seven major areas of organisational behaviour, I shall first describe the different types of writing which are available.

THE MAIN TYPES OF VAILABLE LITERATURE

An increasing numbr of *general textbooks* on organisational behaviour have become available in recent years. Most of these are American in origin and in the material they include, such as Peter M. Blau and W. Richard Scott's *Formal organisations* (Routledge and Kegan Paul, 1963), Joe Kelly's *Organisational behaviour* (Irwin-Dorsey, 1969) and Richard H. Hall's *Organisations: structure and process* (Prentice-Hall, 1972) and *The Organizational world* by Harold J. Leavitt, William R. Dill and Henry B. Eyring (Harcourt Brace Janovich, 1973). Among British books which take a broad look at organisations are D. S. Pugh, D. J. Hickson and C. R. Hining's *Writers on organisations* (2nd ed., Penguin, 1971), Cyril Sofer's *Organisations in theory and practice* (Heinemann Educational, 1972) and Geoffrey Hutton's *Thinking about organisation* (2nd ed., Tavistock, 1972). While not textbooks as such, two distinctive and divergent approaches to the analysis of organisations are provided by *Systems thinking*, edited by F. E. Emery (Penguin, 1969) and by David Silverman's *The theory of organisations* (Heinemann Educational, 1970), which is critical of regarding organisations as systems.

In addition to textbooks, quite a few *collections of readings* have now been produced which cover the whole field or substantial parts of it. Koya Azumi and Jerald Hage in their *Organisational systems* (Heath, 1972) have produced a text with readings which adopts a sociological perspective. Walter A. Hill and Douglas M. Egan have edited *Readings in organisational theory* (Allyn and Bacon, 1966) with a more distinctive emphasis on behaviour within organisations. These are two examples of American readings, and there are not as yet many books that include a substantial number of British articles. *Industrial society: social sciences in management*, edited by Denis Pym (Penguin, 1968), does present original British contributions which demonstrate the relevance of research for management practice. A new Open University reader, *People and organisations*, edited by Graeme Salaman and Kenneth Thompson (Longmans, 1973), also includes a number of British writings of a more academic nature.

Organisational behaviour draws, as we have seen, upon several underlying disciplines and seeks to integrate different levels of analysis. There are therefore *textbooks and readings in the contributory disciplines* which can help us a great deal in our understanding of organisation. Daniel Katz and Robert L. Kahn's *The social psychology of organisations* (Wiley, 1966) is an important example of a social psychological approach to the subject which uses the concept of organisations as open systems. Michael Argyle, a British social psychologist, has produced a text on *The social psychology of work* (Allen Lane, The Penguin Press, 1972) which also makes a useful contribution from one of the underlying disciplines. On the sociological side, a text such as S. R. Parker, R. K. Brown, J. Child and M. A. Smith's *The sociology of industry* (2nd ed., Allen and Unwin, 1972) serves to place the study of organisations into its broader social and institutional contexts. A range of sociological research and discussion on modern organisational life is contained in the contributions to *Man and organisation*, edited by John Child (Allen and Unwin, 1973). Some time ago Harvey Leibenstein explored the relation of economic analysis to organisational analysis in his *Economic theory and organisational analysis* (Harper, 1960) but this lead has only been followed up by a few writers, including Richard M. Cyert and James G. March in *A behavioural theory of the firm* (Prentice-Hall, 1963).

A fourth type of literature on organisational behaviour is the *research monograph* and the *research paper*. (Chapter 8 provides a general discussion of research literature.) Many of these writings are highly specialised, although some published research reports are of general interest to those concerned with management. One example is Tom Lupton's *On the shop floor* (Pergamon, 1963), which provides an insightful account of worker behaviour, including restriction of output, and an analysis of its possible causes. Another is Peter A. Clark's *Organisational design: theory and practice* (Tavistock, 1972), which describes research on the problems of collaboration between social scientists and managers in designing and implementing new forms of organisation. Useful monographs, research reports and occasional papers are also published at regular intervals by the

Institute of Personnel Management, the British Institute of Management and the Association of Teachers of Management.

Both published and unpublished papers of interest are available in reprint or working paper series. Among the main institutions which produce such a series and include work on organisational behaviour are:

1. The Institute of Industrial Relations, University of California, Berkeley
2. The European Institute for Advanced Studies in Management, Brussels
3. The Organisational Behaviour Research Group, London Graduate School of Business Studies
4. The University of Aston Management Centre, Birmingham
5. The International Institute of Management, Berlin

A number of American universities now make doctoral theses on management subjects available, including some in the field of organisational behaviour. All American doctoral dissertations since 1970 are now available on microfilm from the British Lending Library at Boston Spa. These may be consulted through a major library such as that of the London Graduate School of Business Studies, which can also provide full information on access to reprints of articles and unpublished working papers.

Many research monographs on organisational behaviour are richly described and analysed *case studies*, such as Peter M. Blau's *The dynamics of bureaucracy* (2nd ed., Chicago University Press, 1963) and E. J. Miller and A. K. Rice's *Systems of organisation* (Tavistock, 1967), in which systems analysis is applied to a number of cases of organisational change. In addition, case studies written more specifically for purposes of teaching students or developing managers' awareness of organisational behaviour are available either in published collections or from the bibliographies of the Harvard Business School Case Clearing House and of the new British Case Clearing House at the Cranfield Institute of Technology. Published collections of cases are mostly American, such as Gene W. Dalton, Paul R. Lawrence and Larry E. Greiner's *Organisational change and development* (Irwin-Dorsey, 1970), *Behavioral science concepts in case analysis*, by Renato Tagiuri *et al.* (Harvard Business School, 1968), and Richard N. Farmer, Barry M. Richman and William G. Ryan's *Incidents for studying management and organisation* (Wadsworth, 1970). Two collections of British cases include some which illustrate organisational behaviour problems: *Case studies in management*, edited by Michael Ivens and Frank Broadway (Business Publications, 1964), and *Bradford exercises in management*, edited by Thomas Kempner and Gordon Wills (Nelson, 1966).

Finally, mention must be made of the main *journals* and *works of reference* which contain articles on organisational behaviour. *Management Today*, published monthly, contains a wealth of journalistic reports on company happenings and on new management thinking about organisational matters. *Management Education and Development* contains articles on behavioural approaches to executive and organisational development, while the *Journal of Management Studies* also includes reports of research. These journals are all British, the last two being published quarterly, as are those mentioned next. These are the more academic British journals which contain relevant articles: the *British Journal of Industrial Relations*, *Human Relations*, the *Industrial Relations Journal*, *Occupational Psychology* and *Sociology*. Three American academic journals which define their subject matter entirely in terms of organisational behaviour are the *Administrative Science Quarterly*, *Organisational Behaviour and Human Performance* and the *Journal of Applied Behavioural Science*. Among works of reference, three regular publications of abstracts include articles on organisational behaviour: *Management Abstracts*, *Psychological Abstracts* and *Sociological Abstracts*. A definitive source of reference for the subject is *Handbook of organisations*, edited by James G. March (Rand McNally, 1965), and the same publisher has since produced another major reference in *Handbook of industrial and organisational psychology*, edited by M. D. Dunnette (Rand McNally, 1973). Finally, in 1966 the journal *Current Sociology* published a review of literature on 'The study of organisations', written by Renate Mayntz.

SELECTIONS FROM THE LITERATURE

Some of the textbooks and collected readings which provide a substantial coverage of organisational behaviour have been listed in the previous section. What follows is a selection of literature, a reading of which would give a good coverage of the seven main topics I have listed. In making the selection I have given preference to British books, but American and other work which makes an outstanding contribution has also been included. While many of the citations have been published recently, some are older works which are important statements or research landmarks. In the field of behaviour in organisations, much analysis and research remains valid for some considerable time. Bearing this in mind, together with the fact that most research work is eventually reported in book form, the following selection concentrates on books rather than on work which may first have appeared in journals.

Work and the individual

The outstanding text on this subject is by an American author: Victor

H. Vroom's *Work and motivation* (Wiley, 1964). The same author together with Edwrd L. Deci has more recently edited a set of readings on this topic entitled *Management and motivation* (Penguin, 1970). A collection of original British contributions covering subjects such as individual performance, accidents, selection, motivation, the man–machine interface and participation is edited by Peter B. Warr in *Psychology at work* (Penguin, 1971). An influential theory of motivation at work, which has stimulated experiments in job enrichment, is Herzberg's, developed in *The motivation to work*, by F. Herzberg *et al.* (2nd ed., Wiley, 1959), and F. Herzberg's *Work and the nature of man* (World Publishing, 1966).

Two volumes edited by R. Fraser, *Work: twenty personal accounts* (Penguin, 1968, 1969), provide rich descriptions of people's experiences in different occupations. *The affluent worker: industrial attitudes and behaviour*, by John H. Goldthorpe *et al.* (Cambridge University Press, 1969), analyses research on workers in Luton and criticises current theories about work and the individual. W. W. Daniel's *Beyond the wage–work bargain* (Political and Economic Planning, 1970) also reviews explanations for employee attitudes and behaviour in the light of his investigations of productivity bargaining. There is relatively little British writing on managers and work, the fullest account being Rosemary Stewart's *Managers and their jobs* (Macmillan, 1967; Pan, 1970). An American study, John P. Campbell, Marvin D. Dunnette, Edward E. Lawler and Karl E. Weick's *Managerial behaviour, performance and effectiveness* (McGraw Hill, 1970) synthesises a large number of studies and gives a review of American personnel practices. *The nature of managerial work*, by Henry Mintzberg (Harper and Row, 1973) also reviews the field and reports the author' own research.

An important aspect of an individual's behaviour within organisations concerns his carreer pattern and mobility between jobs. There are several British studies of managers' careers, such as R. V. Clements's *Managers: a study of their careers in industry* (Allen and Unwin, 1958) and D. G. Clark's *The Industrial manager: his background and career pattern* (Business Publications, 1966). Cyril Sofer's *Men in mid-career: a study of British managers and technical specialists* (Cambridge University Press, 1970) reviews research on managers' careers and experience of work as well as reporting on his own studies. Robert N. Rapaport's *Mid-career development* (Tavistock, 1970) explores how individual patterns of career development relate to managers' organisational environments and to their experience of training in a management college. S. Birch and B. Macmillan's *Managers on the move* (British Institute of Management, 1972) presents data on patterns of job-changing among British managers. The major studies so far of occupational choice and mobility among non-managerial employees have been carried out in the USA, such as J. A. Davis's

Undergraduate career decisions (Aldine, 1965) and B. G. Glaser's *Organisational scientists: their professional careers* (Bobbs-Merrill, 1964).

Major studies of the association between technology and individual behaviour include Joan Woodward's *Industrial organisation: behaviour and control* (Oxford University Press, 1970), Jon M. Shepard's *Automation and alienation* (MIT Press, 1971) and Robert Blauner's *Alienation and freedom* (University of Chicago Press, 1964). Geoffrey K. Ingham's *Size of industrial organisation and worker behaviour* (Cambridge University Press, 1970) examines the consequences for worker behaviour of differences in the structures of large and small-scale industrial organisations.

Finally, a good review of the interrelationship between type of work, work behaviour and leisure is contained in Stanley Parker's *The future of work and leisure* (MacGibbon and Kee, 1971; Paladin, 1972).

Working in groups

The importance of the internal dynamics of working groups for setting norms of individual behaviour (for instance, about levels of productivity) and in providing social satisfactions for their members was first analysed in the classic report on the famous Hawthorne Experiments: F. J. Roethlisberger and W. J. Dickson's *Management and the worker* (Harvard University Press, 1939). An up-to-date review of the great amount of research into working groups that has been carried out since Hawthorne is contained in Peter B. Smith's *Groups within organisations* (Harper and Row, 1973).

Some of the most important work of the Tavistock Institute of Human Relations has focused on ways of allowing cohesive and autonomous working groups to form in technological conditions of mass production where the logic of engineering is towards individual specialisation, social isolation and control by the machine. This research has employed the sociotechnical system approach and its results are described in *Organisational choice*, by E. L. Trist *et al.* (Tavistock, 1963), which records experiments in British coal mines, and in A. K. Rice's *The enterprise and its environment* (Tavistock, 1963), which describes experiments in Indian plants; while Miller and Rice's *Systems of organisation* (already listed) analyses the results of experiments in reshaping task and social groups at work in a range of British organisations. A collection of readings which includes reports on experiments in restructuring work groups to provide individuals with greater satisfaction and autonomy, as well as reports on the design of individual jobs, is *Design of jobs*, edited by Louis E. Davis and James C. Taylor (Penguin, 1972).

The study of group dynamics has led to an appreciation of how experiences in groups can provide an individual with the means to gain a deeper appreciation of himself and of his relationships with others. The ways in which group experiences can unfreeze a person's defensive resistance to self-awareness or to the acceptance of new ideas has led to their use for personal development, and this has been extensive among managers. The literature on training ('T') groups includes M. L. and P. J. Berger's *Group training techniques: cases, applications and research* (Gower Press, 1972), C. L. Cooper and I. L. Mangham's *T-Groups: a survey of research* (Wiley, 1971), and L. P. Bradford, J. R. Gibb and K. D. Benne's *T-group theory and laboratory methods* (Wiley, 1969).

Leadership and social skills

T-group training is often used in an attempt to improve a person's capacity to fulfil a leadership role, as a manager or supervisor. This is described in A. K. Rice's *Learning for leadership* (Tavistock, 1965). The study of different leadership styles and their possible relation to the effectiveness of subordinates goes back much longer—again to the Hawthorne Experiments. The Hawthorne Experiments suggested that democratic and participative styles of leadership would increase not only employees' involvement with the organisation but also their productivity. This remains basically the theme developed in Rensis Likert's *New patterns of management* (McGraw-Hill, 1961) and in his *The human organisation* (McGraw-Hill, 1967). Douglas McGregor's writing has been in similar vein, arguing that managers should adopt a more positive view of people's motivation in *The human side of enterprise* (McGraw-Hill, 1960) and in *Leadership and motivation* (MIT Press, 1966). The attention managers give to accommodating the needs of their subordinates has often been contrasted with the concern they have for production; R. R. Blake and J. S. Morton, in *The managerial grid* (Gulf Publishing, 1964), argue that the two concerns should and can be integrated. A more sophisticated view is that the effects of particular leadership styles, especially in regard to the balance between concern for people and for tasks, depends on the situation—this is developed by Fred E. Ficdler in *A theory of leadership effectiveness* (McGraw-Hill, 1967). Fiedler has also pointed out that managers who have a given type of personality may find it hard to adopt certain leadership styles which are out of keeping with that personality.

These books are all American: there has been relatively little British work on leadership—even Frank A. Helter's *Managerial decision-making* (Tavistock, 1971) reports research on American managers by a British investigator. However, Michael Argyle has conducted research into interpersonal behaviour and social skills which he reports along with other work in *The psychology of interpersonal behaviour* (Penguin, 1967) and *Social interaction* (Methuen, 1969).

Organistional processes

Alfred D. Chandler's *Strategy and structure* (MIT Press, 1962) provides a seminal analysis of how big American corporations developed over the course of time; a more personal account of the process of corporate change is given in A. P. Sloan's *My years with General Motors* (Doubleday, 1964). Two classic statements on the process of managing are given by Mary Parker Follett in *Dynamic administration*, edited by H. C. Metcalf and L. Urwick (Harper, 1941), who was primarily a political theorist, and by C. I. Barnard in *The functions of the executive* (Harvard University Press, 1938), who was a senior American executive of long experience.

Organisational processes of communicating, processing and sometimes withholding information, of internal conflicts and politicking, of shifts in the power accruing to people's roles, and so forth, often become more exposed to the observer during periods of change, when the organisation is, as it were, subject to pressure and even crisis. R. H. Guest's *Organisational change* (Dorsey, 1962) and A. W. Gouldner's *Patterns of industrial bureaucracy* (Free Press, 1954) are two case studies of the organisational processes stemming from a change in chief executives. Philip Selznick's *TVA and the grass roots* (University of California, 1949; Harper, 1966) is a detailed analysis of the processes by which the Tennesse Valley Authority accommodated itself to its local environment and clientele. Studies of the introduction of new technology, such as Enid Mumford and Olive Bank's *The computer and the clerk* (Routledge and Kegan Paul, 1967) also provide an insight into how organisations adjust to change with different degrees of success. A study such as Melville Dalton's *Men who manage* (Wiley, 1959) serves to remind us, however, that change, bargaining and conflict are endemic rather than exceptional features of life within organisations.

One of the most central processes within organisations is the securing and evaluation of relevant information as a basis for taking decisions. Harold L. Wilensky's *Organisational intelligence* (Basic Books, 1967) demonstrates through a wealth of American case material how the quality of information available to organisational decision-makers can shape their policy formulations; where information is inadequate, policies may become disastrously out of tune with environmental realities. *The politics of organisational decision making* (Tavistock, 1973), by Andrew Pettigrew, provides a study of how specialist personnel can influence major organisational decisions through their control over the provision of technical information. James G. March and Herbert A. Simon's path-breaking synthesis of research on *Organisations* (Wiley, 1965) gave a great deal of attention to the cognitive limits on rationality in decision-making and the problem of searching for relevant information, an issue further developed in Cyert and March's *Behavioural theory of the firm*, cited earlier.

Organisation structure and systems of management

The structure and processes of an organisation are likely to be intimately related. Tom Burns and G. M. Stalker's *The management of innovation* (Tavistock, 1966) is a pioneering study of Scottish electronics companies moving into more dynamic environments, which demonstrates how inappropriate structures can give rise to processes and behaviour inimical to effective company performance. H. J. Leavitt's *Managerial psychology* (3rd ed., University of Chicago Press, 1972) describes experiments which demonstrate how the formal structure of relationships between roles can influence patterns of communication and, hence, the speed and quality of decisions.

PA Management Consultants' *Company organisation theory and practice* (Allen and Unwin, 1970) draws upon theory, research and consulting experience to suggest practical guidelines on organisation structure for managers. Wilfred Brown's *Organisation* (Heinemann Educational, 1971) builds upon the author's experience at the Glacier Metal Company and in public life. Michael Z. Brooke and H. Lee Remmers's *The strategy of multinational enterprise* (Longman, 1970) presents research into the organisation and management systems adopted within large multinational corporations, while John Stopford and Louis T. Wells's *Managing the multinational enterprise* (Longman, 1972) is another comparative study on the same subject. Leonard R. Sayles and Margaret K. Chandler's *Managing large systems* (Harper and Row, 1971) is a major study of the administration of the National Aeronautics and Space Administration (NASA) which provides considerable insight into ways of organising corporations of giant size and complexity, such as the development of matrix structures.

The effects of different structures and management systems upon behaviour within organisations has not yet been thoroughly researched. Chris Argyris in *Personality and organisation* (Harper, 1957) and in later books such as *Integrating the individual and the organisation* (Wiley, 1964) puts the case that traditional bureaucratic forms of organisation have deleterious effects on their members' capacities to find fulfilment in their employment. An early study by Argyris examined *The impact of budgets on people* (Controllership Institute, 1952). An important article by Lyman W. Porter and Edward E. Lawler has reviewed research on 'Properties of organisation structure in relation to job attitudes and job behaviour'. This appeared in the *Psychological Bulletin*, July, 64 (1965).

Systems of payment can be regarded as an aspect of the structure of management control. The conditions under which different forms of payment system give rise to particular behaviours among employees is a question that has long attracted interest, especially among British writers. R. Marriott's *Incentive payment systems: a review of research and opinion* (Staples, 1968) compares the evidence from many studies. W. Baldamus's *Efficiency and effort* (Tavistock, 1961) is a perceptive analysis, while important British research on payment systems and shopfloor behaviour is reported by Lupton's *On the shop floor* (already cited) and by Sheila Cunnison's *Wages and work allocation* (Tavistock, 1967). Tom Lupton and Dan Gowler attempt to provide a systematic approach to *Selecting a wage payment system* (Engineering Employers' Federation, 1969), which pays due regard to the complexities of practical situations. Elliot Jaques's *Equitable payment* (Heinemann Educational, 1961; Penguin, 1967) argues that shared norms about 'fair pay' which his research has identified should be used as a baseline for an agreed national policy on income differentials.

Organisational design

As research progresses, it is becoming evident that the performance of organisations is enhanced if the design of their structures and management systems takes account of the particular circumstances under which they are operating. There is surprisingly little literature on organisational performance as yet, although James L. Price's *Organisational effectiveness* (Irwin-Dorsey, 1968) has made a start by listing an inventory of propositions gleaned from 50 studies, while Paul E. Mott's *The characteristics of effective organisations* (Harper and Row, 1972) explores the correlates of organisational performance with data from several types of American institution.

However, studies of the forms of organisation adopted under different environmental conditions, with different technologies and sizes of enterprises, have usually made explicit, or at least implicit, reference to performance. Thus, Paul R. Lawrence and Jay W. Lorsch's *Organisation and environment* (Harvard Business School, 1967) present research evidence that shows how successful companies adopted different degrees of internal differentiation and types of co-ordinative mechanisms according to the dynamism of the environment. On the basis of their findings they developed the practical approach to improving organisational design described in their *Developing organisations: diagnosis and action* (Addison-Wesley,

1969). Joan Woodward's *Industrial organisation: theory and practice* (Oxford University Press, 1965) found that more successful firms were those which varied their structures according to their dominant forms of production technology. Charles Perrow's *Organisational Analysis: a sociological view* (Tavistock, 1970) also argues that different organisational designs are appropriate to different technologies. Studies such as Peter M. Blau and Richard A. Schoenherr's *The structure of organisations* (Basic Books, 1971), which find a high degree of association between the size of organisations and the nature of the structures they adopt, suggest that this also represents an accommodation to the requirements for administrative effectiveness.

Books are now beginning to appear which focus specifically on the considerations that should enter into the design of organisation. For example, Gene W. Dalton and Paul R. Lawrence's *Organisational structure and design* (Irwin-Dorsey 1970) presents American cases and guidelines, while *Studies in organisational design*, edited by Jay W. Lorsch and Paul R. Lawrence (Irwin-Dorsey 1970), contains further reports of experience in American companies. Sayles and Chandler's *Managing large scale systems* (already cited) provides valuable guidelines on methods and problems of managing matrix systems of organisation.

The challenge of change

A further contingency in designing organisation is, of course, provided by the members: their abilities, their needs and their aspirations. I have already cited writings such as those of Chris Argyris which maintain that this has become an urgent problem in the development of contemporary organisation structures. There is a growing awareness that the world of work is experiencing considerable pressures for change not only from the increasing aspirations of people to partcipate in a more meaningful and responsible work life, but also from market developments, technical advances and governmental intervention. Consequently, there is now a considerable interest in the problems of designing organisations and jobs in order that they should be more adaptive to meet increasing change. The commitment and contribution of employees is all the more necessary to achieve this degree of organisational flexibility. How to develop organisations to a point where this objective is secured has been the theme of a series of books published by Addison-Wesley on *Organisation development*. The keynote for this series is set by Warren G. Bennis's *Organisation development: its nature, origins and prospects* (Addison-Wesley, 1969). *Personal and organisational development*, edited by Richard Hacon (McGraw-Hill, 1972) is a useful collection of articles on the same issue.

Several good texts on organisation development have now appeared, among them *Organizational change: techniques and applications* by N. Margulies and J. Wallace (Scott Foresman, 1973) and *Organisation development*, by W. L. French and C. H. Bell (Prentice-Hall, 1973).

Two books by Peter A. Clark examine the processes of collaboration by social scientists with managers in the introduction of new or changed organisational systems. His *Organisational design: theory and practice* (already cited) is a detailed report of his own and colleagues' experience, while his *Action research and organisational change* (Harper and Row, 1972) analyses reported research and experience. Philip Sadler and Bernard Barry also report on *Organisational development: case studies in the printing industry* (Longman, 1970).

Attempts to redesign jobs in order to permit employees to exercise more responsibility and initiative are described in Louis E. Davis and James C. Taylor's *Design of jobs* (cited earlier), and also in Margaret Butteriss's *Job enrichment and employee participation* (Institute of Personnel Management, 1971). W. J. Paul and K. B. Robertson's *Job enrichment and employee motivation* (Gower Press, 1970) describes the results of experiments among employees in ICI which were stimulated by Herzberg's theory of work motivation. Lynda King Taylor's *Not for bread alone* (Business Books, 1972) provides further cases of the application of job enrichment in British and European companies. W. W. Daniel and Neil McIntosh's *The right to manage?* (Macdonald, 1972) argues that British management must catch up with changes in its labour force which require the enrichment of jobs, the extension of participation in decision-making and the reform of payment systems.

Finally, automation and the introduction of computers has been a major source of change in organisations for some while now. The problems and opportunities attendant on the introduction of automation are considered by Philip Sadler in *Social research on automation* (Heinemann, 1968) and by H. A. Rhee in *Office automation in social perspective* (Blackwell, 1968). E. Mumford and T. Ward's *Computers: planning for people* (Batsford, 1968) is specifically concerned with planning the introduction of computer systems and securing the acceptance of consequent changes by employees. Mumford has also studied job satisfaction among computer specialists in *Job satisfaction: a study of computer specialists* (Longmans, 1972).

CONCLUSION

This chapter has provided a selection of literature on organisational behaviour. The range of topics and titles has been extensive, and it is apparent that most books are confined to specialised aspects of the total field. A more holistic approach is, however, attracting increasing interest, and we can expect in the future to see a growing volume of literature which will adopt the interdisciplinary and integrated concept of organisational behaviour outlined at the beginning of the chapter.

14

The Literature of Manpower Management and Industrial Relations

Ray Loveridge and *Stuart Timperley*

The practice of management may be defined in terms of a universally recognised social need to exercise control over resources—both physical and human. While control over physical resources often demands great technical expertise, the ability to control human resources requires the ability to *influence* the attitudes and behaviour of others. Technical control over physical and financial resources is much more amenable to systematic programming than is control over human beings. Manpower management is therefore often the source of considerable frustration to less skilled practitioners, who fail to realise the complementary of the technical and motivational aspects of management and the dependency of the one on the other.

The area of study of Manpower Management is the recruitment, allocation and motivation of a labour force within an industrialised society. As such, it extends beyond the study of work organisations to an analysis of the contextual social, legal, political and economic structure within which the employment contract is struck. Its primary focus is nevertheless this contract between the individual employee, or group of employees, and the employer.

For at least 50 years the study of Manpower Management has been carried out by writers ranging through psychologists, production engineers, political scientists, economists, lawyers and, more recently, social anthropologists and sociologists. Within their work a strong functionally oriented interest in the Personnel aspects of management has emerged on the one hand and, on the other, a concern for labour markets and collective procedures generally entitled Industrial Relations. The growth in recognition given to professional examinations in Personnel Management and to under-graduate and postgraduate degree courses in Industrial Relations has reinforced and accelerated the growing tendency to functional specialisation in this area of management. Over the last 10 years this nascent professional-ism has in turn produced a vast expansion in the literature available to the general reader. Its very abundance makes the problem of selection a difficult one; more particularly because, in spite of the growth in pro-fessionalism, the number of good integrative textbooks available to English audiences are still relatively scarce.

Nor are the professional biases always helpful to the general reader. The writer on Personnel Management will normally treat Industrial Relations, like Manpower Planning, Training, etc., as a specialist sub-division of the functionally oriented discipline of Personnel Management. Yet for many academic writers the field of Industrial Relations is seen to cover all aspects of the employment relationship. It, and not Personnel Management, is the over-spanning discipline: for these authors Industrial Relations is seen to treat all possible factors affecting the form and method of job regulation—of which Personnel Management is only one. Indeed, for reasons explained below, writers on Industrial Relations have tended until recently to discount the role of the personnel manager.

This antipathy is not, of course, true of academic psychologists. Both occupational psychologists (selection, development, etc.) and industrial psychologists (work place) have been major contributors to the core of Personnel Management thought and literature. Yet in itself this professional alliance has created a deep gulf between these professional psychologists writing on individual and small group characteristics (normally described as Human Relations) and academic economists, lawyers and sociologists. The latter have usually chosen to concern themselves with the workings of labour markets, and institutions analysed as collective phenomena. The involvement of psychologists, or 'behaviouralists', in the design of manage-ment controls and in training management in the use of such controls has been a source of approbation among other social scientists until comparatively recently.

Thus, as well as the usual barriers to communication between academics and management that are presented by differences in habit and language, one finds that, within academic disciplines, specialisms are so narrow as sometimes to result in a certain 'ivory tower' naivety in the researcher's approach to management problems. The psychologist will sometimes write as if trade unions or the fear of redundancy never happened; the labour economist, as if productivity were related to marginal changes in wages; the labour lawyers, as if extrapolations from eighteenth century case law could 'solve' problems of highly involved human relationships.

Fortunately, this impression is now being mitigated by the case study research undertaken by social scientists in recent years. This work has been given impetus by the, not universally popular, intervention of statutory agencies such as the National Board for Prices and Incomes, the Commission on Industrial Relations and the National Training Agency, and also by the work of consultants. The innovations were, however, those made by a small group of industrial sociologists and social anthropologists at the University of Liverpool during the 1950s headed by Professor W. H. Scott, and published in, for example, books such as *Technical change and industrial relations*, by W. H. Scott and others (Liverpool University Press, 1956). The contributions made then and subsequently by the alumni of this group have influenced the whole course of research and study in the manpower area. Contemporary in time and equally important from the point of view of personnel design and practice has been the work of the Tavistock Institute and Clinic. Quite apart from the contributions that the Tavistock team have made to occupational psychology—see, for example, 'The process of occupational choice', by S. White (*British Journal of Industrial Relations*, **4**(2), 166–184, 1968) —the development of the concept of the 'socio-technical system' as both a framework of organisational analysis and a basis for prognosis has stemmed from the work of the Institute and has been published in such books as, for example, *Organisational choice*, by E. L. Trist and others (Tavistock Press, 1963). The work of these groups has proliferated to many universities, colleges and management training schools.

To an increasing extent students of manpower management have become aware of the need for a more embracing conceptual umbrella than that provided by either personnel management or industrial relations. The cross-fertilisation of ideas in the manpower studies has led to the formation of a group of researchers and practitioners each of whom has more in common with the others than with his particular discipline. On the other hand, the trend to increasing specialisation in such fields as manpower planning and the psychology of negotiating and gaming has tended to be centrifugal in its effect rather than integrative. Neither does one anticipate that such valuable contributors to management thinking as labour economists and labour lawyers will willingly surrender their professional allegiances to any new integrative discipline.

Nevertheless, there has been a change in the focus of much of the literature from a concern with intuitive 'principle' and anecdotal 'practice' to an emphasis on properly researched diagnosis of organisational problems and a rational planning of manpower requirements. The authors of this chapter will deliberately give weight to this new type of literature in their selection. We do not, however, subscribe to the erection of new professional barriers, since we believe that the frontiers of knowledge can only be extended by being kept open to all comers. The reader must therefore assume an eclectic approach to the selection of his reading. Whoever has treated the employment relationship as his subject for study is eligible to appear in this chapter.

The framework for this chapter is a simple one. The first section comprises a guide to the literature in industrial relations. The next focuses on personnel management. A third suggests an integrative approach to the framework preparation of learning media in the area of manpower management, and on the basis of this framework we make suggestions on present omissions from the literature.

The content of the literature takes three forms. The first is concerned with distilling present knowledge and presenting it in an integrated manner. A second category is that which attempts to suggest modified and 'improved' methods of management. In the best examples of this literature the author looks for explanations of managerial problems through scientific study and analysis. Equally valuable in a different way are contributions by distinguished practitioners who can structure their experience so as to provide lessons for others in the field. Lastly, there is the vast output of literature used in the day-to-day operation of any functional area of management but more particularly in the manpower area. Collective agreements, training documents, labour market statistics and the analysis of these provided by trade associations, government agencies and consultants are all vital to an understanding of the operation of personnel or industrial relations systems.

INDUSTRIAL RELATIONS

For many years the study of industrial relations in the UK has been based on or around extramural university teaching for trade union members. In the post-war era the emergence of interventionary Government strategies has brought about an increasing concern among academics and practitioners with evolving means to meeting *community* priorities rather than those of direct participants. There has therefore been a noticeable shift in the focus of the literature away from recording the history of protest and early unionisation to analyses and even propagation of the concepts of 'fairness', 'participation' and 'partnership' in the management of the economy as a whole. While the institutions of collective bargaining remain at the centre of this concern, the emphasis has been on the control of the regulatory system of bargaining itself either by statutory means or through external investigation designed to stimulate a self-generated change within industry, company or plant industrial relations systems.

Over this period the study of social history and evolutionary processes within industrial relations has given place to a consideration of the design of new or modified systems of joint regulation. Although this emphasis upon systematic approaches to the analysis of the subject has been historically related to the need to design *national* regulatory structures, spillover to management has been very real. The teaching and literature in the field are slowly but with increasing momentum becoming geared to the vocational needs of the practitioners. We propose to give some brief insight into the literature of industrial relations under the headings of general textbooks; work place bargaining; trade unions; shop-stewards; labour markets; industrial law; and, finally, employer associations and specific industrial conditions. A separate section is given to journals and miscellaneous source material.

General textbooks

This type of book has been written by most major scholars at some time in their career. The latest and most encyclopaedic is indubitably that of Professor H. A. Clegg, *The system of industrial relations in Great Britain* (2nd ed., Blackwell, 1972). A more compact book of readings edited by W. E. J. McCarthy, *Industrial relations in Britain* (Lyon Grant and Green, 1969), has been produced for Henley Administrative Staff College; while one of the present authors has produced a one-chapter survey of the system, *Collective bargaining by national employees in the UK*, by R. Loveridge (Ann Arbor, 1971). However, the most lucid analysis to be obtained is still that of the *Report of the Royal Commission on Trade Unions and Employer Associations*, 1965–68, under the Chairmanship of Lord Donovan (HMSO, 1968). If this book is taken as a text, it must obviously be supplemented by one of the many books written on the 1971 *Industrial Relations Act.*

For the management teacher or trainer R. Lowndes's book *Industrial relations: a contemporary survey* (Holt, Reinhart and Winston, 1972) is an attempt to marry a systems approach to industrial relations with behavioural theory through the use of long quotations from a wide variety of source literature. A number of managerial practitioners are also beginning to write of their experiences, distinguished examples being *The manager's guide to industrial relations*, by L. F. Neal and A. Robertson (Allen and Unwin, 1969) and Lord Robens's *Engineering and economic progress* (Oxford University Press, 1965). In general, these books can provide valuable insights into the way theory and practice combine with the idiosyncratic values and needs of practitioners believed by their contemporaries to be successful managers.

Work place bargaining

Since the move to work place negotiations has been a major feature of UK industrial relations in the post-war period, it is difficult to escape this subject under any heading. The history of this movement is traced in a reader edited by Professor B. C. Roberts, *Industrial relations: contemporary problems and perspectives* (Methuen, 1968). The change brought about through participative methods of bargaining was explored by Alan Flanders's pioneering *The Fawley productivity agreements* (Faber, 1964). Other authors, such as W. W. Daniel in his *Beyond the wage-work bargain* (PEP Broadsheet 519, July 1970), have produced valuable empirical evidence of new innovations in bargaining together with a behavioural analysis of its effects. More recently B. Towers, T. Whittingham and A. W. Gottschalk have brought together a valuable collection of readings on new forms of plant regulation *Bargaining for change* (Allen and Unwin, 1973). From such collections of the varied evidence and research findings one can trace the emergence of a new text, less concerned with the structure of rules and regulations, and more able to analyse the processes by which they were arrived at.

Trade unions and the role of the shop steward

The process of plant bargaining cannot, however, be understood without a clear analysis and understanding of the role of the shop steward. W. E. J. McCarthy's analysis *The role of the shop steward in British industrial relations* (Research Paper No. 1, HMSO, 1966) provides the content of the first of a series of Research Papers prepared for the Royal Commission on Trade Unions and Employer Associations. A wider discussion based on a survey of shop stewards has been prepared by J. F. B. Goodman and T. Whittingham, *Shop stewards in British industry* (Pan Books, 1973) and another study by S. W. Lerner and J. Bescoby, *Shop steward combine committees in the British engineering industry* (*British Journal of Industrial Relations*, July 1966) covers 'combines' or federations of stewards.

W. E. J. McCarthy has written the most original work on the 'closed shop', *The closed shop in Britain* (Blackwell, 1964), while Professor H. A. Turner has related this aspect of union tactics to the strategy and structure of their organisation in his *Trade union growth, structure and policy* (Allen and Unwin, 1962). A more discursive little book on unions is that of Professor Alan Flanders, *Trade unions* (Hutchinson, 1965), while W. E. J. McCarthy's Penguin collection of readings, *Trade unions* (Penguin Books, 1972), provides a useful pot-pourri. A notable omission, however, is Professor V. L. Allen's fundamentally important work on union leadership and union democracy, *Trade union leadership* (Longmans Green, 1957). Occupational change in the labour market and in company recruiting patterns has brought a growing concern with the problems of white-collar workers. Professor G. S. Bain has written what is probably the definitive work on white-collar unionisation, *The growth of white collar unionism* (Clarendon Press, 1970), while several other surveys have begun to contribute to our knowledge in this area.

Labour markets

One of the more interesting books on general market conditions is that of L. C. Hunter and D. J. Robertson, *Economics of wages and labour* (Macmillan, 1969). L. C. Hunter has also written, with G. L. Reid, a comprehensive survey of the literature on labour market mobility, *Urban worker mobility* (Paris, OECD, 1968). An attempt to analyse local wage structures in economist's terms has been made by Derek Robinson in *Local labour markets and wage structures* (Gower Press, 1970). Wage payment systems have been analysed by behavioural scientists on many occasions, but Robinson's book attempts to provide an integrated framework. Hours of work, overtime and shift-working are examined in various texts from the diverse viewpoints of economists, psychologists and sociologists with little attempt at integration, and a good example of this is *Manpower policy and employment trends*, edited by B. C. Roberts and J. H. Smith (Bell, 1966). Restrictive or protective practices have also been examined through these different approaches brought together in *Restrictive practices* (Research Paper No. 4 of the Royal Commission, 1967). Redundancy and other less traumatic aspects of economic and technological change are examined by a number of contemporary scholars as well as by practitioners.

Industrial law

The *Industrial Relations Act* of 1971 has of course resulted in a spate of publications. These range from short guides to the workings of the Act issued by employer associations, such as the Engineering Employers' Federation, through more extensive check-lists in layman's language, such as P. Patterson's *Employer guide to the Industrial Relations Act* (Kogan Page, 1971), to even more extensive and learned analyses written by lawyers—for example, N. M. Selwyn's *Guide to the Industrial Relations Act* (Butterworths, 1971). The text combines experience in the working of the Act with legal analysis has yet to be written and of course cannot be written until sufficient case-law has been established to make the writing of such a text worthwhile. A number of good texts exist on industrial law as it has evolved within the tradition of British common law prior to the 1971 Act and these must be read to understand the framework within which industrial relations has evolved in the UK.

Possibly of more importance in the day-to-day servicing of industrial relations is the structure of law relating to employment, safety and welfare. This has been well treated by Mrs. O. Aikin and Mrs. J: Reid in the first of the Penguin Foundations of Law Series, *Employment, welfare and safety at work* (Penguin Books, 1971); but this volume has of course to be supplemented by the recent *Report of the Select Committee on Safety and Hygiene* (HMSO, 1973) under the Chairmanship of Lord Robens, and by the *Industrial Relations Act* itself.

Industrial bargaining

Employer associations have been greatly neglected in the literature. Professor Clegg and R. Adams have written a historical account of employer federations in the engineering industry, *The employers' challenge* (Blackwell, 1957), and A. Marsh has provided a meticulous historical examination of procedures within the industry, *Industrial relations in engineering* (Pergamon Press, 1965). We must again resort to the Research series of the Royal Commission to find a more comprehensive coverage of other industries, *Employers' associations*, by V. G. Munn and W. E. J. McCarthy (Research Paper No. 7, Royal Commission, HMSO, 1967). For a similarly wide review of procedures one has to go back to the badly dated *Industrial relations handbook* of the Ministry of Labour (1961). A number of accounts exist of the *workings* of such procedures, most notably H. A. Turner, G. Clack and G. Roberts's *Labour relations in the motor industry* (Allen and Unwin, 1967).

Journals, periodicals and miscellaneous sources

To the practising manager concise reviews of the 'state of play' are invaluable. Two services set out to provide up-to-date information on industrial relations together with précis of legal cases and the latest agreement and commentaries on long term trends. *Incomes Data Service* began in 1966 on the rising tide of productivity bargaining and the consequent need for information of a more sophisticated kind than was then available. The *Industrial Relations Review and Report* is an imitator of the former publication which came out 2 years later; it aimed to place more emphasis on expert commentary, particularly on legal matters. A later 'stable-mate' is the *Industrial Relations Law Report* from the same publisher. The first two reviews are published at fortnightly intervals and the *Law Report* monthly. All three publications fill gaps in officially produced information services which remain woefully inadequate. This is particularly true of the activities of the Industrial Tribunals and the National Industrial Relations Court set up under the 1971 Act. The recorded verdicts of the latter institution may be obtained from the Court or in the daily Law Reports, in *The Times* and *The Daily Telegraph*. It is, however, impossible to find any cheap and easily accessible central record of Industrial Tribunal verdicts or analysis of their verdicts such as is provided by the National Labour Relations Board in the USA.

The reports of the *Commission on Industrial Relations* appear at regular intervals. These are often reports of investigations into plant recognition or bargaining procedures which have been referred to the CIR by the Secretary of State under the terms of the 1971 Act or which have been undertaken at the invitation of the parties concerned. However, most of the recent references have been on issues of wider significance, such as shop steward facilities (Report 17) or industrial relations training (Reports 33 and 33a). These, together with the research reports and policy indicators of the Department of Employment, the Manpower Commission and other more transitory Government bodies, have provided a new and very high level of discussion on industrial relations topics. Publications range from *Training for the management of human resources* (1972) to *Equal opportunities for men and women* (1973). A standing order at HMSO and the Department of Employment are well worth while. (A similar subscription to the US Department of Labor will still provide an idea of the service that should be possible in the UK.) The monthly *DEP Gazette* contains a range of useful labour statistics and short articles on trends and recent developments.

Unfavourable comparisons might also be made between the publications of employer associations in the UK and the associations (or local conference boards) in the USA and Europe. However, mention has to be made of the efforts of the British Institute of Management in the training area; the Management Education Information Unit is a particularly good guide in industrial relations, as in other areas of management. A number of industrial employer groups, most notably those in printing and chemicals, have also produced excellent information services. For some time the Engineering Employers Federation published work based on sponsored research programmes (see our later reference to Lupton *et al.*) and these are still available. Local associations such as the Coventry Engineering Employers Association also deserve an honourable mention. Needless to say, a standing order for the publications of the Institute of Personnel Management is extremely valuable, as is contact with the TUC publications department and the production and research departments of the major trade unions.

Outside of employer associations and unions, there exist a range of peripheral organisations supplying information in pursuit of their various objectives. Most notable is that of The Industrial Society, whose aim is to reduce industrial conflict through improved 'communications'. In recent times the Society has gained a high and steadily improving reputation for professional consultancy and this is beginning to appear in its literature. More transitory organisations range from Working Together, which has produced interesting work on job evaluation and other subjects, to Common Cause, which *inter alia*, reports on the alleged political activities of unionists. Much of this peripheral literature gives 'flavour' to one's knowledge of the field.

An international perspective may be gained by means of an annual subscription to the International Institute of Labour Studies at Geneva; for trainers its documentary exchange scheme provides useful source material and training exercises—free! On the same 'academic' plane the *British Journal of Industrial Relations* (London School of Economics) and the *Industrial Relations Journal* (University of Nottingham) provide the profession with its main means of communications. For the less insular the *Industrial and Labor Relations Review* (Cornell University) and *Industrial Relations* (University of California, Berkeley) are often conducive to new thoughts on familiar domestic problems.

Manpower management

As we mentioned in the introduction to this chapter, it is only recently that the personnel management field has begun to develop its own literature. This is particularly true of the UK, where, unlike their American counterparts, British personnel specialists have been slow in developing an organised and integrated body of material. In particular, the dichotomy between prescriptive work based on well-established normative 'principles and practice' on the one hand and analyses of real-life situations by social scientists on the other hand is still very evident.

The basic functions of personnel—the recruitment, the induction, the allocation and the motivation of manpower—can be expounded within a strictly procedural manner accompanied by general statements on 'the one best way' to carry through these procedures. Conversely, it is possible to examine these same procedures in operation under a variety of differing circumstances, for example, and to note that there is no one best way but only particular forms of *analysis*, some more appropriate than others in pursuit of given organisational goals. This latter way—the social scientists' way—is not easily transplanted in the psyche of many of the most hardened practitioners, who, in spite of the variety of their day-to-day experiences, prefer the absolute nature of generalised principle.

General texts

There are signs, however, that the situation with regard to personnel management literature is changing in this country. There are now a number of textbooks in existence albeit in many cases of an introductory nature. They nevertheless represent a useful base upon which to build a more substantial literature. J. V. Grant and A. Smith, in their *Personnel administration and industrial relations* (Longmans, 1969), have produced a sensible introductory text for students which includes chapters on the major personnel specialisms. J. Munro Fraser's compact volume, *Introduction to personnel management* (Nelson, 1971), is also helpful for the newcomer and is illustrated by easily understood cases, as is T. P. Lyons's *The personnel function in a changing environment* (Pitman, 1971), which is written from the practitioner's standpoint (and all the more welcome for that). Like the previous books, this latter text provides an excellent starting point for the newcomer.

A much wider and socially aware view of the field is taken by Anne Crichton in her examination of the implications of the changing environment for personnel management, *Personnel management in context* (Batsford, 1968). The nature of industrial organisation, the development of unions and professions, as well as the impact of the developments in the social sciences are taken into account. Although the author is not very explicit about her interpretation of such implications, she does present a comprehensive review of the main work and contributions in each of these areas, a helpful list of recommended further readings and an analysis of the role of personnel specialists. Similarly, a rather wider perspective than is found in most texts is provided by the book of readings in personnel management edited by D. E. McFarland for the Penguin Modern Management series, *Personnel management* (Penguin Books, 1971). There is some unevenness of choice in this reader, but it is basically a problem-centred volume which attempts to cover relevant issues.

Finally, on the general aspects of personnel management, it is worth mentioning two excellent introductory booklets, one by David Barber, *The process of personnel management* (IPM, 1971), and the other by J. Collingridge and M. Ritchie, *Personnel management: problems of the smaller firm* (IPM, 1970). The former outlines the function and process of personnel management, and the latter focuses on problems in the smaller firm. They are both in the Institute of Personnel Management series of pamphlets. Like other titles in this series, these booklets provide clearly written outlines of an introductory nature.

All these booklets are predominantly British sources and it is felt that there is some merit in providing references that are culturally specific. However, there are many concepts and techniques which are common across culture and a number of American texts are still the standard works on the subject. The classic reference is still the general text *Personnel administration*, by P. Pigors and C. A. Myers (McGraw-Hill, 1969), now in its sixth edition. Two other standard American works are G. Strauss and L. R. Sayles's *Personnel: human problems in management* (Prentice-Hall, 1967), and W. L. French's *Personnel management process* (Houghton Mifflin, 1970) (both in their second editions). All these books share the dubious distinction of undertaking a comprehensive coverage of the field in a most predictable way. An even greater drawback is perhaps the fragmented and disintegrated treatment of each of the major areas. It is perhaps significant that when similar ground is given a distinctly psychological bias, as in J. B. Miner's book *Personnel psychology* (Macmillan, 1960) the text is more satisfactory. The rigour of treatment and presentation is notable.

Manpower planning

Increasingly it is being accepted that any action in the personnel field should take place within a planning framework, and this is reflected in, or is perhaps a consequence of, the relatively recent publications on manpower planning. Two of the shortest, but possibly the best, are in booklet form: the first, by the Edinburgh Group of the IPM, *Perspectives in manpower planning* (IPM, 1967), deals succinctly with most aspects of manpower planning—the motivation for it, manpower analysis, utilisation and forecasting—at all levels. The second is by the Department of Employment, *Company manpower planning* (HMSO, 1968), and although specifically organisational in intention, it is nonetheless a most useful and practical document. The realisation that every aspect of organisational planning cannot be divorced from manpower planning is the basis of an informative book by G. Mcbeath, *Organisation and manpower planning* (Business Books, 1969). More specialised manpower planning, that for high-talent manpower and executive development, is dealt with very thoroughly by E. W. Vetter in his *Manpower planning for high talent personnel* (University of Michigan Press, 1967). Also in this area there are some useful books of readings which draw together quantitative and qualitative writings and research findings: two such are N. A. B. Wilson and D. Bartholomew's *Manpower research* (English Universities Press, 1969), and A. R. Smith's *Manpower and management science* (English Universities Press, 1972). Finally, the excellent bibliography edited by C. G. Lewis, *Manpower planning: a bibliography* (English Universities Press, 1970), is really indispensable for those concerned to explore in more detail this area.

Within the planning framework referred to above are contained the various personnel policy areas, and for the purpose of this chapter we propose to examine the literature in three of the key areas—the areas of rewards and payments, of recruitment and selection and of training and development.

Rewards structures

The nature of an organisation's reward system does not of course refer solely to financial and other material rewards; status and authority, for example, are often given and taken as rewards. Promotion and other sorts of mobility can therefore be seen as part of the system of organisational rewards. These factors are effectively covered in the literature on manpower planning which has already been mentioned. However, it is worth highlighting the fact that there is a well-developed literature on careers and occupation which deals with such issues. Two particularly good books by social scientists (i.e. not prescriptive) are Cyril Sofer's *Men in mid career* (Cambridge University Press, 1970), which is a discussion of executives in mid-career, and *Occupational sociology*, by L. Taylor (Oxford University Press, 1969).

To return more specifically to the area of payment, there is certainly no shortage of literature on the types and effects of payment systems. The now defunct National Board for Prices and Incomes produced a number of excellent reports on all aspects of employment, and two particularly useful ones were *Payment by results systems* (Report no. 65, Cmnd 3627 HMSO, 1968) and *Salary structures* (Report No. 132, Cmnd 4187, HMSO, 1969). One of the most systematic approaches to the design of rewards and reward structures is the booklet by Professor T. Lupton and D. Gowler, *Selecting a wage system* (Engineering Employers' Federation, 1969), which is part of the Engineering Employers Federation's research series—this attempts to list the situational factors to be taken into account when considering the introduction and appropriateness of a payment system. Written for practitioners, it represents a significant social science contribution to the design tools of the operational manager. The use of job evaluation techniques for assisting wage payment system design is now extensively practised. An introductory but fairly comprehensive booklet for personnel managers is George F. Thomason's *Personnel manager's guide to job evaluation* (IPM, 1968). A major work on the subject for those wishing to specialise much more has been written by T. T. Paterson and is called *Job Evaluation*, Vol. 1 (Business Books, 1972). To complete one's study of the relationship of wage payment systems to job evaluation and to productivity issues it is necessary to extend one's reading to works such as T. B. North and G. L. Buckingham's *Productivity agreements and wage systems* (Gower Press, 1969).

In contrast to the many studies of wage payment systems, there are few good books on salaries and executive remuneration systems. G. Mcbeath and D. N. Rand's *Salary administration* (2nd ed., Business Publications, 1969) is a practical and systematic account of the design and management of remuneration structures. The broad policy issues involved in management compensation are more extensively discussed by

G. Mcbeath in a separate work called *Management remuneration policy* (Business Books, 1969). Finally, the recent booklet *Salary structures for management careers* by A. Bowley (IPM, 1972) is a helpful guide in relating, as the title suggests, salary structures to management careers.

Recruitment, selection and induction

It is surprising that the input process, whereby people are recruited and selected for organisational positions, has not been given even more attention than it gets. We would contend that the way organisations choose potential managers, and equally the choice of potential employers by individuals in the labour market, are crucial for organisational effectiveness. To a considerable extent these reflect the identity and nature of an organisation, and, hence, the type of employment policies that operate subsequent to entry. Although there are obviously references to these subjects in many publications on recruitment and selection, there is little systematic attempt to relate the induction process to all other organisational attempts to influence the later behaviour of employees. Probably the most relevant work in this context is, again, Sofer's study of men in mid-career, mentioned above, which is set within a framework of the interrelated nature of personnel policies.

Most of the publications on recruitment and selection are prescriptively oriented towards specific procedures and techniques, some more general in their recommendations than others. For example, the booklet by R. A. Denerley and P. R. Plumbley, *Recruitment and selection in a full employment economy* (IPM, 1968), is an account of relevant approaches to the recruitment and selection of different types of employee under current conditions of full employment. *Recruitment handbook*, edited by B. Ungerson (Gower Press, 1970), is another useful reference book for the manager. Personnel selection and placement is discussed by M. D. Dunnette in his useful text *Personnel selection and placement* (Tavistock, 1966), which is extended to cover the evidence for adopting particular selection methods. More specialised areas in selection, such as interviewing techniques and psychological testing, are covered by two comprehensive references: one by E. Sidney and M. Brown, *The skills of interviewing* (Tavistock, 1961); and another, a now standard work on psychological testing, by A. Anastasi, *Psychological testing* (3rd ed., Collier-Macmillan, 1968).

Training and development

Much of the literature on training and development consists of surveys of the 'what is being done and shouldn't we do more' form: for example, the Department of Employment's publication entitled *Survey on management training and development* (HMSO, 1971). The other main category consists of discussions around the problem of the evaluation of the effectiveness of training. Such discussions are mainly to be found in articles: an exception is the book by P. Warr, M. Bird and N. Rackham, *Evaluation of management training* (Gower Press, 1970). A review of evaluations of management training produced by M. Whitelaw for the IPM booklet series, *The evaluation of management training: a review* (IPM, 1972), gives a surprisingly detailed account of the methodological problems and prescriptions for evaluations. In the well-established Tavistock Institute series of books the study by B. M. Bass and J. A Vaughan, *Training in industry: the management of learning* (Tavistock, 1968), is up to the high professional standards of that institution. Although again psychologically oriented, it is a useful and informative technical guide to what can be accomplished. The articles referred to above will be found in a variety of management and personnel journals, and we do not intend to mention such articles specifically (there are so many); rather we will briefly review the journals in this field and the reader can refer to these directly.

Journals

Apart from the social scientific journals which we referred to elsewhere in this chapter and which do occasionally contain articles of interest to the personnel specialist, there are a number of more specialised journals which provide between them considerable coverage of the personnel field. Undoubtedly the best source for keeping up to date on employment issues (all aspects of personnel, training and industrial relations) is the journal *Personnel Management*, published monthly by Business Publications for the Institute of Personnel Management. This consists of short, and usually highly readable and informative, articles with sections for sensible book reviews. In addition, a short Digest is published monthly containing primarily job advertisements but also updating recent personnel 'events'. The academic journal of personnel management—and again under the auspices of the IPM—is *Personnel Review*. This relatively new journal has made an impressive start under the joint editorship of Professor Enid Mumford and Karen Legge. It examines key issues affecting human resources—manpower planning, payment, selection, and so on—in some depth, as well as acting as a forum for what might be called the applied behavioural sciences. On the training side, the publication *Industrial Training International*, edited by Eric Frank and Peter Smith, is a useful reference for training specialists. The publications emanating from the various Industrial Training Boards usually have a usefulness which extends beyond the industry for which they have been produced. The Air Transport and the Travel Industry Board, for example, produce excellent reports of applied research. The newly created Institute of Manpower Studies based on the London School of Economics and the University of Sussex publish a regular survey of their activities under the title of *Monitor,* which is available on subscription.

The Association of Teachers of Management not only produce their own journal, *Management Education and Development,* which contains many relevant and informative articles of interest to practitioners as well as academics, but also a series of *Occasional Papers.* Most leading management journals and newspapers, such as the *Financial Times,* carry regular feature articles on the latest developments in manpower management. Through such media many managers have received a smattering of the new thinking on the subject which can be pursued in more specialised journals listed above.

CONCLUSIONS

The emergence of professionalism in manpower management is not an unmixed blessing; one important effect, however, is, that in content and form the literature of both personnel management and industrial relations has become more relevant to the work of the practitioner. From a certain 'wooliness' in content that reflected the author's concern with establishing long-term principles, or an excessively detailed exposition of techniques (not usually tested for the recommended universal applicability), the literature is turning to a new concern for hard situational analysis.

The form of publication is also changing. Most major publishers are issuing both new and old works in paper-back covers. Readings selected and brought together by distinguished scholars have been published in a number of series such as those in the *Penguin Modern Management Series.* Series of new works on industrial relations and personnel are also being compiled by *Pan Management Series* but an interesting new development is the publication of case studies such as T. Lane and K. Roberts's *Strike at Pilkingtons* by Fontana and others designed to appeal to a wide audience. All these paper-back contributions have so far tended to raise rather than lower standards of discussion. The field of study and research, however, is being carried forward by series such as those started by the SSRC Research Unit at the University of Warwick and by the London School of Economics Industrial Relations Department— both published by Heinemann Educational Books.

These series are just a few of the many started and carried on by universities and other professional bodies. Over a period of time they should acquire an identity and distinctive place in the literature. Much will obviously depend upon the continued acquisition and retention of an interested and increasingly sympathetic audience.

15

The Literature of Marketing

P. J. S. Law

INTRODUCTION

As Robert Louis Stevenson said, 'Everyone lives by selling something', and men have been practising marketing ever since the first caveman exchanged a portion of his latest kill for a couple of flint arrow-heads. However, the formal study of marketing has been of much more recent origin. It is really only in this century that scholars have differentiated marketing from other kinds of social and economic behaviour and have begun to accumulate knowledge and to build a theoretical framework to support their observations and relate them one to another. The science of marketing is a young science, and its literature must be read in that context. Impatience, inexperience, jumping to conclusions, all the faults of youth are to be found in abundance. The good qualities are there too, and there is plenty of evidence of enthusiasm and a willingness to explore new ideas. My main wish is that more writers would be more honest, both with their readers and with themselves. Too many new 'laws' of marketing are based on inadequate or half-baked evidence, too many crude thoughts are presented as the ultimate answers rather than exploratory questions. The arrogance with which this is often done provokes hostility in the reader, and genuine advances may be ignored or rejected.

DEVELOPMENT OF MARKETING THOUGHT

Marketing arose at the beginning of the twentieth century as a result of the failure of economic theory to explain economic activity or to provide guidance for businessmen and government authorities in market-place behaviour. Some markets were characterised by the absence of competition; demand and supply were no longer closely linked but were separated by increasingly complex channels of distribution; and wholesalers were exercising greater power over these channels. New interpretations were needed, and these needs led to the creation of marketing.

The first writings were mainly descriptive. The institutions in the channel were described, and an analysis was made of the functions performed at each level, such as stockholding, sorting and transportation. There were also specialised studies of advertising and selling, both important topics as the sellers' markets of the nineteenth century became saturated and manufacturers found it harder to dispose of their production.

In the second decade of the century marketing writing took a more analytical turn, and a number of different approaches were tried. Writers such as P. H. Nystrom, in *The economics of retailing* (Ronald Press, 1915), and L. D. H. Weld developed the institutional approach. Another group of writers concentrated on the functional aspects of marketing. Recognising that certain marketing activities were common to a wide range of situations, they identified and described 'elements' of marketing, such as selling, buying, credits and collections. This approach was typified by Paul Cherington in *The elements of marketing* (Macmillan, 1920). The commodity approach was mainly concerned with the marketing of agricultural produce, but manufactured goods were included later.

Other writers described marketing in terms of the economic concept of utility, suggesting that the creation of utility of time and place and, later, of possession was the *raison d'être* of marketing activity. The continued importance of advertising and selling was reflected by the number of books on these topics which appeared at this time, such as J. G. Frederick's *Modern sales management* (Appleton-Century, 1919).

In the 1920s and 1930s writers concentrated on the managerial and decision-making aspects of the subject. A body of empirical knowledge was being built up, and it was becoming possible to make generalised statements about cause and effect. These statements could then be used to suggest decision rules for managers, the 'principles' of marketing which emerged in the writings of men such as P. W. Ivey and F. E. Clark. Marketing was seen as an economic activity, affected by economic and social conditions in the market, and involving the performance by marketing establishments of all the activities involved in the distribution of goods from producers to consumers. This classical description of marketing is found in Paul D. Converse's book *Elements of marketing* (Prentice-Hall, 1930).

At this time, and not surprisingly, the first attempts at classification emerged. Goods were classified into convenience, shopping and speciality goods, according to the way in which they were purchased. The list of marketing functions was refined, and such things as providing market information included. Wholesaling and retailing were examined more closely. A series of books were produced on all aspects of retail management, such as buying credit, store operation and management, and merchandising. *Retail merchandising, planning and control*, by J. L. Fri (Prentice-Hall, 1925), was the first book in this 'Retailing Series'. T. N. Beckman defined more precisely the differences between wholesaling and retailing in such books as *Wholesaling* (Ronald Press, 1937).

Market research was another area in which significant developments took place. Attention was paid to the techniques of data collection, and at the same time the results of large-scale surveys began to be available. This enabled writers to back their qualitative judgments with quantitative evidence. L. O. Brown, in *Market research* (Ronald Press, 1937), made a major contribution in this field.

It was after the war that today's patterns of thought began to emerge. The emphasis on management continued and the idea of the marketing mix was put forward to show that marketing consisted of the conscious management of a range of interrelated variables in order to achieve specified objectives. The most significant change, however, was the development of the 'marketing concept'. In the early part of the century businessmen had been mainly concerned to improve their production, this being the era of 'scientific management' and such writers as F. W. Taylor. In the inter-war years increased production capacity was faced by shrinking markets and the main problem was how to get rid of everything that was made. Hence, attention was turned to improving methods of selling, advertising and distribution. After the post-war boom, markets again became saturated in the early 1950s, but this time the response was different. The customer was seen as the starting point for all marketing planning. Management's job was to identify and interpret their customers' needs and wants and then put together a marketing system, embracing distribution, selling, etc., and also the product itself, which met those needs. One of the leading exponents of this approach, which has come to be known as the 'marketing concept', is Theodore Levitt. His ideas have been summarised in a recent book, *The marketing mode: pathways to corporate growth* (McGraw-Hill, 1969). Current writers take this a stage further and define marketing's task as meeting the needs of society in general, for such things as freedom of choice, or at least adequate information on which to base choice, and freedom from pollution.

The 1960s were also characterised by an epidemic of model-building. Computers made it possible to handle vast quantities of data and mathematical models of varying degrees of complexity were produced to allocate advertisements between media, plan salesmen's calls, etc. At the same time the interests in customers' thought processes was demonstrated by the number of models of consumer behaviour that were proposed.

For those who wish to take this subject further Robert Bartels has written an excellent book, *The development of marketing thought* (Irwin, 1962), on which much of this section is based.

CURRENT APPROACHES

Marketing is a complicated subject. It all boils down eventually to people's behaviour, to their response to the words and pictures in an advertisement, to the interactions within a group of people responsible for the purchase of a power station, to the communication between a salesman and his prospect. Unfortunately, behavioural science is nowhere near ready to help the marketing decision-maker in the way that, say, thermodynamics helps the chemical engineer. Economists have for years claimed that fewer people will buy a product as the price is increased. This seems intrinsically reasonable, although the experimental evidence is rather limited, and leads to the downward-sloping demand curve which appears in Chapter 1 of every economics textbook. But how do people perceive the relationship between price and quality? What happens in times of rapid inflation? Do people have a threshold below which they are insensitive to price movements? These are the questions that marketing writers and managers have to struggle with to earn a living, and clear-cut answers are rarely to be found.

The literature of marketing is complicated, too. It seems, at times, as if there are as many ways of writing about the subject as there are writers. This is hardly surprising if one considers that it is not often taught at undergraduate level, and tends to attract people from a wide range of disciplines and with a wide range of experience. The applied mathematician looks on marketing as an exercise ground for his complicated mathematical models; the psychologist is interested in an individual's response to a variety of marketing stimuli; and the engineer seeks a practical and economical solution to a complicated problem. In this section I shall discuss some of the current approaches.

'Marketing literature offers its readers very few true and important "principles" or "theories" . . .'.* The situation is more or less the same today as it was in 1948, in spite of the continuing interest shown by writers in the development of a theory of marketing. This point is well illustrated by *Theory in marketing*, edited by Reavis Cox, Wroe Alderson and Stanley J. Shapiro (Irwin, 1964). The editors commissioned original essays from the leading American scholars of the day. The result is an interesting volume, but, as the editors say in their introduction: 'It would be most encouraging if the essays in this symposium showed beyond

---

*Wroe Alderson and Reavis Cox, 'Towards a theory of marketing' (*Journal of Marketing*, **13**(4), 139, 1948).

serious doubt that students of marketing are making substantial progress toward setting up a systematic and disciplined theory of their own to supplement and possibly to supplant the offerings of related disciplines. Unfortunately, the essays do not demonstrate this fact.' This is not really surprising, nor is it depressing.

There are a number of stages in the process of setting up a theory. The first stage is observation of a phenomenon. This observation is very often crude. For example, the ancients knew that there were certain heavenly bodies that moved relative to the fixed stars, and they were able to make quite accurate measurements of their changes in position over time. The next stage is the formulation of a hypothesis, an attempt to explain why things behave as they do. If one assumes that the earth is the centre of the universe, the observations of planetary position can only be explained by assuming that they move in a complicated set of interlocking cycles and epicycles. In spite of Aristarchus, this view held sway for some 1500 years. The next stage is experimentation, the testing of the hypothesis. Many people, of whom Copernicus is probably the best-known, had doubted the geocentric theory of planetary motion, but it was not until Tycho Brahe had completed his series of meticulous observations that Kepler was able to substantiate an alternative hypothesis, that planets moved round the sun in elliptical orbits, at non-uniform speeds. Finally, Newton, 'standing on the shoulders of giants', was able to reduce all observable motion in the universe to four basic laws, the laws of Inertia, of Acceleration under an impressed force, of Reciprocal Action and Reaction, and of Gravity. One should move on from here to Einstein and Heisenberg, but this chapter is concerned with marketing, not astronomy.

The point is that marketing theory now is at about the same stage of development as astronomical theory was at the end of the sixteenth century. Tycho Brahes there are in abundance. Nielsen researchers are questioning housewives and recording their purchases; MEAL are counting advertisements and publishing how much each firm spends month by month; and a host of PhD students are measuring everything in sight. There are some Keplers around, but they are few in number, and as for Newton, he is nowhere in sight.

This situation can be illustrated by a brief review of the literature of consumer behaviour. This is a topic of fundamental importance to marketing managers. Virtually everything they do, whether it be the planning of an advertising campaign, the choice of distribution channels or the packaging of a product, is done in an effort to communicate with an audience. Unless they can identify that audience, and understand how it behaves, there can be little basis other than hunch on which to decide such things as the content of an advertising message, its timing or the medium by which it is transmitted. A study of the literature reveals two things: firstly, the diversity of the approaches made to the problem, and secondly, that comparatively little use has been made of the hardest and most abundant of the data, the records of the actual purchases made by the consumers themselves. J. A. Howard and J. N. Sheth, in *The theory of buyer behaviour* (Wiley, 1969), construct an elaborate model on the basis of various psychological theories of learning and exploratory behaviour. A consumer, influenced by a number of 'exogenous variables' such as social class and culture, is exposed to inputs from the product itself. These variables and inputs are processed in various ways inside the consumer and the result is an output of purchase behaviour. Like the economist's demand curve, the model seems to be reasonable but cannot yet be tested as Farley and Ring discovered.* The same criticism can be levelled at the model F. M. Nicosia described in his book *Consumer decision processes, marketing and advertising implications* (Prentice-Hall, 1966). Consumer decision-making is depicted as a cycle. Messages from the environment impinge on a consumer's attributes to induce an attitude. He then goes through a search process, the result of which is a motivation. Finally, there is a purchase, leading to experience of the product, which feeds back into his attributes. The loop can, of course, be broken at any stage. Nicosia describes how this process can be simulated on a computer, but does not establish a close link between simulated and observed behaviour.

The problem of how a consumer chooses between brands has also been studied in depth. The sequence of an individual's purchases of the various brands within a product has been studied, and a number of explanations proposed for the patterns which develop. F. Harary and B. Lipstein, in 'The dynamics of brand loyalty: a Markovian approach' (*Operations Research*, **10**(1), 17, 1962), and J. D. Herniter and J. D. Magee, in 'Customer behaviour as a Markov process' (*Operations Research*, **9**(1), 105–122, 1961), suggest that there is an underlying probability of a consumer switching from one brand to another and that his choice of brands over time can be explained as a Markov process. When that didn't work semi-Markov and dynamic inference models were proposed, e.g. R. A. Howard, 'Dynamic inference' (*Operations Research*, **13**(5), 712–733, 1965). The Markovian Epicycles ground on while A. S. C. Ehrenberg and others took a fresh look at the data, with minds uncluttered by the myth of brand loyalty. An impressive list of publications culminated in Ehrenberg's book *Repeat-buying* (North-Holland, 1973). In this he proposes, among other things, that in many markets a consumer buys a portfolio of brands as they are all virtually the same in his eyes. Furthermore, his purchases over time can be predicted by a set of simple mathematical laws based on the negative binomial distribution. These laws, while saying nothing about the state of the consumer's mind before or

---

*J. U. Farley and L. W. Ring, 'An empirical test of the Howard–Sheth model of buyer behaviour' (*Journal of Marketing Research*, 7(4), 427–438, 1970).

during the act of purchase, are based on actual data, have wide generality and are strikingly robust. This is more than can be said for many of their predecessors.

A second approach to marketing is the managerial one. Here the emphasis is on normative rather than positive models, on presenting alternative courses of action rather than explaining phenomena, although, of course, these cannot be entirely separated. Many general marketing texts fall into this category. The best-known of these is Philip Kotler's *Marketing management: analysis, planning and control* (Prentice-Hall, 1972). Whatever one feels about Kotler's style, and the book could hardly be described as easy to read, almost every significant contribution to marketing thought appears somewhere in its 850 pages. Another massive and comprehensive treatise is the *Handbook of modern marketing* (McGraw-Hill, 1970), edited by V. P. Buell and C. Heyel. The editors commissioned 120 articles from leading writers and practitioners. Section headings include 'Planning the Product Line', 'Marketing Management' and 'Market Communications'. As with all books of readings, it lacks cohesion, but it is an invaluable reference text, and most of the sections include a short bibliography, so the reader can dig deeper into a topic if he wishes to.

Particular aspects of marketing have also been written about from a managerial point of view. F. A. Pessemier's *New product decisions* (McGraw-Hill, 1966), *Business logistics* (Ronald Press, 1964), by J. L. Heskett, R. M. Ivie and N. A. Glaskowsky, and *Management of the sales force*, by W. J. Stanton and R. H. Buskirk (Irwin, 1964), are typical of this class of book. The emphasis is on techniques of problem-solving and decision-making.

In recent years there has been a growth in the application of mathematics, and a move away from the 'How I did it' type of book. Computers have made it possible to handle large amounts of data and Bayesian statistics, decision theory and game theory all have their devotees among marketing writers. D. B. Montgomery and G. L. Urban have produced two books in this vein, *Management science in marketing* (Prentice-Hall, 1969), and *Applications of management science in marketing* (Prentice-Hall, 1970). W. R. King, in *Quantitative analysis for marketing management* (McGraw-Hill, 1967), showed how even the most complicated marketing problems can be reduced to a fairly simple mathematical formulation. While models of this kind produce solutions which are by no means optimum, the clarity and logic necessitated by this approach can have a profound effect on managerial thinking. Managers are forced to be explicit about the factors they take into account when making decisions, and to distinguish between what is assumed, what is known and what can be inferred. Apart from a few simple examples, it has not yet been possible to reproduce in model form the way in which a manager makes up his mind. On any one occasion, 30 or more pieces of information may have to be gathered and analysed before a decision can be made. The manager will take a view on the state of the market, the strengths and weaknesses of the competition, the effectiveness of his own promotional policies, etc., and will combine these in some gestalt way in order to arrive at a decision. This is usually known as judgment. The very complexity of this process has so far defied analysis, but management scientists and decision theorists have lifted one or two corners of the veil. They have encouraged managers to state what the important variables are and to quantify the relationships between them. This information is then used to construct a model of the decision-making process. At the least, by facilitating routine decisions, these models can make a manager's life easier. Their strength lies in their ability to process a wider range of inputs faster than an individual brain can, and to answer the question 'What if?' This point is well made by P. Kotler in *Marketing decision making: a model building approach* (Holt, Rinehart and Winston, 1971). Earlier books on the same topic include *Mathematical models and marketing management* (Harvard Business School, Boston, 1964), by R. D. Buzzell, and *Marketing models: quantitative and behavioural*, by Ralph L. Day (International Textbook Co., 1964).

Another approach to writing about marketing can, for want of a better word, be called the interdisciplinary approach. Theories, models and practices developed in other fields are applied to marketing situations. As might be expected, the behavioural sciences have been a particularly rich source of ideas. For example, Leon Festinger's *Theory of cognitive dissonance* (Stanford Press, 1957) has been applied to a wide range of purchase and post-purchase situations and has given rise to such articles as those by G. Bell, 'The automobile buyer after the purchase' (*Journal of Marketing*, 31(3), 12–16, 1961), and S. Oshikawa, 'The measurement of cognitive dissonance: some experimental findings' (*Journal of Marketing*, 36(1), 64–67, 1972). Some idea of the range of borrowings can be gained from books of readings such as *Consumer behaviour in theory and action* (Wiley, 1970), edited by S. H. Britt, and *Perspectives in consumer behaviour*, edited by H. H. Kassarjian and T. S. Robertson (revised ed., Scott, Foresman, Glenview, Ill., 1973). Both books discuss concepts from psychology, such as perception and learning; from sociology, such as group dynamics and class; and from anthropology, such as culture. Britt's book is undoubtedly stronger on the theory than on the action, and this highlights the problems of borrowing. Concepts developed within one frame of reference may often give valuable insights when used within another frame, but can rarely, if ever, be translated directly into practice. There remains a major need for marketing theorists to interpret and apply ideas from other disciplines.

Systems theory is proving to be another fruitful source of ideas. Models have been developed in the past for a wide range of specialised marketing decisions. Examples of this are: 'A model for marketing and pricing under competitive bidding', by K. Simmonds (*New Directions in Marketing*, AMA 48th Conference, S–9, June 1965), or 'Demon: a management model for marketing new products', by A. Charnes *et al.* (*California Management Review*, **11**(1), 31–46, 1968). These are comparatively straightforward representations of the reality of decision-making, and there are many more complex ones, but all of them make certain simplifying assumptions and leave out certain aspects of the environment which will have an effect on the final decision. Furthermore, a manager is seldom faced with an isolated decision. He has to manipulate all the marketing variables at his command in order to achieve the optimum performance in the market-place. This may mean that he will settle for less than best in some areas, in order to produce the best over-all result. In short, he is faced with a system. Such books as *Systems analysis for marketing, planning and control* (Scott, Foresman, 1972), by S. F. Stasch, attempt to apply the concepts of systems theory to the solution of marketing problems. Given that marketing is an open system and therefore naturally unstable and changeable, the systems specialists have tended to confine their activities to relatively minor problems. The enormous task of combining all these into an over-all systems approach has yet to be tackled.

Finally, there are a number of writers who have adopted a comparative approach. They study market processes in a number of situations and attempt to isolate the similarities and differences between them. Once this is done, they can move on to the next stage, which is to ask why these similarities or differences exist, what intervening variable, if any, is the cause. This, for the social sciences, is the equivalent of the experimental method in the natural sciences. Experiments are merely comparisons where the cases to be compared are produced to order under controlled conditions. Comparisons can be made over time, such as the historical analysis of the development of a distribution system; or geographically, comparing marketing phenomena in spatially separated locations, such as cities, countries, or continents. It is not sufficient just to list the phenomena. This is interesting, and a study of marketing in 10 countries may be useful background material for students of international marketing. The comparative approach requires that the various systems be contrasted explicitly and the appropriate conclusions drawn. *Comparative marketing systems: a cultural approach*, edited by M. S. Sommers and J. B. Kernan (Appleton-Century-Crofts, 1968), contains a number of descriptions of different geographical markets, but leaves much of the analysis to the reader. J. Boddewyn, in *Compardtive management and marketing* (Scott, Foresman, 1969), adopts a more rigorous approach, but deals much more with management than with marketing.

MARKETING TOPICS

The previous section described various ways in which marketing writers shape their thoughts: this section discusses some of the subjects they write about. The various activities that go to make up marketing are usually described as the marketing mix. Most general textbooks cover all the elements of this mix and will not be described here. Instead, attention will be given to specialist writings in the various areas.

Most economics textbooks deal with pricing at some length. A classic in this field is Joel Dean's *Managerial economics* (Prentice-Hall, 1951). A marketing manager cannot afford to take a narrow, economist's view of the subject, but he is not well served by the literature. There are a number of descriptive texts, such as *Pricing in big business: a case approach*, by A. D. H. Kaplan, J. B. Dirlan and R. F. Lanzilotti (The Brookings Institution, Washington, DC, 1958), and *Product analysis pricing*, by Wilfrid Brown and Elliot Jaques (Heinemann, 1954). For a normative approach, he would have to rely on D. V. Harper's book *Price policy and procedure* (Harcourt, Brace and World, 1966) or *Pricing for higher profit: criteria, methods, applications*, by S. A. Tucker (McGraw-Hill, 1966). There is as yet no textbook on competitive bidding. K. Simmonds has published a number of articles on this subject and these, among others, are listed in R. M. Stark's 'Competitive bidding: a comprehensive bibliography' (*Operations Research*, **19**(2), 484, 1971).

Product policy is almost inextricably mixed with corporate strategy, and books such as *Corporate strategy*, by H. Igor Ansoff (Penguin, 1970), devote much of their time to a discussion of the firm's choice of products. Theodore Levitt's classic article 'Marketing myopia' (*Harvard Business Review*, **38**(4), 45–56, 1960), perhaps the most widely quoted article in the whole of marketing literature, must also be included under this heading. D. W. Foster's book *Planning for products and markets* (Longmans, 1972) deals more specifically with problems of product management, and for a book of reading, albeit by now somewhat dated, there is *Product strategy and management*, edited by T. L. Berg and A. Schuchman (Holt, Rinehart and Winston, 1963).

There is no shortage of books on advertising and promotion: *Advertising*, by A. W. Frey (Ronald Press, 1963), *Advertising procedure*, by O. Kleppner (Scott, Foresman, 1973), and *Promotional decisions using mathematical models*, by P. J. Robinson (MSI and Allyn and Bacon, 1968), to name but a few. More specialised books include such titles as *Media planning*, by J. R. Adams (Business Books, 1971). As each new advertising panacea arises, whether it is game theory, or linear programming techniques for media selection, it is followed by a host of articles in the learned journals. The trouble is that they all say so little, as no one really knows how advertising works. This is a sobering thought when one remembers that it is now an industry spending a thousand million pounds a year.

There are a number of books on selling techniques, but for a managerial approach one must turn to the Stanton and Buskirk work mentioned above (p. 272), R. V. Butt's *Sales effort and marketing strategy* (American Management Association, 1969) or *Control of the field sales force*, by D. W. Smallbone (Staples Press, 1966). Articles such as D. A. Newton's 'Get the most out of your sales force' (*Harvard Business Review*, **47** (5), 130–143, 1969). and D. B. Montgomery and F. E. Webster's 'Application of operations research to personal selling strategy' (*Journal of Marketing*, **32**(1), 50–57, 1968) deal with specific issues, but all writers seem to have avoided the most important topic of all, the estimation of sales potential and consequent territory allocation. For a view from the other side of the fence there is Hugh Buckner's classic book *How British industry buys* (Hutchinson, 1967).

The logistics aspect of distribution is well covered by such books as *Physical distribution management: logistics problems of the firm*, by D. J. Bowersox, E. W. Smykay and B. L. LaLonde (Macmillan, 1968), but little serious attention has been paid to the equally important problem of channel selection. Comparative studies, such as N. A. H. Stacey and A. Wilson's *The changing pattern of distribution* (Pergamon Press, 1968) and *Distribution in Great Britain and North America*, by Hall, Knapp and Winsten (Oxford University Press, 1961), are of some assistance, but for an analytical approach one has to turn to B. E. Mallen's book of readings *The marketing channel—a conceptual viewpoint* (Wiley, 1967).

It is difficult to choose between the various available texts on market research. One of the latest and most comprehensive is the *Consumer market research handbook*, edited by R. M. Worcester (McGraw-Hill, 1972), and the British point of view is expressed in A. R. Davies's *The practice of marketing research* (Heinemann, 1973). The different problems encountered in industrial markets are discussed in *The assessment of industrial markets*, by A. Wilson (Hutchinson, 1968).

The application of information theory and information processing techniques to marketing is a comparatively new topic. V. J. Cook and J. D. Herniter give a general view in 'A manager's guide to model based information systems in marketing' (*American marketing association Conference Proceedings*, 121, June 1969), and two books on this subject are *Marketing research and information systems*, by R. D. Buzzell, D. F. Cox and R. V. Brown (McGraw-Hill, 1969), and *Marketing research, information systems and decision making*, by K. P. Uhl and B. Schoner (Wiley, 1969).

THE LITERATURE ITSELF

Reference has been made throughout this chapter to textbooks of various kinds, and these will not be discussed further in this section. For teaching purposes, there is a growing number of books of case studies. These either take the form of alternate text and cases, such as *Problems in marketing*, by M. P. Brown, W. B. England and J. B. Matthews (McGraw-Hill, 1961), or consist entirely of cases like K. Simmonds and D. Leighton's *Case problems in marketing* (Nelson, 1973).

Marketing articles can be found in three main types of journals. Firstly, there are the specialist, academic journals. The American Marketing Association publish both the *Journal of Marketing*, for the more general, normative type of articles, and the *Journal of Marketing Research*, for the more specialised, quantitative articles. They also publish the proceedings of their biannual conferences, under a range of titles such as 'New Directions in Marketing'. These documents are a valuable guide to up-to-date work. The British equivalent of the *Journal of Marketing* is the *European Journal of Marketing*, a publication which is gaining in stature as it grows older. Marketing research is, as might be expected, well served by journals published on this side of the Atlantic, such as the *Journal of the Market Research Society* (formerly *Commentary*), the *European Marketing Research Review* and, in the industrial field, the *IMRA Journal*. In the advertising field the leading journals are the *Journal of Advertising Research* and the *Advertising Quarterly*.

A second group of magazines, with a managerial slant, includes *Marketing; monthly journal of the Institute of Marketing*, Campaign and *Adweek*. The Institute of Marketing publishes a more recent research-oriented journal, *Marketing Forum*, which comes out six times a year.

Finally, as is apparent from the references given earlier on in this chapter, marketing articles appear in a wide range of business journals, such as the *Journal of Business, Harvard Business Review, Operations Research Quarterly*, etc. Details of these and other management and business journals are given in Chapter 6.

Information about markets is contained in a wide range of Government and private publications. Government publications include the *Annual Abstract of Statistics, Social Trends*, etc., and such organisations as the British Bureau of Television Advertising, A. C. Nielson and Co., and the British Market Research Bureau publish market data. This is too complex a field to be dealt with adequately in a chapter of this length but it has been dealt with more fully by Miss J. Harvey in Chapter 10. The best guide-book is *Sources of UK marketing information*, edited by G. Wills (Nelson, 1969).

The *Journal of Marketing* publishes, in each issue, abstracts of articles from a wide range of journals. They also review recent books. Other abstracting journals are the Market Research Society's *Market Research Abstracts* and, from the USA, the *Marketing Information Guide*— details of these and other abstracting journals are given in Chapter 5. The most comprehensive bibliography available is Georges Sandeau's *International bibliography of marketing and distribution* (4th ed., Staples Press, 1972).

Other bibliographies include the *Bibliography on physical distribution management* (Marketing Publications Inc., Washington DC, 1969), a *Bibliography of market surveys* (GATT International Trade Centre Geneva, 1967) and *The quantitative approach to marketing—a selected bibliography* (Warwick University, 1972), by R. W. Fisher and M. Hirst.

CONCLUSION

It is difficult, within a comparatively short space, to do justice to the literature of marketing. Its very diversity defies adequate classification. The selection of topics and references in this chapter is a personal one, and it would be easy to suggest additions in both areas. For a British book, the preponderance of American material is regrettable, but that reflects the greater effort put in, in both time and people, across the Atlantic. It is hoped that there is enough material here to enable students and practitioners of marketing to dig deeper into a fascinating subject.

16

Computers and Management

J. D. Dews

In the 15–20 years in which computers have been commercially available, their use has pervaded almost every aspect of daily life and they are now indispensable to the running of all but the smaller businesses. The increasing bulk of normal business transactions by banks, insurance companies, airlines, public utilities and local authorities makes it scarcely conceivable that commercial life could continue even at its current level without computers. Inevitably the manager working in any such organisation finds his life and work affected in some way by computers: he has been presented with a tool the potentiality of which is limited only by the ingenuity of human beings in finding new ways of using it. Yet as the hardware becomes ever more powerful, faster and more reliable, there are signs that the full benefit of the technology that already exists is not fully realised. Fifteen years is long enough for a technological revolution, but it may well take rather longer to change the habits of thinking and working of responsible people in organisations. As early printed books were modelled on the manuscripts of the previous age, and early railway carriages were similar in design to the coaches used on roads, there is a tendency for computers to be used to do work previously done by people in much the same ways, only faster and more accurately. This is probably inevitable, and since the work has to be done—invoices have to be produced and workers' pay has to be calculated—considerable savings may be realised in this way. If a decision can be logically specified, it can be programmed for the computer, which is less likely to apply the rules incorrectly than a person.

For the manager, however, the computer's ability to process vast amounts of data offers the possibility of providing him with information which may otherwise not be obtainable, which will help him to make the decisions which are not programmable: the real gains to be had may well lie in improvements in his planning and forecasting capabilities. The design and implementation of systems which will be of real help to the manager in his task of managing an enterprise, or part of it, require a deeper understanding of the problems and objectives of the organisation, and of the relationships between the various activities, than do the routine applications to the processing of data. It is the senior members of any organisation who have the deepest understanding of its objectives: managers of all types must be increasingly concerned with the computer if it is to be used successfully, and the evidence seems to show that senior management involvement and understanding of the computer is an important factor in the success of any application.

This chapter therefore discusses the books on computers which are of particular relevance to managers and students of management, on the assumption that they must know enough about computers, as well as their own businesses, to make decisions on the acquisition of computing facilities, and to manage those facilities successfully. The books are mentioned in the following categories: introductory books; literature on the management uses of the computer; the impact of the computer on management; the management of the computer; information systems; library information systems; social aspects of the computer. The range of periodicals available is then discussed, and some of the abstracts and bibliographies, by means of which further information may be sought. The literature mentioned is available in the UK, though not confined to UK publications. US and international publications are included where relevant.

For those who start from a position of relative ignorance of computers, it is worth mentioning some introductory works. Probably the best brief introduction to computers is that by F. J. M. Laver, *Introducing computers* (HMSO), of which a second edition was published in 1973. *Electronic computers,* by S. H. Hollingdale and G. C. Toothill (2nd ed., Penguin, 1970), is a more comprehensive introduction, with considerable emphasis on the hardware. The hardware aspects are also readably dealt with in *Introduction to computers,* by K. London (new ed., Faber, 1970).

There are a number of introductions to the computer written with the manager in mind. *An executive's guide to computer concepts,* by Y. E. Monsma and K. E. Powell (Pitman, 1970), provides in easily assimilable form an understanding of the kind of thinking required to design a program and execute it, without going into detail about the hardware. *The effective use of computers in business,* by P. A. Lesty (Cassell, 1969), also aims to provide the 'busy manager' with the information essential to an understanding of computing, without excessive detail. A good textbook is *Computers in business: an introduction,* by D. H. Sanders (2nd ed., McGraw-Hill, 1972).

USE OF THE COMPUTER BY MANAGEMENT

Each manager will find a different use of the computer according to his function, but will also find it useful to know something of the range of uses to which the computer may be put.

New power for management, by David B. Hertz (McGraw-Hill, 1967), shows how the computer may be used to implement the application of management science in decision-making, long-term planning, capital investment analysis, production—distribution—marketing analysis, building marketing models and management control. *Computers, science and management dynamics*, by Robert J. Fahey and others (Financial Executives Research Foundation, New York, 1969), similarly deals with the use of computers for management control in production, distribution, finance, manpower, etc. Laura Tatham, in *The use of computers for profit: a businessman's guide* (McGraw-Hill, 1969), gives fairly detailed explanations of the main management applications of the computer, in non-technical language.

A readable survey of ways in which computers are used by management is *Computers for management*, edited by H. Stuart and R. Yearsley (Heinemann, 1969). The chapters vary in quality but the chapter on production is especially lucid, and there is a description of the management control system used by the National Coal Board. *Computer applications in management*, edited by J. Birkle and R. Yearsley (Staples Press, 1969), also deals with a number of applications in a more general way.

In production work the computer can help with materials planning, stock control, control of work in progress and work scheduling. Even a simple stock control system is likely to be beneficial in reducing costs, but a complete production control system is likely to be complex and requires very careful planning. The National Computing Centre published *Computer aided production control* in 1967, and more recently there is *Production control by computer*, by J. D. C. Truster (Machinery Publications, 1970). In 1973, however, the NCC published the results of a survey of production control systems in the UK, which showed that development is slow in this field: *Computerguide No. 9: Production control* (National Computing Centre, 1973).

Two fairly well-defined applications in the production engineering field are numerical control and process control. In the former the computer produces a paper tape which can be used to control a machine tool as it cuts or forms a complex part. *Fundamentals of numerical control*, by F. B. Lockwood (Machinery Publications, 1970), and *Numerical control*, by N. O. Olester (Wiley/Interscience, 1970), deal with this topic in detail. Special programming languages have been developed to implement numerical control programs and some of these are described in *Numerical control programming languages*, by W. H. P. Lestie (North-Holland, 1970). *A selective bibliography on numerical control*, by R. A. Kelby, was published as an insert to this last book.

In a process control system the computer monitors the conditions at each point in a continuous process, such as chemical manufacture or oil-refining, and makes continual adjustments to the process on the basis of instrument readings, so as to ensure that the process is kept in balance.

The marketing manager may look to the computer for assistance with transport and distribution problems, warehousing, stock control, delivery scheduling, control of the sales force, sales accounting, analysis and forecasting, market research survey analysis, analysis of advertising media or simulation of different marketing strategies. *Marketing and the computer*, edited by W. Alderson and S. J. Shapiro (Prentice-Hall, 1964), deals with some of these applications, and a smaller book of the same title by I. St. J. Hugo (Pergamon, 1967) covers the ground in a more general and superficial way. A more specialised work is *Computer simulation of competitive market response*, by A. E. Amstutz (MIT Press, 1967), and *Computers in transport planning and operation*, by A. Wren (Ian Allan, 1971), deals with vehicle scheduling.

The computer's ability to store large amounts of data and select from it quickly is also useful to the personnel manager with large numbers of staff records to control. Details of pay, age, sex, qualifications, etc., may be stored and used for selection of particular individuals who meet the precise specifications for particular jobs, but also for the analysis of trends in labour turnover, for manpower planning and other analyses of the work force. A number of pamphlets have been produced by the Institute of Personnel Management, such as *The computer in personnel work*, by E. Wille (1966), and *Personnel records and the computer*, by J. Springall (1971). A fuller treatment of the computerisation of personnel records, with a description of a generalised data management language, GEDAN, is *Personnel systems and data management*, by G. A. Bassett and H. Y. Weatherbee, published by the American Management Association in 1971.

Some of the earliest applications of computers in business were in the financial area, but these were mainly mechanisation of routine processes, such as payroll calculation, invoicing and costing. These are still basic jobs for the computer, and probably the first areas of work to which computerisation is applied in the firm. In recent years, however, the use of the computer for budgetary control, investment analysis and corporate financial modelling is more common. *Accounting, computers, management information systems*, by David H. Li (McGraw-Hill, 1968), is a textbook of computing from the accountant's point of view and develops the concept of the accounting function as an information system for management.

THE IMPACT OF THE COMPUTER ON MANAGEMENT

Perhaps the most extensive research into the effect of computers on management in the UK is that of Rosemary Stewart, *How computers affect management* (Macmillan, 1971), based on case studies of operational systems of varying types and sizes. The effect on management varied with the application, but it usually resulted in more work for middle managers during the development process. One of the implications drawn is the need for knowledge on the part of managers, both of computers and of the problems of the organisation.

The impact on management is likely to be least where the applications are routine, except that when the computer is used only in this way it is likely to become an expensive luxury which may have an unfortunate effect on the profitability of the company. If it is used as an aid to management, however, in the ways mentioned above it should result in the manager's working more effectively because he will be better informed. It will usually mean also that he will have a better understanding of his objectives and practices if he has been involved in the specification of the system—the penalties for error at this stage are likely to be heavy.

The computer sampler: management perspectives on the computer, edited by W. F. Boore and J. R. Murphy (McGraw-Hill, 1968), is a book of readings from the (American) periodical literature on business which 'focus on the managerial dimensions of exploiting computer technology within a business enterprise' and contains papers on the effect of the computer on management. *The impact of computers on management*, by C. A. Myers (MIT Press, 1967), deals with the effect of the computer on organisational structure and control, with particular reference to the total systems concept, and the changes which such systems could bring about. Changes in the structure and behaviour of organisations as well as individuals is dealt with also in *The real computer: its influence, uses and effects*, by F. G. Withington, published by Addison-Wesley in 1969.

MANAGEMENT OF THE COMPUTER

So far the relationship between computers and management has been dealt with from the point of view of the use of computers *by* management. The computer in an organisation, however, poses its own problems and itself requires managing. Management of the computer implies not only the management of the machine itself, and the people who run it, but management of the changes in the organisation which the progessive introduction of mechanisation into the work of the firm bring about, and of the relationships between the user departments and the computer staff. The installation of the computer brings into the firm a category of staff of which the organisation may not have had previous experience.

Handbook of computer management, edited by R. B. Yearsley and G. M. R. Graham (Gower Press, 1973), deals with methods of obtaining computing services—choosing a computer, software, consultancy services, standards, training personnel; and also briefly explains most of the business applications in finance/accounting, production, inventory management, marketing and information retrieval. Each chapter is written by a contributor with expertise in the aspect dealt with.

A practical book which discusses in detail the methods and techniques of introducing and maintaining computer systems is *Managing the introduction of computer systems*, by R. Tomlin (McGraw-Hill, 1970). The effectiveness of the computer depends heavily on proper planning and control in the EDP department, and this book outlines some of the methods which ensure good management.

The mere presence of a computer in an organisation is not sufficient to ensure that its use will be profitable or beneficial, and there have been many examples of computers not justifying the high hopes placed on them. Manufacturers were somewhat inclined to oversell their equipment in the early days. Since then a number of surveys of computer use have been done to identify the factors which lead to successful computer use in some organisations while in others the computer has become an expensive failure. A book based on such research in a number of countries is *How to manage computers for results*, by D. N. Chorafas (Gee, 1969). The main causes of failure to derive adequate benefit from the computer are identified as lack of attention to cost effectiveness, failure to rethink the problems in computer terms and lack of detailed planning. A brief and readable pamphlet on the same lines was produced by McKinsey and Company in 1966, *Unlocking the computer's profit potential* (McKinsey and Co., 1968), and the British Institute of Management also conducted a survey in British companies, published in 1971 as *Achieving computer profitability: a survey of current practice in 102 companies*, by H. Johannsen and S. Birch.

INFORMATION PROCESSING

The usefulness of the computer to management lies primarily in the assistance it can give in decision-making, at all levels and in all areas of activity. The quality of a decision depends very largely on the amount of relevant information available at the time. The computer, because of its ability to process the large amounts of data from which the information is derived, makes available more relevant information. From the management point of view, therefore, the computer is an information processing machine. The distinction between data processing and information processing is likely to be somewhat blurred, since even the most routine data-processing application will usually provide some information of use to management, but the deliberate emphasis on information processing is likely to result in more profitable use of the computer. The practical difficulties, organisational rather than technical, are greater than might have been thought at first, and the quality of the design of the information systems is crucial.

There has been in the past few years a vogue for 'management information systems', and a considerable number of books and articles have been written for and against them. Anything from a single programme providing on-line interrogation of an inventory or personnel file is likely to be called a management information system, while, on the other hand, the concept of the top manager using a terminal for instant access to all the information he needs for decision-making has been put forward as a possibility of the near future. Many books whose titles include the words 'management information system' are in fact introductory textbooks on computing with some emphasis on information processing.

A management information system is here taken to mean a series of related sub-systems operating on a common data base in such a way that the same data are used to derive information for a variety of purposes and make it available to the managers who require it, when they require it. Since senior managers are concerned with strategic decisions which rarely need immediate access to the very latest detailed information, the response time in their case need not be instantaneous and on-line access is not required; whereas the manager making operating decisions has more need of up-to-date information and fast response. A feature of a management information system, however, is that all the information which has a bearing on a decision is taken into account, so that the relationships between the sub-systems require careful consideration and the analysis of these relationships is a major factor in the success of the system.

The complexity of the relationships is well shown in *Management information systems: a framework for planning and development*, by S. C. Blumental (Prentice-Hall, 1972), which describes the stages of planning and development which must be gone through in the development of a large system. The need for careful consideration of the needs of the user of the system is emphasised in *Management oriented management information systems*, by Jerome Kanter (Prentice-Hall, 1972), which also makes a serious attempt to define the management information system. *Information systems for modern management*, by R. G. Murdock and Joel E. Ross (Prentice-Hall, 1971), aims to bridge the gap between management and the computer specialists by relating information system to a general system theory of management, while *Computer based management information systems*, by L. I. Krauss, published by the American Management Association in 1970, contains more practical advice and guidelines for dealing with many of the problems encountered in the development of such systems from the point of view of the general manager. *Computers, management and information*, by David Firnberg (Allen and Unwin, 1973), discusses the type of data from which information is derived, and how these may be handled to provide the information to the manager who needs to use it, with an emphasis on the use of visual display units. A book which assumes little previous knowledge of computers is *Computer based information systems in organisations*, by H. C. Lucas (Science Research Associates, 1973).

Information processing in libraries

Libraries, too, are making increasing use of computers to help cope with the ever-increasing flood of publications. Computing in libraries is somewhat different, however, from that in the firm. Libraries themselves are information-processing institutions; their work is not so much with books and documents as with records of them, and the computer provides the possibility of more rapid and accurate processing of these records, and of retrieving the required records more quickly than with conventional tools. The library, therefore, aims to automate its own functions, and library automation is in fact data processing rather than information processing, but the data to be processed are particularly complex. The management uses of the computer of the kind outlined in this chapter are insignificant compared with the purely processing activity, which is characterised by massive amounts of data and heavy output costs. The on-line terminal brings the possibility of interrogation of a computer file, but the costs of storing a library data base in random access storage is still prohibitive for most libraries. However, computer storage is becoming cheaper and this may well be feasible in the not too distant future.

Library records have traditionally been of books, periodical articles, reports and other documents, which are relatively crude 'units' so far as information is concerned. A book contains at least as much information as is recorded in its own index, and even periodical articles contain information on many more topics than may be deduced from their titles. True information retrieval would necessitate the indexing and recording of these much smaller units of information—a task which is at present far beyond the resources of most libraries, even though automation will enable them to carry out more detailed indexing than hitherto. But such micro-indexing may be conceivable on a national or international basis, and the future of information processing in libraries may well lie in the direction of more centralisation of indexing and cataloguing functions, with individual libraries subscribing to a central agency for access to a massive on-line data base through a remote terminal.

There is now quite a large number of agencies which have built up data bases (such as INSPEC, MEDLARS, *Chemical Abstracts*) from which they supply published information services in the form of abstracting journals, selective bibliographies and selective current-awareness services, and experiments are in progress for providing on-line access to these through a terminal. The on-line data bases are at present limited, but there is no reason to think that the experiments will not be successful and the data bases extended as the cost of equipment falls.

The library of the not too distant future, then, is likely to use the computer as a tool in its day-to-day processing of books and other information in its own stock, to reduce the load of routine work and free the staff for more active assistance for readers; it may also buy information on magnetic tape for processing on its own machine, such as the catalogue data provided by the BNB MARC service, or it may even buy the catalogue of its own stock, processed entirely outside the library; and it will have access to a number of other data bases external to the library, from which it may obtain lists of documentation on sought topics on behalf of its readers. The obtaining of the documents themselves will also be facilitated by the maintenance of computer records of the holdings of a large number of libraries, so that the whereabouts of a particular document may be traced. The key problem for libraries, however, as information-processing institutions, is the same whether they are auto-mated or not, and this is the development of adequate 'indexing languages' which will ensure that the terms applied to any document or record of information match the terms used by the person who later requires and seeks that document. This is an intellectual problem which, like mechanical translation, has not yet yielded to solution by the computer. Research is being carried out on such problems, and although some success has been achieved in a research environment, practical results are likely to be some time in realisation.

SOCIAL ASPECTS OF THE COMPUTER

The introduction of a computer into an organisation inevitably affects the work of many of the staff. For some it may bring an opportunity to change to more interesting work, but for others it may mean relegation to more tedious work or even redundancy. Management bears a responsi-bility to so organise the introduction of computing that disruption and disaffection of staff are reduced to a minimum. Such extreme insensitivity as keeping the purchase of a computer secret from the staff until it arrived is probably unlikely today, although it happened in the early days. The changed science may be due in large part to the researches of Enid Mumford and others.

An early survey published in 1967, *The computer and the clerk*, by

Enid Mumford and Olive Banks (Routledge, 1967), studied the change in attitudes of staff before and after the installation of computer systems in two firms. The results of research were given more practical form in *Computers: planning for people*, by Enid Mumford and T. B. Ward (Batsford, 1966), in which the human relations problems were discussed, with a practical example of the analysis of these problems. *Computers, planning and personnel management*, also by Enid Mumford (IPM, 1969), outlines the role of the personnel manager in the planning processes leading to the introduction of computers into the organisation.

Apart from the problems concerning the existing staff on the introduction of computing, there is now a need to consider the personnel management of the new type of staff which has grown up with the computer—systems analysts, programmers, keyboard operators and computer operators, on whom the success of a computer system will depend in the future—and a contribution to the understanding of the management of such people is *Job satisfaction: a study of computer specialists*, also by Enid Mumford (Longman, 1972).

The use of computers by managers, whether in business or any other form of enterprise, necessarily produces an effect on everyone else, and the social effects of the computer have been far-reaching. Several books therefore have appeared which consider the computer from this point of view. *Computers, managers and society*, by Michael Rose (Penguin, 1969), describes in general terms what the computer does and discusses some of its effects, especially on office workers.

There are also a number of books which review the probable future of computers in society and sound some warning notes about the need to control their use. *The computerised society*, by J. Martin and A. R. D. Norman (Prentice-Hall, 1970), looks ahead 15 years to some of the changes which are foreseeable now. Malcolm Warner and Michael Stone, in *The data bank society* (Allen and Unwin, 1970), are concerned with the threat to privacy of the individual which the use of computers presents. *Computers and society*, by Stanley Rothman and Charles Mosmann (Science Research Associates, 1972), is a textbook which presents information about the technology and the social implications together, on the assumption that either cannot be adequately understood without a knowledge of the other. *Computers and the year 2000*, edited by Lord Avebury and others (National Computing Centre, 1973), looks at the developments foreseeable in a wide variety of fields of application of computers.

PERIODICALS

Some of the books on computers relevant to managers have now been mentioned, but in such a rapidly developing field reliance only on books as sources of information would leave the manager less than well-informed. For up-to-date information it is essential to scan some at least of the many journals in the field. A large number of articles about computers and computing appear in journals devoted to management and business, with which it is assumed that the reader is familiar, having read this book to this point, but there are a number of journals in the computing field which should be mentioned. There are probably over 700 periodicals directly concerned with computers and computing, but a rather small proportion of these need be mentioned here. In 1971 the National Computing Centre published a *World list of computer periodicals*, giving locations in some 50 libraries in the UK.

The periodicals may be roughly classified into four main groups, which are not mutually exclusive, but are useful for purposes of description. These are academic, commercial, house journals and newsletters.

Of the academic type a few only will be mentioned, largely on account of their pre-eminence in the field. In Great Britain the *Computer Journal*, published since 1958 by the British Computer Society, is the leading journal in this category. It has a strong bias towards the mathematical and theoretical aspects of computing, although it also contains articles of more general interest (a useful feature of the arrangement of each issue is that the articles of more general interest appear towards the front). The British Computer Society also published the *Computer Bulletin* (quarterly, 1957–1968; monthly 1968–1972), containing shorter and less technical articles and society news, but this was replaced in 1973 by *Computing*, a newspaper-type publication. Publication of *Computer Bulletin* was resumed in 1974.

In the USA, the Association for Computing Machinery is the oldest and most important society publishing academic journals, which are among the most frequently cited in the field. *The Journal of the ACM* (quarterly, 1954–) contains the most technical and theoretical papers, while *Communications of the ACM* (monthly, 1958–) contains more general articles, news, correspondence and also algorithms (methods of programming particular tasks). *Computer Surveys* (quarterly, 1969–) is a relatively recent venture, in which each issue contains a long survey article on a particular topic, as for example 'Sorting', 'Table look-up techniques', 'On-line text editing'.

The commercial journals are perhaps of more interest to the manager, as they tend to deal more with the business applications of computers; their articles are usually brief and possibly superficial surveys of topics of current interest or particular applications, and a good deal of space is devoted to news of new equipment. *Data Systems*, formerly *Data and Control Systems* (monthly, 1959–), and *Data Processing* (bi-monthly, 1959–) are probably the leading journals of this type in Great Britain, while in the USA *Datamation* (monthly 1961–1969; semi-monthly

1970–) is the most widely read, and *Data Processing Magazine* (monthly 1958–) is another well-established journal. *Computers and Automation* (monthly 1951–) was one of the first commercial periodicals in the USA. Recently this journal has tended to concentrate on the social issues raised by automation, and in recognition of this, changed its title in 1972 to *Computers and Automation and People* with the intention of changing it again to *Computers and People* in the future. A journal of the same type and level of interest as those just mentioned is *Data Management* (monthly, 1954–), which is the official journal of the (American) Data Processing Management Association. *The EDP Analyser* (monthly, 1963–) has one longer article only in each issue dealing with a specific topic, as for example 'Improvement in system analysis and design', 'Managing the systems effort'.

There are a number of publications of the newspaper type. *Computing* has already been mentioned. The *Computer Weekly* is the leading example in this country, published since 1966. As well as news of new equipment, new contracts, orders placed for machines and movement of executives within the industry, it comments on the development of the computing industry and its relations with government. There is a periodic insert containing international news, and each issue contains at least one full-page article on a specific application. Half its space is devoted to personnel advertisements. Similar journals are *Data Week* and *Computer Digest*.

Yet another type of journal is published by computer manufacturers and other firms in the industry. These vary considerably in format and content. Some, such as the *Journal of Research and Development* and *Systems Journal*, from IBM, are of high technical standard and may be ranked as academic journals. The *Honeywell Computer Journal* also contains technical articles. Others are limited to news items directly relevant to the users of the company's product, and are exemplified by IBM's *Link* and ICL's *Computer International*.

CONFERENCE PROCEEDINGS

A number of regular conferences are held, the proceedings of which form an important channel of publication of new work. Those of the American Federation of Information Processing Societies (AFIPS) are some of the most long-standing. The Fall Joint Computer Conference and the Spring Joint Computer Conference have been held since 1953, although until 1961 they were named the Western and the Eastern Joint Computer Conferences, respectively. Their proceedings are published regularly, in numbered volumes of which there are now over 40. The Association for Computing Machinery holds an annual conference, and the Data Processing Management Association holds them semi-annually, the proceedings being published under the title *Data Processing*. The most important international conference is that of the International Federation for Information Processing, which is held in a different location every 3 years. The 1971 conference was held in Ljubljana and that of 1974 in Stockholm. The proceedings are published as *Information Processing*.

ABSTRACTING SERVICES

Access to the considerable volume of literature represented by the periodicals mentioned above is best achieved by the use of the abstracting services with which the computing field is well endowed.

Services which have a bias towards business and management aspects of computing are *Accounting and Data Processing Abstracts*, *Computer Journal Abstracts* and *New Literature on Automation*.

Accounting and Data Processing Abstracts is one of the five more specialised services into which *Management Services Abstracts* was split in 1970. Published by ANBAR Publications, this is one of the most useful abstracting services for the practising manager, being selective and evaluative, with brief critical abstracts, appearing very soon (2–3 months) after the primary publication. The editorial policy of abstracting only those articles which in the opinion of the abstracter say something new on their subject, and only articles deemed useful to the practising manager, is continued in the four separate publications. The emphasis is therefore on data-processing applications of computers, and on the less technical literature. The arrangement of the abstracts is alphabetically by the source journal, but there is a classified index (semi-annual and annual) based on the classification specially developed for ANBAR, and an annual author index. The service includes a bibliography of books reviewed in any of the journals abstracted.

Computing Journal Abstracts began as an internal service for members of staff of the National Computing Centre, but was made available more widely from Vol. 3 in 1971. This is a weekly service, and abstracts about 60 articles a week. The journals abstracted are those received in the library of the NCC (about 400) so that a number of 'fringe' journals are abstracted selectively. The arrangement is systematic, with a table of contents in each issue which lists the titles of the articles.

New Literature on Automation (monthly) is another service based on a library—that of the Netherlands Centre for Informatics (Nederlands Studiecentrum voor Informatica), Amsterdam. Before 1968 it was published as *IAG—Literature on Automation*, and effectively forms a supplement to the catalogue of the library, published as *International computer bibliography*, described below. Books as well as articles are abstracted, and periodicals in languages other than English are covered. Abstracts are usually in the language of the original. The abstracting is selective, but oriented towards business applications. The arrangement is systematic, according to a classification developed specially by the Studiecentrum, with an author index in each issue. A cumulative author and subject index for 1961–64 was published in 1966 and for 1965–68 in 1970.

It is not proposed to mention all the abstracting services covering computing here. A survey of them by A. R. Dorling, *A guide to abstracting journals for computers and computing*, was published by the National Reference Library for Science and Invention in 1972. The holdings of the NRLSI are noted, and there is a section giving details of coverage of computing in services primarily concerned with other subjects. Two of the more general services should be mentioned, however, because of their relatively wide coverage and their standing in the field. These are *Computer Abstracts* and *Computing Review*.

Computer Abstracts began as *Computer Bibliography*, but took its present title in 1960. It is published monthly, by Technical Information Co. Ltd of St. Helier, Jersey, with author, subject and patent indexes, these indexes being cumulated annually. The subject index is detailed, semi-systematic. About 150 periodicals are abstracted, and there is good coverage of the more technical aspects of the subject, and programming for scientific applications. The abstracts are on the whole rather longer than those of the services already mentioned, and the indexes make this service useful for retrospective searching.

Computing Reviews, also monthly, is published by the Association for Computing Machinery, of New York. As the title implies, the entries are more in the nature of reviews than abstracts, longer than any of the other services, critical and signed. The whole field of computing is covered, including applications in the humanities, but only the more academic material is selected for review. Foreign-language journals are covered, and theses are also reviewed, as well as books. The reviews are arranged in subject sections. Bibliographies of specialised subjects are also included periodically.

BIBLIOGRAPHIES

The most important bibliography in the field is the *International computer bibliography*, published jointly by the National Computing Centre in Manchester and the Netherlands Automatic Information Processing Research Centre (Nederlands Studiecentrum voor Informatica) in Amsterdam. The bibliography is actually the catalogue of the library of the latter institution and is international in scope. The main volume was published in 1968, and a supplementary volume covering the period from 1969 to the first half of 1970 appeared in 1971. A further volume is in preparation.

Both volumes are arranged by the special classification developed for the library of the Studiecentrum and nearly all entries have annotations, either in English or in the language of the book. Although the coverage of the literature is wide, the Studiecentrum itself has a special interest in business and data processing. The bibliography requires some effort to use effectively, but this effort will be repaid.

Before the publication of the Studiecentrum catalogue, the main bibliography was probably W. W. Youden's *Computer literature bibliography 1946–1963* (National Bureau of Standards, 1964), to which a supplement, *Computer literature bibliography 1964–1967*, was published in 1968. This is a computer-produced KWIC (Keyword in Context) bibliography which lists exhaustively articles and papers from a relatively small number of journals, but also from a large number of conference proceedings and from books. Each volume contains about 5000 references.

More recent is the rather oddly entitled *KWIC index: a bibliography of computer management*, by Malcolm H. Gotterer, published in 1970 by Brandon/Systems Press, Princeton. About 900 references are listed, both books and articles, with a strong emphasis on the management *of* computers, although items on the use of computers *by* managers are included. The usefulness of the KWIC method of indexing is somewhat limited, especially if one requires a systematic view of the subject, and relies heavily on the sought term being included in the title of a relevant article. However, it is a comparatively easy form of index to produce by computer.

Another American work, suffering as many do from an almost exclusive concentration on the American literature, is *Computers and data processing: information sources*, by Chester Morril (Gale Research, Detroit, 1969). This is systematically arranged and annotated, and therefore more useful than a KWIC index.

A continuing bibliography is the *Quarterly Bibliography of Computers and Data Processing*, published by Applied Computer Research of Phoenix, Arizona, since 1970. This cumulates on rather a complex pattern, the final cumulation period apparently being 2 years. An interesting feature is that it scans and indexes many of the 'business' journals, such as *Journal of Business*, *Financial Executive*, etc. The subject headings are broad, and it indexes books as well as articles.

In this section also may be mentioned *A guide to computer literature*, by A. Pritchard (2nd ed., Bingley, 1972). This provides a comprehensive survey (in narrative form) of all the varied types of publication which go to make up the literature of computing, and is an invaluable chart for anyone embarking on a detailed study of any aspect of computing.

CONCLUSION

The bibliographical control of computer literature is relatively good; there is sufficient literature which is relevant to the manager's needs to enable him to make effective use of it in his work, and to ensure that the tasks for which the machine is used do in fact assist him in his work of planning and control. Developments in the use of computers for business management will depend on the ingenuity of managers in specifying, and assisting in the design of, relevant tasks, and it is hoped that the works mentioned in this chapter will help him to do so.

17

Quantitative Methods and Production

Howard Thomas

INTRODUCTION

What are quantitative methods?

One of the most fundamental changes in business management since World War II has been the rapid expansion of computer facilities, and of departments of management science, operations research and systems analysis within firms. To many managers the mechanics of computers and OR models are often incomprehensible, and specialists in management science areas sometimes find difficulty in implementing their quantitative approaches to problem-solving because of management scepticism about quantitative concepts. The growth and development of the use of operational research and quantitative methods in business has thus made it desirable that managers and students of business and administration should be exposed to quantitative methods, in order to improve their appreciation and understanding of the available methods.

Many reports, in both the UK and the USA, have reviewed business education and the need for thorough training not only in functional areas, such as financial management, but also in basic discipline areas—for example, quantitative methods.

'Quantitative methods' is a general term for quantitative techniques and mathematical methods which can find application to business decision problems. There are four main methodological disciplines in quantitative methods: (1) mathematics, (2) statistics and statistical methods, (3) mathematical methods and operational research, and (4) computational methods.

This definition of quantitative methods excludes such areas as managerial accounting and finance, which are sometimes defined as quantitative techniques in business school syllabuses. Using, therefore, the four headings cited above, a suggested list of relevant quantitative techniques is given below.

Mathematics

1. Differential and integral calculus
2. Linear algebra
3. Finite mathematics and applications
4. Constrained optimisation, including the logic of linear and mathematical programming

Statistics

1. Statistical description, e.g. sources of statistics and information
2. Data reduction and handling
3. Probability theory
4. Data collections and sampling methods
5. The logic of statistical inference and hypothesis testing
6. The analysis of multivariate data, e.g. regression analysis
7. Methods of data analysis
8. Statistical decision analysis

Mathematical Methods and Operational Research

1. Model-building and implementation
2. Mathematical programming
3. Decision-making under uncertainty
4. Simulation
5. Some simple stochastic process models
6. Inventory and production processes
7. Forecasting

Computational Methods

1. Flow diagramming
2. Methods of numerical analysis
3. Use of on-line terminals
4. Use of available packages

The differential need for numeracy

There is a problem in reviewing the quantitative methods literature for an audience whose requirements may not be homogenous. It is clear, for example, that the need for the various types of available literature sources in quantitative methods must vary within different managerial levels and professions. Middle managers and members of professions probably find short managerially based textbooks and articles in broadly based journals more to their taste. Potential MBAs and research students will probably need to use more narrowly defined textbooks and research monographs, and to keep in touch with current research through articles in very specifically defined learned journals.

For these reasons, in the literature survey which follows, we shall identify certain types of literature sources: (a) general textbooks for the practising manager; (b) general textbooks for the research student /MBA; (c) research monographs; (d) case study volumes; (e) survey and expository articles; (f) research-based articles; and (g) readings volumes, which are essentially collections of some of the major articles and contributions in particular fields.

Theory versus application

An additionally useful classification in the literature is to treat the *theoretical side* and the *applied side* of the subject separately. There are many textbooks, articles, etc., which concentrate on the *techniques* of quantitative methods *per se* and can reasonably be classified as *theoretical contributions*. On the other hand, there are a continually increasing number of contributions to the literature which apply quantitative techniques to problem areas in business and particularly in the functional areas of marketing, finance, production and business policy. These can reasonably be classified as *applied contributions*.

The main *theoretical contributions* in areas of mathematics, statistical methods, mathematical methods, OR and computing will be reviewed in terms of the seven categories outlined in the numeracy section.

The same seven categories will then be used to review the applications of quantitative methods in: (a) marketing, (b) production, (c) finance, (d) business policy, (e) managerial economics, (f) organisational behaviour, (g) research and development and (h) management information and planning systems.

THEORETICAL CONTRIBUTIONS

Introduction

Inevitably, this section concentrates upon those theoretical contributions which are of greatest relevance to the application of quantitative methods in business. For this reason, those requiring a more detailed theoretical review will have to refer to some of the individual learned journals listed in this chapter.

The organisation of this section is under four main headings: (1) theoretical contributions to mathematical methods; (2) theoretical contributions to statistical methods; (3) theoretical contributions to operational research; and (4) theoretical contributions in the area of computing.

Mathematical methods

In the over-all introduction we specified the main mathematical techniques which are of interest in understanding the application of quantitative methods to business problems. In summary they are: calculus, linear algebra, finite mathematics and the mathematics of optimisation.

In this area there are many more suitable student textbooks than textbooks which would have appeal to a managerial audience. The classic textbook for managers is undoubtedly the series of texts that were developed for the General Electric In-company Training Program in the USA. They are now available in a four-volume set entitled *Mathematics for management*, edited by C. H. Springer *et al.* (Irwin, 1968). A useful text, which has an appealing practical ring about it, is *Mathematics in management,* by A. Battersy (Penguin, 1970). With student textbooks there are clearly any number of excellent choices. R. Courant's two-volume *Differential and integral calculus* (Blackie, 1937; reprinted 1966) is a fundamental reference work for calculus methods. Many students find a short paperback, *Calculus made easy,* by S. P. Thompson (Macmillan, 1965), a useful adjunct in that it highlights the main concepts and techniques in a repetitive learning fashion.

In the field of linear algebra George Hadley's *Linear algebra* (Addison-Wesley, 1961) is well written, and gives many examples and exercises, by means of which the student can check his progress. It is preferred by students to the more mathematically elegant *A survey of modern algebra,* by G. Birkhoff and S. Maclane (3rd ed., Collier-Macmillan, 1965), which nevertheless is the fundamental reference for those who wish to take the subject further.

To some extent, partial coverage of the literature of finite mathematics is given in Birkhoff and Maclane; but in nothing like as elegant a fashion as the approcah of J. G. Kemeny and L. Snell's *Introduction to finite mathematics* (2nd ed., Prentice-Hall, 1966). Kemeny and Snell collaborated with two business academics, A. Schleifer and G. Thompson, to produce a text called *Finite mathematics with business applications* (2nd ed., Prentice-Hall, 1972), which places the mathematics of set theory and symbolic logic in a business context, and, undoubtedly, many students find this approach very relevant to their needs.

When one reviews the literature on mathematics for optimisation, the problem is one of seeing the wood from the trees. The selection of books from the large set available inevitably must reflect the personal biases of the reader. George Hadley, whose name has been referred to already, has a gift as a textbook writer. His books on linear programming and non-linear and dynamic programming, published by Addison-Wesley, illustrate the value of texts for students which have plenty of worked examples and exercises sequenced intelligently within the text. One of the texts in the London Business School Series by T. A. J. Nicholson, *Optimisation in industry* (2 vols., Longmans, 1971), is a concisely written review of both the theory and application of optimisation techniques in business. It covers algorithms such as 'branch and bound' and 'hill climbing', combinatorial methods and heuristic approaches, which are not formally covered in any depth in Hadley's texts.

There is a class of books in mathematical methods which try to cover the whole range of techniques itemised in the above section. These texts are written primarily for business school courses in basic mathematics and mathematical methods, which are prerequisites which the student must take in order to develop competence in the basic languages and approaches of mathematics. Perhaps the best example of this global type of book is *Mathematical analysis for business decisions*, by J. Howell and D. Teichroew (Irwin, 1971). A new edition to the London Business School Series called *Mathematics for business decision*, by R. F. Huddie and H. Thomas promises to be a more complete answer as the compendium kind of text, and its development has been centred firmly around the evolution of the quantitative methods courses in the London Business School.

Statistical methods

The recently revised standard reference work and text in the area of statistical methods is the meticulously thorough *Advanced theory of statistics*, by M. G. Kendall and A. Stuart (3 vols., Griffin, 1968–73). Almost every theoretical contribution, at least up until the late 1960s, is itemised in this book, and is synthesised into the main stream of each appropriate chapter. Perhaps for the student it suffers from the disadvantage of being too detailed, and texts on individual subject areas within statistics often find favour with students. To give some examples of these more narrowly based texts in the field of probability theory, there are two contributions which deserve attention. They are *Introduction to probability theory*, by W. Feller (2 vols., Wiley, 1968–71), which is an extremely comprehensive survey, and a more selective, but perhaps more readable, book by D. V. Lindley called *Introduction to probability and statistics from a Bayesian viewpoint*, again in two volumes (Cambridge University Press, 1965). The extensive work in statistical decision theory which has developed very strongly over the last 15 years is represented in the work of R. O. Schlaifer, *Probability and statistics for business decisions* (McGraw-Hill, 1959), a text which has a sampling theory orientation. Also similar work, which has a more theoretical orientation, is shown in H. Raiffa and R. O. Schlaifer's *Applied statistical decision theory* (Harvard, 1961) and *Introduction to statistical decision theory*, by J. W. Pratt, H. Raiffa and R. O. Schlaifer (preliminary ed., McGraw-Hill, 1965). Summaries of this work in statistical decision theory are given in two excellent monographs, one entitled *Decision analysis*, by H. Raiffa (Addison-Wesley, 1968), and the other *The theory of decision making*, by D. V. Lindley (Wiley, 1970).

There are two excellent series of monographs in statistics which provide a very good source of student textbooks in areas such as multivariate analysis, time series analysis and data analysis. The first is the Methuen monograph series, an exciting example of which is the volume entitled *Foundations of statistical inference*, edited by L. J. Savage (1962). The other monograph series is that published by Griffin and an example of one of their texts is the excellent volume *Fundamentals of statistical reasoning*, by M. H. Quenouille (Griffin, 1965). Inevitably the whole range of available texts has not been covered here, but for the more research-oriented and student reader enough references have been given for appropriate texts to be found.

For the manager, however, there is not such a great abundance of suitable texts. A very short monograph by G. G. W. Kalton called *Introduction to statistical thinking* (Chapman and Hall, 1967) bears careful reading, as it aims to emphasise concepts rather than techniques. Two other books attempt to do this—D. J. Bartholomew and E. E. Bassett's *Let's look at figures* (Penguin, 1971) is an attempt to implant the relevance of statistical thinking, whereas M. J. Moroney's *Facts from figures* (Penguin, 1969) reviews the range of appropriate statistical methods, but in a much more technique-oriented way. The complaint made by many managers on executive programmes is that few textbooks seem to be motivated towards highlighting the relevance of statistical thinking in business. There are, at the moment, a number of texts being developed from executive teaching, and a notable example of this approach is *Statistical thinking*, by T. Cass and H. Thomas, which is based upon experience of teaching in the Cranfield and London Business Schools. Cass's other volume, *Statistical methods in management* (Cassell, 1969), is a good example of a successful text for managers which is perhaps too technique-oriented.

In statistical methods a very useful source of knowledge for both students and executives is the survey or expository article about a particular subject area. Surveys of this kind can be found in journals such as the *Journal of the Royal Statistical Society, . Series A (General)*, and also in the *Journal of the American Statistical Association*. Typically, these surveys are commissioned either when a new area emerges, or when there is a feeling that an existing area of statistics needs clarification because of a rapid expansion of research-based articles. As an example, a paper was given in the *Journal of the Royal Statistical Society, Series A*, **132** (3) (1969), on 'A survey of control theory', by David Wishart, and this reflected the increasing interest of statisticians in applying control theory (essentially an engineering tool) to statistical problems.

The main research in this area can be found in a limited number of journals. The *Journal of the American Statistical Association* and the *Journal of the Royal Statistical Society* give an adequate coverage of the research field. However, specialist journals such as *Econometrica*, *Biometrika*, *Technometrics* and the *Journal of Applied Probability* itemise research contributions in multivariate analysis, biometrics, technical applications and probability theory. A useful additional journal is the *Bulletin of Applied Mathematics and its Applications*, which, to some extent, is largely concerned with mathematical methods, but nevertheless has many useful statistical developments within its pages.

Operational research

There is a parallel with the theoretical literature in statistics in that Harvey Wagner has produced a thorough and meticulous guide to operational research in much the same way as Kendall and Stuart provided a reference source for statistical methods (see p. 299). H. M. Wagner's book, *Principles of operational research* (Prentice-Hall, 1970), is a review of the whole of the literature on operational research, with a tremendous number of practical examples drawn in large part from Wagner's consulting work with McKinsey and Co. and such organisations as the Rand Corporation in the USA. As a result, it is much appreciated by the more mathematically inclined students who wish to see the directions in which operational research proceeds in both a theoretical and an application-oriented domain. There is no doubt that Wagner's book has no parallel in the literature, but those who might like a more concise text on operational research could try an excellent book by F. S. Hillier and G. J. Liebermann, *Introduction to operations research* (Holden-Day, 1965).

For the manager or for the less numerate reader, there are a number of excellent reviews of the literature on operational research. W. E. Duckworth's *A guide to operational research* (Methuen, 1967) reviews in a broad-brush way the kinds of applications of operational research and some of the theoretical issues in a survey which reflects the state of OR in the early 1960s. Patrick Rivett's *Concepts in operational research*, in the New Thinkers Library series (C. A. Watts, 1968), attempts to develop in a logical way the main concepts underlying the operational research approach, and a further text by Rivett in association with Russell Ackoff, *A manager's guide to operational research·* (Wiley, 1963), is somewhat of a cross between Duckworth's book and *Concepts in operational research.*

The concept of model-building is fundamental in the operational research literature. Another book by B. H. P. Rivett, who can be regarded as one of the main philosophers in operational research, *Principles of model building* (Wiley, 1972), attempts to explain the rationale of model-building in very much a decision analysis framework, and even if it does not completely succeed, it is worthwhile reading for both the manager and the serious student of operational research.

Before we turn to books which have been written about various of the main techniques of OR, mention should be made of a book by Professor P. G. Moore, *Basic operational research* (Pitman, 1968), which is a very worthwhile attempt to present the main techniques of operational research for executive or managerial students. Experience has shown that many students of OR, in addition, like the book because it sets out to explain the logic as well as the mathematics of each technique.

There are many books which aim to present the techniques of OR individually. They can usefully be divided into managerial treatments and research monograph papers. The best treatment of stock control for a managerial audience is the book entitled *A guide to stock control*, by A. Battersby (2nd ed., Pitman, 1971). Pitman also have a series of texts on topics of operational research which appeal both to managers and to students, provided that they are sufficiently numerate. E. M. L. Beale's *Mathematical programming and practice* (Pitman, 1968) is a very useful introduction to linear programming and can be recommended wholeheartedly. A good introduction to the literature of probability theory and decision-making under uncertainty is provided by H. Thomas's *Decision theory and the manager* (Pitman–Times Management Library, 1972). A recent paperback in the Penguin series by G. Jones entitled *Simulation and business decisions* gives a very useful introduction to the use of simulation in operational research. This was published in 1973. A more mathematical treatment suitable for students is given by K. D. Tocher's *The art of simulation* (English Universities Press, 1961). Battersby has written an interesting text on forecasting entitled *Sales forecasting* (Penguin, 1970), whereas G. E. P. Box and G. M. Jenkins's *Time series analysis: forecasting and control* (Holden-Day, 1970) is now a widely accepted classic in the field of forecasting.

For the serious student of OR research monographs are often published by John Wiley and Sons, in association with the Operations Research Society in America. The publications in this series have ranged from Conference Proceedings to commissioned monographs in new or developing areas of OR. An example of such a monograph was the volume *Bayesian decision theory and Markov chains*, by J. J. Martin (Wiley, 1971), which looked at the interrelationship between statistical decision theory and stochastic processes. Some specialist publishers—for example, Springer-Verlag in Germany, and North-Holland and Elsevier—publish research monographs in this field. An example of such a monograph is the excellent treatment by M. J. Beckmann, *Dynamic programming and economic decisions* (Springer-Verlag, 1968), in which many valuable results for the application of dynamic programming are developed.

For those interested in obtaining an overview of operational research from a survey article, Professor P. G. Moore's contribution 'A survey of operational research' in the *Journal of the Royal Statistical Society, Series A*, **129**, 399–417 (1966) is a valuable reference source. The *Royal Statistical Society Journal* and the *American Statistical Association Journal* are important sources for survey articles of new areas within this field. J. Hampton *et al.* reviewed 'Subjective probability and its measurement' in the *Journal of the Royal Statistical Society, Series A*, **136**(1), 21–42 (1973), and this is a good example of such a survey article. Sometimes, managerially based surveys of techniques of OR appear in the *Journal of Management Studies*. Two good examples are the article entitled 'Resource allocation, by A. W. Pearson (1968) and P. G. Moore and H. Thomas's 'Measurement problems in decision analysis' (1973). Occasionally surveys can also be found in journals such as *The Operational Research Quarterly*, *Management Science* and *Operations Research*. *Omega*, which is a new international journal of management science, has as its major rationale the provision of survey articles in all the fields of management science and OR, and should prove to be a welcome source for survey articles in the future.

The main research-based articles tend to be found in the *Operational Research Quarterly*, *Operations Research*, *Management Science*, the *SIAM Review*, the *Naval Research Logistics Quarterly* and *Decision Sciences*. Occasionally articles on operational research find their way into *Applied Statistics*, *Series C* of the *Journal of the Royal Statistical Society*, and the *Journal of the American Statistical Association*. However, these contributions are usually cross-referenced by the main publications in the OR field mentioned above.

Computing

It is very true to say that a knowledge of computing is gained through 'learning by doing'. The role of formal textbooks and managerially based books is, in the main, to introduce students to concepts of flow diagramming and programming, and to develop an appreciation of appropriate numerical methods for solving mathematical formulations of business problems.

Textbooks can therefore usefully be divided into those which try to get a student to program and those which attempt to develop an appreciation of numerical methods, given experience or ability in programming. Most of the computer manufacturers—for example, IBM and ICL—produce for their clients material from which an appreciation and knowledge of computer programming can be gained. McGraw-Hill, in fact, publish one of these introductions to a programming language, namely *A programmed introduction to FORTRAN*, by J. C. Plumb (1965), which is an excellent example of a text produced by an education division of a computing company.

Reference can always be made to the education division of the main computing companies for recommendations about the appropriate methods of learning flow diagramming and computing languages. There are, however, two books which seem to develop the necessary expertise on a non-'learning by doing' basis. The first is Kemeny, Snell, Schlaifer and Thompson's *Finite mathematics with business applications* mentioned earlier (p. 298), which is a very useful aid for developing skills in flow diagramming and in demonstrating to students areas in which computing methods can very successfully be applied in business. The second, G. B. Davis's *Introduction to electronic computers* (2nd ed., McGraw-Hill, 1971), is a representative example of a text primarily for students, which explains both the workings of computers and techniques of flow diagramming and programming.

There are many books on numerical methods and, again, a choice is inevitable. A. D. Booth's *Guide to numerical methods* is available from HMSO and is a cheap but nevertheless splendid reference guide, whereas Hamming's *Introduction to applied numerical analysis* (McGraw-Hill, 1971) is a much more wide-ranging mathematical treatment.

Computing is a field characterised by research efforts within both Universities and firms. In business our interest is not in analogue computing but in digital computing. Therefore the research literature in the digital computing area only is of relevance here. There are several research Institutes in this country from which computing research is generated. The Atlas Computer Laboratory in Chilton has a monograph series, as also do the computer centres set up under the Flower Report in Manchester University, Edinburgh University and London University. These institutes are all willing to send research monographs to interested parties. In this area it is also useful to keep track of the main research departments in computing, and these tend to be concentrated around London, Manchester and Edinburgh. A fine example is the department of Machine Intelligence and Perception in the University of Edinburgh, which is doing fundamental research work into conversational languages such as Pop 1 and Pop 2, and also into simulating the cognitive and information processing facets of the human brain within computer technology. There are obviously parallel institutes in the USA, but there is not sufficient space here to mention them. It should be noted that some of the algorithms developed for computing are sometimes published in journals, and indeed *Applied Statistics: Journal of the Royal Statistical Society, Series C* has a regular series devoted to new algorithms.

Since business applications are important to us, no literature review would be adequate without mentioning the work on computer programming carried out within the Harvard Business School. Bob Schlaifer, one of the pioneers of modern decision analysis, has written an extensive set of program, *Computer programs for elementary decision analysis*, which were published by the Division of Research of Harvard Business School in 1971. Currently Bob Schlaifer and Art Schleifer have just finished a volume of computer programs for analysing qualitative data, which should soon be published by the Division of Research at the Harvard Business School.

The main Journals that should be perused in this area are the British Computer Society's *Computer Journal*, and the *Journal of the Association of Computing Machinery*. These are largely theoretical Journals but the *Computer Journal* often has management-oriented articles. Occasionally some of the research literature in computing finds its way into the main statistical and operations research journals.

Summary and conclusions

Within this section a careful review of the literature in the main areas of mathematical methods, statistical methods, operational research and computing methods which is of relevance to business has been undertaken. They have been classed as theoretical contributions, because the literature tends to have a technical orientation *per se* rather than a strongly defined application orientation. While this review is not comprehensive, it should provide the reader with a number of staging posts which will aid him in finding references of most value in his studies.

In the next section we look at the literature on quantitative methods which has an applied orientation, and which is therefore looking at applications of quantitative methods in the various areas and disciplines of business.

APPLIED CONTRIBUTIONS

Introduction

In this section the main intention is to provide the reader with an insight into the direction in which quantitative methods and applied techniques are progressing in business applications. A classification of these contributions by business subject area, e.g. marketing, finance, etc., is attempted, and this is intended merely to be a useful categorisation for searching through the literature of business studies. There is every reason to suspect that many quantitative contributions are interdisciplinary in nature and cross subject areas. However, it would be extremely difficult to devise a meaningful classification to encompass the increasing number of applied situations of an interdisciplinary nature.

In this section, therefore, the contributions are reviewed in the following sequence: marketing, production, finance, business policy, managerial economics, organisational behaviour, research and development, and management information in planning systems.

Marketing

Marketing is, by definition, an interdisciplinary subject. To some business school students it is 'all things to all men', but it has significant inputs from economics, social psychology and quantitative methods. One of the main pioneers in the use of quantitative methods in marketing has been Dr. Paul E. Green, one-time business development manager with the Du Pont Company in the USA and now a Professor of Marketing in the University of Pennsylvania. Together with Ronald Frank, a Professor at Stanford University, he has written the two best guides for managers and students who require a broad-brush appreciation of the impact of quantitative techniques on marketing: *A manager's guide to marketing research* (Wiley, 1967) gives a good, very general introduction to the subject area, whereas *Quantitative methods in marketing* (Foundations of Modern Marketing Series, Prentice-Hall, 1968) gives a technique-oriented introduction and concentrates on decision theory, linear programming, experimental design and sampling. These texts are particularly useful for those dealing in marketing decision-making.

For the interested student, an earlier volume by F. M. Bass and R. D. Buzzell, *Mathematical methods and models in marketing* (Division of Research, Harvard Business School, 1963), presents the role of model-building and quantitative thinking in marketing in a much more analytical manner. A later text by R. D. Buzzell and D. Cox, *Marketing research and information systems* (Prentice-Hall, 1968), attempts to develop a more systems-oriented view of marketing and to relate it to information systems within the firm. A less useful book by George Fisk called *Marketing —a systems approach* (Prentice-Hall, 1966) took essentially the same view.

Books of readings are very common in the area of marketing model-building. Two good examples are *Marketing models*, edited by R. L. Day (International Textbook Co., 1966), and a more recent volume,

Quantitative analysis in marketing, edited by P. Kotler (Holt, Rinehart and Winston, 1973). However, the astute reader will notice that there has been relatively little development of new quantitative applications in marketing, although in recent years there have been attempts to apply techniques such as multidimensional scaling and the theory of stochastic processes to marketing problems.

Research in quantitative marketing can, to some extent, be classed as the frenzied application of quantitative techniques to decision problems which do not fit those techniques. Some researchers, notably Andrew Ehrenberg from the London Business School, have tried to provide a theoretical or law-like basis for the development of marketing thought. Some empirical generalisations have emerged and it is clear that quantitative techniques find an easier home once the theoretical basis of a subject is well-known and established. Therefore in the next 5 years or so a predictable trend in market research will be the greater awareness of marketing relationships, and this will tend to foster a growth of meaningful quantitative applications.

In research there are three directions which have currently produced a large amount of original quantitative thinking. Consumer behaviour is an area of research which has been given an uplift by John Howard's book *A theory of buyer behaviour* (Wiley, 1970), and it has generated a considerable volume of work in the quantitative direction. One direction of research exemplified by A. S. C. Ehrenberg has been to discover law-like relationships in marketing. The other direction has been to apply stochastic process models to consumer behaviour and two books are extremely important here. A. S. C. Ehrenberg's *Repeat buying* (North-Holland, 1972) applies the negative binomial and logarithmic series distribution, whereas W. F. Massy, D. B. Montgomery and A. Silk's *Stochastic process models in consumer behaviour* (MIT Press, 1972) looks at a wider range of methods and reviews some of Ehrenberg's work in the course of the book's development. Still in the area of marketing, the third direction has been in the application of multidimensional scaling or, as it is sometimes known, preference analysis. This has been useful in the assessment of consumer preferences for the range of features of a new car, to quote just one example. P. E. Green and D. S. Tull's *Research for marketing decisions* (3rd ed., Prentice-Hall, 1970) has four chapters which give a thorough review of this literature, and can be regarded as a very detailed text on the extent of quantitative thinking in marketing.

Research of this kind is always found in the main journals—for example, the *Harvard Business Review*, *European Journal of Marketing*, *Journal of Marketing*, *Journal of Marketing Research*, *Journal of the Market Research Society* and the *Journal of Business*. The *Journal of Marketing Research* is particularly noteworthy as it covers most of the original American thinking, whereas the *Journal of the Market Research Society* reflects the newer thinking in the UK. Occasionally, surveys of the literature appear in conference publications or commissioned articles in journals. An article, 'Quantitative methods in marketing', by H. Thomas, in the *Proceedings of the Marketing Conference* (Harrogate, 1967) gives a quantitative flavour in its treatment of the major applications up until 1966. *Applied Statistics* devoted the entire contents of its Summer 1966 issue to the application of quantitative techniques in marketing. This particular issue was edited by R. J. Lawrence, Professor of Marketing in the University of Lancaster, and contributions were included on law-like relationships (A. S. C. Ehrenberg) and Bayesian decision analysis (R. Green). Ehrenberg's article 'Towards an integrated theory of consumer behaviour' (*Journal of the Market Research Society*, 11(4), 305–337, 1969) is an excellent summary of both his law-like relationships and stochastic process work. It provides the reader with the core of the implications for marketing theory that have emerged from his quantitative work. Quite apart from articles, research tends to be propogated in monograph series. An example of such a series is the Reports of the Marketing Science Institute in Cambridge, Mass. These Reports cover research commissioned by the Institute and have, in recent years, included treatments of consumer behaviour, multivariate analysis and decision analysis. The Division of Research at Harvard Business School publishes research contributions in this area from time to time. Rex V. Brown's research volume entitled *Research and the credibility of estimates* (Harvard, 1970) is one of these volumes and presents a decision theoretic view of the marketing research process. Other research reports are published on an occasional basis by professional institutes and societies within the field — for example, the Advertising Association in the UK has for some time been interested in the effectiveness of advertising, and recently published a monograph on *The effect of advertising on sales and brand shares*, by Professor J. M. Samuels of Birmingham University. Marketing is an area in which case studies proliferate, many of which concentrate on policy issues and therefore are not treated here; indeed, very few give examples of quantitative applications. A recent British volume of cases entitled *Case problems in marketing*, edited by Professor K. Simmonds of the London Business School (Nelson, 1973), quotes a number of examples such as Meridian and British Electrical Supplies, which illustrate quantitative applications in bidding and decision analysis. Buzzell's book *Marketing research and information systems*, outlined earlier (p. 306), includes cases such as Aliad A and B, developed by R. V. Brown, which look at quantitative techniques in market research. Some of the volumes of readings collected from articles in the *Harvard Business Review* and published in series by the *Harvard Business Review* themselves, give useful case material — for example, the *Marketing Decision Series*. Included in this series is Fritz Edelman's *The art and science of competitive bidding*, which discusses models which have been applied in the area of bidding for competitive tenders. Obviously many other case volumes exist, and the reader must select from them for himself relevant information about quantitative thinking in this area. It is an undisputed fact that many other applications of case situations of a quantitative type will emerge over the next 10 years.

In summary, there is a wide range of sources for the quantitative marketing literature. If a single starting point had to be identified, then it would have to be the *Harvard Business Review*, if only because a large number of references exist in most of the articles written there.

Production

In many ways production management could be regarded as the 'Cinderella' of management activities. Whereas techniques such as inventory control and production systems have received much attention in the literature of management, there has not been the same level of implementation of such systems into business practice. This probably reflects a combination of an overly theoretical approach to production in business schools and a dogmatic approach to production management in industry, born of the short-fall of new recruits into production management. Currently, production has much greater managerial emphasis in its teaching content within universities, and this can only lead to the more ready induction of good quality students into production and thus to the increased development of production management systems within industry.

Production management as an activity covers the management of the total production operation within the company, and thus has increasingly a strong behavioural dimension. The newer textbooks in the area reflect this view and, indeed, the current research on production management tends to be much more interdisciplinary in nature.

Two textbooks deserve mention as general texts in this field. Professor Martin K. Starr's *Production management systems and synthesis* (Prentice-Hall, 1966) gives a valuable general treatment of the area, whereas Ray Wild's recent text, *The techniques of production management* (Holt, Rinehart and Winston, 1973), is more of a technique-oriented approach. Read in parallel, these two books provide a fine introduction to both the management and the theoretical aspects of production and should prove rewarding for both managers and students. The main research efforts in production are reported in journals. The leading journals in this field are the *International Journal of Production Research*, the *Operational Research Quarterly*, Operations Research and *Management Science*. Research contributions are also reported in the proceedings of international conferences on operations research. Examples of such conferences are the American operational research conferences, most of which have been edited by Professor D. B. Hertz, and published by Wiley for the Operations Research Society of America. New directions in production thinking are given reasonable coverage in the *Journal of Systems Engineering*, published by the University of Lancaster.

Managerial articles and surveys are often available in the *Harvard Business Review*. This *Review* publishes collections of previous articles, and its *Production Management Series* is a source of broadly based articles on research in production management.

The majority of the research effort in case production has until very recently been concentrated on a small number of Schools in the USA. Harvard in particular has generated much of the case work, and some of it is given in James L. McKenney and R. S. Rosenbloom's *Cases in production and operations management* (Irwin, 1966). In this volume linear programming, inventory control and quality control applications can be found very easily. Currently considerable research efforts in the UK are leading to the development of UK cases in production. A notable team specialising in this sphere is the Production Research Group at the London Business School, under the direction of Professor T. A. J. Nicholson.

An additional source of literature is the small text, which covers either research or the description of a production technique. An example of the latter is Allan Huitson's *Essentials of quality control* (Griffin Monograph, 1964). The former kind of monograph—for example, on inventory control —has been published in the Operations Research Society of America Series, mentioned earlier.

In summary, it is fair to say that production management is developing away from a direct quantitative treatment to a more broadly based inter-disciplinary treatment. As a result, in future years it is reasonable to expect quantitative techniques to be judged in production in terms of their relevance for the solution of the production·problems rather than in terms of their intrinsic theoretical merit.

Finance

The revolution in the teaching of financial management and in developments in financial management practice, have undoubtedly resulted in the application of quantitative techniques to financial decision problems. The stock market and banking have been areas in which significant quantitative research contributions have been made. Current interest in financial management in the UK is enormous, and this has recently been reflected in a large number of donations being made to the London Business School to establish an Institute of Finance within its walls.

Because of this rapid revolution, much of the older literature in this area, exemplified perhaps by Pearson Hunt's books from Harvard Business School, can now be considered out of date. James van Horne's *Fundamentals of financial management* (Prentice-Hall, 1971) was one of the texts which took a quantitative approach to problems of financial management, although it was intended as a general guide to the whole area of financial management. J. C. T. Mao's *Quantitative analysis of financial decisions* (Collier-Macmillan, 1969) concentrated much more on showing the areas in which quantitative analysis could usefully be applied. However, perhaps the fundamental contribution in the financial management literature has been the recent volume by E. F. Fama and M. H. Miller, *The theory of finance* (Holt, Rinehart and Winston, 1972). This book puts forward the Chicago hypothesis of efficient markets, and concentrates very heavily on the capital asset pricing theory. For the managerial reader, G. P. Clarkson and B. J. Elliott's *Managing money and finance* (2nd ed., Gower Press, 1972) gives sufficient insight into areas in which numerate methods can be applied.

The rapidly developing character of financial management as a discipline inevitably means that the research monograph is an essential source for those interested in working at the frontiers of the subject. R. A. Brealey's *Introduction to risk and return on common stocks* (MIT Press, 1969), synthesises a great deal of the research on the stock-market carried out at the Centre for Research in Security Prices, at the University of Chicago. A companion volume of Brealey's from the same stable, i.e. MIT Press, summarises later work in this area. The publishing firm of North Holland have recently issued a number of important volumes on research in capital budgeting. Professor F. S. Hillier's *The evaluation of risky inter-related capital investments* (1969) is essentially a piece of research work that has made a significant contribution to the treatment of risk and uncertainty in capital investment appraisal. Prentice-Hall very recently published a Doctoral Dissertation Series in which the Ford Foundation Doctoral Dissertation Prize Winning Theses were recorded. Four theses in this particular series are worthy of mention: Professor David Meiselman's *The term structure of interest rates*, Professor G. P. E. Clarkson's *The trust investment decision process*, Professor D. E. Farrar's *Investment analysis under uncertainty* and H. M. Weingartner's *Mathematical programming and capital budgeting*. All of these were pioneering pieces in their own areas. Meiselman's was an example of the Chicago School on interest rates; Clarkson's represented an example of the Carnegie School's 'behavioural theory of the firm' approach; Farrar's used some of Markowitz's earlier work on portfolio selection; and Weingartner's looked at the problem of using mathematical programming in selecting a portfolio of projects in capital budgeting. Currently research monographs tend to be published much more by firms within the USA than by UK publishers. John Wiley and Sons in America have published monographs that emerged from the work of the Cowle's Commission for Research in Economics. Perhaps the most important of these monographs, at least in the area of finance, is Professor H. M. Markowitz's *Portfolio selection*, which is at the root of most of the current contributions in research in portfolio theory and the stock market. Another recent research monograph which has far-reaching applications is Professor K. J. Arrow's *Essays in the theory of risk bearing* (Yale University Press, 1971). This monograph has encouraged and stimulated study of the treatment of risk in financial analysis and should be read alongside work on modern decision analysis, developed by Professors Pratt, Raiffa and Schlaifer at the Harvard Business School.

Research articles are equally important in finance because of its rapid change as a subject area. The main journals in the USA are the *Journal of Finance* and the *Journal of Financial and Quantitative Analysis*. The *Journal of Business* and the *Journal of Political Economy* of the University of Chicago, while not primarily financial journals, repeat much of the work that comes from the Chicago School of Finance. Occasionally articles on quantitative finance also appear in the *Journal of the American Statistical Association*, Applied Statistics, the *Operational Research Quarterly* and *Management Science*.

There is a proliferation of readings volumes about aspects of finance. At the moment four can be recommended for quantitative applications. Firstly, *The theory of business finance: a book of readings*, edited by S. R. Archer and E. D'Ambrosio (Macmillan, 1967), covers a broad range. Secondly, Professor Paul H. Cootner's *An introduction to the random characteristic of Stock Market prices* (revised ed., MIT Press, 1967) includes all the early research on quantitative Stock Market analysis. Thirdly, R. A. Brealey and J. Lorie's *Modern development in investment management* (Praeger, 1972), uses Cootner's book as a base and presents the newer thinking about the capital asset pricing model, drawn mainly from Professor W. F. Sharpe's 'Capital asset prices' *(Journal of Finance*, **19**, 425–442, 1964.) Fourthly, Professor K. J. Cohen and F. S. Hammer's *Analytical methods in banking* (Irwin, 1966) presents many applications of quantitative methods in the banking area. In this reviewer's opinion, case volumes are not an important literature source in quantitative finance, for developmental reasons already mentioned. However, case volumes do exist, and those interested can refer to the *Case problems in finance from the Harvard Business School*, published by Irwin or the collection of articles in finance regularly published from the *Harvard Business Review*.

All in all, quantitative finance is an area in which there will be rapid developments of much interest for research students. It is an area which has a magnetic quality about it at the moment, and if this article had been written in 5 years time, there would be a considerable number of very interesting quantitative research topics to discuss.

Business policy

'Policy' is an umbrella title which covers the study of how decison-makers should formulate and evaluate strategies about decision problems.

Most of the literature in the policy field tends to be case histories or case studies of business decision problems in which the strategies were either difficult to categorise or very diffuse in terms of ultimate analysis. There has therefore been very little in the way of quantitative thinking in this area, although there are signs from recent research contributions that quantitative thinking is becoming more developed. H. I. Ansoff's thoughtful text *Corporate strategy* (Penguin, 1970), which was first published in 1965, attempts to provide an overview of strategy problems, but, more important, offers a framework for policy analysis which can be used as a base for applying quantitative models.

The techniques of modern decision analysis, which can be found concisely explained in H. Thomas's book *Decision theory and the manager* (Pitman, 1972), have very much in them that is of relevance for policy analysis. There have been a series of research contributions from Harvard Business School which have used decision analysis to attack a number of public sector problems—for example, H. Ellis's thesis *The design of an air pollution program for New York City* (Division of Research, Harvard 1972). Further work in the analysis of public sector policy problems has been presented in a recent volume entitled *Analysis of public systems*, edited by A. W. Drake, R. L. Keeney and P. M. Morse (MIT Press, 1972).

In the private sector of the business policy field, a recent book called *Decisions, strategies and new ventures*, edited by W. Byrnes and K. Chesterton (Allen and Unwin, 1973), highlights the use of decision analysis in policy analysis within Unilever. The authors present a number of cases— for example, Transistors in Alterland—which, although disguised, illustrate how the realistic formulation of alternatives, and the sensible assessment of risk and uncertainty, can be of great value to the decision-maker in assessing the differences between the policy choices which he has to consider.

The development of quantitative thinking in business policy will soon be shown in the contributions to the main journals in this area. The *Harvard Business Review* is probably the most useful journal for general articles, whereas journals such as *Policy Sciences* and the *Journal of Business Policy* tend to be slightly more research-oriented. *Long Range Planning*, a UK journal, presents studies which show the interconnection between policy and planning. Occasionally articles appear in the *Operational Research Quarterly* and *Management Science*, which report upon the quantitative analysis of policy alternatives.

At the moment, the literature on the quantitative analysis of policy is very small. It will develop in three main directions: (1) through the publication of a number of current or very recent doctoral theses in the research monograph series; (2) through articles in the main journals; and (3) through the increasing interest which is being shown, on the one hand, by Government in policy analysis tools such as programme analysis and review (PAR) and planning programming and budgeting systems (PPBS) and, on the other hand, by an increasing number of businesses using tools of decision analysis as a means of evaluating policy choices.

Managerial economics

Microeconomics as a science developed very much as a theory of how markets operate and not as a theory of how firms operate, either internally or within markets. Managerial economics as a discipline concentrates more closely upon economics at the level of the firm, and thus on an understanding of how individual units within the firm operate.

The Carnegie School fathered *The behavioural theory of the Firm*, by R. M. Cyert and J. G. March (Prentice-Hall, 1963), which was an attempt to overcome some of the deficiences of microeconomic theory through incorporating notions of modern organisational theory into economic analysis. Other attempts to modify the theory of the firm exist, and W. Fellner's *Probability and profit* (Irwin, 1966) uses the ideas of modern decision analysis at the level of the individual firm. These additions to the theory of the firm should be regarded more as conceptual and theoretical devices than as predictive devices. Managerial economists will have to test the effectiveness of various theories, and until that stage is reached, differential effectiveness in terms of prediction cannot be used as a means of differentiating between competing theories.

A short text on *Managerial economics* has recently been provided by D. E. Farrar and J. R. Meyer in the Prentice-Hall Foundation of Modern Economics Series. This series is a comprehensive collection of guides to many other areas in economics which may be of interest to the businessman. A case-oriented student text, *Managerial economics—text and cases*, by C. Christensen, N. Harlan and R. Vancil (Irwin, 1968), surveys the whole field of managerial economics and includes a number of cases which apply decision analysis and other quantitative techniques to economic decision-making at the level of the firm.

The Penguin Readings in Modern Economics Series has provided us with a very appealing volume *Managerial economics*, edited by Professor G. P. E. Clarkson, in which many quantitative contributions to managerial economics are presented. More up-to-date articles can be found in journals such as *Applied Economics*, *Economica*, *Journal of Political Economy*, *Management Science* and *Econometrica*.

The Prentice-Hall Doctoral Dissertation Series, which was mentioned earlier in the context of research in finance, has also produced a number of relevant theses in the managerial economics field. The monographs from the Centre of Business Research in the University of Manchester, published by Allen and Unwin, have given us an insight into how investment decisions are made—in B. R. Williams's *Investment proposals and decisions* (Allen and Unwin, 1965)—and the way in which pricing decisions are made in business—in D. C. Hague's *Pricing in business* (Allen and Unwin, 1971). Other research on managerial economics can be obtained from the monograph series of the Centre for Mathematical Studies in Business and Economics of the University of Chicago, of the Centre of Operational Research in Economics in the University of Louvain, and of the European Institute of Advanced Studies in Management, Brussels.

In summary, the literature on managerial economics will develop in the future through the application of two different sets of disciplines to the existing framework. Firstly, the techniques of modern decision analysis have already led to the development of a wide range of cases in managerial economics, which have been published by McGraw-Hill in *Cases in managerial economics*, edited by R. D. Schlaifer. This can be read as a companion volume to his text *Analysis of decisions under uncertainty* (McGraw-Hill, 1969). There will undoubtedly be further case applications and developments in this particular field. Secondly, then, a number of existing mathematical models for resource allocation will be applied to more micro-problems in economics. An example of such a mathematical model would be linear programming.

Organisational behaviour (OB)

The only literature sources which are relevant for identifying the presence of quantitative thinking in this area are the research monograph, specilaised textbooks and research articles.

There are two textbooks which stimulated the interest of sociologists and psychologists in mathematical approaches. The first is Professor J. S. Coleman's comprehensive reference source, *An introduction to mathematical sociology* (Free Press, 1964), which reviews the whole range of quantitative techniques and gives examples of the ways in which they can be applied in the sociological area. The volume *Mathematical psychology*, by C. H. Coombs, A. Tversky and R. Dawes (Prentice-Hall, 1970), does a similar job for psychological applications. These books can be regarded as the fundamental sources for research students and those working at the frontiers of quantitative applications. An example of research in quantitative OB is the work of Professor D. Bartholomew, *Stochastic models and manpower planning* (Wiley, 1967), which applies the range of stochastic process models to the allocation and deployment of manpower resources within organisations.

A new area of research in this field has been the general area of behavioural decision theory or, in simpler terms, the study of the way in which businessmen make decisions. Much of the literature is summarised in an excellent book by Wayne Lee called *Decision theory and human behaviour* (Wiley, 1971), while earlier research is covered in a book of readings, *Decision making*, edited by Ward Edwards and Amos Tversky (Penguin, 1968). To some extent, the work of the Carnegie School—for example, Cyert, March and Simon—should be mentioned, as they have concentrated more on business decision contexts than have Ward Edwards or Wayne Lee. The main journals to study are *Organisational Behavior and Human Performance*, the *Journal of Experimental Psychology*, the *Journal of Abnormal and Social Psychology*, the *Journal of Mathematical Psychology*, the *Journal of Mathematical Sociology*, the *British Journal of Sociology*, the *American Sociological Review*, the *British Journal of Industrial Relations* and the *Administrative Science Quarterly*. Occasionally, management-oriented articles appear in the *Journal of Management Studies*, the *Journal of Business* and the *IEEE Transactions in Engineering Management* (USA).

In summary, quantitative thinking is developing in a piecemeal fashion in this area. If anything, it is limited by the obvious problems and pitfalls which concern a researcher in modelling, in any controlled kind of way, human or social phenomena.

Research and development

Quantitative thinking in research and development management has been directed towards issues of resource allocation. Questions such as how to assess the worth of research projects, how to select the optimum portfolio projects, and how to plan and control research and development activity are some of the key questions to which operational research specialists sought answers.

A management-oriented text which looks at some of these quantitative issues is T. S. MacLeod's *The management of research and development* (Gower Press, 1969), while Burton V. Dean's *Planning and controlling research and development activities* (American Management Science, 1964) gives a comprehensive review of all the quantitative approaches that have been devised in relation to research and development planning.

The approach which has had the greatest influence on the management of research and development has been the R & D approach of the Sloan School of Management, Massachusetts Institute of Technology. While the contributions of authorities such as Professor D. Marquis and Professor

T. J. Allen have been organisational in nature, Professor E. B. Roberts has provided, in his book *The management of research and development* (MIT Press, 1964), a quantitative approach based on systems dynamics notions for planning and controlling R & D. In the UK a number of groups have been working actively in the area of research and development: for example, the R & D Research Unit at Manchester Business School; the Operational Research Branch of the British Iron and Steel Research Association (BISRA); the Mathematical Services Branch of ICI; and some of the nationalised industries, such as the Gas Council and the Electricity Council. A comprehensive text, *Quantitative management in R & D*, edited by R. Reader *et al.* (Allen and Unwin, 1972), emerged from the work at BISRA. The other research efforts have been reported in the main journals in this field, the most notable of which, *R & D Management*, has presented much of the work of the Manchester Unit.

In this developing area, therefore, it is sensible to identify some of the more important research articles. A detailed survey of the scope of quantitative thinking was given in the article 'Operations research in R & D', by E. Ritchie (*Operational Research Quarterly*, 1972). An article by Professor O. L. Davies entitled 'Some statistical considerations in the selection of research projects' appeared in *Applied Statistics* in 1962, but still has a tremendous relevance for anybody interested in the applications of quantitative methods to areas such as pharmaceuticals. The application of modern decision analysis methods in research and development is well treated by W. Abernathy and R. S. Rosenbloom in 'Parallel path strategies in development projects' (*Management Science*, 1969). A thorough survey of issues of project worth and portfolio selection in R & D can be found in H. Thomas's 'The assessment of project worth with applications to R & D', in *Cost Benefit and Cost Effectiveness*, edited by J. N. Wolfe (Allen and Unwin, 1973). The mathematical programming approach can be followed up by looking at articles by D. C. Bell and A. W. Read in issues of *R & D Management* in 1971 and 1972.

A particularly interesting direction in the literature has been the discussion of the extent of estimation error in forecasting the worth or value of research and development projects. This research is relevant when one considers efforts such as the RB 211 failure at Rolls-Royce and the currently embarrassing situation with Concorde. This work was started at the Rand Coporation in the USA, and is best exemplified by W. Marshall and A. Meckling's contribution in the volume *Rate and direction of inventive activity*, edited by R. R. Nelson (Princeton for NBER, 1963). A further important contribution came from R. Summer's work in a volume *Strategy for R & D* (Springer-Verlag, 1968), edited by T. Marschak *et al.* These two contributions emphasised the extent of cost escalation in Government-sponsored R & D, for projects such as the Polaris Missile

Programme. Some recent parallel work has been carried out in the UK by two major authorities. Firstly, K. P. Norris of Manchester Business School has published a number of articles in *R & D Management* which summarise his work with a series of industrial firms concerning the cost escalation on their applied research and development projects. H. Thomas, on the other hand, has published evidence in two articles in *R & D Management* (June, 1971, and February, 1972) which present rarer evidence about inaccuracies in estimates of benefit factors, such as prices and quantities sold of products derived from research and development, as well as the normal findings of cost escalation.

Apart from *R & D Management*, the main journals which should be studied for reports on quantitative applications of research and development are the *Operational Research Quarterly*, *Operations Research*, *Management Science* and the *IEEE Transactions in Engineering Management*. Survey articles occur from time to time in these publications, particularly in the *IEEE Transactions in Engineering Management*. For example, M. Baker and W. Pound's 'Project selection—where we stand' (*IEEE Transactions in Engineering Management*) is a comprehensive survey of mathematical programming applications.

The Operational Research Society in the UK sponsors the work of an OR Study Group in R & D and they present their work at sessions of the annual conference. Some of their reports are available on request from the Operational Research Society. B. V. Dean's edited volume *Operations research in research and development* (Wiley, 1964) published the research contributions of a R & D Study Group of the Operations Research Society of America.

As time progresses, many of the current efforts at quantitative research in this field will become operational management tools. The current state of the art can always be found in the issues of the *Harvard Business Review* and in the *R & D Management Series* of collective articles occasionally published by that *Review*.

Management information and planning systems (MIS)

MIS is another of those umbrella areas which are essentially interdisciplinary in nature. Computer specialists tend to regard MIS as their area, but, in all frankness, most of them lose sight of the organisational and implementation problems involved in the development of such systems. A computer-oriented guide to systems analysis is given in a book by P. Kilgour, *The students systems analysis* (Edward Arnold, 1968), whereas a more broadly based view is given in R. G. Murdick and J. E. Ross's *Information systems for modern management* (Prentice-Hall, 1968). While some people will find these texts appealing, this reviewer recommends two main books: Igor Ansoff's *Corporate strategy* (Penguin, 1970) gives an overview of, and framework for, planning systems, whereas J. C. Emery's *Organisation planning and control systems* is an excellent and thoughtful treatment of the organisational and implementation problems. In neither of these is computer technology emphasised, and this is correct, since computer technology is only a means to an end, once the design of the system for management information and control has been effected.

A research monograph by R. Anthony, *Planning and control systems* (Division of Research, Harvard Business School, 1963), gives an insight into the financial planning system and its relation to the design of the overall planning activity. Buzzell and Cox's text on marketing information systems, mentioned earlier (p. 306), does the same job in the marketing context. C. P. Bonino's simulation of information and decision systems within the firm (Doctoral Dissertation Series, Prentice-Hall, 1963) develops a model for planning and control which relies heavily on organisational considerations developed in the Carnegie Behavioural Theory Approach, and he also develops a number of useful computer algorithms for simulation in this area.

Turning to research articles, one which can be recommended wholeheartedly is really a survey. It is Russell L. Ackoff's 'Management misinformation systems' (*Management Science*, 1964), which carefully examines structures for planning and factors which need to be included in information systems. J. B. Kidd and J. R. Morgan in 'Predictive management information systems' (*Operational Research Quarterly*, 1969) looked at many of the issues which are involved in using subjective quantities within information systems, and concisely assesses the application of modern decision analysis methods in this field. A new textbook, based on research in McKinsey and Company and on work at the London Business School, by D. B. Hertz and H. Thomas, *The future of planning under uncertainty* (Wiley, 1975) will look at the design implementation of real-life management information systems.

The main journals in which research can be found are *Management Science*, the *Operational Research Quarterly*, the *Journal of the British Computer Society*, the *Journal of Management Studies*, the *Harvard Business Review*, *Operations Research* and the *Sloan Management Review*. The management-oriented journal here is the *Harvard Business Review*, whereas the others tend to report the up-to-date research applications.

Readings volumes are not very useful in this context largely because it is important that the editor should have a realistic view about the nature of management information systems. Few editors currently have had a sensible view of management information systems as opposed to computer information systems. There are too many readings volumes on computer information systems and few, if any, which talk about the nature of management information. A possible exception is the volume on *Management information systems*, edited by I. W. Macrae, in the Penguin Modern

Management Readings Series. The literature must, in future, reflect a much greater awareness of design and implementation issues in relation to MIS.

Summary and conclusions

This can only be a brief conclusion to what is already a very wide-ranging section. It should be clear that all the comments on literature sources are coloured by personal views about directions in which quantitative thinking should move in each of the functional and applied areas of management. Other specialists in quantitative methods might disagree with some of my categorisations, and with some of my predictions. However, while these are personal ideas, they are based on thorough practical experience in each of these areas, and should at least encourage the reader to develop alternative viewpoints. Indeed, this has been my main aim in writing this section.

Index

This is primarily a subject index which includes references to all types of publications discussed and the names of the libraries and organisations described in Chapter 3 and elsewhere. It also includes the titles of abstracting and indexing publications described in Chapter 5 and the periodicals in Chapter 6. Other titles of reference works and statistical publications are included only when there is any appreciable description of them in the text. Textbooks, monographs and the names of all authors are excluded because they are too numerous.